DATE DUE

Egypt after Mubarak

PRINCETON STUDIES IN MUSLIM POLITICS

Dale F. Eickelman and Augustus Richard Norton, Editors

Diane Singerman, *Avenues of Participation: Family, Politics, and Networks in Urban Quarters of Cairo*

Tone Bringa, *Being Muslim the Bosnian Way: Identity and Community in a Central Bosnian Village*

Dale F. Eickelman and James Piscatori, *Muslim Politics*

Bruce B. Lawrence, *Shattering the Myth: Islam beyond Violence*

Ziba Mir-Hosseini, *Islam and Gender: The Religious Debate in Contemporary Iran*

Robert W. Hefner, *Civil Islam: Muslims and Democratization in Indonesia*

Muhammad Qasim Zaman, *The 'Ulama in Contemporary Islam: Custodians of Change*

Michael G. Peletz, *Islamic Modern: Religious Courts and Cultural Politics in Malaysia*

Oskar Verkaaik, *Migrants and Militants: Fun and Urban Violence in Pakistan*

Laetitia Bucaille, *Growing up Palestinian: Israeli Occupation and the Intifada Generation*

Robert W. Hefner, editor, *Remaking Muslim Politics: Pluralism, Contestation, Democratization*

Lara Deeb, *An Enchanted Modern: Gender and Public Piety in Shi'i Lebanon*

Roxanne L. Euben, *Journeys to the Other Shore: Muslim and Western Travelers in Search of Knowledge*

Robert W. Hefner and Muhammad Qasim Zaman, eds., *Schooling Islam: The Culture and Politics of Modern Muslim Education*

Loren D. Lybarger, *Identity and Religion in Palestine: The Struggle between Islamism and Secularism in the Occupied Territories*

Bruce K. Rutherford, *Egypt after Mubarak: Liberalism, Islam, and Democracy in the Arab World*

Egypt after **Mubarak**

LIBERALISM, ISLAM, AND DEMOCRACY
IN THE ARAB WORLD

Bruce K. Rutherford

PRINCETON UNIVERSITY PRESS
PRINCETON AND OXFORD

Published by Princeton University Press, 41 William Street, Princeton, New Jersey 08540
In the United Kingdom: Princeton University Press, 6 Oxford Street, Woodstock,
Oxfordshire OX20 1TW

Library of Congress Cataloging-in-Publication Data

Rutherford, Bruce K.
Egypt after Mubarak : liberalism, Islam, and democracy in the Arab world /
Bruce K. Rutherford.
p.   cm. — (Princeton studies in Muslim politics)
Includes bibliographical references and index.
ISBN 978-0-691-13665-3 (hardcover : alk. paper)
1. Egypt—Politics and government—21st century—Forecasting.
2. Islam and politics—Egypt—Forecasting. 3. Democracy—Egypt.
4. Liberalism—Egypt. 5. Jam'iyat al-Ikhwan al-Muslimin (Egypt)—
Political activity. 6. Lawyers—Egypt—Political activity. 7. Egypt—
Economic policy. I. Title.
JQ3881.R87 2008
320.962—dc22   2008019455

British Library Cataloging-in-Publication Data is available

This book has been composed in Postscript Galliard Typeface

Printed on acid-free paper. ∞

press.princeton.edu

Printed in the United States of America

10 9 8 7 6 5 4 3

To the Memory of My Parents

Contents

Acknowledgments

THIS PROJECT began as a doctoral dissertation on the emergence of constitutionalism in Egypt. My dissertation advisor, David Apter, provided many suggestions that helped to frame the research and develop the argument. I also received helpful advice from several other members of Yale University's political science department, including Joseph LaPalombara, Ian Shapiro, Rogers Smith, Stephen Skowronek, and Juan Linz.

Fieldwork in Cairo was funded by the J. William Fulbright Program (IIE), the American Research Center in Egypt, the Social Science Research Council, and the Research Council at Colgate University. Several organizations provided additional funding that supported my study of the Arabic language, particularly the Social Science Research Council, the Yale Center for International and Area Studies, the Center for Arabic Study Abroad (CASA) at the American University in Cairo, and the Foreign Language and Area Studies (FLAS) program of the United States Department of Education.

In addition, I benefited from postdoctoral fellowships at the Institute for Transregional Study of the Contemporary Middle East, North Africa, and Central Asia at Princeton University; the Center of International Studies at Princeton University; and the Islamic Legal Studies Program at Harvard Law School. I am deeply grateful to these organizations for providing the time and resources needed to complete my work. I especially wish to thank their directors, who offered valuable encouragement and advice: Abdellah Hammoudi, Aaron Friedberg, Richard Ullman, Frank Vogel, and Peri Bearman.

I have had the good fortune of enjoying the kindness, insight, and support of many scholars in Egypt and the United States. I am especially grateful to Eva Bellin, Nancy Bermeo, Nathan Brown, Mona Makram Ebeid, Leila Fawaz, Andrew Hess, Michael Johnston, Robert Kraynak, Vickie Langohr, Ellen Lust-Okar, Tamir Moustafa, Augustus Richard Norton, Michele Penner Angrist, M. Anne Pitcher, Carrie Rosefsky Wickham, Mustafa Kamal al-Sayyid, Emad El-Din Shahin, Suad Sharqawi, Samer Shehata, Adel Omar Sherif, and John Waterbury.

Naseema Noor provided superb research assistance and has become a fine scholar in her own right. I also received valuable assistance from Ismail Fayed, 'Umar al-Barjisi, Dahlia Rizk, Mozn Hassan, Fatma Imam, Lauren Robinson, Melissa Zoock, and Nazia Moqueet. I owe a special thank-you to Letta Palmer.

Portions of chapters 3 and 4 appeared previously in the *Middle East Journal* under the title, "What Do Egypt's Islamists Want? Moderate Islam and the Rise of Islamic Constitutionalism." This material is used with permission from the *Journal*.

Hamilton, New York
December 15, 2007

Egypt after Mubarak

CHAPTER ONE

Hybrid Regimes and Arab Democracy

ON APRIL 30, 2006, the Egyptian Parliament voted by a large majority to renew the emergency law. This law grants the president extraordinary powers to detain citizens, prevent public gatherings, and issue decrees with little accountability to Parliament or the people. The vote was a familiar ritual: the Egyptian Parliament has routinely approved the emergency law for most of the past forty years.[1] However, this acquiescence to presidential power is not universal. A few months prior to the April vote, the Supreme Constitutional Court issued a ruling that substantially limited the scope of the president's authority under the emergency law. The Court's decision prohibited the president from using the emergency law to assert government control over private property in non-emergency situations, and admonished the prime minister for applying it in a manner that disregarded the constitutional rights of Egyptians.[2] Many civil society groups also challenged the law, especially the Muslim Brotherhood. It organized several demonstrations to protest the parliamentary vote and criticized the law extensively in the media. Its parliamentary delegation denounced the measure as contrary to the principles of Islam because it ignored the wishes of the Egyptian people and failed to serve the public interest.[3]

These events illustrate a growing contradiction in contemporary Egypt. An observer could easily conclude that the country is a classic example of

---

[1] The emergency law was invoked during the June 1967 war. It has been in force ever since, with only a brief interruption from May 15, 1980 until October 6, 1981. For details of the emergency law, see A. Seif El-Islam, "Exceptional Laws and Exceptional Courts," in *Egypt and Its Laws*, ed. Nathalie Bernard-Maugiron and Baudouin Dupret (New York: Kluwer Law International, 2002), 364–66. Amendments to the Constitution in March 2007 incorporated many of the powers of the emergency law into the Constitution. These amendments will be discussed in chapter 6.

[2] SCC decision 74 for Judicial Year 23, issued January 24, 2006. This decision supplemented earlier rulings by the administrative courts that narrowed the president's authority to arrest citizens under the emergency law and further limited the types of property that could be seized. See High Administrative Court, Cases 675 and 797, Judicial Year 22, issued May 27, 1978; High Administrative Court, Case 830, Judicial Year 20, issued December 29, 1979; High Administrative Court, Cases 1435, 1310, 1271, 126, and 810, Judicial Year 28, March 12, 1985. These cases will be discussed in greater detail in chapter 2.

[3] "Bayan al-Ikhwan al-Muslimin 'an Qanun al-Tawari'" (Cairo: n.p., April 2006). Also see the coverage of the parliamentary vote in *al-Misri al-Youm*, May 1, 2006.

stable authoritarianism. The regime controls much of the media, dominates political life, and suppresses its opponents with a vast array of legal
and extra-legal tools. It also carefully monitors and manipulates civil society groups and political parties. And yet, Egyptian political life includes
several features that suggest a different picture. The country has a vibrant
and aggressive judiciary whose rulings constrain the regime.[4] It also has
an increasingly assertive judges' association (the Judges' Club) that openly
confronts the executive and lobbies for legal and political reform. In addition, Egypt has a large and well-organized Islamist organization (the Muslim Brotherhood) that calls for increased governmental accountability,
greater respect for law, and improved protection of citizens' rights. Although the Brotherhood has no formal capacity to constrain the state, it
regularly challenges and delegitimizes abuses of power by invoking Islamic principles of law and governance.[5]

Some analysts may be inclined to dismiss these critics of executive power
as marginal actors with little substantive impact on politics. However, this
view neglects a fundamental change in the character of Egyptian politics
since the early 1990s. The statist order created during the Nasser era has
been undermined by economic crises, economic restructuring, and integration into the global economy. These changes have weakened key institutions of state control, particularly the public sector and the subsidy system. They have also eroded the ideology that legitimates the regime. This
does not mean that the state is fading away. However, the state no longer
dominates the economy and society. This situation has created opportunities for competing ideologies and institutions to emerge—most notably,
a liberal conception of law within the judiciary and an Islamic conception
of governance within the Muslim Brotherhood. These new approaches
to constitutional order have grown into meaningful alternatives to the
declining statism of the regime. Furthermore, these two alternatives share
important features. Their agendas converge around a core set of reforms
that embody the key features of classical liberalism, including constraints
on state power, strengthening the rule of law, and protecting some basic
rights. This set of reforms has also gained support from parts of the business community and the reformist wing of the ruling party. This development suggests that Egypt's political future may include a steady deepening
of liberalism and, possibly, democracy.

[4] For example, Egypt's courts have issued decisions that dissolved the Parliament on two
occasions, reduced regime-sponsored electoral fraud, created twelve political parties, and
overturned government orders to close opposition newspapers and silence critical journalists.
These cases will be discussed in chapter 2.

[5] Each of these topics will be discussed in greater depth in chapters 2 through 4.

THE IMPERATIVE OF ARAB DEMOCRACY:
CHANGING INTERNATIONAL AND DOMESTIC PRIORITIES

The possibility of sustained liberal and democratic development is novel in the Middle East. For most of the post–World War II period, political reform has been a low priority for both local leaders and the international community. The United States has a particularly undistinguished record in this regard. One of its earliest interventions during the Cold War occurred in Iran in 1953, when American agents assisted a coup that overthrew a popularly elected leader (Mohammad Mossadeq) and restored the authority of the shah. The United States then provided extensive military and economic aid to the shah's regime over the next twenty-six years. The United States has also provided substantial support to other monarchies in the region, particularly in Saudi Arabia, Jordan, Kuwait, and Morocco. Its willingness to back autocracy reached a peak in the 1980s, when the United States provided military and intelligence assistance to Saddam Hussein's Iraq in order to strengthen its hand against Iran.[6] The U.S. secretary of state at the time, George Shultz, candidly explained that "the United States simply could not stand idle and watch the Khomeini revolution sweep forward."[7]

As Shultz's comment suggests, U.S. policy toward the region was guided by its core strategic interests, namely, access to adequate supplies of oil at stable prices; the security of Israel; and the minimization of Soviet influence. With the success of the Iranian revolution in 1979, the containment of radical Islam—in its Shi'a and, later, Sunni variants—was added to this list. Building stable democracies was considered a secondary objective, at best. Whenever the issue of democratization arose, the prevailing view was, "Why rock the boat?"[8] Democratization would almost certainly produce a period of transition that would increase instability. This instability, in turn, might jeopardize the smooth flow of oil and could provide opportunities for anti-American groups to expand their political influence. It simply made little sense to jeopardize global economic prosperity in order to embark on an uncertain path of political reform. When there

---

[6] Amatzia Baram, "US Input into Iraqi Decisionmaking, 1988–1990," in *The Middle East and the United States: A Historical and Political Reassessment, Fourth Edition*, ed. David W. Lesch (Boulder, CO: Westview Press, 2007), 352. Also, Alan Friedman, *Spider's Web: The Secret History of How the White House Illegally Armed Iraq* (New York: Bantam Books, 1993).

[7] George P. Shultz, *Turmoil and Triumph: My Years as Secretary of State* (New York: Scribner's, 1993), 237.

[8] William B. Quandt, "American Policy toward Democratic Political Movements in the Middle East," in *Rules and Rights in the Middle East: Democracy, Law, and Society*, ed. Ellis Goldberg et al. (Seattle: University of Washington Press, 1993), 166.

were opportunities to promote democracy, they were pursued either half-heartedly or not at all. For example, in late 1991 and early 1992, Algeria's president made the surprising decision to allow relatively free parliamentary elections. They led to widespread losses for the ruling party and unexpected success for an Islamist movement, the Islamic Salvation Front (FIS). In order to block the FIS from gaining control of the Parliament, the Algerian military intervened by declaring a state of emergency, canceling the election results, and imprisoning the leaders and activists of the FIS. The United States offered no objection. Speaking a few years later, the U.S. secretary of state at the time (James Baker) recalled that the United States chose not to defend the democratic process because it would have produced a government with views hostile toward the United States. In his words, "We didn't live with [the election results] in Algeria because we felt that the fundamentalists' views were so adverse to what we believe in and what we support, and to the national interest of the United States."[9] The United States had an even better opportunity to promote democracy during the Gulf War of 1990–91. Iraq under Saddam Hussein had invaded and annexed Kuwait in August 1990. The United States and its allies intervened with over 500,000 troops to expel Iraqi forces and restore the Kuwaiti monarchy. Some American politicians and analysts argued that American military action should be conditioned on Kuwait's ruling family, the al-Sabah, agreeing to a specific timetable for democratization. In this view, American troops should not risk their lives to defend a feudal monarchy.[10] Such reasoning was not incorporated into American policy. President George H. W. Bush's speech on the eve of the American air war against Iraq is striking for its lack of reference to any political goal beyond the restoration of the Kuwaiti monarchy.[11] A senior policy maker at the time observed, "I am among the unregenerate few who believe that American foreign policy must serve the national interest—which is not in every case to be confused with the furtherance of American ideals overseas."[12]

This view that democratization takes a back seat to core strategic concerns has played an important role in the U.S. relationship with Egypt.

[9] "Looking Back on the Middle East: James A. Baker III," *Middle East Quarterly* 1, no. 3 (1994): 83. Interestingly, the Algerian coup is not even mentioned in Baker's memoirs. See James A. Baker, *The Politics of Diplomacy: Revolution, War, and Peace, 1989–1992* (New York: G. P. Putnam's Sons, 1995).

[10] For examples of this argument, see David Ignatius, "In the Coming New Gulf Order, We Must Help the Arab World Join the Global Democratic Revolution," *Washington Post*, August 26, 1990; Caryle Murphy, "Gulf States' Next Test: Democracy," *Washington Post*, September 15, 1990.

[11] See the text of George H. W. Bush's speech, "President Bush Assures American People: We Will Not Fail," *Washington Post*, January 17, 1991.

[12] The official is quoted in Thomas L. Friedman, "A New U.S. Problem: Freely Elected Tyrants," *New York Times*, January 12, 1992. The name of the official is not given.

This relationship is shaped by the strategic interests mentioned earlier—oil, Israel, the Soviet Union (until 1991), and radical Islam. It is also influenced by the United States' eagerness after 1979 to sustain the Camp David peace agreement and, if possible, to extend this peace to other Arab regimes.[13] In pursuit of these goals, the United States began substantial levels of economic aid in the mid-1970s.[14] The assistance started with $370 million in economic aid in 1975. By 1978, this figure had risen to $943 million. It then rose further in 1979, to $1.1 billion, as a result of the peace agreement with Israel. A whopping $1.5 billion in military assistance was also added to the package. Throughout the 1980s and 1990s, U.S. military and economic aid averaged roughly $2.2 billion per year. In 2000, the United States began to cut back on economic aid at a rate of 5 percent per year with the goal of reducing economic assistance by 50 percent over ten years. This reduction was part of a broader strategy to shift the U.S.-Egyptian economic relationship from "aid to trade." In 2006, economic assistance had fallen to $490 million. Military assistance remained at its well-established level of roughly $1.2 billion per year. By the end of 2006, the United States had sent over $62 billion in economic and military assistance to Egypt over the previous thirty-one years (in nominal dollars).[15]

Despite this extraordinary level of assistance, the United States never used aid as a lever for accelerating political reform. Indeed, the United States was skeptical of the value of democratization from the earliest days of the Nasser regime. At the time of the Free Officers' coup in 1952, the U.S. ambassador concluded that Egypt was "not ready for democracy."[16] He believed that greater freedoms and free elections would merely provide opportunities for communists to expand their influence, and might produce social disorder that communists could exploit.[17] This sentiment per-

---

[13] Roger Owen, "Egypt," in *The Pivotal States: A New Framework for U.S. Policy in the Developing World*, ed. Robert Chase et al. (New York: W. W. Norton, 1999), 133; Alfred L. Atherton, *Egypt and U.S. Interests* (Washington, DC: Foreign Policy Institute, 1988), 5–7.

[14] The impetus for starting this assistance was Sadat's decision in 1972 to sever Egypt's military ties with the USSR. It was reinforced by Sadat's willingness to engage in a dialogue over Egyptian-Israeli security concerns in the wake of the 1973 Arab-Israeli war, particularly with regard to the orderly disengagement of Egyptian and Israeli troops in Sinai.

[15] All aid figures are taken from Jeremy M. Sharp, "Egypt: Background and U.S. Relations" (Washington, DC: Congressional Research Service, January 10, 2007), 31–33. For discussion of the strategy to shift the U.S.-Egyptian economic relationship from aid to trade, see "Strategy Introduction" in *USAID-Egypt 2000–2009 Strategy*, p. 1. The United States has announced plans to continue military aid at a level of $1.3 billion per year through 2017. Robin Wright, "U.S. Plans New Arms Sales to Gulf Allies," *Washington Post*, July 28, 2007.

[16] Kirk J. Beattie, *Egypt during the Nasser Years: Ideology, Politics, and Civil Society* (Boulder, CO: Westview Press, 1994), 99.

[17] Ibid. The United States also believed that a military regime was better able to undertake key social reforms (particularly land reform) needed to stimulate economic development and

sisted over the next five decades. In the late 1980s, a former U.S. ambassador to Egypt (Alfred Atherton) wrote a careful and thorough discussion of the U.S.-Egypt relationship without even mentioning democracy promotion.[18] Similarly, a former National Security Council official who specializes in Egypt (William Quandt) wrote a seventy-seven-page essay on U.S.-Egyptian relations in 1990 without addressing the issues of democracy or political reform.[19]

Democracy and human rights were sometimes mentioned in official documents. For example, the U.S. State Department issued an annual report on human rights that drew attention to the Egyptian government's record of torture, electoral fraud, and suppression of civil society.[20] It also issued periodic statements that encouraged Egypt to develop more representative and accountable government. It even allocated some USAID funds for this purpose.[21] However, political reform was understood by both sides as being subordinate to the strategic concerns that lay at the heart of the U.S.-Egyptian relationship.

This view of democratization in Egypt and the Arab world underwent a significant change following the terrorist attacks of September 11, 2001. Prior to September 11, U.S. policy makers assumed that stable and friendly authoritarian regimes in the Arab world were the best guarantee of American security and economic interests. In the wake of the attacks, U.S. leaders from both parties concluded that terrorism by radical Islamists was partially a result of the repression and economic stagnation of Arab dictatorships. These suffocating conditions produced a large pool of frustrated, hopeless, and angry young men who yearned for greater dignity and purpose in their lives. They were easy recruits for terrorist ideologues promising honor and martyrdom in a struggle against injustice.[22]

---

prevent a peasant revolution. Ibid., 141. Also, Joel Gordon, *Nasser's Blessed Movement: Egypt's Free Officers and the July Revolution* (New York: Oxford University Press, 1992), 195.

[18] He wrote briefly that "Egypt has today a good record in the field of human rights . . . Egypt has made important advances, especially under Mubarak, toward establishing democratic institutions and reducing corruption." He makes no mention of whether democracy promotion should be a goal in the U.S. relationship with Egypt. Atherton, *Egypt and U.S. Interests*, 19.

[19] The book focuses primarily on economic reform and the Arab-Israeli peace process. William B. Quandt, *The United States and Egypt* (Cairo: American University in Cairo Press, 1990).

[20] These reports were prepared by the Department of State's Bureau of Democracy, Human Rights, and Labor. The recent reports are available on the State Department's website: http://www.state.gov/g/drl/rls/hrrpt/.

[21] Beginning in the 1990s, USAID began allocating funds to support "institutional reform." These programs focused on legal reform, judicial training, and strengthening the Parliament's administrative capabilities. See "Strategic Plan 1996–2001" (Cairo: USAID/Egypt, September 1996), iii–iv.

[22] President Bush articulated this view in a speech to the National Endowment for Democracy in November 2003. He stated, "As long as the Middle East remains a place where

For advocates of this view, the key to defeating terrorism lay in ending repression and poor governance in the Arab world. In the words of the secretary of state, "for sixty years the United States pursued stability at the expense of democracy in the Middle East—and we achieved neither. Now, we are taking a different course. We are supporting the democratic aspirations of all people."[23] In November 2003, President George Bush proclaimed that the United States had adopted a "forward strategy of freedom in the Middle East" that would be a central feature of American foreign policy.[24] This posture was part of a broader plan to promote democracy throughout the world. The administration's National Security Strategy, issued in March 2006, stated in its first paragraph, "The goal of our statecraft is to help create a world of democratic, well-governed states that can meet the needs of their citizens and conduct themselves responsibly in the international system."[25] It further argued that democratic regimes are more stable, more economically prosperous, and more peaceful toward their neighbors than any alternative form of government. As a consequence, promoting democracy is "the best way to provide enduring security for the American people."[26] This view was shared by other prominent Republicans, particularly John McCain.[27]

The Middle East was clearly the primary focus of this strategy. From 2002 to 2006, the administration allocated over $400 million to the

---

freedom does not flourish, it will remain a place of stagnation, resentment, and violence ready for export. And with the spread of weapons that can bring catastrophic harm to our country and to our friends, it would be reckless to accept the status quo." George W. Bush, "Speech on Democracy and Freedom in the Middle East," presented at the National Endowment for Democracy, November 6, 2003.

[23] Condoleezza Rice, "Remarks at the American University in Cairo," June 20, 2005. The Undersecretary of State for Political Affairs reaffirmed in April 2005 that "The U.S. plans to make—as a permanent feature of its policy in the region—a broad and substantial program to help the peoples of the Middle East reach a more secure and democratic future." R. Nicholas Burns, "A Transatlantic Agenda for the Year Ahead," speech delivered at the Royal Institute for International Affairs, London, April 6, 2005.

[24] George W. Bush, "Speech on Democracy and Freedom in the Middle East," presented at the National Endowment for Democracy, November 6, 2003.

[25] *The National Security Strategy of the United States of America* (Washington, DC: The White House, 2006), 1. Bush struck a similar theme in his second inaugural address, where he concluded that "the survival of liberty in our land increasingly depends on the success of liberty in other lands." George W. Bush, "Inaugural Address," January 20, 2005.

[26] *National Security Strategy of the United States*, 1.

[27] McCain was a cosponsor of the Advance Democracy Act in 2005. When introducing the Act, he proclaimed that "the promotion of democracy and freedom is simply inseparable from the long-term security of the United States. When the security of New York or Washington or California depends in part on the degree of freedom in Riyadh or Baghdad or Cairo, then we must promote democracy, the rule of law, and social modernization just as we promote the sophistication of our weapons and the modernization of our militaries." He has also backed legislation supporting democratic reform in Iraq, Jordan, Russia, Central America, Haiti, Fiji, Kosovo, Burma, and Afghanistan. See McCain's official website: http://mccain.senate.gov. Accessed August 15, 2007.

newly created Middle East Partnership Initiative (MEPI) that seeks to increase the fairness of elections, support civil society groups, strengthen judiciaries, and improve protection of women's rights.[28] Another $250 million has been proposed by Congress under the Advance Democracy Act, with most of it earmarked for the Middle East.[29] USAID's budget for democracy promotion in the Middle East also increased sharply, from $27 million in 2001 to $105 million in 2005.[30] And, the United States invaded Iraq. The war was justified, in part, as an effort to bring democracy to the region. The administration argued that the democratic transformation of Iraq would "serve as a beacon of liberty, inspiring democratic reformers throughout the Middle East."[31]

The goal of building democracy in the Middle East has attracted bipartisan support. Democrats voted in large numbers to fund the democracy promotion programs put forward by the Bush administration.[32] The democrats' deputy leader in the Senate, Richard Durbin of Illinois, stated in 2004, "I agree wholeheartedly with the president that one of the most important things this country can do to fight terrorism is to promote democracy in the Middle East. The lack of democracy in many Middle Eastern countries has led directly to Islamic extremism."[33] Hillary Clinton asserted in a 2006 speech that "human freedom and the quest for individuals to achieve their god-given potential must be at the heart of American approaches across the [Middle East]. The dream of democracy and human

[28] A more detailed list of the MEPI's programs is available at http://mepi.state.gov/c16050.htm. Also see Jeremy M. Sharp, *The Middle East Partnership Initiative: An Overview* (Washington, DC: Congressional Research Service, July 20, 2005).

[29] The program is described in a press release from one of its co-sponsors, Senator Joe Lieberman, at: http://lieberman.senate.gov/newsroom/release.cfm?id=232762.

[30] Roughly 70 percent of this funding went to democracy promotion programs in Iraq. See Tamara Cofman-Wittes and Sarah E. Yerkes, "The Middle East Freedom Agenda: An Update," *Current History* 106, no. 696 (January 2007): 35.

[31] Remarks by Stephen Hadley, assistant to the president for national security affairs, before the Center for Strategic and International Studies, December 20, 2005. Hadley further concluded that the resulting spread of democracy in the region would "lead to a Middle East that is more peaceful, more stable, and more inhospitable to terrorists and their supporters."

[32] Funding for the Middle East Partnership Initiative encountered some resistance in the Congress but, ironically, this resistance came primarily from Republicans. They objected to what they considered the MEPI's lack of clear objectives. They were also concerned that some of its programs duplicated existing programs already supported through USAID funding. See Jeremy M. Sharp, *The Middle East Partnership Initiative*; also, "The Middle East Partnership Initiative: Promoting Democratization in a Troubled Region." Hearing before the Subcommittee on the Middle East and Central Asia of the Committee on International Relations, House of Representatives, March 19, 2003.

[33] Durbin made these comments during a floor statement regarding the Syria Accountability Act in 2004. The statement is available at http://durbin.senate.gov/issues/syria.cfm. Accessed June 15, 2007.

rights is one that should belong to all people in the Middle East and across the world . . . we must stand on the side of democracy wherever we can help it take hold."[34] Barack Obama held a similar view, claiming that the key to defeating radical Islam lay in "provid[ing] the kind of steady support for political reformers and civil society that enabled our victory in the Cold War."[35] Obama was also one of six cosponsors of the Advance Democracy Act, which called for the expansion of democracy promotion in the Middle East.

When the democrats gained control of the House of Representatives and the Senate in 2006, they sought to bring some of this rhetoric into reality. They incorporated funding for MEPI into their signature bill on national security, the "Real Security Act of 2006."[36] Several prominent democrats also initiated an effort to withhold $100 million in military assistance to Egypt, which provided further opportunity to voice their support for human rights and democracy in Egypt and the Arab world.[37]

America's calls for democracy in the Middle East were joined by equally convinced—though less effusive—European allies. The German foreign minister, for example, agreed that the fight against terrorism required a much broader conception of security that included "social-cultural modernization issues, as well as democracy, the rule of law, women's rights and good governance."[38] The European Security Strategy, adopted in December 2003, states that "the quality of international society depends on the quality of governments that are its foundation. The best protection of our security is a world of well-governed democratic states."[39] The European Union Commission president reiterated this view,[40] as did other European

[34] "Challenges for U.S. Foreign Policy in the Middle East—Remarks of Senator Hillary Rodham Clinton at Princeton University's Woodrow Wilson School of Public and International Affairs," January 19, 2006.

[35] Barack Obama, "Renewing American Leadership," *Foreign Affairs* (July/August 2007), 11. Also see page 14.

[36] See the description of the Real Security Act at http://democrats.senate.gov/ newsroom/record.cfm?id=262588.

[37] The effort was initiated by David Obey, the chair of the House Appropriations Committee. He proposed the amendment because, in his words, "I am increasingly concerned that Egypt is headed in a direction domestically that puts at risk not only U.S. interests in the region but the very stability of Egypt." See Obey's statement attached to the House report on bill 109–486—Foreign Operations, Export Financing, and Related Programs Appropriations Bill, 2007. For a record of the debate on the bill in June 2007, see Congressional Record—House, volume 153, number 100 (110th Congress, 1st Session).

[38] The remarks were made by the German foreign minister, Joschka Fisher, at the 40th Munich Conference on Security Policy, February 7, 2004.

[39] "A Secure Europe in a Better World: European Security Strategy." Issued December 12, 2003. Available online at: http://ue.eu.int/uedocs/cmsUpload/78367.pdf.

[40] The Commission president, Jose Manuel Barroso, noted during his visit to the White House in October 2005 that the United States and Europe share a strategic partnership that

leaders such as Tony Blair.[41] The EU's efforts are carried out primarily within the framework of the Euro-Mediterranean Partnership, which includes funding to strengthen civil society groups, human rights, and the rule of law. The funding for these programs increased substantially after the terrorist attacks of 2001.[42] Individual European countries have also undertaken bilateral efforts to promote the rule of law and human rights in Arab countries, with Britain, Denmark, France, and Sweden taking the lead.[43] In addition, European nations have cooperated with the United States on an annual conference in the region, the Forum for the Future. This event brings together G-8 ministers, ministers from Arab governments, businessmen, and civil society leaders to develop programs for political and economic reform.[44] It is currently the only setting that allows democracy advocates to interact directly with government ministers and business leaders.

Of course, the United States and Europe still defend the strategic interests mentioned earlier. Democracy promotion has not trumped these interests. At times, it takes a back seat to them, which leads to variations in

---

seeks to "promote democracy, human rights, the rule of law, and the market economy around the world." "European Commission President Barroso meets U.S. President Bush at the White House," EU press release, October 15, 2005.

[41] See, for example, Tony Blair's speech before the U.S. Congress on July 17, 2003. He states that, "The spread of freedom is the best security for the free. It is our last line of defense and our first line of attack. Just as the terrorist seeks to divide humanity in hate, so we have to unify it around an idea, and that idea is liberty."

[42] John Calabrese, "Freedom on the March in the Middle East—and Transatlantic Relations on a New Course?" *Mediterranean Quarterly* (2005): 45–46. From 1995 through 2004, the total funding for the Partnership was $1 billion per year. This funding was applied to programs in three areas: economic development, political reform, and cultural development. The Partnership underwent a thorough review on its tenth anniversary in 2005. As a result of this review, total funding was increased to $1.2 billion per year and programs for political reform were given higher priority. Daniel Dombey and Roula Khalaf, "Euro-Med Leaders Look to Build on Barcelona Process," *Financial Times*, November 26, 2005.

[43] Michael Emerson and others, "The Reluctant Debutante—The EU as Promoter of Democracy in its Neighborhood," in *Democratisation in the European Neighborhood*, ed. Michael Emerson (Brussels: Center for European Policy Studies, 2005), 203–8. Also, Richard Youngs, "Europe's Uncertain Pursuit of Middle East Reform," in *Uncharted Journey: Promoting Democracy in the Middle East*, ed. Thomas Carothers and Marina Ottaway (Washington, DC: Carnegie Endowment for International Peace, 2005), 234–35. The EU has also undertaken bilateral agreements for political reform with Jordan, Morocco, and the Palestinian Authority. It is negotiating such agreements with Egypt and Lebanon. Haizam Amirah-Fernandez, "EU: Barcelona Process and the New Neighborhood Policy," *Arab Reform Bulletin* 4, no. 1 (2006), 5–6.

[44] These conferences take place under the heading of the Broader Middle East and North Africa Initiative, which is also called the Forum for the Future. The first conference occurred in Rabat, Morocco in December 2004. The second was held in Manama, Bahrain in November 2005. The third meeting occurred in Jordan in December 2006.

the strength of Western advocacy for democracy over time and between countries.[45] However, this normal ebb-and-flow of interests should not be construed as insincerity. Since 2001, democratization has been elevated from an appealing afterthought among policy makers to a strategic objective in itself. True, it is only one objective among many. But it now carries significant weight among policy makers in the United States and Europe. Major Western governments now argue with increasing conviction that the absence of democracy in the region has a direct impact on regional and global security.[46]

This change on the international stage has been matched by a serious effort among Arab intellectuals and activists to promote democratic reform. The most systematic work in this regard is the Arab Human Development Reports (AHDR) of 2002, 2003, 2004, and 2005.[47] These reports were prepared by a team of prominent Arab intellectuals under the auspices of the United Nations Development Program. They received wide distribution—for example, over 1 million copies of the 2002 report were downloaded from the UNDP's website.[48] The reports focus on three "deficits" that plague the Arab world: a lack of freedom, insufficient rights for women, and inadequate educational systems. They emphasize that all people are entitled to the full range of civil and political rights, and that each citizen has the right to participate in his own governance. The reports assert that these principles are fundamental to human freedom which, in turn, is the foundation for economic growth and human development.[49]

[45] For example, Secretary of State Condoleezza Rice visited Egypt in January 2007 and held a long meeting with President Mubarak. During her visit, she made no effort to encourage political reform. Rather, she focused on gaining Egypt's support for American policy toward the Arab-Israeli conflict, Iraq, and Iran. This stands in sharp contrast to her visit in June 2005, when she publicly called for more rapid democratization. For her speech in June 2005, see Condoleezza Rice, "Remarks at the American University in Cairo," June 20, 2005. For her remarks during her visit in January 2007, see Condoleezza Rice, "Remarks with Egyptian Foreign Minister Aboul Gheit," January 15, 2007. Available on the State Department's website: http://www.state.gov/. Accessed June 12, 2007.

[46] As Henry Kissinger put it, "The advocates of the important role of a commitment to democracy in American foreign policy have won their intellectual battle." Henry A. Kissinger, "Intervention with a Vision," in *The Right War? The Conservative Debate on Iraq*, ed. Gary Rosen (Cambridge: Cambridge University Press, 2005), 53.

[47] *Arab Human Development Report 2002: Creating Opportunities for Future Generations* (New York: United Nations Development Program, 2002); *Arab Human Development Report 2003: Building a Knowledge Society* (New York: United Nations Development Program, 2003); *Arab Human Development Report 2004: Towards Freedom in the Arab World* (New York: United Nations Development Program, 2005); *Arab Human Development Report 2005: Towards the Rise of Women in the Arab World* (New York: United Nations Development Program, 2006).

[48] *Arab Human Development Report 2003*, i. The report was cited by *Time* magazine as the most important publication of 2002.

[49] *Arab Human Development Report 2004*, 2–3.

The reports also argue that the Arab world confronts several acute problems that can be managed only through skilled and accountable governance. The most formidable of these problems include the following:

A demographic "youth bulge." Roughly 38 percent of the region's population is under the age of fourteen. The region will need 50 million new jobs by 2010 in order to accommodate them. This demographic challenge draws attention to two core weaknesses of the current order: the poor quality of state-led economic management, which has produced weak economic growth; and the absence of political institutions that can represent the interests of these young people and respond to their concerns quickly and effectively. In the view of the AHDR, democratization addresses both of these problems. It increases the transparency and accountability of government decision making, thereby improving economic policy and performance. It also provides an orderly and reliable mechanism for including citizens in political life.

The political repercussions of economic restructuring. In order to improve economic performance, many countries in the region have adopted market-oriented economic reforms that shrink the public sector and reduce state subsidies. In the short term, these measures cause severe hardship, particularly to public-sector workers and unskilled labor. In the view of the AHDR, democratic reforms are essential for creating political institutions that can respond to the needs of these workers and provide a peaceful avenue for expressing and managing their dissent.

The growing power of Islamist groups. Throughout the Middle East, Islamist groups have developed broad popular support, effective social service networks, and a formidable capacity to mobilize their followers. The appeal of these groups is likely to increase in the future. In the view of the AHDR, democratic reforms are the only way to integrate these groups into the political process and give them a stake in peaceful change.

The authors of the AHDR believe that the current political structures of the Arab world are simply not up to these challenges. If the region is to cope effectively, democratization is essential. If it does not occur, Arabs face the prospect of "intensified social conflict . . . violent protest . . . [and] internal disorder."[50]

Support for democratization is not limited to the small circle of intellectuals who wrote the AHDR. Opinion polls indicate significant public backing for democratic principles. A poll by the World Values Survey in Egypt, Jordan, Morocco, and Algeria found that over 85 percent of respondents considered democracy "better than any other form of govern-

[50] Ibid., 19.

ment."[51] The percentage of respondents who considered democracy the best form of government exceeded that of any other region in the developing world.[52] The Arab respondents also expressed the highest rate of rejection (80 percent) of authoritarian rule.[53] A poll conducted by the AHDR indicates that Arabs place a high value on freedom of thought, expression, and belief.[54] Additional survey research reaches similar conclusions and suggests that the Arab public supports many democratic values, with the important exception of women's equality.[55]

Public advocacy of democratization has also become widespread and forceful. Meetings of intellectuals, civil society organizations, and business groups frequently include declarations of support for democracy.[56] The Arab media also increasingly advocates democratization, with satellite television stations leading the way. The most popular satellite station, *al-Jazeera*, has made political reform a central theme of its programming. A recent study of its broadcasts since 1999 found that roughly one-third of its talk show programs deal with this topic. They frequently include harsh attacks on the regimes of the region and vigorous demands for democratic change. In the view of the study's author (Marc Lynch), *al-Jazeera* has helped to transform Arab political discourse by creating an intellectual climate where challenging political authority is not only tolerated, but

[51] Respondents were presented with the statement: "Despite its problems, democracy is better than any other form of government." In each of the four Arab countries studied, over 85 percent of the respondents either "strongly agreed" or "agreed" with this statement. The results of the survey with regard to the Middle East are summarized in Mark Tessler, "Do Islamic Orientations Influence Attitudes Toward Democracy in the Arab World? Evidence from Egypt, Jordon, Morocco, and Algeria," in *Islam, Gender, Culture, and Democracy*, ed. Ronald Inglehart (Willowdale, ON: deSitter Publications, 2003), 13.

[52] *World Values Surveys Four-Wave Integrated Data File, 1981–2004.* Downloaded from the Inter-University Consortium for Political and Social Research.

[53] The question involved asked whether the respondent would accept a "strong leader who does not have to bother with parliament and elections." Ibid.

[54] The survey is summarized in the *Arab Human Development Report 2004*, 98–99.

[55] *The 2002 Gallup Poll of the Islamic World* (Princeton, NJ: Gallup Organization, 2002). This poll was conducted in December 2001 and January 2002. It included 4,300 Arab respondents from Jordan, Kuwait, Lebanon, Morocco, and Saudi Arabia. Also, James J. Zogby, *What Arabs Think: Values, Beliefs, and Concerns* (New York: Zogby International, 2002), especially pp. 33–42. This poll involved 3,800 Arabs in eight countries. Also, Pew Global Attitudes Project, *Views of a Changing World: June 2003* (Washington, DC: Pew Research Center for the People and the Press, 2003), especially pp. 47–70. This poll deals with only two Arab countries, Lebanon and Jordan. Also see Amaney Jamal and Mark Tessler, "Attitudes in the Arab World," *Journal of Democracy* 19, no. 1 (January 2008): 97–110.

[56] The most prominent declarations are: the Sana'a declaration of January 2004, which was produced by the Regional Conference on Democracy, Human Rights, and the Role of the International Criminal Court; and the Alexandria Charter of March 2004, which was the result of a conference of Arab civil society organizations entitled "Arab Reform Issues: Vision and Implementation."

encouraged. It is "building the foundation of a more democratic Arab political culture."[57]

In addition, civil society groups and activists increasingly undertake demonstrations and other acts of public resistance in support of political change. For example, the *Kifaya* ("enough") movement in Egypt organized thousands of demonstrators in the spring of 2005 to call for an end to President Mubarak's rule and the convening of competitive presidential elections. The Muslim Brotherhood mobilized thousands of its followers to participate in these demonstrations. It also organized separate demonstrations to support political and constitutional reform. In Lebanon, the "March 14th" movement brought 1.2 million people onto the streets in 2005 to protest Syria's presence. They organized several subsequent demonstrations to advocate political reform and national reconciliation.[58] Significant public mobilization in favor of political reform has also occurred in Morocco and Jordan, despite the threat of imprisonment and fines.[59]

What is the Future of Democracy in the Arab World?

For the first time in the region's history, there are strong indigenous demands for democracy backed by significant international support. These pressures have not yet led to democratic transitions. However, there have been some meaningful steps toward political reform. Improvements in electoral procedure and monitoring have produced more competitive elections in Algeria, Kuwait, Lebanon, Jordan, and Morocco. Judicial independence has increased in Egypt, Kuwait, Jordan, and Morocco.[60] Judges in Egypt and Kuwait, in particular, have shown a willingness to challenge

[57] Marc Lynch, "Shattering the 'Politics of Silence.' Satellite Television Talk Shows and the Transformation of Arab Political Culture," *Arab Reform Bulletin* 2, no. 11 (2004): 3; also, Marc Lynch, *Voices of the New Arab Public: Iraq, Al-Jazeera, and Middle East Politics Today* (New York: Columbia University Press, 2006).

[58] Paul Salem, *Lebanon at the Crossroads: Rebuilding an Arab Democracy* (Washington, DC: Brookings Institution, 2005); Oussama Safa, "Lebanon Springs Forward," *Journal of Democracy* 17, no. 1 (2006): 22–37.

[59] For further information on Morocco, see: Andrew R. Smith and Fadoua Loudiy, "Testing the Red Lines: On the Liberalization of Speech in Morocco," *Human Rights Quarterly* 27, no. 3 (2005): 1069–1119; Marina Ottaway and Meredith Riley, *Morocco: From Top-Down Reform to Democratic Transition?* (Washington, DC: Carnegie Endowment for International Peace, 2006). For further information on Jordan, see: George Joffe, *Jordan in Transition* (London: Hurst and Co., 2002); Russell E. Lucas, "Deliberalization in Jordan," *Journal of Democracy* 14, no. 1 (2003): 137–44; Anne Marie Baylouny, "Jordan's New 'Political Development' Strategy," *Middle East Report* 35, no. 3 (2005): 40–43.

[60] Nathan Brown, "Arab Judicial Reform: Bold Visions, Few Achievements," *Arab Reform Bulletin*, October 2004.

executive power.[61] Parliaments have gained greater authority to question members of the executive and remove ministers in Jordan and Morocco. Changes in legislation and procedure have made it easier to form political parties in Morocco and Egypt. Strong civil society groups calling for political reform have emerged in Egypt, Lebanon, Morocco, and Jordan. And, press freedom has improved in Bahrain, Morocco, and Jordan.[62]

In addition, several countries in the region have undergone economic restructuring that carries important repercussions for political change. The massive welfare states that enhanced regime legitimacy in many countries have proven financially unsustainable. Persistent budget deficits and fiscal crises have forced cutbacks in key institutions of state control such as the public sector, the subsidy system, and the civil service. This is particularly the case in Egypt, Morocco, and Jordan.[63] The state in these countries is certainly in no danger of collapsing. However, its capacity to control the economy and society has declined.[64] At the same time, new institutions are emerging within the state (such as independent judiciaries) and within civil society (such as Islamist groups). These institutions challenge and constrain state power. As noted earlier, they may also offer an alternative conception of political order that competes with the regime's ideology.

Although these developments are encouraging, we must be careful not to exaggerate their significance. As one might expect, there have been setbacks. Lebanon, in particular, has suffered from a recent descent into sectarian rivalries and violence. In addition, the autocrats of the Arab world have adopted countermeasures to protect their power and frustrate reform. The still-formidable ruling elites of the region have a substantial

[61] Most recently, the Kuwaiti Constitutional Court voided fifteen clauses of the Public Gatherings Law, which restricts public gatherings that convene without prior permission from the authorities. It held that the clauses violated the right to freedom of assembly guaranteed by the constitution. The ruling marked the first time that a court had challenged the emergency powers of the emir. See *Arab Reform Bulletin*, May 2006 (issue 4). For discussion of the Egyptian judiciary, see chapter 2.

[62] These points are gleaned primarily from a review of the monthly *Arab Reform Bulletin* from September 2003 through May 2006. The *Bulletin* is published by the Carnegie Endowment for International Peace.

[63] The Egyptian case is discussed in chapter 5. For further information on economic restructuring in Morocco, see *Fostering Higher Growth and Employment in the Kingdom of Morocco* (Washington, DC: World Bank, 2006). For information on Jordan, see Katherine Blue Carroll, *Business as Usual? Economic Reform in Jordan* (Lanham: Lexington Books, 2003); Warwick M. Knowles, *Jordan since 1989: A Study in Political Economy* (London: I. B. Tauris, 2005).

[64] For further discussion of the changing character of the state in the Arab world, see Hassan Hakimian and Ziba Moshaver, eds., *The State and Global Change: The Political Economy of Transition in the Middle East and North Africa* (Richmond: Curzon Press, 2001).

arsenal of tools at their disposal.[65] Autocratic institutions are not being swept away in dramatic popular upheavals comparable to the "people power" of the Philippines or the colored revolutions of central Europe. Rather, the tools of centralized state power are gradually eroding. As this unfolds, new institutions emerge alongside these weakened—but still functioning—state institutions. In Egypt, for example, the country's powerful security institutions and the legal codes that empower them are not being dismantled. Instead, increasingly assertive administrative and constitutional courts challenge their power and limit their authority.[66] In Jordan, the state's social service institutions and educational system are not shutting down. Instead, they continue to function in a fragmentary and incomplete fashion, and are supplemented by independent Islamic institutions that perform the same functions.[67] Some institutions (such as independent judiciaries) may be products of the regime's policies, but this does not mean they are controlled by the regime. Rather, they develop and function alongside the autocratic institutions of the state and often constitute a meaningful constraint on it.

The net political result of this process is neither authoritarianism nor democracy. Rather, the outcome is a hybrid regime that shares characteristics of both an autocratic order (characterized by a powerful executive with few formal checks on his authority) and a democratic order (which includes institutions that constrain the state and increase governmental accountability). Furthermore, these democratic institutions are often supported by Islamic thinkers and activists. Islamic political and legal thought plays an increasingly important role in defining and legitimizing the institutional alternatives to autocracy.

A full transition to democracy is not likely in any contemporary Arab regime. However, for regimes with these hybrid characteristics, a reversion to full authoritarianism is equally unlikely. In order to understand the future of democracy in the Arab world, we need to understand how these hybrid regimes emerge, why they remain stable, and whether they will transition toward democracy. The theoretical literature on hybrid regimes provides a valuable starting point for this analysis.

---

[65] For further discussion of the tactics of Arab authoritarianism, see Eberhard Kienle, *A Grand Delusion: Democracy and Economic Reform in Egypt* (New York: I. B. Tauris, 2001); Maye Kassem, *Egyptian Politics: The Dynamics of Authoritarian Rule* (Boulder, CO: Lynne Rienner, 2004); Russell Lucas, *Institutions and the Politics of Survival in Jordan: Domestic Responses to External Challenges, 1988–2001* (Binghamton: State University of New York Press, 2005); Ellen Lust-Okar, *Structuring Conflict in the Arab World: Incumbents, Opponents, and Institutions* (New York: Cambridge University Press, 2005).

[66] These court rulings will be discussed in chapter 2.

[67] Janine A. Clark, *Islam, Charity, and Activism: Middle-Class Networks and Social Welfare in Egypt, Jordan, and Yemen* (Bloomington: Indiana University Press, 2004), 82–114.

HYBRID REGIMES AND POLITICAL CHANGE

Scholars of authoritarianism have long been aware of regimes that contain both autocratic and democratic institutions. Linz's classic study of authoritarianism discusses this topic in some detail.[68] Diamond, Linz, and Lipset also examine it in their extensive multi-country study of democratization. They begin by observing that all democracies fall short of the democratic ideal. However, some regimes fall so far short that they cannot be described as democratic. The authors identify several types of regimes that fall within this "grey zone" between democracy and autocracy: "semidemocracy," in which competitive elections occur among multiple parties but there are serious flaws in the electoral process or sharp restrictions on the powers of representative institutions; "low-intensity" democracy, in which vibrant and relatively fair elections take place, but governments lack meaningful accountability during the period between elections; and "hegemonic party systems," in which free elections occur, but one party thoroughly dominates the electoral process and precludes any meaningful competition for power.[69] Each of these is an example of a hybrid regime that exhibits a different mix of authoritarian and democratic institutions.[70] Ottaway describes hybrid regimes in similar terms.[71] They may contain legislatures, independent judiciaries, and civil society organizations. However, they do not allow the transfer of power through elections and, therefore, are not fully functioning democracies.[72]

[68] Juan J. Linz, *Totalitarian and Authoritarian Regimes* (Boulder, CO: Lynne Rienner, 2000), 58–61.

[69] Larry Diamond, Juan J. Linz, and Seymour Martin Lipset, "Introduction: What Makes for Democracy?" in *Politics in Developing Countries: Comparing Experiences with Democracy,* ed. Larry Diamond, Juan J. Linz, and Seymour Martin Lipset (Boulder, CO: Lynne Rienner, 1995), 7–8.

[70] A variety of other terms appear in the literature to describe this type of mixed regime, including: virtual democracy, pseudodemocracy, illiberal democracy, semi-authoritarianism, soft authoritarianism, electoral authoritarianism, and "partly free." See Steven Levitsky and Lucan A. Way, "The Rise of Competitive Authoritarianism," *Journal of Democracy* 13, no. 2 (2002), 51. Also, Ariel C. Armony and Hector E. Schamis, "Babel in Democratization Studies," *Journal of Democracy* 16, no. 4 (2005), 113.

[71] Marina Ottaway, *Democracy Challenged: The Rise of Semi-Authoritarianism* (Washington, DC: Carnegie Endowment for International Peace, 2003), 3.

[72] This discussion of hybrid regimes draws attention to the importance of distinguishing between liberalism and democracy. Western analysts are accustomed to seeing these two principles merged into a single idea—"liberal democracy." However, they are different concepts. Liberalism is a set of institutions and institutional relationships that constrain state power and protect citizens' civil and political rights. These institutions include a clear and unbiased legal code, the separation of powers, checks and balances among these powers, an independent judiciary, and effective legal institutions that implement the law. Democracy is the process of selecting a country's leaders through free and fair elections. In many hybrid regimes, the

Hybrid regimes have been part of the political landscape for several decades.[73] However, their number grew dramatically after the end of the Cold War. The demise of the Soviet Union led to the withdrawal of external support from many of the world's dictatorships. Russia had neither the resources nor the will to continue supporting communist regimes around the world. With the Soviet menace gone, the United States had little reason to support right-wing dictatorships that counterbalanced communist influence. This termination of external support precipitated severe economic crises in many dictatorships in Africa, Asia, and Latin America. Autocrats had little choice but to open their political systems in order to retain power, but they did so in a manner that fell short of full democratic transition.[74] The result was a sharp increase in hybrid regimes.

The Soviet Union's collapse also left the West in a position of political and economic preeminence. Communist and socialist models of development had lost their credibility and popularity. The Western democratic model swept the global competition of ideas and became the natural choice for advocates of political reform in authoritarian regimes. Furthermore, after the collapse of the USSR, the West held a virtual monopoly on economic assistance. Autocrats who wanted a piece of this pie would need to show at least rhetorical support for the principles of democracy and accountability. Several Western countries went a step further and explicitly incorporated democracy promotion into their foreign policies. As noted earlier, this was particularly the case for the United States and the members of the European Union.[75]

These measures were reinforced by a growing network of transnational civil society groups that promoted democracy and human rights.[76] These

---

institutions of liberalism have emerged and constrain some dimensions of executive power. However, the core institution at the heart of democracy—free elections—remains weak or nonexistent. This distinction between liberalism and democracy is particularly important for understanding the Egyptian case. It will be discussed in further detail in chapter 6.

[73] Particularly long-lived examples include Mexico before 1997 and post-independence Malaysia. The following discussion of the history of hybrid regimes draws on Levitsky and Way, "The Rise of Competitive Authoritarianism," 61–63.

[74] Bratton and van de Walle offer a particularly clear discussion of this phenomenon in Africa. See Michael Bratton and Nicolas van de Walle, *Democratic Experiments in Africa: Regime Transitions in Comparative Perspective* (New York: Cambridge University Press, 1997), 97–122.

[75] Thomas Carothers, *Aiding Democracy Abroad: The Learning Curve* (Washington, DC: Carnegie Endowment for International Peace, 1999), 6; Katerina Dalacoura, "U.S. Democracy Promotion in the Arab Middle East since 11 September 2001: A Critique," *International Affairs* 81, no. 5 (2005): 963–79; Ana Echagüe and Richard Youngs, "Democracy and Human Rights in the Barcelona Process," *Mediterranean Politics* 10, no. 2 (2005): 233–38; Richard Gillespie and Richard Youngs, eds., *The European Union and Democracy Promotion: The Case of North Africa* (London: Frank Cass, 2002).

[76] Margaret E. Keck and Kathryn Sikkink, *Activists Beyond Borders: Advocacy Networks in International Politics* (Ithaca, NY: Cornell University Press, 1998); Marina Ottaway and

organizations included human rights groups, international party foundations, and media advocacy groups. They drew international attention to
human rights abuses and lobbied Western governments to monitor and
punish autocratic regimes.[77] Some of the groups also sought to protect
and strengthen pro-democracy forces through lobbying, funding, and
training.[78] In addition, international election observers became an important force for identifying and documenting electoral fraud. Their efforts led to substantial improvements in the fairness and transparency of
elections.[79]

These changes in the international setting dramatically increased the
incentives for authoritarian leaders to adopt at least the trappings of democracy. As Levitsky and Way conclude, "for most governments in lower-
and middle-income countries, the costs associated with the maintenance
of full-scale authoritarian institutions—and the benefits associated with
adopting democratic ones—rose considerably in the 1990s."[80] Diamond
reaches the same conclusion and observes that "one of the most striking
features of the 'late period' of the third wave [of democratization] has
been the unprecedented growth in the number of regimes that are neither
clearly democratic nor conventionally authoritarian."[81] He estimates that,
by 2001, roughly one-third of the world's regimes could be described as
"hybrids."[82] Furthermore, these regimes have shown remarkable durability. Many hybrid regimes have existed for fifteen years or longer, which
exceeds the life span of most bureaucratic-authoritarian regimes in Latin
America.[83] This durability suggests that hybrid regimes cannot be charac-

---

Thomas Carothers, eds., *Funding Virtue: Civil Society Aid and Democracy Promotion* (Washington, DC: Carnegie Endowment for International Peace, 2000).

[77] Keck and Sikkink, *Activists Beyond Borders*, 12–13.

[78] Ibid.; Thomas Risse, Stephen C. Ropp, and Kathryn Sikkink., eds., *The Power of Human
Rights: International Norms and Domestic Change* (New York: Cambridge University
Press, 1999).

[79] Thomas Carothers, "The Observers Observed," *Journal of Democracy* 8, no. 3 (1997):
17–31.

[80] Steven Levitsky and Lucan A. Way, "Autocracy by Democratic Rules: The Dynamics of
Competitive Authoritarianism in the Post–Cold War Era." Paper presented at the confer-
ence, "Mapping the Grey Zone: Clientelism and the Boundary between Democratic and
Democratizing." (New York: Columbia University Press, 2003), 6.

[81] Larry Diamond, "Thinking about Hybrid Regimes," *Journal of Democracy* 13, no. 2
(2002): 25.

[82] Diamond identifies three categories of hybrid regimes: competitive authoritarian
(in which competitive elections exist within a stable authoritarian regime), hegemonic electoral authoritarian (in which a single party dominates regular elections), and "ambiguous
regimes" that straddle the boundary between democracy and authoritarianism in other ways.
Ibid., 26.

[83] Steven Levitsky and Lucan A. Way, *Competitive Authoritarianism: International Link-
age, Organizational Power, and Hybrid Regimes in the Post–Cold War Era* (New York: Cambridge University Press, forthcoming), chap. 1.

terized as "stalled" or "prolonged" or "incomplete" transitions to democ-racy.[84] Rather, they are a distinct regime type that needs to be understood on its own terms.[85]

As hybrid regimes became more numerous and long-lived, scholars of comparative democratization began to study them with greater care. Levitsky and Way undertook a project that analyzed thirty-seven of these regimes. They found that traditional authoritarian regimes assume a hy-brid character through the emergence of four arenas where opposition forces challenge autocratic incumbents: elections, in which opposition candidates run successfully against members of the regime; legislatures, where opposition parliamentarians challenge and constrain the govern-ment; the judiciary, where judges repeal repressive laws and limit the scope of executive power; and the media, where independent journalists investi-gate and expose abuses of power by the regime.[86] Their careful study of change in each of these arenas suggests that hybrid regimes emerge through three processes:

Elite calculations for survival: Ruling elites in autocratic regimes often confront periods of crisis brought on by poor economic performance, mil-itary defeat, excessive repression, or a similar event. They may also face external demands to democratize as a condition for economic aid or mem-bership in international organizations. In order to cope with these pres-sures, ruling elites may adopt limited reforms such as releasing political prisoners, expanding civil and political rights, and allowing some political competition. These measures are carefully calibrated to enhance the re-gime's legitimacy and international stature without allowing genuine competition for power.

Change in the relative power of institutions within the state and society: Authoritarian regimes are based upon control of several key institutions. The most obvious are the security services and police, which provide the "hard power" to maintain order and repress opponents. However, these regimes also rely on "soft power," which shapes the priorities of citizens by providing them with incentives to support the existing order. At the heart of this "soft power" are economic institutions such as the public sector, the subsidy system, and the bureaucracy. These institutions provide jobs, food, housing, education, and a host of other important services. A successful authoritarian regime utilizes them to maintain the loyalty and cooperation of its supporters. These institutions are also valuable tools for co-opting or harassing the regime's opponents.

---

[84] Levitsky and Way study 37 cases of hybrid regimes from 1990 through 2005. Of these, only 14 underwent a transition to democracy. Ibid., chap. 1.

[85] Thomas Carothers, "The End of the Transition Paradigm," *Journal of Democracy* 13, no. 1 (2002): 5–21.

[86] Levitsky and Way, "The Rise of Competitive Authoritarianism," 54–57.

These institutions may be undermined by economic crises, economic mismanagement, or economic restructuring. When these institutions are weakened, the regime's patronage network erodes and it can no longer provide the services that are essential for preserving its legitimacy and power. This can lead to two institutional outcomes that contribute to the development of a hybrid regime. First, governing elites may allow the emergence of new institutions within the state in order to enhance the regime's economic performance. They may, for example, allow the development of an independent judiciary in the hope that it will create a more attractive investment environment by protecting property rights and ensuring reliable enforcement of contracts. Second, the weakening of the institutions that provide public services creates an opportunity for private service organizations to emerge and grow. These may take the form of charitable organizations, religious groups, or commercial firms. They help to meet the basic needs of society in fields such as housing, medical care, and education. Thus, a hybrid regime may emerge through the combination of autocratic institutions weakening and alternative institutions expanding within the state and civil society.

Erosion of the political ideas that legitimate the regime: Autocratic regimes often rely on a set of ideas to justify their centralization of power and their denial of civil and political rights. For example, the Institutional Revolutionary Party (PRI) in Mexico stressed the goal of reordering society to achieve the justice and equity promised by the Mexican revolution. Tanzania under Julius Nyerere tried to implement African socialism, which was based on Nyerere's unique mix of socialist and tribal principles. Egypt under Nasser sought to advance Arab nationalism, which combined Egyptian nationalism, anti-colonialism, and aspirations for regional leadership. Political ideas such as these may not be sufficiently rigorous or systematic to warrant the label "ideology." Nonetheless, they matter for legitimating an autocratic regime and justifying its monopoly on power. These legitimating ideas often erode due to the death of the founding leader, poor economic performance, excessive repression, military defeats, and other practical failures of governance. As these ideas erode, alternative views of political order have the opportunity to develop and build support within the state and society. The growth of these alternative conceptions of law and governance is another important step in the creation of a hybrid regime.

Thus, hybrid regimes emerge through a combination of elite calculations, institutional change, and ideational competition. However, as scholarly interest in hybrid regimes increased, research tended to concentrate only on the short-term maneuvering of autocratic elites.[87] The litera-

---

[87] See, for example, Maxwell A. Cameron, *Democracy and Authoritarianism in Peru: Political Coalitions and Social Change* (New York: St. Martin's Press, 1994); William Case, "Can the 'Halfway House' Stand? Semidemocracy and Elite Theory in Three Southeast Asian

ture focused particularly on the role of elections in authoritarian regimes. Works by Schedler, Magaloni, Geddes, Pripstein Posusney, Lust-Okar, Lucas, Brownlee, and others examined the tactics and political dynamics of elections under authoritarianism with care and precision.[88] However, this literature leaves several important aspects of hybrid regimes underexplored and unconceptualized. While providing insight into the short-term calculations that sustain these regimes, it neglects the longer-term institutional interaction and ideational competition that produce them, determine their stability, and shape their development. These institutional and ideational considerations include: changes in the size and functions of the state; deterioration of the state's capacity to monitor and control society; erosion of the political ideas that legitimate the regime; and the emergence of competing ideas and institutions that constrain the state and further weaken its legitimacy. These longer-term processes are the underlying explanation for the emergence of a hybrid regime. Elections are merely a symptom of the regime's weakness and a tactic for managing it. This does not render them unimportant. However, analysis of this tactic for regime survival tells us relatively little about the underlying institutional and ideational dynamics that determine the regime's character and stability.

In a similar vein, the focus on elections has tilted the literature toward study of elite calculations at a given moment in time within a fixed set of institutional and ideational constraints. It does not analyze the origins of

Countries," *Comparative Politics* 28, no. 4 (1996): 437–64; Michael McFaul, "The Fourth Wave of Democracy and Dictatorship: Noncooperative Transitions in the Postcommunist World," *World Politics* 54, no. 2 (2002): 212–44.

[88] For examples from the literature on comparative authoritarianism, see Andreas Schedler, ed., *Electoral Authoritarianism: The Dynamics of Unfree Competition* (Boulder, CO: Lynne Rienner, 2006); Andreas Schedler, "The Nested Game of Democratization by Elections," *International Political Science Review* 23, no. 1 (2002): 103–122; Andreas Schedler, "The Menu of Manipulation," *Journal of Democracy* 13, no. 2 (2002): 36–50; Beatriz Magaloni, *Voting for Autocracy: Hegemonic Party Survival and Its Demise in Mexico* (New York: Cambridge University Press, 2006); Barbara Geddes, "Why Parties and Elections in Authoritarian Regimes?" Paper presented at the annual meeting of the American Political Science Association, Washington, DC, September 2005; William Case, "Southeast Asia's Hybrid Regimes: When Do Voters Change Them?" *Journal of East Asian Studies* 5, no. 2 (2005): 215–238; Todd A. Eisenstadt, *Courting Democracy in Mexico: Party Strategies and Electoral Institutions* (New York: Cambridge University Press, 2003). For examples dealing specifically with the Middle East, see: Marsha Pripstein Posusney, "Multiparty Elections in the Arab World: Election Rules and Opposition Responses," in *Authoritarianism in The Middle East: Regimes and Resistance*, ed. Marsha Pripstein Posusney and Michele Penner Angrist (Boulder, CO: Lynne Rienner, 2005), 91–118; Jason Brownlee, "The Double Edge of Electoral Authoritarianism: A Comparison of Egypt and Iran." Paper presented at the annual meeting of the American Political Science Association, San Francisco, September 2001; Bradford Dillman, "Parliamentary Elections and the Prospects for Political Pluralism in North Africa," *Government and Opposition* 35, no. 2 (2000): 211–36; Curtis R. Ryan and Jillian Schwedler, "Return to Democratization or New Hybrid Regime? The 2003 Elec-

the institutional and ideational context that shapes the options open to elites, affects their choices, and influences how those choices unfold. The literature also assumes that these institutional and ideational constraints are constant when, in reality, they are undergoing steady change in many hybrid regimes.

In addition, the concentration on elections has steered analysis into an arena of politics where the regime has extensive capabilities to manipulate the outcome. In most hybrid regimes, the government controls every dimension of how elections unfold. It determines who may register to vote. It defines the nature of the electoral campaign, including which candidates may participate, the amount of money they may spend, the size and frequency of their rallies, and their degree of access to the media. It also controls the polling process itself, including who may have access to the polls, who counts the votes, how the results are announced, and how the electoral outcome is translated into political power (number of seats in parliament, in municipal councils, etc.). Concentrating only on elections produces two biases in our understanding of hybrid regimes. First, it yields an exaggerated sense of the regime's capacity to control the polity. It gives the impression that the regime can manipulate every corner of political life as thoroughly as it controls the electoral process. Second, a focus on elections neglects those aspects of political competition that are not part of the electoral process. These include institutional dynamics that can constrain the power of an autocratic state (such as the emergence of an independent judiciary) and ideational competition that involves actors who are either excluded from elections or whose participation is tightly constrained (such as Islamists).

This emphasis on elections is largely the product of scholars assuming that hybrid regimes are transitioning toward democracy. This assumption leads many scholars to base their research upon the theoretical literature on democratization. This literature argues that democracies emerge through a two-stage sequence. The first stage is a democratic transition, which is defined as the holding of free and fair elections. The second stage is a protracted process of democratic consolidation. This entails forming institutions that constrain executive power (such as an autonomous legislature), increase transparency (such as independent media outlets), and establish the rule of law (such as an independent judiciary). Consolidation also involves the widespread adoption of democratic political ideas such as popular sovereignty, equality before the law, and governmental accountability.[89]

---

tions in Jordan," *Middle East Policy* 11, no. 2 (2004): 138–51; Lucas, *Institutions and the Politics of Survival in Jordan*; Lust-Okar, *Structuring Conflict in the Arab World.*

[89] This sequence is explained with particular clarity in Juan J. Linz and Alfred Stepan, *Problems of Democratic Transition and Consolidation: Southern Europe, South America, and*

Scholars of hybrid regimes have implicitly accepted this sequence and focused tightly on elections, which are the first step along the road to democratic transition and consolidation. However, hybrid regimes are not necessarily in transition. They occupy a stable middle ground between democracy and autocracy. They *combine* the institutions of autocracy and democracy. As a consequence, institutions that scholars of democratization defer to later in their analysis—such as independent judiciaries, strong civil society groups, and independent media outlets—assume a prominent and early role in the analysis of hybrid regimes. Similarly, political ideas that are generally associated with the consolidation phase of democratic development—such as regime accountability, popular sovereignty, and respect for individual rights—may emerge quite early in a hybrid regime and develop support within parts of the state and civil society.

The key feature of a hybrid regime is that these democratic institutions and ideas emerge alongside the institutions and ideas of an autocratic regime and co-exist with it. Furthermore, this phenomenon is not simply the outcome of careful calculations by autocratic elites who manipulate the political arena to their advantage. It is also the result of institutional and ideational competition. It is the product of an autocratic regime's declining power amid the emergence of institutional and ideational alternatives. The regime may tolerate this development, often because it lacks the power to stop it or the cost of stopping it is unacceptable. But, this acquiescence does not mean that the regime controls it or supports it.

In order to more fully understand hybrid regimes, we need a framework that pays due attention to the short-term calculations of elites. However, it must also place these calculations within the broader context of institutional development and ideational competition. Historical institutionalism offers the basis for such a framework.

UNDERSTANDING THE EMERGENCE OF HYBRID REGIMES: A HISTORICAL INSTITUTIONALIST APPROACH

The defining feature of a hybrid regime is the development of democratic institutions alongside well-entrenched authoritarian institutions. This phenomenon of a polity containing multiple—and conflicting—institutions has received considerable attention from scholars of historical institutionalism, particularly Skowronek, Hall, Skocpol, Steinmo, Mahoney, Pierson, and Thelen.

Post–Communist Europe (Baltimore: Johns Hopkins University Press, 1996), 3–15. Also see Larry Diamond, *Developing Democracy: Toward Consolidation* (Baltimore: Johns Hopkins University Press, 1999), 1–23.

One of the leading scholars of this approach, Peter Hall, defines institutions as "the formal or informal procedures, routines, norms and conventions embedded in the organizational structure of the polity or political economy."[90] The historical institutionalists regard the polity as an interlocking set of institutions that were created at different times, often to serve different purposes.[91] This mosaic of clashing institutions is a persistent feature of the political landscape that pushes development along particular paths. It creates a structural context that defines the relative power of actors and the range of options available to them.[92]

In the historical institutionalist perspective, political change occurs as a result of critical junctures that weaken old institutions and strengthen others. There are different types of critical junctures, which produce different opportunities for change. The major types include the following:

Military defeat: Loss of a war can smash a regime's legitimacy and rob it of the resources needed to govern, thereby setting the stage for institutional change. Argentina's defeat in the Falklands war is a good example.

Succession crises: The legitimacy of newly established regimes is often built around the charismatic appeal of a single national leader, such as Nasser in Egypt, Khomeini in Iran, or Attaturk in Turkey. To the extent that these leaders construct institutions, they are usually designed to reinforce and extend the personal power of the leader rather than create a rational-legal basis for authority. The death of the charismatic leader often

---

[90] Peter A. Hall and Rosemary C. R. Taylor, "Political Science and the Three New Institutionalisms," *Political Studies* 44 (1996): 938. Practitioners of historical institutionalism generally accept this definition. For a slightly different perspective on how to define institutions, see Theda Skocpol, "Why I Am an Historical Institutionalist," *Polity* 28, no. 1 (1995): 105.

[91] Stephen Skowronek, "Order and Change," *Polity* 28, no. 1 (1995): 95; Karen Orren and Stephen Skowronek, "Institutions and Intercurrence: Theory Building in the Fullness of Time," in *Political Order*, ed. Ian Shapiro and Russell Hardin (New York: New York University Press, 1996): 111–46; James Mahoney and Dietrich Rueschemeyer, "Comparative Historical Analysis: Achievements and Agendas," in *Comparative Historical Analysis in the Social Sciences*, ed. James Mahoney and Dietrich Rueschemeyer (Cambridge: Cambridge University Press, 2003), 3–40; Paul Pierson and Theda Skocpol, "Historical Institutionalism in Contemporary Political Science," in *Political Science: The State of the Discipline*, ed. Ira Katznelson and Helen V. Milner (New York: W.W. Norton, 2002), 693–721. Historical institutionalists also use the metaphor of "layering" of institutions. This results from new institutions being established on top of existing institutions, rather than replacing them. The product is an increasingly complex set of institutions—resembling a layered cake—that often work at cross purposes with each other.

[92] Kathleen Thelen, "Historical Institutionalism in Comparative Politics," *Annual Review of Political Science* 2 (1999): 369–404; Sven Steinmo and Kathleen Thelen, "Historical Institutionalism in Comparative Politics," in *Structuring Politics: Historical Institutionalism in Comparative Analysis*, ed. Sven Steinmo et al. (Cambridge: Cambridge University Press, 1992), 1–32; Ira Katznelson, "Structure and Configuration in Comparative Politics," in *Comparative Politics: Rationality, Culture, and Structure*, ed. Mark Irving Lichbach and Alan S. Zuckerman (New York: Cambridge University Press, 1997), 81–112.

leads to a period of crisis, as potential successors compete for power and as institutions seek to secure the resources and authority needed to sustain their influence.

Economic decline: Rampant inflation and unemployment can undermine public confidence in a political and economic order and produce social despair that fuels calls for change. It can also sap the state of the resources needed to sustain key institutions, patronage networks, and social services. The collapse of the Weimar Republic and the rise of German fascism occurred amidst this type of critical juncture.

Technological change: The introduction of new technologies can weaken the state and strengthen opposition groups, thereby facilitating the decline of a political order and stimulating the emergence of new institutions. For example, improvements in communications technology in Iran in the 1970s greatly aided the dispersion of radical Islamic doctrine that undermined the legitimacy of the shah's regime and contributed to its overthrow in 1979. More recently, the widespread dispersion of satellite television in the Middle East since the early 1990s weakens the state's monopoly on the dissemination of information and exposes citizens to alternative conceptions of politics and society. This development erodes state power and legitimacy and creates opportunities for change.[93]

The direction of change at one of these critical junctures is shaped by two factors:

1. The relative strength of major institutions, which is the result of institutional histories and the effects of the critical juncture. The strength of an institution is a function of its degree of adaptability, complexity, autonomy, and coherence.[94]

2. The conception of politics embedded[95] in each of the clashing institutions.[96] The range of political ideas on offer at a specific critical juncture defines the menu of choices available to political actors. The amount of influence exerted by an idea is shaped by the strength of the institution in which it is embedded.

[93] Lynch, *Voices of the New Arab Public: Iraq, Al-Jazeera, and Middle East Politics Today.*

[94] This approach to assessing the strength of an institution is taken from Samuel P. Huntington, *Political Order in Changing Societies* (New Haven, CT: Yale University Press, 1968), 12–23.

[95] By "embedded," I mean integrated into the norms and policies of the institution as reflected in its publications, training programs, and speeches by leading officials. For a useful discussion of how ideas become embedded in an institution, see Kathryn Sikkink, *Ideas and Institutions: Developmentalism in Brazil and Argentina* (Ithaca, NY: Cornell University Press, 1991), 26–27.

[96] Hall and Sikkink explore the role of ideas in particular detail. See: Peter Hall, "The Movement from Keynesianism to Monetarism: Institutional Analysis and British Economic Policy in the 1970s," in *Structuring Politics: Historical Institutionalism in Comparative*

Thus, in order to understand the direction of change, we need to analyze changes in the strength of major institutions and the ideas of political order embodied in these institutions.[97] It should be stressed that this approach emphasizes the importance of *both* ideas and institutions. Ideas exert a sustained impact on politics only when they are embedded in an institution that provides financial resources, personnel, and an effective organizational structure.

This historical institutionalist perspective suggests that an authoritarian regime can develop into a hybrid regime through the following scenario:

- Critical junctures (such as an economic crisis or a military defeat) weaken key institutions of state power. The institutions affected may include political institutions (such as the presidency), security institutions (such as the armed forces), or economic institutions (such as public-sector companies or the subsidy system).

- Regime elites try to preserve their power under these new conditions by adopting political, legal, and economic reforms. For example, they may strengthen the judiciary and the rule of law in the hope that this step will improve the efficiency of the state and attract essential foreign investment. Or, they may adopt laws that expand civil and political rights in the hope that these measures will enhance the regime's popularity. These reforms create opportunities for competing conceptions of the polity to emerge and grow.

- Institutions that espouse alternative conceptions of the polity (such as the judiciary or Islamist groups) exploit these opportunities. They may be joined by other actors—such as lawyers, human rights activists, intellectuals, and businessmen—who support political change due to their normative beliefs or their self-interest (or both). This interaction between reformist institutions and key actors in civil society broadens and deepens the constituencies for political change. It also defines the agenda for reform and determines which institutions command the greatest influence as the reform process unfolds.

- The government permits this process to proceed either because it is unable to stop it, or because the reforms it produces provide benefits to the regime. These benefits might include economic growth stemming from a strengthening of the rule of law, or enhanced regime legitimacy produced by improvements in civil and political rights.

Analysis, ed. Sven Steinmo et al. (Cambridge: Cambridge University Press, 1992), 90–113; Sikkink, *Ideas and Institutions.*

[97] For further discussion of the sources of institutional change, see Kathleen Thelen, "Time and Temporality in the Analysis of Institutional Evolution and Change," *Studies in American Political Development* 14 (2000): 102–9; Kathleen Thelen, "How Institutions Evolve: Insights from Comparative Historical Analysis," in *Comparative Historical Analysis in the Social Sciences,* ed. James Mahoney and Dietrich Rueschemeyer (Cambridge: Cambridge University Press, 2003), 208–40; Kathleen Thelen, *How Institutions Evolve: The Polit-*

- The resulting hybrid regime not only tolerates multiple conceptions of the polity. Its operation is grounded in the regular interaction of these competing ideas and the institutions that embody them. In this environment, political entrepreneurs can pursue several strategies: they may look for opportunities to broaden their support by cooperating with major institutions and co-opting their ideas; they may regard existing institutions and ideas as threats to their power and seek to isolate and weaken them; or, they may try to create entirely new institutions that break new conceptual ground and mobilize new groups into the political process. The mix of cooperation, conflict, and innovation determines both the stability of the hybrid regime and the trajectory of change from it. In order to understand the development of this regime, we must trace the changes in the relative strength of major institutions, the ideas that these institutions embody, and the behavior of political entrepreneurs.

This is an analytical approach that not only examines key actors and the tactics that they employ to maximize their interests. It also considers the institutional setting that constrains these actors and the ideas that these institutions espouse. It explicitly analyzes the institutional and ideational context that shapes the interests, options, and decisions of the major actors within the polity.

This perspective suggests the following strategy for studying the emergence of a hybrid regime:

1. Delineate the major conceptions of political order that compete for preeminence in the polity. These constitute distinct schools of constitutionalism that offer alternative visions of the country's political future.[98] In order to understand these distinct conceptions of politics, the analysis will focus on each school's ideas in two areas:

- Its approach to governance, which includes its views regarding constraints on state power, governmental accountability, protection of civil and political rights, and public participation in political life.
- Its conception of law, which consists of its ideas regarding three issues: the institutions that are empowered to draft, interpret, and implement law; the source of law's legitimacy (whether it lies with the people, the state, or God); and the purpose of law. This last point asks: is law intended primarily to protect citizens from the state and regulate their interaction with each other?

---

ical Economy of Skills in Germany, Britain, the United States, and Japan (New York: Cambridge University Press, 2004).

[98] This project utilizes the definition of constitutionalism put forward by Stephen Holmes. He defines constitutionalism as "a method of organizing government that depends on and adheres to a set of fundamental guiding principles and laws." Stephen Holmes, "Constitutionalism," in *The Encyclopedia of Democracy*, ed. Seymour Martin Lipset (Washington, DC: Congressional Quarterly, 1995), 299.

Or, is it primarily an instrument of state power that aids the implementation of policy? Or, is it a reflection of divine will that aims to create a divinely guided community on earth?

2. Identify the institutions that espouse these competing conceptions of constitutionalism and analyze their development.

3. Study the critical junctures that weaken the autocratic institutions of the state. These include military defeats, succession crises, economic crises, and moments of disruptive technological change.

4. Examine the regime's efforts to adapt to these critical junctures through political, legal, and economic reforms.

5. Assess how these reforms strengthen institutions that compete with the regime and create opportunities for alternative conceptions of constitutionalism to broaden their support within the state and society.

6. Examine how these competing conceptions of constitutionalism produce a distinctive trajectory of political change. This entails studying their points of convergence and difference regarding the character of governance and the source and purpose of law. Interaction in these two arenas determines the nature of the hybrid regime, its stability, and the type of regime it will transition toward.

THE PATH AHEAD

The following volume applies this analytical framework to Egypt. This country is a particularly insightful and important case for understanding the prospects for democracy in the Middle East. All three conceptions of political order that compete for preeminence in the Arab world—liberal, Islamic, and statist—have deep historical and institutional roots in Egypt. Furthermore, the competition among them has been relatively open. It can be examined through study of sources that are easily accessible and through interviews with relevant actors. Thus, the Egyptian case provides an opportunity to analyze the competition among ideas and institutions that shapes the entire region. Furthermore, Egypt is the key to promoting democracy in the Middle East. It has the Arab world's largest population (81 million in 2008), largest military, and second largest economy. It is the cultural leader of the region and an important source of Sunni religious thought and tradition. The country also serves as a model for political development in other Arab states. Its political and legal institutions have been emulated to varying degrees in Kuwait, the United Arab Emirates, Jordan, Iraq, and Syria. All of these factors give Egypt unique stature and influence. Its experience with liberalism, Islam, and democracy will exert a profound demonstration effect on its neighbors. It will shape the timing, character, and success of democratization throughout the Arab world.

The analysis of Egypt begins in chapter 2, which studies the emergence of liberal constitutionalism. It examines the historical foundations of Egyptian liberalism in the late nineteenth and early twentieth centuries, and observes that this conception of governance became tightly integrated into the development of the legal profession. As a consequence, lawyers and judges became the most dedicated advocates of liberal reform. The Bar Association played a leading role in promoting the liberal cause for most of the twentieth century. However, changes in its membership and steady regime repression eventually fragmented the Bar and undermined its effectiveness. The judiciary, in contrast, has retained a strong sense of liberal identity and has developed a robust conception of liberal constitutionalism. In order to understand this approach to law and politics, the chapter studies the decisions of Egypt's major courts (the Supreme Constitutional Court, the administrative courts, and the Court of Cassation). It uses this body of jurisprudence to analyze the judiciary's views with regard to four core elements of constitutionalism: the rule of law, constraints on state power, protection of basic rights, and public participation in governance.

Chapter 3 examines the development of Islamic constitutionalism, which is based in the Muslim Brotherhood. The chapter begins by studying the re-emergence of the Brotherhood since 1970 and the political pressures that have pushed it toward a moderate conception of Islamic governance. It then analyzes the writings of four contemporary thinkers who play a critical role in defining the Brotherhood's view of constitutional order: Yusuf al-Qaradawi, Muhammad Salim al-'Awwa, Kamal Abu al-Majd, and Tariq al-Bishri. The analysis focuses on their positions regarding the same four aspects of constitutionalism discussed in the previous chapter: the rule of law; constraints on state power; protection of civil and political rights; and public participation in politics.

Chapter 4 begins with a concise summary of the statist conception of political order that underlies Egypt's current autocratic regime. It then documents the economic contradictions that brought this order to the point of crisis in the early 1990s. In response to this crisis, the regime adopted reforms that enabled liberal constitutionalism and Islamic constitutionalism to broaden their influence and support. The analysis examines the growth of these two alternative views of constitutionalism through the actions of their most determined advocates: the de facto professional association for judges (the Judges' Club—*Nadi al-Quda*) and the Muslim Brotherhood. The analysis finds that political competition under Egypt's repressive regime has pushed advocates of liberal constitutionalism and Islamic constitutionalism toward common ground. Their political agendas converge in several areas, particularly with regard to key elements of liberalism such as constraints on state power, strengthening the rule of law, and protection of civil and political rights.

Chapter 5 observes that the implementation of market-oriented economic policies since 1991 has strengthened the political influence of the business community. Egypt's most powerful businessmen have used this opportunity to articulate a distinctive conception of market liberalism through the publications of a prominent think tank, the Egyptian Center for Economic Studies. The chapter documents and analyzes this view of the state, law, and the economy. It also notes that this approach to market liberalism has been adopted by the ruling National Democratic Party and implemented by the reformist prime minister who assumed power in 2004 (Ahmad Nazif).

Chapter 6 observes that the path of institutional change advocated by these market liberals shares important areas of agreement with the reforms advocated by supporters of liberal constitutionalism and Islamic constitutionalism. Each of these groups favors the creation of a more liberal state with effective constraints on its power, a clear and unbiased legal code, and protection of civil and political rights. However, there is no comparable degree of consensus on the value of broadening public participation in politics. This fact suggests that liberalism and democracy have become de-linked in the Egyptian case. Liberalism is likely to progress steadily in the future, while democracy is likely to advance slowly and unevenly. This trajectory may eventually lead to democracy at some point in the future, particularly if liberalism enhances the private sector's independence from the state and leads to a more autonomous and politically active middle class. However, this outcome is not inevitable. Recent amendments to the Constitution in 2007 were particularly disappointing to democrats. They suggest that Egypt is likely to remain a hybrid regime that contains some legal and institutional constraints on executive power, but which falls short of Western norms of democracy.

CHAPTER TWO

Liberal Constitutionalism

PRESERVING AND ADAPTING EGYPT'S LIBERAL TRADITION

> Egypt's judges are the guardians of the rule of law. It is our
> duty to enforce the law consistently and fairly among citizens
> and the government. We also have a duty to protect the rights
> of Egypt's citizens . . . after decades of performing these duties
> with dedication and courage, we have become the conscience
> of the nation. For this reason, we have an obligation to partici-
> pate in public discussions over laws and the judicial system.
> —*Zakariyya 'Abd al-'Aziz*[1]

These remarks, by the president of the de facto professional association for
judges (the Judges' Club), reaffirmed the judiciary's role as the standard
bearer of Egypt's liberal tradition. This tradition has its foundations in
the legal and educational reforms of the late nineteenth century. It was
marginalized during the Nasser period, but remained integral to the professional identity of both lawyers and judges. It reemerged after 1970 as
one of the primary alternatives to the statist ideology of the Nasser era.

The Historical Roots of Egyptian Liberalism

Egypt's liberal tradition incorporates the core principles of classical liberalism: a clear and unbiased legal code, the division of state power into separate branches, checks and balances among these branches, and respect for
basic civil and political rights.[2] The earliest statutory expression of this

---

[1] Zakariyya 'Abd al-'Aziz, "Istiqlal al-Quda," *al-Quda*, Special Issue, June 2005, 2.

[2] Classical liberalism was first defined in the works of John Locke, especially *Two Treatises
of Government* (Cambridge: Cambridge University Press, [1690] 1988). For a useful discussion of the intellectual history of liberalism, see Guido de Ruggiero, *The History of European
Liberalism* (Boston: Beacon Press, 1959). Also, J. Salwyn Schapiro, *Liberalism: Its Meaning
and History* (Princeton, NJ: Van Nostrand, 1958). In contemporary scholarship, the term
"liberalism" has taken on a wide variety of other meanings. For a valuable analysis of
these other forms of liberalism (neoclassical, welfare, libertarian, epistemological, egalitarian,
political, Rawlsian, neo-Rawlsian, etc.), see Paul Kelly, *Liberalism* (Cambridge: Polity
Press, 2005).

view was the "Fundamental Law,"[3] adopted in February 1882. It stated that members of Parliament[4] would be chosen through elections rather than being appointed by the Khedive.[5] It also gave Parliament the authority to convene on its own accord, without Khedival proclamation. It further granted Parliament the authority to impose or cancel taxes and to review the state's budget.[6] For the first time, the Egyptian Parliament could monitor and constrain executive spending.

However, this experiment with constitutionalism was short-lived. Popular anger toward foreign influence in Egypt was growing steadily and led to large anti-British demonstrations in Cairo and Alexandria in June 1882. The British Consul wrote to his superiors that "anarchy" had descended on Egypt, and that British lives and interests were at risk. The British were also worried that a more representative government in Egypt would lack the fiscal discipline needed to restore solvency to the Treasury. This combination of concerns led the British to invade in September 1882. They crushed Egypt's nascent nationalist movement and prevailed on the Khedive to abrogate the Fundamental Law. These steps initiated the British military presence that lasted until 1956.[7]

The British began the occupation by proclaiming, through the Khedive, an Organizational Law[8] in May 1883. This law created a Legislative Council composed of thirty members—sixteen elected by prominent landowners and fourteen chosen by the Khedive. In principle, the Council held the power to examine the budget, review legislation, and hold ministers to account. In practice, it served only an advisory role and had little impact on legislation. Similarly, the Organizational Law created a General Assembly with eighty-two seats, consisting of ministers, members of the Legislative Council, and forty-six members elected by landholders.[9] However, the Assembly met only every other year and had little impact on policy. Lord Cromer, the British Consul-General in Egypt, stated candidly

[3] The Arabic original of the Fundamental Law is published in *Al-Dasatir al-Misriyya, 1805–1971: Nasus wa Tahlil* (Cairo: Markaz al-Tanthim wa al-Mikrufilm, 1977), 79–89.

[4] In Arabic, the Parliament was called *Majlis al-Nuwwab*—literally, Council of Representatives.

[5] Articles 1 and 6 of the Fundamental Law. The document does not specify how the elections would occur.

[6] Articles 33 and 36 of the Fundamental Law.

[7] For an insightful discussion of the politics of this period, see Juan R. I. Cole, *Colonialism and Revolution in the Middle East: Social and Cultural Origins of Egypt's 'Urabi Movement* (Princeton, NJ: Princeton University Press, 1993).

[8] In Arabic, it is *al-Qanun al-Nithami al-Misri*—literally, the Egyptian Organizational Law. Sherif and Boyle translate it as the "organic law." Kevin Boyle and Adel Omar Sherif, *Human Rights and Democracy: The Role of the Supreme Constitutional Court of Egypt* (London: Kluwer Law International, 1996), 5–6.

[9] Boyle and Sherif, *Human Rights and Democracy*, 5–6.

that neither of these bodies was intended to create representative government in Egypt.[10] Their goal was to "give the Egyptian people an opportunity of making their voices heard, but at the same time not to bind the executive Government by parliamentary fetters, which would have been out of place in a country whose political education was so little advanced as that of Egypt."[11]

Though these institutions were intended as largely symbolic talking shops, they provided a forum for Egypt's landed elite to congregate and identify issues of shared concern. This Western-educated aristocracy continued to call for liberal reforms, and increasingly demanded that the Legislative Council and the General Assembly be converted into strong political institutions empowered to formulate legislation and supervise the executive. The proponents of these reforms were emboldened by developments in Istanbul, where the sultan accepted a new Constitution and Parliament in 1908. The monarch in Persia also accepted a constitutional government in 1909. Cromer consistently opposed similar steps in Egypt, fearing that a stronger and more representative legislative body would limit Britain's power and serve as a forum for anti-British nationalist groups. In 1913, Cromer's successor adopted a more conciliatory posture and issued a new Organizational Law. It merged the Legislative Council and the General Assembly into a single body, the Legislative Assembly. This body consisted of eighty members, sixty-six of whom were elected by landowners and fourteen appointed by the Khedive. The new assembly possessed greater authority to veto government proposals for taxation, and was empowered to question ministers at length regarding their policies. Though the body existed for only two years (until Britain declared martial law in 1915), it provided vital experience in public debate for advocates of liberalism. The political relationships formed in this assembly would provide the foundation for the constitutionalist movement that emerged after World War I.[12]

Britain also made important modifications to the judicial system that aided the development of more liberal government. Judicial reform was

[10] Writing in 1908, Cromer believed that Egypt lacked "statesmen capable of controlling Egyptian society and of guiding the very complicated machine of government . . . at some future period the Egyptians may be rendered capable of governing themselves without the presence of a foreign army and without foreign guidance in civil and military affairs . . . but that period is far distant." Earl of Cromer, *Modern Egypt* (New York: Macmillan, 1908), vol. 2, 567; also, 277–78. See also P. J. Vatikiotis, *The History of Modern Egypt: From Muhammad Ali to Mubarak* (Baltimore: Johns Hopkins University Press, 1991), 177; and, Afaf Lutfi al-Sayyid, *Egypt and Cromer: A Study in Anglo-Egyptian Relations* (London: John Murray, 1968), 165.

[11] Cromer, *Modern Egypt*, v. 2, 274.

[12] Boyle and Sherif, *Human Rights and Democracy*, 6; Robert L. Tignor, *Modernization and British Colonial Rule in Egypt, 1882–1914* (Princeton, NJ: Princeton University Press, 1966), 315–16.

considered essential to improving the quality of administration. Lord Dufferin, the British Resident immediately after the occupation in 1882, believed: "One of the chief causes of discontent in the country was the lack of well-defined laws and a system of courts for settling disputes cheaply and efficiently. Before Egypt could become an orderly country, it would have to have a modern set of laws and courts serving the mass of the population."[13]

Initially, the British worked within the framework of reforms based on French law that were undertaken by Khedive Ismail in the 1860s and 1870s. The most important of these reforms was the creation of the "Mixed Courts" in 1876.[14] These courts were staffed largely by European judges and held jurisdiction over any case involving a foreigner or foreign interests. They employed a slightly modified version of the Napoleonic code.[15] In 1883, the British oversaw the establishment of the National Courts, which extended the codes and procedures of the Mixed Courts to the entire Egyptian judicial system.[16]

Cromer regarded French law as ill-suited to the backward state of Egyptian affairs, but accepted its preeminence in the Egyptian legal system until 1890. At that time, a series of corruption scandals and a rise in the crime rate led him to conclude that additional judicial reform was necessary.[17] He appointed a British judicial advisor and instructed him to devise a plan for integrating the Anglo-Indian procedural code into the Egyptian legal system. In practice, this plan involved simplifying the rules of evidence, ending the use of multiple-judge courts, establishing summary courts to deal with small civil cases without appeal, and granting the judge greater

[13] Observation made by Tignor, *Modernization and British Colonial Rule*, 53–54.

[14] The mixed courts replaced the chaotic judicial system that emerged under the Capitulations, whereby any foreigner in Egypt was entitled to be tried by the laws of his native country. This stipulation meant that every embassy—or Consul—had its own court, which heard any case involving its nationals. See Nathan J. Brown, *The Rule of Law in the Arab World: Courts in Egypt and the Gulf* (Cambridge: Cambridge University Press, 1997), 26–29. Also, Byron Cannon, *Politics of Law and the Courts in Nineteenth Century Egypt* (Salt Lake City: University of Utah Press, 1988); Jasper Yeates Brinton, *The Mixed Courts of Egypt* (New Haven, CT: Yale University Press, 1968).

[15] Six legal codes were prepared by a French lawyer, Maitre Manoury: the Civil Code, the Commercial Code, the Code of Maritime Commerce, the Code of Civil and Commercial Procedure, the Penal Code, and the Code of Criminal Procedure. Michael H. Davies, *Business Law in Egypt* (Boston: Kluwer Law and Taxation, 1984), 27.

[16] Farhat Jacob Ziadeh, *Lawyers, the Rule of Law, and Liberalism in Modern Egypt* (Stanford: Hoover Institution, 1968), 33. Also see Tignor, *Modernization and British Colonial Rule*, 137. Cromer was not enthusiastic about broadening the influence of French law. He suspected that France sought to retain its influence in Egypt by encouraging the country to model itself after French institutions. He blocked the formation of a State Council (modeled on the French Conseil d'Etat) for this reason. Cromer, *Modern Egypt*, v. 2, 273.

[17] Tignor, *Modernization and British Colonial Rule*, 131–32, 392.

discretion to rule on the admissibility of evidence and the assignment of punishment.[18] The British also formed a Committee of Judicial Surveillance, composed of three senior European judges, who supervised the operation of the judicial system. In addition, the British allowed local notables to serve as magistrates and apply traditional law when resolving disputes (in contrast to India, where local magistrates were British civil servants). In order to staff this revamped legal system, the British established several training schools for lawyers and judges and restructured the Egyptian Law School.[19]

After World War I, Britain began seeking ways to reduce the financial cost of administering its empire. In Egypt, this effort included negotiating a reduction in Britain's role in Egyptian affairs while ensuring that it could protect its vital strategic interests. At the same time, Egyptian nationalists (led by Sa'ad Zaghlul and the Wafd party) were pushing for complete and unconditional independence. Negotiations between the two sides dragged on, with Britain exiling Zaghlul on two occasions. Finally, in September 1922, Britain unilaterally declared that Egypt was an independent state. Britain granted itself the right to intervene in Egyptian affairs if it believed its security interests, its citizens, or religious minorities were threatened.[20]

Britain had always been wary of Egyptian nationalism and had worked hard to contain this potential threat. It carefully monitored the military to ensure that Egyptian officers would not assume a leadership role in mobilizing nationalist feeling. With the military effectively isolated from politics, the new class of legal professionals stepped into the breach and became the leaders of the nationalist movement. Lawyers such as Mustafa Kamil and Ahmad Lutfi al-Sayyid, and judges such as Sa'ad Zaghlul, called

---

[18] As noted, these reforms were based on the British experience in India. The official who implemented them—John Scott—had served for eight years in India before coming to Egypt. Ibid., 134. Cromer held a high opinion of Scott's impact: "The establishment of a sound judicial system in Egypt may be said to date from the time of Sir John Scott's assumption of the office of Judicial Adviser." Cromer, *Modern Egypt*, v. 2, 290. See page 520 of that volume for a similar sentiment.

[19] Cromer, *Modern Egypt*, v. 2, 518, 520. Tignor notes that, despite these changes, the legal system remained primarily French in character. However, the changes were significant enough to require a separate Egyptian legal commentary on the system's divergences from the French model. Tignor, *Modernization and British Colonial Rule*, 131, 136, 137, 333, 335–36.

[20] More specifically, Britain reserved for itself the authority to intervene in Egyptian affairs in order to defend any of four strategic imperatives: the security of the communications of the British empire in Egypt (i.e., the Suez Canal); the defense of Egypt against foreign aggression or interference; the protection of foreign interests and the protection of minorities in Egypt; and, the Sudan and its status. Afaf Lutfi al-Sayyid Marsot, *Egypt's Liberal Experiment: 1922–1936* (Berkeley: University of California Press, 1977), 63.

for the expulsion of Britain and the formation of a truly independent government. They stressed that these goals should be achieved through the promulgation of a new constitution that would proclaim Egypt's independence and affirm its distinctive identity. Their interest in constitutionalism was not simply a reflection of their legal training. The pursuit of political change through constitutional reform was also a sound tactical strategy. In the short term, a constitution was a valuable instrument for defining and limiting the scope of Britain's interference in Egyptian affairs. In the long term, a constitution provided an internationally sanctioned mechanism for declaring the country's independence and demanding the withdrawal of British troops. Building the nationalist movement on a legal and constitutional foundation struck at the heart of Britain's justification for its occupation. Britain rationalized its presence in Egypt partly in terms of its desire to bring the blessings of modern governance to the primitive peoples of Egypt. At the heart of this modern governance was the rule of law. If Egyptians expressed the will and the capacity to rule themselves through their own European-style constitution and parliament, it would be difficult for Britain to stand in the way and still claim a moral basis for its occupation.

The lawyers and judges who led the nationalist movement were heavily influenced by the ideals of classical liberalism. This was largely a result of the Egyptian legal profession's long-standing ties to French legal and political thought. The patterning of Egyptian law and courts on the French model created a strong demand for Egyptian lawyers and judges trained in the French language and French law. To meet this need, the Egyptian College of Law was established in 1886 under the deanship of a Frenchman. A French School of Law was created in 1890, which trained many students for two years in Egypt and one year in France.[21] Some of the most promising students completed all of their legal training in France. This approach to legal education continued under the British occupation, as the British also placed a high priority on training Egyptian lawyers and judges to European standards.[22]

By the turn of the century, the legal profession had become a center of liberal discourse and culture within the elite.[23] Lawyers and judges were

[21] The school was established under the auspices of the French government. Ziadeh, *Lawyers, the Rule of Law, and Liberalism*, 150. Also, see Baudouin Dupret and Nathalie Bernard-Maugiron, "A General Presentation of Law and Judicial Bodies," in *Egypt and Its Laws*, ed. Baudouin Dupret and Nathalie Bernard-Maugiron (London: Kluwer Law International, 2002), xxviii.

[22] Donald M. Reid, *Lawyers and Politics in the Arab World, 1880–1960* (Minneapolis: Bibliotheca Islamica, 1981), 17–24.

[23] Some liberal nationalists enrolled in law school primarily because it provided training in liberalism. For example, the prominent nationalist leader Mustafa Kamil chose to attend

immersed in French legal and political thought during their professional training. They also absorbed many other features of French philosophy and culture.[24] Furthermore, the type of work undertaken by lawyers and judges required them to think in terms of concepts central to liberalism, such as rights, duties, authority, sovereignty, and personal freedom. Lawyers and judges became the natural advocates of liberal reform. In the words of a prominent lawyer of the early 1900s, 'Abd al-Khalaq Tharwat:

> We are foremost among those who highly esteem concern with public questions and who consider it a duty laid upon every Egyptian to strive by legal means for the progress of the country and its people. . . . Likewise it is our opinion that among the factors conducive to the progress of nations is criticism of the actions of those in authority. But we cannot concede that a person attain the position of government critic unless he has, in addition to great knowledge and profound wisdom, a faculty of level-headedness in word and deed, so that he might rightly evaluate actions, discern matters with sound thought, and not overstep the bounds of legality.[25]

Tharwat clearly believed that lawyers and judges met this ideal.[26] His views were widely shared.[27] Virtually all of the prominent advocates of liberalism came from these two professions, including Ahmad Lutfi al-Sayyid, Qasim Amin, Ahmad Afifi, and 'Abd al-'Aziz Fahmi.

These lawyers and judges made the transformation of law and institutions along liberal lines an integral feature of the nationalist movement. Their crowning achievement was the Constitution of 1923, issued soon after Britain granted Egypt independence in 1922. This document was modeled on the Belgian Constitution, with some adjustments for the Egyptian situation.[28] It established a two-chamber Parliament (article 73).

---

law school because it was "the school for . . . ascertainment of the rights of individuals and nations." Quoted in Ziadeh, *Lawyers, the Rule of Law, and Liberalism*, 63.

[24] Ibid., 151–52. For example, a prominent lawyer who had studied in France—Qassim Amin—became one of the earliest proponents of women's rights in Egypt. Ibid., 97–98.

[25] Quoted in ibid., 91.

[26] He and others also believed that legal professionals were well prepared to lead the nationalist movement. In this view, the leaders of Egypt's independence movement must have the language skills and the argumentative skills needed to make their case to a world audience. Lawyers and judges were far better prepared for this role than any other members of the elite—certainly more so than either the religious leadership or the military. Ibid., 151.

[27] Ibid., 152. The enthusiasm of lawyers for liberalism can also be attributed to professional self-interest. The legal profession suffered from a high degree of state interference in virtually every aspect of its work. A legal order that placed clear restrictions on the power of the state would reduce this problem. Ibid., 152–53.

[28] Nadav Safran, *Egypt in Search of Political Community: An Analysis of the Intellectual and Political Evolution of Egypt, 1804–1952* (Cambridge, MA: Harvard University Press, 1961), 109–10; Marsot, *Egypt's Liberal Experiment*, 68.

The lower House would be chosen through free elections in which all adult citizens were eligible to vote and to run for office. In the upper House, the president of the House and two-fifths of its members were appointed by the king. The remainder were chosen through free elections involving all adult citizens, but only large landowners were permitted to run for office. The Constitution also specified that the government should be divided into ministries, with the prime minister and his ministers appointed by the king but responsible to the Parliament (articles 57–72). Legislative power was exercised jointly by the king and the Parliament (article 24). Private property was protected and the sanctity of the home affirmed (articles 8 and 9). The Constitution guaranteed freedom of expression and assembly, and asserted the equality of all citizens before the law regardless of race, language, or religion (articles 3, 14, 20, 21). It granted the king the authority to dissolve Parliament and to appoint members of the civil service and officers in the military (article 38 and 43). Yet, it also placed important constraints on the king's power. For example, if the king rejected a proposed law, his veto could be overturned by a two-thirds vote of both chambers of Parliament (article 36). If the king issued emergency decrees while the Parliament was out of session, the Parliament must approve them at its first meeting (article 41). If they were not approved, they were rendered void. The Constitution also prohibited any amendment that modified the parliamentary form of government or restricted the principles of liberty and equality as articulated in the Constitution (article 156).

One of the primary architects of the 1923 Constitution, Ahmad Lutfi al-Sayyid, made it clear that he and his fellow liberal reformers sought to inaugurate a new era in Egyptian political life: "We have no choice but to discard the ideas and traditions that have led to our current state of backwardness. We must change and develop so that we become part of the civilized world. . . . We must discard the fear and ignorance that have prevented us from benefiting from the ideals of civilized countries."[29]

Despite the considerable liberalizing potential of the 1923 Constitution, Egypt failed to establish a genuine liberal order. In January 1924, the first elections under the new Constitution were won handily by the Wafd party and led to ten months of Wafd government under the premiership of Sa'ad Zaghlul. The Wafd pursued a strongly nationalist agenda that called for ending Britain's involvement in Egypt, but it made little substantive progress toward this goal. In November 1924, the British military commander in Egypt was assassinated. The British believed that the Wafd played a role in this assassination, and sought to inflict swift and

---

[29] Ahmad Lutfi al-Sayyid, *Al-Muntakhabat* (Cairo: Maktabat al-Anglo al-Misriyya, n.d.), 60.

heavy punishment on Egypt and Zaghlul. This punishment took the form of a demand for the withdrawal of Egyptian troops from the Sudan and the payment of a large indemnity (500,000 Egyptian pounds [LE]). Zaghlul was unwilling to comply with this ultimatum, and resigned. A new government was formed that excluded the Wafd and adopted a more conciliatory posture toward Britain.

This series of events set an inauspicious example that was repeated several times in the coming years. The Wafd would win an election; the king or the British would object to its strident nationalism and controversial policies; the king would then dismiss the Wafd government and replace it with a government more amenable to the palace, which would rule for a few years but gain little popular support; the king, in an effort to create a more effective and legitimate government, would hold new elections; the Wafd would win, and the cycle would start over again. This pattern occurred three times between 1923 and 1935. In addition, the king abrogated the 1923 Constitution in 1930 and replaced it with a new Constitution that significantly broadened his powers, weakened the Parliament, and narrowed the portion of the population that could participate in elections. Dissatisfied with this level of control, he suspended the 1930 Constitution in 1934. These steps succeeded in keeping the Wafd out of power until 1935 when, under pressure from the British and public opinion, the king reinstituted the 1923 Constitution. New elections were held, which the Wafd won. On this occasion, however, the Wafd had tired of political isolation and adopted a less belligerent stand toward the British. It was prepared to reach a compromise agreement with Britain in order to have its hands free to deal with the king and its internal opponents without fear of British intervention. The Wafd's newly found flexibility resulted in the 1936 Anglo-Egyptian accord. The content of the accord—which marginally expanded Egyptian independence[30]—is less significant than the fact that the Wafd surrendered many of its nationalist ideals in order to reach the agreement. The accord sparked intense debate within the Wafd, and led to defections by several prominent leaders such as Mahmud Nu-

---

[30] The agreement fell far short of traditional Wafd demands for Egyptian independence. For example, it did not bring Sudan under Egyptian sovereignty and it recognized Britain's right to station troops in the Suez Canal zone for the next twenty years. It also made the withdrawal of British troops from Egyptian towns and villages contingent on the Egyptian government building the necessary housing for these redeployed soldiers. The Egyptian government failed to construct this new housing. As a consequence, the British presence in the country was essentially unchanged. This presence served as a constant reminder that the Anglo-Egyptian accord failed to achieve any meaningful improvement in Egyptian independence. Safran, *Egypt in Search of Political Community*, 191.

qrashi and 'Abd al-Razzaq al-Sanhuri.[31] The Wafd compromised its nationalist principles even more dramatically in 1942. At that time, the British had grown increasingly concerned that the king and the government of the day were sympathetic to the Axis cause.[32] In February 1942, the British surrounded the palace and forced the king to appoint a Wafdist government which, the British believed, would be more consistently anti-German. The willingness of the Wafd to take power after what was, effectively, a British coup further discredited the party. The party that had fought so ardently for the nationalist cause was now cooperating fully with the occupying power. When the Wafdist government was finally replaced in 1944, its enemies launched a campaign of vilification against the party that included extensive documentation of corruption, war profiteering, and abuse of power. The Wafd responded with its own campaign of accusations, while also organizing demonstrations and violence in the countryside against the government and the king. Whatever the degree of truth in the charges and countercharges, they destroyed every shred of credibility that remained in the system.[33] When Jamal 'Abd al-Nasser carried out a coup in July 1952, virtually no one was willing to defend the regime. Nasser abrogated the 1923 Constitution in December 1952.

Despite these many challenges, liberal constitutionalism did not die out in the 1930s and 1940s. As Gershoni shows in his analysis of the journal *al-Risala*, several prominent supporters of liberalism remained active and articulate throughout this period. The journal's list of regular contributors includes some of the most eminent intellectuals of the day.[34] They consistently reiterated liberal ideals, developed a philosophical foundation for them within the Egyptian experience, and proposed specific reforms to advance the liberal cause. They also condemned internal developments in Nazi Germany and fascist Italy, and criticized the suggestion that Egypt should emulate the fascist example.[35] *Al-Risala* published these essays throughout the darkest days of the 1930s, as Egypt's political and economic situation deteriorated sharply. Furthermore, the journal was widely read. It

[31] These defections were also due to personality clashes and a continuing struggle over who should succeed Zaghlul as leader.

[32] Vatikiotis, *History of Modern Egypt*, 349–51.

[33] Safran, *Egypt in Search of Political Community*, 190–93. Also, Gordon, *Nasser's Blessed Movement*, 18–38.

[34] Among the regular contributors were Muhammad Husayn Haykal, Taha Husayn, 'Abbas Mahmud al-'Aqqad, Ibrahim 'Abd al-Qadir al-Mazini, Ahmad Amin, Tawfiq al-Hakim, Muhammad 'Abd Allah 'Iman, and 'Abd al-Razzaq al-Sanhuri. Israel Gershoni, "Egyptian Liberalism in an Age of 'Crisis of Orientation': al-Risala's Reaction to Fascism and Nazism, 1933–39," *International Journal of Middle East Studies* 31, no. 4 (1999): 555.

[35] Ibid., 555–70.

had a circulation of 15,000 when it began publication in 1933, and reached 40,000 by the end of the decade.[36] Gershoni concludes that the liberal, anti-fascist stance of *al-Risala* was "in no sense a marginal or exceptional phenomenon: rather, it was a phenomenon that represented hegemonic intellectual forces in the Egyptian print culture of the decade."[37]

The Bar Association and the Defense of Liberalism

In addition to this intellectual support, liberalism gained an institutional base within the Bar Association. Prominent members of the Bar played an essential role in drafting the 1923 Constitution. The Bar Association was also a major force for defending the Constitution against encroachment by the king and illiberal governments in the interwar period.[38]

The Association continued this role after Nasser's ascension to power. It called for the rapid return of the military to its barracks. It also sided with Muhammad Najib in his showdown with Nasser in March 1954. In response, Nasser dissolved its board in April 1954 and appointed a new one. He also modified the law of the Bar Association to require that all candidates for the board must be members of the government-controlled Arab Socialist Union (ASU).[39] This step ensured that pro-government lawyers would gain a strong voice in the Bar's deliberations.[40] In addition, the widespread nationalizations of the Nasser era effectively eliminated private enterprise and, with it, the lucrative retaining fees that most prominent lawyers relied upon for a living.[41] Many had little choice but to represent public-sector companies, which required them to support the government's policies or face dismissal.

The Bar Association began a steady political comeback after the 1967 war. It led public criticism of the regime's performance during the war and called repeatedly for criminal prosecution of the officers responsible for the debacle. The regime responded by passing a law in 1968 that enti-

[36] Approximately one-quarter to one-third of *al-Risala*'s issues were sold outside of Egypt. Ibid., 555.

[37] Ibid., 570. He further concludes that, "It was actually the pro-fascist and pro-Nazi intellectual voices that were peripheral" during this period. Ibid., 570.

[38] Ziadeh, *Lawyers, the Rule of Law, and Liberalism*, 77–98. Also, Reid, *Lawyers and Politics in the Arab World*, 139–43.

[39] Ziadeh, *Lawyers, the Rule of Law, and Liberalism*, 158. Beattie, *Egypt during the Nasser Years*, 186–88.

[40] Nonetheless, Ziadeh's survey of seventy lawyers in 1958 found that a large majority still regarded themselves as defenders of liberalism. Ziadeh, *Lawyers, the Rule of Law, and Liberalism*, 153.

[41] Nasser also abolished private religious endowments (*awqaf*), which were an important source of revenue for lawyers. Ibid., 159.

tled all lawyers working in the legal departments of public-sector firms to become voting members of the Bar. The regime hoped that these public-sector lawyers would toe the government line on most political issues, and thereby soften the Bar's criticism of its policies. However, in the wake of the 1967 defeat, even lawyers from public-sector firms were growing disillusioned with the regime. The political activism of the Bar continued unabated.[42] With the relative openness inaugurated by Nasser's March 30, 1968 declaration, the Bar became an even more vociferous advocate of liberal reforms. This sentiment is exhibited most clearly in the pages of the Association's journal, *al-Muhamah*. The president of the Bar, Ahmad al-Khawaja, authored an article in April 1968 that vigorously condemned the regime's use of exceptional courts and called for the establishment of a constitutional court that would "ensure respect for the rights of citizens and enforce the rule of law."[43] Muhammad Asfur, a long-standing advocate of liberalism who had been silenced by the regime in the mid-1960s, wrote that "socialism is not a substitute for political freedoms. The attainment of these freedoms is also a goal of the revolution."[44] The Bar Association's elections in 1969 also reflected this renewed political mission. Advocates of rapid liberal reform easily defeated the government's supporters and won a majority of seats on the Association's board.[45]

Nasser's death in 1970 created new opportunities for the Bar to expand its influence. His successor, Anwar Sadat, sought to strengthen the legitimacy of his regime by drafting a new Constitution that would show greater respect for the rule of law and human rights. In order to give this effort credibility, he invited several of the Bar's most prominent members to serve on the committee that wrote the new Constitution in 1971. The participants included the president of the Bar (Ahmad al-Khawaja) and the heads of each of the Association's major committees (Ibrahim Darwish, 'Abd al-Hamid Matwalli, and 'Abd al-Nasir al-Mataar). These lawyers—particularly Darwish and Matwalli—became the most assertive advocates of liberalism during the committee's deliberations. Many of the Constitution's clauses regarding political and civil rights were drafted by

[42] Raymond William Baker, *Sadat and After: Struggles for Egypt's Political Soul* (Cambridge, MA: Harvard University Press, 1990), 58; John Waterbury, *The Egypt of Nasser and Sadat: The Political Economy of Two Regimes* (Princeton, NJ: Princeton University Press, 1983), 344.

[43] Ahmad al-Khawaja, "al-Muhamun wa Birnamij 30 Maris," *al-Muhamah*, April 1968, 3–4.

[44] Muhammad Asfur, "Mafhum al-Huriyya fi dawa' al-Qiyam al-Ishtirakiyya," *al-Muhamah*, February 1968, 9. Another prominent advocate of civil rights, Nabil al-Hilali, expressed a similar view in the March 1968 issue. Nabil al-Hilali, "Haq al-Difa'a 'an al-Huriyyat," *al-Muhamah*, March 1968, 126–31.

[45] Beattie, *Egypt during the Nasser Years*, 222.

them. They also routinely challenged the illiberal proposals put forward by representatives of the regime.[46]

After the adoption of the new Constitution in September 1971, the Bar chose Mustafa al-Baradei as its president.[47] The regime had forced al-Baradei out of the presidency in 1966 due to his unrelenting demands for improvements in civil and political rights.[48] His return to power was seen as an important indicator of the Bar's renaissance. When combined with the prominent contribution of Bar members to the drafting of the Constitution, it heralded the return of the Bar to its role as a leading advocate of liberalism.

Al-Baradei embodied the spirit of the revived Bar when he wrote that lawyers must "lead others in defense of the rights of their nation . . . and in maintaining personal freedoms of citizens and the public freedoms of the people."[49] The Bar acted on this sentiment by calling for more rapid liberal reform in 1971, arguing that the resulting increase in public support for the regime would strengthen Egypt for the inevitable clash with Israel. It vigorously supported Sadat's steps toward a multi-party system in the mid-1970s. It also called for greater civil and political rights. When the food riots of 1977 led Sadat to promulgate repressive security laws (such as the Law on Protection of the Internal Front and Social Peace), the Bar was the first to denounce them. It also offered free legal representation to anyone charged with violating the new security laws.[50] In addition, it criticized Sadat's 1977 political parties law on the grounds that it placed too many restrictions on the formation and ideology of parties. At the same time, the Bar became a forum for general discussions of politics. It began a series of weekly seminars about major policy issues that brought together speakers from every corner of the political spectrum to debate economic reform, democratization, and peace with Israel.[51]

[46] Their role is most apparent in the minutes of the committee that drafted the 1971 Constitution. These minutes are available at the library of the *Majlis as-Sha'ab* in Cairo under the title, *al-Lajna al-Tahdiriyya li Wada'a Mashrua'a al-Dustur*. For the contribution of Darwish and Matwalli, see the discussions in the *Lajnat Nitham al-Hukm* and *Lajnat al-Maqawamat al-Asassiyya*.

[47] Robert Bianchi, *Unruly Corporatism: Associational Life in Twentieth-Century Egypt* (New York: Oxford University Press, 1989), 100.

[48] For example, al-Baradei gave a speech before the committee that drafted the 1964 Charter in which he called for constitutional limits on arbitrary state power, a right to form opposition political parties, and expanded freedom of speech and organization. See Baker, *Sadat and After*, 57.

[49] Mustafa al-Baradei, "Thakri al-Duktur 'Abd al-Razzaq al-Sanhuri," *al-Muhamah*, March/April 1972, 155.

[50] Baker, *Sadat and After*, 61, 70.

[51] See Ahmad Faris 'Abd al-Mon'am, *al-Niqabat al-Mihaniyya wa al-Siyasa fi 'Ahdi 'Abd al-Nasser wa-l Sadat* (Cairo: Dar al-Mahrusa, 2005), 233–47, 299–313; Ahmad Faris 'Abd

The Bar played a particularly prominent role in the debate over the law creating the Supreme Constitutional Court (SCC). In 1977, Sadat proposed a draft of the SCC law that would have created a highly politicized court with close ties to the executive branch. The Bar dedicated an entire issue of its journal, *al-Muhamah,* to critiquing the law.[52] The issue included sharply critical essays by the General Assemblies of the State Council, the Judges' Association, and the Courts of North and South Cairo. However, the harshest essay was written by the General Assembly of the Bar. It condemned the proposed method for selecting judges, which would have excluded the judiciary from the nominating process and granted complete control over appointments to the Ministry of Justice. It also objected to the draft law's proposal that justices would serve renewable five-year terms, rather than receiving lifetime appointments. The General Assembly of the Bar concluded that the draft law "does not achieve in any way its stated goals, which are the strengthening of legitimacy and the guaranteeing of effective supervision of the constitutionality of laws . . . [it] achieves the opposite of this. It offends the Constitution and threatens the rule of law."[53] The regime accepted these and other criticisms, and ultimately adopted a law for the SCC in 1979 that granted the Court a remarkable degree of independence in its appointments, internal management, and budget.

The Bar also criticized the Camp David accords in the strongest possible terms. It claimed that the agreement betrayed the Egyptian people, abandoned the Palestinians, and strengthened Israel.[54] Sadat found the intensity of the Bar's criticism so galling that he dissolved the Bar's board in June 1981 and appointed a new one. This action was eventually reversed by a decision of the Supreme Constitutional Court in 1982.[55]

However, the Bar Association's effectiveness as a force for liberal reform declined sharply in the 1980s and 1990s. The roots of the Bar's transformation lie in changes within its membership. As table 1 shows, the membership grew dramatically in the 1980s. The association's membership increased more than elevenfold from 1978 to 1992, at an average rate of almost 10,000 new members per year.

---

al-Mon'am, *al-Dur al-Siyasi li Niqabat al-Muhamiyyin: 1912–1981* (Cairo: n.p., 1984), 178–92, 227–51. The Bar Association also provided the forum in which the Wafd party declared its reestablishment in 1978.

[52] See *al-Muhamah,* January/February 1978.

[53] "Bayan Niqabat al Muhamiyyin 'an Mashru'a Qanun al-Mahkama al-Dusturiyya al-'Uliyya," *al-Muhamah,* January/February 1978, 176.

[54] 'Abd al-Mon'am, *al-Dur al-Siyasi li Niqabat al-Muhamiyyin,* 247–51.

[55] In anticipation of the SCC ruling, the Mubarak regime annulled the relevant law (Law 125/1981).

TABLE 1
Bar Association Membership for Selected Years

	1963	1971	1978	1992
Bar Association Members	6,872	9,816	13,283	150,000

Source: The figures for 1963, 1971, and 1978 are found in Bianchi, *Unruly Corporatism*, 95. They are based on Egyptian government sources (CAPMAS). The figure for 1992 is found in Moheb Zaki, *Civil Society and Democratization in Egypt: 1981–1994* (Cairo: Ibn Khaldoun Center and Konrad Adenauer Stiftung, 1995), 47. It is based on research by Amani Qandil.

This extraordinary growth was due to an unprecedented rise in the number of graduates from Egypt's law schools. In 1980, Egypt's law schools granted approximately 4,000 degrees. In 1990, the figure was 13,000.[56] This sharp increase was a reflection of the general transformation of Egyptian university education since the 1960s. The populist policies of the Nasser era included a guarantee that all citizens who passed the entrance exams for university would be admitted. Nasser was never able to fully deliver on this promise, due to a lack of space at universities and a lack of resources. Sadat, however, made a point of responding to every Egyptian family's dream of having well-educated children. He built seven new universities from 1974 to 1978, nearly tripling the number of national universities (from 4 to 11). As a consequence, 60 percent of those who took the baccalaureate exam in the 1970s were permitted to continue on to university, as opposed to only 40 percent in the 1960s.[57]

The law schools received their share of this increase, and began producing large graduating classes that wildly exceeded the country's actual need for lawyers. Most of these graduates were unable to find employment in the legal profession. Yet, they were qualified to join the Bar Association. They soon swelled the organization's ranks with young, unemployed law graduates. By 1992, 60 percent of the Bar Association's members were under the age of thirty-five.[58] A generation gap emerged between the Bar's "old guard" and this mass of new members, with the old guard generally enjoying secure employment and the younger members either unemployed or underemployed.

[56] See Tamir Moustafa, *The Struggle for Constitutional Power: Law, Politics, and Economic Development in Egypt* (New York: Cambridge University Press, 2007), 112. These figures are based on CAPMAS data.

[57] Carrie Rosefsky-Wickham, *Mobilizing Islam: Religion, Activism, and Political Change in Egypt* (New York: Columbia University Press, 2002), 38.

[58] Carrie Rosefsky-Wickham, *Political Mobilization under Authoritarian Rule: Explaining Islamic Activism in Mubarak's Egypt* (Ph.D. Dissertation, Dept. of Politics, Princeton University, 1996), 645.

There were also class and cultural gaps between the two groups. The old guard was largely the product of an era when law was a highly respected profession that attracted the best minds in the country. Upper-middle-class and upper-class students would pursue a legal career because of its stature, independence, and opportunity to earn a comfortable living. For this generation of lawyers, legal training was rigorous and drew extensively on French law. All graduates could read French and were exposed to French legal and political thought. As a consequence, they had a broad understanding of liberal ideals and, in many cases, developed strong support for these ideals.

When law school enrollments began to explode in the mid-1970s, the quality of legal education fell dramatically. Classes routinely swelled to over six hundred students.[59] Law schools lacked the staff and the resources to maintain a high level of instruction. Furthermore, the quality of students fell sharply as law schools were required to accept any applicant who met the minimum exam score,[60] even if he lacked rigorous academic preparation. Relatively few graduates had the opportunity or the inclination to master French and, as a consequence, were not heavily influenced by French political and legal thought. The younger generation of lawyers was perceived by the older generation as second-rate students who were poorly trained and who failed to measure up to the traditional standards of the profession. The old guard—including the Bar's leadership—wanted nothing to do with them, and made little effort to help them find jobs or develop their careers.

These changes in university enrollment patterns in the 1970s and 1980s transformed the Bar from an upper-middle-class institution with a strong commitment to liberalism into a predominately middle- and lower-middle-class organization whose younger members had little understanding of, or commitment to, liberal ideals. At the same time, the old guard leadership of the Association was becoming divided among themselves. Ahmad al-Khawaja, president of the Bar, had led the organization almost without interruption since 1967. His leadership was challenged from several quarters. The dean of Cairo University Law School, Numan Juma'a, regarded al-Khawaja as a political opportunist who lacked a firm commit-

---

[59] Serag observes that in the 1960s Alexandria University's faculty of law admitted roughly 300 students per year. By 1997, the figure was 7,000. Mohamed Serag, "A Global Legal Odyssey: Legal Education in Egypt," *South Texas Law Review* 43 (2002), 616.

[60] University admission is based on a student's score on the general examinations given in the final year of secondary school (the *Thanawiyya 'Amma*). The prestigious faculties, such as medicine and engineering, require scores above 90 percent. Faculties of literature, political science, and history require scores above 80 percent. The law faculty generally accepts scores in the 70s or below. Personal interview with Mamduh Salah, July 7, 1995. He was vice-dean of Cairo University Law School.

ment to economic and political reform. Juma'a made the first of several attempts to unseat him in 1987. Muhammad Asfur, a prominent Wafdist and civil rights lawyer, also mounted a challenge on the grounds that al-Khawaja failed to advance the Bar's liberal principles within the organization and in its interaction with the regime.[61] Neither of the challenges bore fruit, but they effectively paralyzed the leadership of the Association from 1987 onward. Many old-guard members grew angry and disillusioned with the power struggle, and disengaged from the Bar's activities. Many found that their law firms were thriving amidst the expanding private sector, and saw little reason to dedicate their time and energy to the fractious debates within the Bar. Thus, by the early 1990s, the Bar was divided into a small group of elderly leaders who were largely ineffectual, and a large mass of young and unemployed members who resented the leadership's haughty indifference to their plight.[62]

The Muslim Brotherhood (MB) proved highly effective at organizing among the younger members. During the period when most of the younger members received their university educations, the MB was the largest political group on campus. All of the young lawyers were familiar with it, and many had benefited from its social service programs during their studies.[63] Furthermore, many young lawyers were experienced MB activists. They saw organizing within the Bar as a natural extension of their political activity at university. Several MB activists ran for the board of the Bar Association in 1992 on a platform that emphasized the problems faced by young lawyers. It called for a nationwide job bank, interview training, resume workshops, expanded efforts by the Bar to place new graduates in challenging jobs, and the creation of an emergency fund to provide unemployed lawyers with financial assistance. On election day, the MB provided its supporters with free transportation to the polling site and refreshments after the voting.[64] The MB's efforts were particularly effective because the overall turnout for the election was very low: only about 10 percent of the Bar's total membership participated. The MB's well-organized activists won sixteen of the twenty-four seats on the

[61] The details of these clashes are recounted in the annual reports of the *al-Ahram* Strategic Studies Center from 1987 onward. See al-Sayyid Yasin, ed., *al-Taqrir al-Stratiji al-'Arabi* (Cairo:Markaz al-Dirasat al-Siyasiyya wa-l-Istratijiyya bi-l-Ahram, various years).

[62] In essence, "old guard" lawyers had sufficient skills, status, and connections to navigate the new economic landscape in Egypt without the assistance of the Bar. The Bar became the center of activity for those who lacked these traits.

[63] The MB's program for locating housing for students was particularly popular. al-Sayyid Yasin, ed., *al-Taqrir al-Stratiji al-'Arabi, 1988* (Cairo:Markaz al-Dirasat al-Siyasiyya wa-l-Istratijiyya bi-l-Ahram, 1989), 511–16.

[64] The MB also reportedly paid the overdue membership dues of up to 3,000 of its followers, thereby enabling them to vote in the election. Rosefsky-Wickham, *Mobilizing Islam*, 196.

board.[65] The son of the MB's founder, Seif al-Din Hasan al-Banna, became chairman of the board.[66]

The old guard reacted with shock to the MB's electoral success, and began an extensive campaign to limit its influence. These efforts culminated in a lawsuit filed by fourteen members of the Bar in 1995. It alleged that the board (under MB leadership) had misused Bar funds to support MB activities, such as schools and medical clinics affiliated with mosques. The MB argued that these programs were part of its effort to assist unemployed lawyers and their families. The judge was not persuaded, and the Bar was placed under the supervision of the judiciary in April 1996.[67] It remained under judicial sequestration for the next five years. Elections for a new board were finally held in February 2001, when the Brotherhood won eight of the twenty-four seats. This was not enough for the MB to dominate the Bar's decision making. However, it was sufficient to sustain the long-standing tensions and rivalries among the MB, secularists, Nasserists, and Wafdists. The Bar remains highly divided by ideological and personality differences. As a consequence, it has not regained its former role as a powerful voice for liberal reform.

THE JUDICIARY AND LIBERAL CONSTITUTIONALISM

While the Bar waned during the 1990s, the judiciary remained a steady and articulate proponent of liberal ideals. Unlike the Bar Association, the judiciary has retained its elite status. Only the finest law graduates are eligible to become judges.[68] At the entry and middle levels of the judiciary,

---

[65] The elections were held September 14, 1992. MB candidates won roughly one-half of the votes cast. Rosefsky-Wickham, *Mobilizing Islam*, 196. For coverage of the election, see *al-Wafd* from September 15 and 16, 1992. For general analysis of the Bar Association and of other professional syndicates, see Amani Qandil, *'Amaliyyat al-Tahawwul al-Dimaqrati fi Misr, 1981–1993* (Cairo: Dar al-Amin, 1995).

[66] For a useful discussion of the MB's activities within the Bar from 1992–1995, see Ahmad 'Abd al-Hafiz, *Niqabat al-Muhamiyyin* (Cairo:Markaz al-Dirasat al-Siyasiyya wa-l-Istratijiyya bi-l-Ahram, 2003), 163–72.

[67] For further details on the Bar's clash with the government in the mid-1990s, see: 'Abd Allah Khalil, *Azmat Niqabat al-Muhamiyyin* (Cairo: Cairo Institute for Human Rights Studies, 1999); Baher Alashhab et al., *Clash in Egypt: The Government and the Bar* (Geneva: Center for the Independence of Judges and Lawyers, 1995); Neil Davidson and Pierre Sebastien, *Egypt: The Sequestration of the Bar* (Geneva: Center for the Independence of Judges and Lawyers, 1998).

[68] Roughly 3,000 law school graduates apply to join the judiciary each year. Of this number, 150–250 are selected after undergoing an evaluation process that examines their academic record, moral character, and family background. A newly appointed member of the judiciary works in the office of the public prosecutor until he is thirty years old. If he completes this service successfully, he is eligible for appointment as a sitting judge. Personal

appointments and promotions are handled entirely by professional judges.[69] At the highest levels, the executive branch exerts some influence over appointments but does not dominate them.[70] This degree of judicial control over appointments has created a highly cohesive and insular professional identity. This distinct identity is reinforced by the fact that judges are trained in the same law schools,[71] socialize in the same circles, and often marry within the same families. They also enjoy virtually iron-clad job security and a high degree of autonomy from other state institutions.[72]

---

interview with 'Umar Hafiz, former deputy director of the National Center for Judicial Studies, March 15, 2005.

[69] The specific procedures for appointments vary among Egypt's courts (the ordinary judiciary, the administrative judiciary, and the Supreme Constitutional Court). Nonetheless, the approach to appointments is similar in each case. For example, when a vacancy occurs in the ordinary judiciary, senior judges within the court involved develop a list of candidates. The president of the court then selects from the names on this list. This choice is reviewed and approved by the Supreme Judicial Council, a seven-person board of the country's most senior judges. The Council then prepares a decree of appointment, which is signed by the president of the republic. For further details on the judicial appointment process, see the relevant laws for each court. For the ordinary judiciary, see law 46/1972 as amended by law 35/1984; for the administrative judiciary, see law 47/1972 as amended by law 136/1984; for the Supreme Constitutional Court, see law 48/1979.

[70] When a vacancy occurs for the presidency of a court, the senior members of the court involved develop a list of candidates. The president of the republic then chooses from this list. The only exception to this procedure is the presidency of the Supreme Constitutional Court. In this case, the president of the republic is empowered to choose the appointee without input from other judges provided the candidate has appropriate training and professional experience. This exception applies only to the president of the SCC. When a vacancy occurs for other positions on the SCC, two candidates are nominated—one by the members of the Court, and one by the president of the Court. The president of the republic then chooses from among these two candidates. See article 5 of the law governing the SCC (law 48/1979).

[71] Usually, the "top three" law schools—Cairo University, 'Ain Shams University, and Alexandria University.

[72] By the standards of the developing world, Egypt's courts enjoy a high degree of independence. As noted earlier, judges control most appointments and promotions except at the highest levels, where the executive contributes to the decision but does not dictate it. For many years, judges complained that they lacked financial independence because the budget for the judiciary was administered by the Ministry of Justice. There is no evidence that the ministry used this power to pressure the judiciary to adopt specific rulings. Nonetheless, the leaders of the judiciary—particularly within the Judges' Club—have long protested this potential for executive interference. As a consequence, the government amended the law of the judiciary in 2006 (law 142/2006). The judiciary's budget is now submitted directly to the Parliament without passing through the Ministry of Justice. However, judges believe there is still room for improvement in judicial independence. They continue to call for several reforms, including: greater judicial control over the selection of judges for lucrative postings outside of the judiciary (e.g., as advisors to government agencies or as counselors in the Gulf Arab countries); greater autonomy and power for the de facto professional association of judges (the Judges' Club); and clearer guarantees of an adequate pension for retired judges. The debate over strengthening judicial independence will be discussed in

These conditions do not mean that the judiciary is utterly homogenous. As noted below, there are significant differences of opinion among judges over important legal issues. However, judges share a strong professional identity rooted in liberal ideals and they enjoy substantial institutional autonomy. This combination has enabled them to develop a robust conception of liberal constitutionalism.

The Egyptian judiciary consists of two separate court structures: the ordinary courts, which handle civil, commercial, criminal, and personal status cases; and the administrative courts of the State Council, which deal with noncriminal cases involving the state. These are supplemented by the Supreme Constitutional Court (SCC), which holds exclusive authority to rule on the constitutionality of laws, resolve conflicts of jurisdiction among courts, and provide definitive interpretations of the law. In addition, the country has several specialized courts, including the Emergency State Security Court,[73] the State Security Court,[74] and the Court of Values.[75] It also has a military court system that is sometimes used to try civilians accused of crimes related to national security.[76]

The judiciary's conception of liberal constitutionalism can be traced most clearly in the rulings of the two courts that deal explicitly with the powers of the state and its relationship to the citizenry: the SCC and the administrative courts of the State Council. The opinions of these courts complement each other. The SCC generally issues broad decisions regarding the constitutional principles that delineate the parameters of law. The administrative courts produce the large volume of detailed rulings that give these SCC decisions further substance and specificity. In some areas, the rulings of the ordinary judiciary are also important. This is particularly true for cases involving civil and political rights, where decisions by the highest appeals court for the ordinary judiciary (the Court of Cassation) are often significant.

---

greater detail in chapter 4. For further analysis of judicial independence, see: Brown, *Rule of Law in the Arab World*, 96–98; Muhammad Kamil 'Ubayd, *Istiqlal al-Qada'* (Cairo: Maktabat Rijal al-Qada', 1991).

[73] This court hears cases that entail violation of decrees issued during the state of emergency.

[74] This court specializes in cases involving violations of ordinary laws related to national security, which include economic crimes, certain political crimes, terrorism, theft of public money, espionage, and possession of explosives. Legislation was adopted in June 2003 to abolish the State Security Courts. "State Security Courts to be Abolished," *Arab Reform Bulletin* 1, no. 2 (July 2003). However, the legislation has not yet been implemented and these courts continue to hear cases.

[75] This court was created in 1980 by the Law on Protection of the Internal Front and Social Peace. It focuses on cases involving economic and political crimes that are investigated by the Socialist Public Prosecutor. It will be discussed in greater detail below.

[76] For more detailed discussion of the structure of the judicial system, see Muhammad Fathi Najib, *al-Tanthim al-Qada'i al-Misri* (Cairo: Dar al-Sharuq, 2003).

In order to understand the conception of liberal constitutionalism that emerges from the jurisprudence of these courts, the following analysis will examine their rulings in four areas: constraints on state power, the rule of law (which focuses on the independence of the judiciary and the role of exceptional courts), protection of civil and political rights, and public participation in politics.[77] This is certainly not an exhaustive list of issues relevant to a discussion of constitutionalism. However, these topics define the core features of a political order. They allow us to delineate the essential characteristics of liberal constitutionalism as understood by the Egyptian judiciary.

Constraints on State Power

The SCC and the administrative courts have accumulated a large body of rulings that seek to limit state power and render it more accountable to law. These principles are clearest in the body of jurisprudence dealing with the state's policies toward the economy and, particularly, its power to sequester property. The SCC has been especially active in this area. Its rulings have annulled the land reform laws of 1961 and 1964,[78] required the government to acquire a court order before confiscating property,[79] blocked the government from selling sequestered property without the approval of the owner,[80] and confirmed that the state may sequester only the property of someone convicted of a crime, and not the property of the convicted individual's family.[81] The SCC has also overturned the nationalization laws of 1964 and 1966 on the grounds that they failed to

---

[77] The relevant cases were identified by consulting the case indexes and case summaries of the most widely used scholarly works on Egyptian jurisprudence: 'Awad al-Murr, *al-Riqaba al-Qada'iyya 'ala Dusturiyyat al-Qawanin* (Cairo: Shirakat al-Jalal li-l-Taba'aat, 2003); Faruq 'Abd al-Bir, *Dur al-Mahkama al-Dusturiyya al-Misriyya fi Himayat al-Huquq wa-l-Huriyyat* (Cairo: al-Nasr al-Thahabi li-l-Taba'aat, 2004); and Faruq 'Abd al-Bir, *Dur Majlis al-Dawla al-Misri fi Himayat al-Huquq wa al-Huriyyat al-'Amma - al-Juz al-Thalith* (Cairo: al-Nasr al-Thahabi li-l-Taba'aat, 1998). Research among these sources produced a universe of 128 cases in the Supreme Constitutional Court, the administrative courts, and the Court of Cassation. These cases were then read and analyzed.

[78] SCC case 3, Judicial Year 1, issued June 25, 1983; also, Case 4, Judicial Year 1, issued June 25, 1983.

[79] SCC case 28, Judicial Year 1, issued January 3, 1981.

[80] SCC cases 139 and 140, Judicial Year 5, issued June 21, 1986.

[81] SCC case 68, Judicial Year 3, issued March 4, 1989. For a detailed discussion of the Supreme Constitutional Court's jurisprudence regarding property rights, see Enid Hill, "The Supreme Constitutional Court of Egypt on Property," *Egypte/Monde Arabe: Le Prince et son Juge: Droit et Politique Dans L'Egypte Contemporaine*, no. 2 (1999): 55–92. For a discussion of SCC rulings that limit the state's power to tax, see Moustafa, *Struggle for Constitutional Power*, 134–36.

provide adequate compensation to the owners of property.[82] In the words of the Court, the nationalization laws entailed "excessive use of state power to infringe the property rights of citizens."[83] As such, they represented "an abuse of state power."[84] These SCC rulings reinforced a large body of jurisprudence in the administrative courts that had limited the applicability of these laws for years, long before the SCC formally ruled them unconstitutional.[85]

The courts have also worked vigorously to assert their jurisdiction over the state. During the 1960s, the state often claimed that its major laws and decisions were reflections of the peoples' "revolutionary will" and, as a consequence, could not be subjected to judicial oversight. For example, this line of argument was used to defend presidential sequestration orders from the Nasser era that led to the seizure of substantial tracts of agricultural land. The administrative courts have consistently rejected this line of argument and asserted that "all employees and actions of the state are subject to the law and the jurisdiction of the administrative judiciary."[86] The SCC has adopted a similar position. It has voided several government decrees that authorized the seizure of property, despite government protestations that these actions were essential to public safety and thus were beyond the jurisdiction of the courts.[87] It even challenged the president when he made a similar claim. In September 1981, Sadat issued a series of decrees that imprisoned most of his political opponents and suppressed virtually all of the opposition press. The government argued that these decrees were essential for the country's political stability and that they were beyond judicial scrutiny because the president had declared a "state of necessity." The SCC rejected this assertion and argued that "the executive authority is not free to decide upon the existence of a state of necessity. Rather, it is subject to the control exercised by the Supreme Constitutional

[82] SCC case 1, Judicial Year 1, issued March 2, 1985.

[83] Ibid.

[84] Ibid.

[85] For a thorough discussion of administrative court rulings that deal with property rights, see 'Abd al-Bir, *Dur Majlis al-Dawla al-Misri fi Himayat al-Huquq wa al-Huriyyat al-'Amma - al-Juz al-Thalith*, 761–1008.

[86] Administrative Court case 2571, Judicial Year 26, issued May 7, 1974. The case dealt with a presidential order from 1961 to sequester a plot of land. The government argued that the decision was an integral part of the revolutionary mission of the state and was therefore beyond the jurisdiction of the administrative judiciary. The court disagreed and canceled the order. For a similar line of reasoning and response from the judiciary, see Administrative Court case 2335, Judicial Year 26, issued March 31, 1976; Administrative Court case 959, Judicial Year 22, issued Feb. 21, 1972; High Administrative Court case 573, Judicial Year 20, issued February 28, 1976.

[87] SCC case 16, Judicial Year 1, issued April 30, 1983; also, SCC case 6, Judicial Year 2, issued April 30, 1983.

Court, which ascertains the existence of a state of necessity within the limits specified by the Constitution."[88]

In addition, the courts have asserted their authority to limit the president's powers under the emergency law. Egypt has been ruled under emergency law for all but seventeen months since 1967. This law grants the president broad authority to monitor, arrest, and detain citizens in the name of national security. In 1978, the High Administrative Court significantly limited the application of the emergency law by narrowing the legal definitions of "suspicion" and "sedition."[89] A decision by the same court in 1985 further limited the scope for legitimate arrest under the emergency law by requiring that the person arrested constitute a clear danger to the public at the time of the arrest (rather than simply a "potential" danger). Furthermore, it held that individuals could not be considered dangerous and suspicious indefinitely. New evidence of the danger posed by an individual must be presented to justify each arrest.[90] The High Administrative Court ruled in 1979 that the president could not invoke the emergency law to justify the confiscation of personal property because such action constituted "a major deviation from the law . . . [and] an aggression against personal freedom and the sanctity of private property."[91] It added that the emergency law does not create an "absolute system." Rather, it creates a system that is "constrained by law and the Constitution and by judicial supervision . . . it is still subject to the sovereignty of law and the supervision of the judiciary."[92] It added in another case that the state of emergency is "exceptional, with specific goals . . . it does not grant absolute powers or unlimited mandates."[93] Similarly, the SCC held in 1985 that Sadat had exceeded his legitimate emergency powers when he amended the Law on Personal Status in 1979.[94] It concluded that no emergency existed with regard to personal status matters and, as a result, it was illegal for the president to use his emergency powers to amend the law.[95]

[88] SCC case 15, Judicial Year 18, issued January 2, 1999.

[89] High Administrative Court, cases 675 and 797, Judicial Year 22, issued May 27, 1978.

[90] High Administrative Court, cases 1435, 1310, 1271, 126, and 810, Judicial Year 28, issued March 12, 1985. For further discussion of these cases, see James Rosberg, *Roads to the Rule of Law: The Emergence of an Independent Judiciary in Contemporary Egypt*. (Ph.D. Dissertation, Massachusetts Institute of Technology, 1995), 215–18. Also, High Administrative Court case 671, Judicial Year 30, issued January 1, 1984; High Administrative Court case 1776, Judicial Year 32, issued December 23, 1989.

[91] High Administrative Court case 830, Judicial Year 20, issued December 29, 1979.

[92] Ibid.

[93] High Administrative Court cases 675, 797, Judicial Year 22, issued May 27, 1978.

[94] These amendments were known as the "Jihan laws," after Sadat's wife. They substantially improved the rights of women, particularly with regard to divorce and child custody.

[95] SCC case 28, Judicial Year 2, issued May 4, 1985. It reached a similar conclusion regarding Sadat's decision in 1981 to create a consumption tax by issuing a presidential decree. It

These rulings suggest that the judiciary holds a view of politics and law that is classically liberal. The judges are acutely aware that the state commands vast resources that can compromise the rights and security of individual citizens. Courts must act firmly to monitor and constrain this power.

Yet, as one reads further among the major decisions of the SCC and the administrative courts, there is an element that diverges from the core premises of liberalism. These courts are far more comfortable with a powerful and invasive state than classical liberals. For example, Egypt's courts have a well-developed doctrine of "acts of sovereignty" and "political acts." This doctrine distinguishes between policy decisions (which are beyond the purview of the courts) and administrative actions that implement these decisions (which are subject to judicial supervision). In 1975, the administrative court wrote that "supreme actions taken to defend the existence of the state or to preserve its security"[96] are acts of sovereignty and are not subject to judicial review. The SCC has also adopted this view, ruling that an act of sovereignty includes decisions taken to "preserve the state and its safety domestically or abroad and to preserve its basic interests."[97] For example, the SCC refused to hear a case challenging President Mubarak's decision to hold a referendum to dissolve the Parliament in 1987. In its view, the president's decision was a matter of policy rather than an interpretation or application of the law and thus was not subject to judicial oversight.[98] The courts have also ruled that they have no jurisdiction regarding the executive's decision to call elections, to form a cabinet, to grant political asylum to foreign leaders, to sign international treaties, or to send the country's troops overseas.[99] The executive must

argued that only the legislature can create a tax. It can transfer this power to the president only during a time of national crisis, which "clearly did not exist with regard to the country's tax policies." SCC case 18, Judicial Year 8, issued February 3, 1996. A similar ruling in 2006 held that the president could not invoke the emergency law to limit the redevelopment and renovation of private property. SCC case 74, Judicial Year 23, issued January 24, 2006.

[96] Administrative Court case 377, Judicial Year 20, issued April 5, 1975.

[97] SCC case 3, Judicial Year 1, issued June 25, 1983.

[98] For a discussion of this case and the doctrine of "political acts," see 'Abd al-Rahman Nosseir, "The Supreme Constitutional Court of Egypt and the Protection of Human Rights" (Chicago: Unpublished paper, 1992), 13. While the decision to hold the referendum was considered a political act, the decisions about how to carry it out remained within the jurisdiction of the courts. The administrative courts heard several cases that challenged the organization and execution of the referendum. For example, Administrative Court case 2406, Judicial Year 41, issued April 4, 1987; case 2516, Judicial Year 41, issued March 31, 1987.

[99] See Administrative Court case 3608, Judicial Year 38, May 8, 1984; case 3754, Judicial Year 38, issued May 8, 1984; case 2406, Judicial Year 41, issued April 4, 1987; case 2516, Judicial Year 41, issued March 31, 1987; case 5124, Judicial Year 41, issued October 1, 1987. Also, High Administrative Court case 1939, Judicial Year 30, issued December 12, 1987; High Administrative Court case 659, Judicial Year 32, issued May 15, 1989.

retain unrestrained authority in these areas in order to "preserve the interests of the state and ensure stability."[100]

As one might expect, the courts also tend to defer to state power on matters of national security. For example, the SCC has affirmed the legality of the State Security Court—a controversial body that is staffed only partially by judges and which does not allow defendants full rights of due process.[101] It has also acquiesced to a broadening of the jurisdiction of military courts. In 1993, the regime began transferring civilian cases to these courts in order to achieve quick and harsh sentences against its political opponents, particularly Islamists.[102] The SCC issued an interpretation of the military court's law that formally affirmed the president's power to transfer civilian cases at his discretion.[103] It refrained from issuing a ruling on the constitutionality of the law, despite having a relevant case before it for over ten years. The transfer of civilians to military courts was clearly unconstitutional,[104] but the Court was reluctant to issue a ruling that might be perceived as weakening the president's capacity to confront terrorism.[105]

This judicial deference to the executive may simply be a result of the political environment that judges face. Egypt has an autocratic regime with a president that jealously guards his power, particularly on matters of security. If courts attempted to confront the president on a core security matter, he might retaliate. Many members of the judiciary still remember the "massacre of the judges" in 1969, when Nasser dismissed more than

[100] Administrative Court case 2516, Judicial Year 41, issued March 31, 1987.

[101] At the primary level, the State Security Courts are staffed by professional judges drawn from the ordinary judiciary. However, the defendant is permitted only one appeal, to the Supreme State Security Court. This court consists of a panel of five that can include two military officers. There is no requirement that the officers have legal training or judicial experience. See A. Seif El-Islam, "Exceptional Laws and Exceptional Courts," in *Egypt and Its Laws*, ed. Nathalie Bernard-Maugiron and Baudouin Dupret (New York: Kluwer Law International, 2002), 359–76. Also, Moustafa, *Struggle for Constitutional Power*, 104–6.

[102] These courts provide fewer procedural protections for defendants and no opportunity for judicial appeal. For further detail on their structure, see A. Seif El-Islam, "Exceptional Laws and Exceptional Courts," 372–75.

[103] It issued this interpretation of law 25/1966 on January 30, 1993. It did not, however, attempt to address whether the law was constitutional. It merely affirmed that the law, as written, granted the president the power to transfer individual cases to military courts when a state of emergency is in effect.

[104] This assessment is based on my conversations with three SCC justices in the summer of 1996. The transfer violated the Constitution's guarantee that every citizen has a right to be tried before his "natural judge." In this context, the clause means that a civilian should be tried before a civilian judge.

[105] This issue has since been rendered moot by an amendment in March 2007 to article 179 of the Constitution. The amendment grants the president the authority to refer individual cases to "any judicial body mentioned in the Constitution or the law."

two hundred judges deemed insufficiently supportive of the regime. Although these dismissals were quickly reversed when Sadat came to power in 1970, they remain a constant reminder of the wrath that the executive can unleash.

However, the judiciary's accommodation of state power goes beyond this instrumental tactic for survival. Courts defer to the state on many occasions when no threat of executive retaliation is imminent or even likely. This posture is the product of a carefully reasoned judicial philosophy. Numerous rulings by both the SCC and the administrative courts hold that liberty is possible only when political and social order is maintained. In this view, a powerful state plays the pivotal role in creating liberty. Indeed, in several court decisions, the judges argue that rights do not exist outside the framework of the state. As a consequence, state power is seen as a fundamentally constructive force. However, the state must not be permitted to use its power in a manner that is "arbitrary and excessive,"[106] or which aims to "dominate society" and "bury opposing opinions."[107] The purpose of law is not to limit the state at every turn. Rather, it is to keep the state on a clearly defined path that serves the interests of society.

A strong state can aid society in many ways. For example, the SCC has issued several rulings that support the state's authority to regulate and manage the economy. This role for the state includes maintaining the social insurance system, which is "essential to national prosperity and harmony."[108] It also entails redistributing land in order to achieve the "socially desirable end of reducing inequality" and the social tensions that it produces.[109] In addition, the state should regulate the housing market in order to ensure that the needs of the public are met. This action, in turn, "preserves social solidarity, which leads to the unity and cohesion of the community."[110]

In the SCC's jurisprudence, a strong state also makes a valuable contribution to the moral character of society. It is particularly important for protecting the family. The Egyptian Constitution states, in article 9, that the family is "the foundation of society, based upon religion, morality, and patriotism. The state preserves the genuine character of the Egyptian family and the values and traditions that it embodies, while affirming and developing this character within Egyptian society."[111]

---

[106] SCC case 5, Judicial Year 1, issued May 16, 1981.
[107] SCC case 37, Judicial Year 11, issued February 6, 1993.
[108] SCC case 21, Judicial Year 20, June 3, 2000.
[109] SCC case 28, Judicial Year 6, June 6, 1998.
[110] SCC case 82, Judicial Year 22, issued December 19, 2004.
[111] Article 9 of the 1971 Constitution.

The SCC has taken this principle to heart. In its rulings, the efforts of individual citizens are not sufficient to preserve and strengthen the moral foundations of society. They must be supplemented by an activist state that defends and promotes morality. This view is particularly clear in SCC decisions dealing with educational institutions. The Court has held that the state has a fundamental duty to regulate education in order to ensure that sound ethical and moral principles are conveyed to the next generation.[112] It also has a duty to regulate student conduct—including the clothes that students wear—in order to ensure that children are raised in a manner that conforms to the traditions of the community and with religious values.[113] Several other rulings further clarify the state's role in building the moral character of the community. For example, the SCC overturned a law that prohibited members of the State Council from marrying foreign women. It held that the choice of a spouse was a fundamental step in the formation of the family, and that "the state must protect the family's values and traditions" by ensuring that citizens are free to choose their spouse without restriction.[114] It expressed a similar sentiment in a dispute over how quickly a missing person should be declared legally dead. Two procedures were available, one which led to a relatively quick decision and another that could last several years. The Court held that the quicker procedure was preferable because it reduced the suffering that the family endured. It added that the state should seek to expedite its decisions in this matter due to its obligation to "preserve the genuine character of the Egyptian family and the values and traditions that it embodies, while affirming and developing this character within Egyptian society."[115] Interestingly, the SCC has interpreted this principle to include defending the equality of women and their right to work. It argues that gender equality is fully compatible with Islam and a fundamental component of a just society. Furthermore, the state should actively promote the equality of women as part of its constitutional obligation to "coordinate between the duty of the woman, her family, and her work in society."[116]

This doctrine has produced an interesting twist in the SCC's jurisprudence regarding freedom of expression. Throughout its rulings, the SCC is a strong supporter of a free press. However, it has also asserted that the

---

[112] SCC case 18, Judicial Year 22, issued April 7, 2001.

[113] This case dealt with a dispute over whether the minister of education had the authority to prohibit female students from wearing the *niqab* (face veil). The SCC held that he had the authority to do so. SCC case 8, Judicial Year 17, issued May 18, 1996.

[114] SCC case 23, Judicial Year 16, issued March 18, 1995.

[115] SCC case 107, Judicial Year 21, issued December 9, 2001.

[116] The obligation of the state to play this coordinating role is specified in article 11 of the Constitution. SCC case 18, Judicial Year 14, issued May 3, 1997; Also see SCC case 6, Judicial Year 20, issued April 14, 2002.

Liberal Constitutionalism • 59

state has an important role to play in this arena. In its view, the state ensures that the press does not exceed "the prescribed constitutional limits concerning the preservation of the fundamentals of the society, and the need for the members of civil society to respect them . . . [the state must] prevent the transformation of freedom of expression into an anarchy that could destroy the pillars of society."[117]

The jurisprudence of the High Administrative Court (HAC) reflects a similar view of the state and its role in shaping society. Indeed, the jurisprudence of the HAC suggests a view of state power that resembles that of Rousseau: the state is seen as the embodiment of the public will and, therefore, a fundamental force for good. However, the precise language for conveying this concept is less direct than Rousseau's. The terminology that appears most often asserts that the state "defines and defends the public interest." For example, the administrative court heard a case in 1984 that challenged the authority of the state to seize a vacant lot and use it for construction of a school. The court upheld the state's decision, and further argued that the state has a fundamental duty to "define and defend the interests of the community."[118] The plaintiff appealed, but the High Administrative Court upheld the ruling and added that it is the function of the state to "assess where the public interest lies."[119] A similar line of reasoning emerges in the body of jurisprudence regarding the state's power to carry out sequestrations and nationalizations. The court was willing to accept that the state could play a constructive role in managing the economy and in improving the distribution of wealth and jobs. The problem lay in the state exercising this power in an arbitrary and excessive fashion that led it to "dominate the society and the economy."[120] State leadership and guidance for the economy and society are fine. Indeed, they are desirable if state decisions are the result of careful deliberations by dispassionate experts. But, state domination that is bent on destroying any alternative center of power is not. This unrestricted state power is "a formula for abuse."[121] Similarly, state action designed to benefit the leaders of the state or their allies is "contrary to the public interest and must be met with quick and harsh punishment."[122]

Throughout these decisions, the courts emerge as defenders of a strong state that carefully evaluates the options available and distills them into

[117] SCC case 25, Judicial Year 22, issued May 5, 2001.
[118] Administrative Court case 2296, Judicial Year 34, issued June 2, 1983.
[119] High Administrative Court case 3035, Judicial Year 29, issued November 23, 1985.
[120] High Administrative Court case 571, Judicial Year 18, issued May 12, 1979.
[121] High Administrative Court case 1175, Judicial Year 36, issued July 19, 1992. Also, High Administrative Court cases 2829 and 2909, Judicial Year 36, issued February 16, 1991; High Administrative Court case 2597, Judicial Year 34, November 27, 1994.
[122] High Administrative Court case 1942, Judicial Year 27, issued December 25, 1982.

coherent policies that aid the community. The purpose of constraints on state power is to ensure that the state plays this role and to guarantee that its power is not hijacked to serve the narrow ambitions of an individual or group. The judges do not object to a strong state. Rather, they object to an arbitrary state and (even more vehemently) to a corrupt state. Egypt's judges do not see themselves as simply enforcers of state-drafted law. Rather, they consider themselves the guardians of the public interest. They seek to ensure that the state uses its formidable resources to serve this interest.

In light of this view of the state, one of the key areas of discretion for Egyptian judges lies in determining the boundary between sound and unsound uses of state power. Thoughtful and competent judges disagree on this point and, as a consequence, we see variation in rulings among administrative courts on whether a particular type of state action is acceptable.[123] Similarly, there is variation among courts over the severity of punishment assigned for a given state transgression of the law. Some judges have adopted the view that punishments must be substantial in order to deter future abuses of power. For example, in a 1972 ruling, an administrative court held that a branch of the Ministry of Agriculture that had illegally seized a plot of agricultural land from its owner should be disbanded and its director subjected to criminal prosecution.[124] However, a different administrative court facing a similar case in 1980 (involving the Ministry of Supply) simply fined the ministry a relatively modest sum (2000 LE). The court concluded that awarding a larger sum (as requested by the plaintiff) "would cause unacceptable damage to an essential agency of the state."[125] It further volunteered that the level of compensation for the victim "must be balanced against the need to maintain strong and effective state institutions that can serve the needs of the public."[126] Each of these cases was grounded in the principle that state power should be

[123] For example, there was substantial disagreement among courts over whether the president should have the authority to transfer individual cases to military courts. The administrative court ruled that this power was excessive. In its view, the president should be permitted to transfer categories of crimes to military courts (such as drug-related crimes or terrorism-related crimes). But, the transfer of individual cases constituted a violation of each citizen's constitutional right to be tried before his "natural judge." The Supreme Constitutional Court adopted a different interpretation of the law, ruling that the president holds the authority to transfer individual cases as long as this action serves "the interests of society and . . . the safety of the nation." Administrative Court case 763, Judicial Year 47, issued December 8, 1992; SCC interpretation No. 1, Judicial Year 15, issued in January 1993.

[124] Administrative Court case 1057, Judicial Year 24, issued January 18, 1972. Also see Administrative Court case 1960, Judicial Year 26, issued January 9, 1973 and Administrative Court case 2526, Judicial Year 26, issued January 30, 1973.

[125] Administrative Court case 119, Judicial Year 34, issued June 25, 1980.

[126] Ibid.

exercised in a consistent manner that is accountable to the law. However, there was sharp disagreement over how aggressively the judiciary should act to rein in state power. In the second view, the judges sought to ensure that a strong state was preserved, even if this entailed compromising the rights of an aggrieved citizen.[127]

The Rule of Law

As noted in the previous section, the judiciary stresses that the government should respect the law and be constrained by it. In this view, law is fundamental to ensuring that the state serves justice and the interests of the community. Law can play this role only if judges apply it with consistency and fairness. This can be achieved only when the judiciary enjoys a high degree of independence and professionalism.

Egypt's judges have vigorously defended their independence. For example, the major courts and the Judges' Club took a strong public stand during the debate in 1977 over the law creating the Supreme Constitutional Court. Several different bodies that represent judges wrote detailed criticisms of the proposed SCC law in the Bar Association's journal, *al-Muhamah*. As mentioned earlier, the initial draft of the law sought to create a highly politicized court with close ties to the executive. The clause of the proposed law that granted the executive complete power over appointing justices to the SCC received a sharp rebuke from the General Assembly of the State Council (the representative of the administrative courts), which wrote that this aspect of the law "effectively gives the ruling party complete control over appointments" and thus "brings a political taint to the Court."[128] The Judges' Club was even more vociferous, claiming that the clause "removes from the Court any semblance of judicial character and gives it a political character . . . it makes the Court neither independent nor neutral."[129] The clause that granted justices five-year renewable terms also received criticism. The General Assembly of the Courts of North and South Cairo condemned this passage as a "clear violation of the independence of the court"[130] and called for judges to serve until they reach the mandatory

---

[127] This view seems to borrow from republican thought. It may be a product of the influence of the French republican tradition on the Egyptian judiciary. For an insightful discussion of French influence on Egyptian legal thinking, see Suliman Muhammad al-Tamawi, *al-Nathariyya al-'Amma li-l Qararat al-Idariyya* (Cairo: Dar al-Fikr al-'Arabi, 1984).

[128] "Qararat al-Jam'aiyya al-'Amumiyya li Majlis al-Dawla 'an Mashru'a Qanun al-Mahkama al-Dusturiyya al-'Uliyya," *al-Muhamah*, January/February 1978, 184.

[129] "Bayan Nadi al-Quda 'an Mashru'a Qanun al-Mahkama al-Dusturiyya al-'Uliyya," *al-Muhamah*, January/February 1978, 181.

[130] "Qararat al-Jam'aiyya al-'Amumiyya li Mahkamat Shamal wa Janub al-Qahira 'an Mashru'a Qanun al-Mahkama al-Dusturiyya al-'Uliyya," *al-Muhamah*, January/February 1978, 205.

retirement age of sixty. The judges' overall assessment of the proposed law was equally harsh. The Judges' Club concluded that the draft law "violates the separation of legislative, executive, and judicial power . . . [and] constitutes an assault on the foundations of the judicial system."[131] Each of the bodies that represent judges called on the government to redraft the law, in consultation with Egypt's major courts and the professional associations for judges and lawyers. The final draft of the SCC law—promulgated in 1979—responded to most of their concerns.

The judiciary has produced a substantial body of jurisprudence that further seeks to strengthen the autonomy and integrity of the courts. Many of these cases deal with the jurisdiction and authority of exceptional courts and prosecutors created by the regime, including the Emergency State Security Courts, the Socialist Public Prosecutor, and the Court of Values. These institutions were created largely to circumvent the ordinary judiciary and enable the regime to prosecute its opponents before hand-picked judges using streamlined procedures that increase the likelihood of conviction. They provoked a strong reaction from the judiciary. The administrative courts, in particular, issued a large body of rulings that limit their jurisdiction. For example, a ruling in 1971 held that the government could use the Emergency State Security Courts only in those circumstances where "a clear case could be made of an imminent threat to public safety" that made rapid prosecution essential.[132] Their use was a "deviation from the tradition of Egyptian law and is justified only for temporary periods to deal with specific threats to public safety that cannot be handled effectively by the ordinary judiciary."[133] It argued that, in practice, "there are very few matters of law that cannot be handled by the ordinary judiciary and the administrative judiciary, working in cooperation with the public prosecutor."[134] It further volunteered that the use of special prosecutors and exceptional courts inserts "political considerations into the judicial process" and "erodes public respect for the law and the judicial system."[135]

In 1982, the High Administrative Court asserted its authority to review decisions by the Emergency State Security Courts.[136] It adopted this position despite the fact that the law creating the Emergency State Security Courts stated that cases could not be appealed to other judicial bodies. The administrative courts also ruled that these emergency courts could not be used to try plaintiffs accused of violating the ordinary criminal

---

[131] "Bayan Nadi al-Quda 'an Mashru'a Qanun al-Mahkama al-Dusturiyya al-'Uliyya," *al-Muhamah*, January/February 1978, 181.

[132] Administrative Court case 7, Judicial Year 25, issued November 30, 1971.

[133] Ibid.

[134] Ibid.

[135] Ibid.

[136] High Administrative Court case 1362, Judicial Year 36, issued November 9, 1982.

code. Rather, they could only hear cases involving violation of presidential decrees issued under the emergency law.[137] This decision sharply restricted the type of cases that could be heard before the emergency courts.[138]

The administrative courts have also sought to rein in the Socialist Public Prosecutor (SPP). The SPP was given a vague mandate in the 1971 Constitution to protect society, the political system, and socialism. The 1980 Law of Protection of Values from Dishonor broadened its jurisdiction by allowing it to pursue anyone who had accumulated substantial wealth or criticized public policy. The law also empowered a special court—the Court of Values—to hear all the cases that the SPP compiled. This court had a mixed composition of judicial and nonjudicial personnel.[139]

The administrative courts moved aggressively to limit the SPP's jurisdiction. For example, the SPP attempted to screen candidates for local and union elections and excluded those whom it considered unqualified or unsuited. The High Administrative Court ruled this action illegal and reinstated the candidates. It also provided several of them with compensation.[140] In addition, the administrative courts sought to limit the jurisdiction of the Court of Values. In 1978, they asserted that all decisions of the Court of Values could be appealed before the administrative judiciary.[141] In essence, the ruling argued that the Court of Values was not really a judicial body because it was not composed entirely of judges. Rather, it was a branch of the executive and, as a consequence, its actions fell under the jurisdiction of the administrative courts. The Supreme Constitutional Court upheld this view in 1995.[142] This decision allowed hundreds of victims of sequestration at the hands of the SPP to seek redress from regular courts.

[137] High Administrative Court case 400, Judicial Year 33, issued May 23, 1987. Also, Administrative Court case 6085, Judicial Year 40, December 23, 1986.

[138] The legal shortcomings of these courts lie primarily in their composition. Under existing law, the emergency state security courts can consist entirely of judges, a mix of judges and military officers, or (under some conditions) only military officers. Seif el-Islam, "Exceptional Laws and Exceptional Courts," 369.

[139] Brown, *Rule of Law in the Arab World*, 109–10. The SPP was removed from the Constitution as a result of an amendment to article 179, which was adopted in March 2007. However, it is unclear whether the SPP will continue to function under statutory law.

[140] High Administrative Court cases 396 and 470, Judicial Year 30, issued March 16, 1985; High Administrative Court case 220, Judicial Year 26, issued March 2, 1981; High Administrative Court case 700, Judicial Year 27, issued December 18, 1982. Also, Administrative Court case 1923, Judicial Year 33, issued December 27, 1983; Administrative Court case 466, Judicial Year 35, issued March 3, 1981. Also see Rosberg, 201–4.

[141] Administrative Court case 653, Judicial Year 18, issued February 11, 1978; Administrative Court case 830, Judicial Year 20, issued December 29, 1979.

[142] SCC case 9, Judicial Year 16, issued August 5, 1995. See Moustafa, *Struggle for Constitutional Power*, 133–34.

Along with this effort to preserve the independence and professionalism of the judicial system, there is also a body of rulings designed to preserve public respect for the judiciary. The courts vigorously uphold laws that prevent citizens from publicly criticizing judges or their decisions. The rhetoric in these cases is often quite effusive by the normally staid standards of Egyptian judicial opinions. For example, a ruling in 1985 held that "respect for the state and the institutions of law are the foundation of public order. When someone insults a judge, he is not insulting an individual. He insults the embodiment of our nation and our civilization."[143] Another ruling held that judges are the "conscience of the nation" and hold a sacred obligation to serve the people. Statements that sully the reputation of individual judges, or the judiciary as a whole, threaten their ability to perform this key function.[144] The message in this jurisprudence is clear and consistent. The judiciary sees itself as playing a noble, even sacred, role in serving the interests of the public. Indeed, in the existing political order, some judges go so far as to suggest that the judiciary is the only institution with the public's interests at heart.[145] As a consequence, the protection of its independence and its stature are essential to the nation's well-being. Calls to defend judicial independence and integrity are not just a reflection of a proud profession guarding its turf. They are the product of a deeply held sense of mission. The judiciary believes some parts of the state have been explicitly designed to weaken the rule of law and, thus, threaten the public interest. Judges have a national duty to resist these efforts. This view appears with remarkable consistency in the jurisprudence of the administrative courts, both over time and at the primary and appellate levels. It is a central feature of the judiciary's professional identity.

Protection of Civil and Political Rights

The jurisprudence of the SCC protects a wide range of rights. For example, a substantial body of rulings defends freedom of expression. During the Sadat era, the government adopted legislation that banned political participation by pre-1952 political leaders as well as Sadat's opponents from the 1971 "corrective revolution." The SCC overturned both laws on the grounds that they constituted an unacceptable infringement on

---

[143] Administrative Court case 163, Judicial Year 28, issued February 21, 1985.

[144] Administrative Court case 56, Judicial Year 32, issued March 12, 1992. The Supreme Judicial Council reiterated this view in 2007. It issued a statement reaffirming that only legal experts may comment on court rulings, and that their comments must be limited to the legal issues at hand. They may not question the motives or neutrality of judges. See Mona el-Nahhas, "Muddying the Law," *al-Ahram Weekly*, October 4–10, 2007.

[145] Administrative Court case 56, Judicial Year 32, issued March 12, 1992.

freedom of speech.[146] It also rejected an attempt by the regime to ban political activity by opponents of the Camp David accords.[147] A ruling by the SCC in 1995 significantly narrowed the applicability of the libel law by holding that a public official who is offended by a newspaper article can sue only the author of the article and the editor of the paper, not the chairman of the party that sponsors the paper.[148] The administrative courts have further protected freedom of speech by overturning dozens of government orders to censor or close newspapers. Virtually every newspaper in Egypt has benefited from these rulings, including all of the opposition papers.[149]

The SCC has also acted to strengthen freedom of assembly. In one of its earliest rulings, the Court struck down a decree from the Sadat era that dissolved the ruling council of the Bar Association and replaced it with a presidentially appointed board. The SCC held that the decree represented an unconstitutional infringement on freedom of assembly and the autonomy of professional associations.[150] The SCC later voided a new NGO law (Law 153/1999) that sharply restricted the organization, funding, and operations of civil society groups.[151] The administrative courts have also been active in this area. For example, the Ministry of Interior often refuses to allow public demonstrations to occur because they might disrupt public order. The administrative courts have intervened repeatedly to reverse these decisions and allow the demonstrations to take place.[152] In addition,

---

[146] SCC case 56, Judicial Year 6, issued June 21, 1986; SCC case 49, Judicial Year 6, issued April 4, 1987.

[147] SCC case 44, Judicial Year 7, issued May 7, 1988.

[148] SCC case 25, Judicial Year 16, issued July 3, 1995.

[149] High Administrative Court case 591, Judicial Year 25, January 16, 1982; High Administrative Court case 1470, Judicial Year 40, May 20, 1986; Administrative Court case 504, Judicial Year 37, March 26, 1987.

[150] SCC case 47, Judicial Year 3, issued June 11, 1983.

[151] SCC case 153, Judicial Year 21, issued June 3, 2000. Moustafa notes that the SCC's rationale for overturning the law focused on procedural issues (the law had not been properly vetted by the *Shura* council). However, the ruling contained a long and detailed statement that identified the constitutional flaws in the legislation. Moustafa argues that this approach enabled the Court to communicate its constitutional concerns to the regime without provoking a direct confrontation. Moustafa, *Struggle for Constitutional Power*, 187.

[152] A ruling in 1986 is typical. The case entailed a demonstration in downtown Cairo proposed by critics of the Camp David accords. The Ministry of Interior refused to allow the demonstration on the grounds that the resulting crowds would disrupt social peace. The Administrative Court overturned the Ministry's decision and asserted that the Ministry "cannot restrict freedom of assembly based upon the expectation of disorder without providing clear proof that this expectation is well-founded." Administrative Court case 3696, Judicial Year 40, issued October 28, 1986. For a similar line of reasoning, see the following Administrative Court cases: case 5094, Judicial Year 36, issued September 5, 1982; case 2056, Judicial Year 34, issued August 19, 1980; case 2056, Judicial Year 34, issued April 10,

the administrative courts have overruled numerous efforts by the Ministry of Social Affairs (MOSA) to limit or disband civil society groups. They have also forced the government to be far less arbitrary in how it manages these groups. Several rulings have rejected MOSA decisions to dissolve NGOs on the grounds that the ministry lacked sufficient evidence to justify such harsh action.[153]

Egyptian judicial rulings also contain a large number of cases that protect basic rights of due process. The Court of Cassation has protected citizens' freedom from unauthorized search and seizure,[154] freedom from torture,[155] the right to a prompt and fair trial, and the right of the accused to legal representation.[156] The administrative courts have ruled that an individual may not remain on an official list of suspects indefinitely and, thus, may not be routinely subjected to interrogation or detention without the presentation of specific evidence justifying suspicion of wrongdoing.[157] The same court also held that it has the authority to rule on whether a person's name should appear on the Ministry of Interior's list of those considered dangerous to security.[158] The SCC has issued similar rulings, holding that searches may only take place with a court order[159] and that citizens may not be imprisoned or denied professional opportunities on the basis of mere suspicion.[160] SCC decisions have also affirmed the presumption of innocence as well as a citizen's right to trial, defense counsel, and humane treatment while under arrest.[161]

The extent to which this body of rulings protects individual rights constitutes one of the most liberal features of Egyptian jurisprudence. However, these rulings contain important differences from liberalism. Liberal thought is grounded in the premise that individual rights lie at the heart

---

1984; case 7131, Judicial Year 43, issued August 31, 1989; case 377, Judicial Year 40, issued June 5, 1986; case 7741, Judicial Year 75, issued February 4, 2003.

[153] Administrative Court case 2899, Judicial Year 39, issued December 3, 1985; High Administrative Court case 699, Judicial Year 32, issued October 24, 1987; High Administrative Court case 734, Judicial Year 21, issued June 14, 1980.

[154] Court of Cassation case 1630 of judicial year 48. The ruling held that searches can take place only with a warrant issued by a judge.

[155] Court of Cassation case 3351 of Judicial Year 56.

[156] Court of Cassation case 6241 of Judicial Year 52.

[157] High Administrative Court case 1776, Judicial Year 32, issued December 23, 1989; High Administrative Court case 389, Judicial Year 37, issued January 15, 1995.

[158] High Administrative Court cases 1260 and 1310, Judicial Year 28, issued March 12, 1985.

[159] SCC case 5, Judicial Year 4, issued June 2, 1984.

[160] SCC case 3, Judicial Year 10, issued January 2, 1993.

[161] SCC case 13, Judicial Year 12, issued February 2, 1992; SCC case 3, Judicial Year 10, issued January 2, 1993; SCC case 37, Judicial Year 11, issued February 6, 1993; SCC case 15, Judicial Year 14, issued May 15, 1993; SCC case 13, Judicial Year 15, issued December 17, 1994; SCC case 6, Judicial Year 13, issued May 16, 1992.

of the political order. States are created to protect these rights within a framework of ordered liberty. The state may not infringe on them unless there is a compelling public need to do so. Egyptian jurisprudence lacks this overriding emphasis on individual rights. In the many rulings cited above, the judges make no effort to assert a doctrine of fundamental rights that precedes law and the state. There is no hint at a conception of natural rights. Rather, individual rights are justified in terms of their contribution to the well-being of the community.

For example, consider the body of jurisprudence mentioned earlier regarding individual property rights. In the early 1990s, the SCC overturned several laws that placed arbitrary caps on the level of compensation for nationalized land and buildings. The SCC's reasoning stressed that these caps "deterred national savings and investment." They must be lifted in order to attract investment, facilitate economic growth, and "build national prosperity." There is no effort to assert an inherent right to property. Rather, citizens enjoy property rights because these rights lead to a more prosperous community. To underscore this point, the Court added that property must "serve a social function" in support of the national economy.[162] In a related case, the SCC similarly argued that full protection of property rights should be extended to foreign investors. Again, there is no effort to assert the sanctity of property rights. Rather, there is a pragmatic observation that, if Egypt fails to offer robust protection of property, foreigners may conclude that Egypt does not stand by its international obligations. This development would damage the country's economic growth.[163] The administrative courts apply the same principle. They have issued a large body of rulings that challenge the procedures for sequestering property, the level of compensation provided, and the fact that some government agencies that carry out these measures (such as the Socialist Public Prosecutor) deny their victims an opportunity to challenge the action in court. The line of argument in these cases holds consistently that property rights should be protected because of their constructive "social role" and their contribution to economic growth and prosperity. There is no assertion of an inherent or immutable right to property. Indeed, one ruling expressly addresses and dismisses this line of argument. It holds that a focus on the individual's right to own property "can undermine

---

[162] All quotations are from SCC case 65, Judicial Year 4, issued May 16, 1992. For a similar line of reasoning, see the following SCC cases: case 28, Judicial Year 6, issued June 6, 1998; case 5, Judicial Year 1, issued May 16, 1981; case 1, Judicial Year 1, issued March 2, 1985; case 36, Judicial Year 9, issued March 14, 1992; case 6, Judicial Year 9, issued March 18, 1995; case 4, Judicial Year 15, issued July 18, 1996; case 3, Judicial Year 18, issued January 4, 1997.

[163] SCC case 98, Judicial Year 4, March 5, 1994; Also, SCC case 8, Judicial Year 8, issued March 7, 1992.

national unity by placing the well-being of the individual ahead of the good of society."[164] It adds that an emphasis on personal wealth and property can also lead to corruption. Instead, citizens should focus on the socially constructive role that property plays and the contribution it makes to a "stable and harmonious community."[165]

This emphasis on the community's well-being is also apparent in the SCC's decision in 1997 regarding the constitutionality of privatization. The Egyptian government undertook an ambitious program in the 1990s to privatize public-sector firms. These privatization plans appeared to contradict several articles of Egypt's socialist-era Constitution, particularly articles 30 and 33 which held that the public sector was the "vanguard of progress in all spheres" and "the mainstay of the strength of the homeland."[166] Opponents of privatization argued that these articles gave the public sector the central role in the economy and guaranteed citizens the right to secure and well-paying jobs in public-sector firms. Despite these clauses and arguments, the SCC ruled that the privatization law was constitutional.[167] The chief justice at the time, 'Awad Al-Murr, later acknowledged that the SCC's decision deviated sharply from the language and intent of the Constitution. Nonetheless, he defended the decision because "[our Constitution] cannot be interpreted in any way that will impede our society. . . . Our Constitution must not be construed as hindering our movement in the advance of progress."[168] He clearly believed that privatization and market reform were essential for economic development. In essence, the Chief Justice was prepared to willfully misinterpret the Constitution in order to advance the best interests of society. He adopted this position despite the fact that it clearly violated the constitutional rights of public-sector workers and brought hardship on them and their families.[169] As we will see below, this willingness to disregard the written law in order

---

[164] Administrative Court case 2441, Judicial Year 30, issued May 18, 1985.

[165] Ibid.

[166] This phrasing was removed from the Constitution as a result of amendments adopted in March 2007. For further discussion of these amendments, see chapter 6.

[167] SCC case 7, Judicial Year 16, issued February 1, 1997. It did so with the somewhat contorted reasoning that the term "public sector" in the Constitution should be understood to mean "public investment." In the Court's view, the government is empowered to exercise its discretion regarding the allocation of public investment. This discretion includes selling public assets and directing the proceeds to other socially useful purposes. For further detail on this decision, see Moustafa, *Struggle for Constitutional Power*, 128–32; also, Baudouin Dupret, "A Liberal Interpretation of a Socialist Constitution: The Egyptian Supreme Constitutional Court and Privatization of the Public Sector," in *Politics from Above, Politics from Below*, ed. Eberhard Kienle (London: Saqi, 2003), 167–87.

[168] Speech by 'Awad al-Murr at the American University in Cairo, June 11, 2000. The quotation is recounted in Moustafa, *Struggle for Constitutional Power*, 131.

[169] As an advocate of market reform, the chief justice may well have believed that the reallocation of resources brought about by privatization would lead to improved economic growth and job creation. The workers displaced by privatization would then have the oppor-

to serve the "public interest" has important echoes in Islamic thought. In particular, it resembles the doctrine of *maslaha* that informs much of the legal argumentation of Egypt's contemporary Islamic reformers.

As one might expect, this conceptualization of rights leads to several occasions when individual rights are compromised in order to strengthen the community. This is most apparent in cases that deal with freedom of speech and inquiry regarding religious topics. For example, there is a substantial body of administrative court rulings that uphold the authority of al-Azhar University to review and censor all written, audio, or audiovisual works dealing with Islamic subjects. Several of these rulings defend this practice as essential for preserving the harmony and morality of the community. One holds that "a person's freedom of speech does not extend to offending the most deeply held beliefs of his fellow Egyptians. It also does not extend to raising doubts in them about their faith."[170] This view also led to a separate decision to penalize the speech of a controversial scholar of the Qur'an, Nasr Hamid Abu Zayd. An appeals court held in 1995 that Abu Zayd's analysis of the Qur'an deviated so dramatically from orthodox Islam that it constituted apostasy.[171] The court further held that his marriage of twelve years should be annulled, on the grounds that his Muslim wife could not be legally married to an apostate. To the surprise of most legal observers, this ruling was upheld by the Court of Cassation in August 1996.[172] Abu Zayd's offense did not lie in his unconventional views of the Qur'an. So long as he kept these views to himself, he was not subject to prosecution. However, when he began disseminating these views through his writings and lectures, he was "causing other Muslims to doubt their faith . . . . This posed a serious threat to the well-being of the nation, and constitutes a violation of the law. . . . The exercise of a citizen's freedom of speech must not be allowed to undermine the stability of society or its unity."[173]

The judiciary's emphasis on the well-being of the community also leads to some discrimination against religious minorities. The right of non-Mus-

---

tunity to thrive in this more prosperous economy. However, he did not explicitly present this line of argument.

[170] Administrative Court case 113, Judicial Year 35, issued March 13, 1984. The State Council issued a legal opinion that reiterated this view. See Fatwa 121 of the General Assembly of the State Council, issued February 10, 1994.

[171] Abu Zayd attempted to apply discourse theory to the interpretation of the Qur'an, arguing that many of the key events of the Qur'an should be understood as allegorical metaphors of general principles rather than as literal accounts. For an insightful discussion of Abu Zayd's work, see Navid Kermani, "From Revelation to Interpretation: Nasr Hamid Abu Zayd and the Literary Study of the Qur'an," in *Modern Muslim Intellectuals and the Qur'an*, ed. Suha Taji-Farouki (New York: Oxford University Press, 2004), 169–92.

[172] Court of Cassation cases 475, 478, and 481, for Judicial Year 65, issued August 5, 1996.

[173] Ibid.

lims to live and worship in Egypt is clearly protected in the Constitution. However, the administrative courts have ruled that non-Muslims must practice their faith in a manner that "does not disrupt the harmony of society."[174] This view has led the administrative courts to uphold restrictions on the construction of new Christian churches in predominately Muslim areas.[175] The courts have shown even less tolerance of religious minorities who are not "people of the book"—in other words, religious minorities other than Christians and Jews. These rulings apply primarily to members of the Baha'i faith. In 1979, the administrative court ruled that Bahaism is not one of the heavenly religions and, therefore, cannot be practiced legally in Egypt. Indeed, the practice of the faith was considered a threat to public safety and unity.[176] In 1981, the High Administrative Court ruled that Baha'is were apostates and, as a consequence, could not legally bequeath property to their heirs.[177] As these cases suggest, the courts have not developed a doctrine of an inherent personal right to freedom of religion. Rather, there is only a right to practice specific faiths that are deemed compatible with the values of the broader community.[178]

---

[174] Administrative Court case 7, Judicial Year 2, issued March 1, 1975. A similar line of argument was used in a 1975 decision by the Supreme Court (the predecessor to the Supreme Constitutional Court). This ruling held that non-Muslims could practice their faith as long as it "conforms to the traditional values of Egyptians, does not jeopardize national security, and does not violate accepted social norms." Supreme Court case 7, Judicial Year 2, issued March 1, 1975.

[175] Administrative Court case 615, Judicial Year 5, issued December 16, 1952.

[176] Administrative Court case 84, Judicial Year 31, issued May 16, 1979. Also see Fatwa 271 of the General Assembly of the State Council, issued May 19, 1957. An administrative court decision in April 2006 granted Baha'is the right to list their religion on official documents. However, this decision was reversed on appeal. See High Administrative Court cases 16834 and 18971, Judicial Year 52, issued December 16, 2006. Another administrative court decision in January 2008 allowed Baha'is to leave the "religion" box on official documents blank. It is unclear whether the government will appeal this ruling. See Fathiyya al-Dukhakhani and 'Ali Wail, "The Search for 2000 Baha'is to Benefit from a Ruling that Recognizes their Civil Rights," al-Misri al-Youm, April 7, 2006; Sha'ma al-Qarshawi, "The Supreme Administrative [Court] Cancels the Ruling that Recognizes Bahaism and Concludes that it is Impermissible to State This on Official Papers," al-Misri al-Youm, December 17, 2006; "Egypt: Refusal to Recognize 'Bahaism' and a Call for Changing Religion from Muslim to Christian," al-Hayat, January 29, 2008; Sha'ma al-Qarshawi, "The Interior Ministry is Forced to Produce Identity Cards for Baha'is with 'No Religion' or a Blank," al-Misri al-Youm, January 30, 2008; Majdi Soman, "Human Rights Watch Welcomes the Decision of the Administrative Judiciary to the Benefit of the Baha'is . . . and the Interior Studies Challenging It," al-Misri al-Youm, January 31, 2008.

[177] High Administrative Court case 599, Judicial Year 19, issued January 25, 1981. Also, Rosberg, Roads to the Rule of Law, 219–21.

[178] For further discussion of restrictions on religious freedom in Egypt, see Egypt -- Prohibited Identities: State Interference with Religious Freedom (New York: Human Rights Watch, November 2007).

Some scholars interpret this approach to rights as highly positivistic: the courts enforce the rights that are granted by law without making much effort to assess whether the law is substantively or morally sound.[179] However, the reasoning presented in these rulings suggests a deeper philosophical foundation for the judges' decisions. These decisions articulate a doctrine of communal solidarity that resembles the core features of communitarianism in Western legal and political thought. This view is not inherently illiberal. Indeed, as noted above, it can lead to protection of a wide range of individual rights. However, the justification for these rights lies on a different foundation. In liberal thought, rights are derived from a bedrock belief in natural rights that accrue to all persons simply by virtue of their humanity. The communitarian doctrine developed by Egyptian courts derives individual rights from the contribution they provide to the well-being of the community. This approach provides a less robust philosophical basis for the protection of individual rights and liberties than one finds in the liberal tradition.

Public Participation in Politics

The SCC and the administrative courts have accumulated an impressive record of decisions that strengthen the procedures and institutions of democracy. This is apparent in their rulings regarding political parties. In 1988, the SCC rejected a law that prohibited the establishment of political parties that opposed the Camp David accords.[180] This ruling allowed the formation of three political parties that criticize the accords. Administrative courts have also been active in this area. For example, the government attempted to block the establishment of the New Wafd party on the grounds that it had dissolved itself in 1978 and its license was, as a result, invalid. An administrative court ruled against this view in 1983, and thus made possible the re-emergence of Egypt's largest legal opposition party.[181] In eight other cases, the government attempted to block the formation of new parties by claiming that the party's platform failed to offer an ideological position that distinguished it from other parties or that its platform was at odds with the Constitution. In each of the eight cases, administrative courts held that the government failed to interpret the

---

[179] Brown, *Rule of Law in the Arab World*, 118, 128.

[180] SCC case 44, Judicial Year 7, issued May 7, 1988.

[181] Administrative Court case 115, Judicial Year 38, issued October 29, 1983. The government appealed this ruling, but its petition was denied on January 2, 1984. For a detailed discussion of the legal maneuverings surrounding the reemergence of the Wafd, see 'Abd al-Bir, *Dur Majlis al-Dawla al-Misri fi Himayat al-Huquq wa al-Huriyyat al-'Amma - al-Juz al-Thalith*, 1299–1308.

law properly and that the parties should be granted licenses.[182] Thus, twelve of Egypt's political parties have come into existence through rulings by the judiciary.

The judiciary has also been active in attempting to improve the quality of elections. Egypt has long suffered from electoral malfeasance of myriad forms, including flawed voter registration lists,[183] voters casting multiple ballots, manipulation of vote counting, and the use of government security forces to block opposition voters from reaching the polls.[184] The judiciary has issued a large body of decisions that seek to address these and other problems. The SCC voided the parliamentary electoral law on two occasions (1987 and 1990) on the grounds that it failed to provide independent candidates with an equal opportunity to run for office.[185] Each of these rulings led to the dissolution of the sitting Parliament and the convening of new elections. In 1989, it voided the laws governing *Shura* council elections and municipal elections on the same grounds.[186] The SCC also ruled in July 2000 that parliamentary elections must be fully supervised by the judiciary. This decision ended a long-standing procedure whereby representatives of the Ministry of Interior supervised elections.[187] It marked a significant step toward reducing electoral fraud, although flaws in Egyptian elections remained.[188]

The administrative courts have also been active in monitoring the conduct of elections. They have asserted their jurisdiction in cases involving electoral irregularities or fraud, thereby giving opposition politicians a forum in which to challenge dubious electoral outcomes. They also claim the authority to review the process for nominating candidates, the determination of which parties have won seats in the People's Assembly, and

---

[182] The parties involved are: the *al-Umma* party, Young Egypt, the Green Party, the Federalist Party, the People's Party, the Arab Nasserist Party, the Social Justice Party, and the Solidarity Party. For details regarding each of these cases, see 'Abd al-Bir, *Dur Majlis al-Dawla al-Misri fi Himayat al-Huquq wa al-Huriyyat al-'Amma - al-Juz al-Thalith*, 1191–1334.

[183] Some lists reportedly contain the names of deceased persons, or list the name of the same person several times.

[184] For a more detailed discussion of electoral fraud, see *A Testimony for History: Monitoring the Egyptian 2005 Parliamentary Elections* (Cairo: Independent Committee for Elections Monitoring, December 2005).

[185] SCC case 131, Judicial Year 6, May 16, 1987; and case 37, Judicial Year 9, issued May 19, 1990.

[186] SCC case 23, Judicial Year 8, April 15, 1989; SCC case 14, Judicial Year 8, April 15, 1989.

[187] SCC case 11, Judicial Year 13, issued July 8, 2000. For an excellent discussion of the politics surrounding this ruling and its implementation, see Moustafa, *Struggle for Constitutional Power*, 191–98.

[188] See Jason Brownlee, "The Decline of Pluralism in Mubarak's Egypt," *Journal of Democracy* 13, no. 4 (2002): 6–14.

the distribution of seats among parties.[189] In 1985, the High Administrative Court overturned efforts by the Socialist Public Prosecutor to exclude members of the opposition from parliamentary elections.[190] In the same year, this court further ruled that the government's conduct of parliamentary and local elections violated the law by placing opposition candidates at a systematic disadvantage.[191] The administrative courts took an even more dramatic step in the 1995 parliamentary elections, holding that electoral procedures in 47 percent of the districts were so flawed that the outcome should be annulled. The Court of Cassation also found extensive evidence of electoral malfeasance.[192] The speaker of Parliament disregarded these rulings on the grounds that only the Parliament has the authority to decide who may legitimately occupy a seat.[193] However, the administrative courts awarded compensation to the victims—usually in the range of 25,000–100,000 LE.[194]

These rulings on parties and elections show a clear commitment by the judiciary to strengthening the procedures of democratic participation. Yet, throughout this jurisprudence, the judges express consistent reservations about democracy. For example, consider the administrative court rulings that favor the formation of new parties. These rulings stress that parties are desirable because they bring "structure" to public participation in political life. One ruling speaks at some length about the danger

[189] High Administrative Court case 4387, Judicial Year 35, issued May 31, 1992; High Administrative Court case 340, Judicial Year 23, issued April 9, 1977; High Administrative Court case 15, Judicial Year 23, issued April 9, 1977; High Administrative Court case 791, Judicial Year 23, issued January 28, 1978; Administrative Court case 3423, Judicial Year 41, issued April 21, 1987; Administrative Court case 3059, Judicial Year 41, issued March 31, 1987; Administrative Court case 3042, Judicial Year 41, issued March 31, 1987. The administrative courts draw a distinction between the counting of votes and the administrative procedures associated with the election. The former is "directly related to the wishes of the voters and the accurate expression of their will." As a consequence, it is not subject to judicial review—all disputes over vote tallies must be directed to the Parliament, in accordance with article 93 of the Constitution. However, all other aspects of the electoral process are considered administrative acts that are subject to the jurisdiction of the administrative courts. High Administrative Court case 2080, Judicial Year 50, December 5, 1995; High Administrative Court case 580, Judicial Year 42, November 17, 1996.

[190] High Administrative Court cases 396 and 470, Judicial Year 30, issued March 16, 1985.

[191] High Administrative Court case 3096, Judicial Year 30, issued May 25, 1985. The Ministry of Interior allowed candidates from the ruling NDP to hold rallies, display campaign posters, and canvas with few restrictions. Opposition candidates, however, faced restrictions in all of these areas.

[192] See *The Independent Commission for Electoral Review Report on the 1995 Parliamentary Elections* (Cairo: ICER, January 10, 1996). Also, Moustafa, *Struggle for Constitutional Power*, 160–61.

[193] This assertion is based on article 93 of the 1971 Constitution.

[194] Moustafa, *The Struggle for Constitutional Power*, 161.

posed by "mass politics" that can lead to instability and disorder.[195] Another ruling adds that parties are essential for "bringing organization to the public's participation in public life" and ensuring that this participation is "orderly and compatible with the safety and security of the nation."[196] The rulings return repeatedly to the theme that public participation in political life holds the potential to spiral out of control and lead to social disorder and weakened government. As a consequence, there is a need to carefully manage public participation through the formation of "responsible" political parties that convey the concerns of citizens in a peaceful and orderly fashion. In this view, political parties are as much an instrument of control as of political mobilization. Indeed, the courts seem quite nervous about the repercussions of widespread political mobilization. In a similar vein, a 1992 administrative court ruling expressed reservations about the capacity of the average Egyptian to exercise sound judgment on matters of politics and policy. It notes that the average Egyptian has relatively little education and is "easily swayed by individuals with strong personalities."[197] Political parties are essential for ensuring that experienced and educated persons can organize and represent popular opinion in a responsible manner.[198]

The implication is that Egyptians are not yet fully ready to participate in their own governance. The rulings do not assert a fundamental right to public participation in politics, or even the concept of popular sovereignty—although there were many opportunities to invoke these ideas, and language in the Constitution supports them. A similar sentiment emerges in several of the rulings on electoral disputes. They emphasize the importance of efficient and credible electoral procedures as a means to "avoid mass politics that can be exploited by charismatic speakers or persons with powerful personalities."[199] One ruling goes so far as to explicitly refer to the "previous era" (i.e., the Nasser era) when mass politics enabled a small elite to "dominate the political process and suppress political competition."[200] It concludes that elections are a "ritual for including citizens in the process of government."[201] This participation strengthens the legitimacy of government and the stability of society. However, decision making should lie with persons who command "relevant education, experience,

[195] Administrative Court case 639, Judicial Year 39, issued June 6, 1993.

[196] Administrative Court case 66, Judicial Year 37, issued April 19, 1992.

[197] Administrative Court case 3783, Judicial Year 38, issued May 29, 1984.

[198] Ibid.

[199] Administrative Court case 2974, Judicial Year 41, issued March 28, 1987.

[200] Administrative Court case 3414, Judicial Year 41, issued April 21, 1987.

[201] Ibid. Also see Administrative Court cases 3385, 3453, 3483, Judicial Year 41, issued April 21, 1987.

and knowledge."[202] These leaders carefully weigh the strengths and weaknesses of the options available and arrive at the policy solution that best serves the public interest. If parties and elections function properly, they will naturally favor persons with the education and judgment needed to play this role. This is, obviously, an idealized view of politics and political competition. Nonetheless, it is the ideal that informs the judiciary's decisions. Judges clearly favor a highly educated elite as the guardians of politics and society, and regard the disorder of unstructured political competition as a threat to social stability.

• • •

The rulings discussed in this chapter suggest that the judiciary is more supportive of horizontal accountability of government than vertical accountability. Judges work with great energy and consistency to define the institutional boundaries between the various parts of the state. As noted earlier, this is particularly the case with regard to the independence of the judiciary. These limits on institutional power—defined by law and enforced by the judiciary—are the key to regulating the state and holding it accountable to law. In contrast, the judges are ambivalent about the concept of government accountability to the people. They regard public participation in elections as important for enhancing the legitimacy of the regime. However, the substance of governing and meaningful accountability should lie with those citizens who have the relevant training, knowledge, and experience. This natural elite serves as the trustee of the public interest, which it defines through careful deliberation and study—not through consultation with the people.

This body of jurisprudence has produced a distinctive conception of liberal constitutionalism. Like classical liberalism, it calls for a constrained and accountable state, the rule of law, and the protection of individual rights. It supports the core institutions of classical liberalism, including a clear and impartial legal code, the separation of powers within the state, checks and balances among these powers, an independent judiciary, an autonomous legal profession, and property rights. However, it has several unique features. It tolerates a more powerful and invasive state than is suggested by liberal thought. It also places greater emphasis on strengthening the community and affirming communal solidarity. Liberal constitutionalism in Egypt does not share the intense focus on personal liberty that characterizes classical liberalism. This does not suggest an indifference to individual rights. Rather, it indicates a greater willingness to balance

[202] High Administrative Court case 1900, Judicial Year 33, issued April 29, 1989. Also see High Administrative Court cases 1920 and 1922, Judicial Year 33, issued April 29, 1989.

individual rights with the interests of the community. Finally, the judiciary holds a relatively weak commitment to public participation in political life and remains wary of the disorder that can arise from mass politics.

This conception of constitutionalism provides a clear ideological alternative to the unbridled statism of the regime. As we will see in chapter 4, it is the guiding force behind the Judges' Club's campaign for political and legal reform. However, it is not the only alternative view of political and legal order in contemporary Egypt. The country also has a sophisticated Islamic conception of constitutionalism, which is our next focus of attention.

CHAPTER THREE

Islamic Constitutionalism

THE POLITICAL GOALS OF MODERATE ISLAM

As MUHAMMAD 'AKIF walked into the auditorium in downtown Cairo, the assembled journalists were both skeptical and curious. 'Akif had been a relatively unknown figure in the Muslim Brotherhood. Now, in March 2004, he was the newly appointed General Guide of the organization. As he began his opening remarks, he addressed the issue that concerned most Egyptians: What, exactly, does the Brotherhood want? 'Akif declared that the Brotherhood seeks "a republican system of government that is democratic, constitutional, and parliamentary and that conforms with Islamic principles."[1]

With this statement, 'Akif asserted the Islamic alternative to both the regime and the liberal constitutionalists of the judiciary. He also affirmed the Brotherhood's role as the primary advocate of a moderate Islamic conception of politics and law. However, the Brotherhood has not always been a proponent of this view. Indeed, it has avoided issuing a clear statement of its ideology and political objectives for most of its history. The moderate posture adopted by 'Akif is largely a product of the last fifteen years, and reflects the Brotherhood's adaptation to the constraints and opportunities of the Egyptian political scene. In response to these pressures, the organization's reformers have borrowed ideas from Egypt's most prominent theorists of Islamic constitutionalism. These ideas provide a window on the emerging political doctrine and goals of the Brotherhood. They also delineate the distinctive form of liberalism and democracy advocated by Egypt's growing Islamist movement.

THE RISE, FALL, AND REBIRTH OF THE MUSLIM BROTHERHOOD

Founded in 1928 as a discussion group and charitable organization, the Muslim Brotherhood (MB) grew within a decade into the largest and

---

[1] The purpose of the press conference was to announce the release of the Brotherhood's Reform Initiative. 'Akif's statement reiterates the view presented in the Initiative. See *Mubadirat al-Ikhwan al-Muslimin hawwal Mabad' al-Islah fi Misr* (Cairo: Dar al-Manara, 2004), 12–13.

best-organized social movement in Egypt. The organization's founder, Hasan al-Banna, had a simple and powerful message: the people of Egypt had wandered from the spiritual and moral principles of Islam. As a consequence, the country had become poor, divided, and corrupt. Britain exploited these weaknesses to maintain a painful and humiliating occupation. The only hope for rebuilding the nation's pride and power lay in a return to Islam and, particularly, the implementation of *Shari'a*. Al-Banna wrote that, without the *Shari'a*, Muslims were "a people without direction." With it, they acquired a sense of strength and purpose "deeply rooted in our history, our society, and our circumstances."[2]

Al-Banna was vague regarding the Brotherhood's specific political objectives. Indeed, in its early years, the Brotherhood more closely resembled a Sufi order than a political movement.[3] The organization was built around the charismatic authority of al-Banna and a small group of disciples who dutifully implemented his instructions. The few details of the organization's objectives emerged only gradually through the sermons and letters of al-Banna.

In 1945, these were codified into a set of bylaws.[4] They state that the Brotherhood pursues five goals: precise explanation of the Qur'an based on its original meaning while accommodating "the spirit of the age"; unification of Egypt and the Islamic world based on the principles of the Qur'an; strengthening Egyptian society by increasing national wealth, reducing inequality, and providing social services; liberating all Arab countries of any foreign presence; and pursuing world cooperation and peace based on freedom, human rights, and Islam.

The Brotherhood would utilize four methods to achieve these goals:

- Missionary work (*al-da'wa*) that would spread the Brotherhood's views through preaching, pamphlets, newspapers, magazines, and books.
- Education (*al-tarbiya*) for the Brotherhood's followers and the population as a whole.
- Indoctrination (*al-tawjih*) of all Egyptians to the principle that *Shari'a* must govern every aspect of life.
- Action (*al-'amal*) that would include building mosques, schools, hospitals, and social service clinics.

---

[2] Hasan al-Banna, "Dusturna" in Hasan al-Banna, *Majmu'aat Rasa'il al-Imam al-Shadid Hasan al-Banna* (Cairo: Dar al-Nashr al-Islami, n.d.), 35.

[3] Brynjar Lia, *The Society of the Muslim Brothers in Egypt: The Rise of an Islamic Mass Movement, 1928–1942* (Reading: Ithaca Press, 1998), 37. For an interesting discussion of al-Banna's views on Sufism, see Richard P. Mitchell, *The Society of the Muslim Brothers* (New York: Oxford University Press, 1993), 214–16.

[4] *Qanun al-Nitham al-Asasi li Hay't al-Ikhwan al-Muslimin* (Cairo: Dar al-Ansar, 1945).

Al-Banna elaborated several other goals for the organization through additional statements, letters, and sermons. He called for banning all political parties,[5] ending corruption in government, strengthening the independence of the judiciary, and expanding the government's role in supervising education and public morality.[6]

Al-Banna further argued that Egypt suffered from two forms of imperialism. The first was the obvious, external variety at the hands of Britain. It entailed a large British troop presence and de facto British control over Egyptian politics and policy. The second was a more insidious form of "internal colonialism" carried out by local elites who shared Britain's goals and benefited from its presence. In order to achieve true independence, Egyptians must defeat both of these forms of imperialism. This view led the MB to undertake military action against both the British colonial forces and their Egyptian allies. In the late 1940s, the MB's "secret apparatus" was held responsible for the assassination of a judge and a prime minister, the bombing of several government buildings, and a plot to overthrow the government.[7] Al-Banna denied that the Brotherhood was behind these acts. Nonetheless, he was assassinated in 1949 by members of the secret police seeking revenge for the murder of the prime minister.

Under al-Banna's leadership, the Brotherhood developed into two movements. The "secret apparatus," led by Ahmad Sanadi, favored military confrontation with the regime. A less belligerent faction, led by Hasan al-Hudeibi, called for education and preaching that would develop the spiritual awareness of the Egyptian people and gradually build public support for implementing *Shari'a*. Al-Banna was able to avoid a clash between these two factions largely because of his personal charisma and his credibility as founder of the movement. His death led to a protracted internal battle between them. Al-Hudeibi eventually assumed the post of General Guide, but he never gained the obedience of the more violent Sanadi faction.

Nonetheless, the Brotherhood remained the most effective civilian opposition to the Monarchy and the British. It was the only civilian group that Nasser and his fellow Free Officers chose to include in the 1952 coup.[8] Indeed, Nasser initially regarded the Brotherhood as a natural ally. It was a long-standing advocate of many positions that were central to the Free

[5] He believed that political parties aggravated social and class divisions within society.

[6] These points are raised repeatedly in his speeches and letters. See *Majmu'aat Rasa'il*, especially pp. 120–74.

[7] Mitchell, *Society of the Muslim Brothers*, 61–69.

[8] The MB's role was to block the road from Ismailia to Cairo, thereby ensuring that the British could not reinforce the King's supporters. The MB also protected the foreign embassies in Cairo to ensure that the British could not intervene on the pretext of protecting foreign citizens from harm. Beattie, *Egypt during the Nasser Years*, 57; Gordon, *Nasser's Blessed Movement*, 54.

Officers' agenda, including opposition to the British occupation, support for a clean parliamentary system, and economic reforms that narrowed the gap between rich and poor. This similarity of views led Nasser to include the MB in his regime. A member of the MB was made Minister of Religious Endowments, and a prominent MB supporter was appointed Minister of Justice. He also pardoned all MB members who had been imprisoned for attacks on the pre-1952 regime, reopened the investigation into the assassination of Hasan al-Banna, and named three members of the MB to the Committee of fifty that would draft the new constitution.[9]

However, the Brotherhood also constituted a significant potential threat to the regime. On each of the key policy goals mentioned above, the Brotherhood had a longer and more impressive record of achievement than the Free Officers. It also had greater popularity, a larger organization, an effective paramilitary wing, and supporters in the army and police. The MB was aware of its power and began pressing for a prominent position in regime decision making as early as August 1952. It formally asked for the role of "guardian" of the revolution, which would empower it to monitor the regime's policies and ensure that they were consistent with Islam.[10] When the Free Officers rejected this proposition, the MB organized demonstrations at Cairo University calling for constitutional reform.[11] It also orchestrated a large demonstration in support of Muhammad Najib's appeal for new elections.[12]

By December 1953, the Free Officers were deeply concerned about the MB. They were beginning another round of negotiations with Great Britain over its troop presence in Egypt, and feared that the Brotherhood would organize protests against any compromises needed to reach an agreement. The MB also showed signs of further strengthening its ties to Muhammad Najib, the largely symbolic prime minister who appeared to support some of the Brotherhood's goals. The Free Officers attempted to

[9] Gordon, *Nasser's Blessed Movement*, 76, 100–101.

[10] The MB had sought this guardianship role before the coup. This posture led to some tension with the Free Officers and the eventual ouster of the MB's liaison to the Free Officers in early 1952. Gordon, *Nasser's Blessed Movement*, 53. The MB again sought a guardianship role when Hudeibi met with Nasser on July 30, 1952—one week after the coup. On August 2, the MB published a manifesto stating the reforms that it supported. It called for the dissolution of political parties, promulgation of a new constitution based on Islam, nationalization of the Ahli Bank, outlawing of interest, closure of the stock exchange, land reform, expansion of free education, and free public health services. Beattie, *Egypt during the Nasser Years*, 73.

[11] It coordinated these rallies with demonstrations organized by the communists, raising further concern among the Free Officers that an anti-regime alliance was emerging at the universities. Gordon, *Nasser's Blessed Movement*, 105.

[12] Beattie, *Egypt during the Nasser Years*, 94.

weaken the MB by recruiting its rank-and-file members to the regime's new mass party, the Liberation Rally. The MB vigorously resisted this effort. In January 1954, a clash between MB supporters and members of the Liberation Rally at Cairo University led the regime to formally dissolve the Brotherhood.[13] In March 1954, the MB organized a large rally backing Muhammad Najib's claim to lead the country. The Free Officers reacted by arresting most of the MB's leadership and unleashing a barrage of public criticism of the organization.

Tensions came to a head with Nasser's signing of a tentative withdrawal agreement with the British on October 19, 1954. The agreement allowed Britain to maintain troops in Egypt for at least six more years. The MB strongly criticized both the agreement and the regime. A militant faction of the Brotherhood attempted to assassinate Nasser on October 26, 1954. He responded with a thorough crackdown on the MB, arresting over 30,000 members and executing several of the organization's senior leaders.[14] He also used the assassination attempt as an excuse to arrest Muhammad Najib, on the unlikely charge that he had plotted with the MB to attain power.

Despite this crackdown, the MB managed to survive. In the early 1960s, a new and more radical theological trend emerged within the organization under the leadership of Sayyid Qutb. Qutb argued that Egypt's government defied even the most basic precepts of Islam and, as a consequence, the country was in a state of pre-Islamic ignorance.[15] He concluded that devout Muslims had an obligation to forcibly overthrow this corrupt regime. Any tolerance of it, or cooperation with it, was sinful and hopeless.[16] Qutb attracted followers in both the military and the police. He also had considerable success in recruiting supporters among the middle class.

Nasser confronted this MB threat quickly and brutally. In August 1965, he claimed that Qutb and his disciples were involved in a plot to assassinate him and take over the government. He arrested over 18,000 MB members and sympathizers and executed twenty-six of its leaders, including Qutb.[17] By 1966, the MB was in a state of disarray. Its key leaders were arrested

[13] The Brotherhood was dissolved on the grounds that it was a political organization, and was thus subject to the regime's ban on all such organizations. Gordon, *Nasser's Blessed Movement*, 105.

[14] The government also took control of the Brotherhood's social service programs, thereby eliminating its primary source of popular support. Mitchell, *Society of the Muslim Brothers*, 127.

[15] Qutb described it as a "jahiliyya" society, a term used to describe Arabia prior to the rise of Islam.

[16] The clearest exposition of this view is in Sayyid Qutb, *Ma'alim fi-l-Tariq* (Cairo: n.p., 1964).

[17] Waterbury, *The Egypt of Nasser and Sadat*, 341.

or dead, its branches were dissolved, and its wealth was confiscated. The organization's few remaining leaders fled into exile, mostly to Saudi Arabia or Europe.

Egypt's defeat in the 1967 war provided the MB with an opportunity to rise from the ashes. The defeat shook the ideological foundations of the regime. Nasser had come to power with sweeping plans for prosperity, strength, and dignity. The defeat at the hands of Israel revealed the hollowness of these promises. Nasserism had produced a weak and divided regime that not only failed to defend the country, but lost territory in Sinai as well as the Holy City of Jerusalem. As the country searched for explanations, supporters of political Islam naturally argued that the catastrophic defeat was due to the secular and leftist character of the regime. A return to Islam would revive the nation's unity, strength, and sense of purpose.[18]

Nasser responded to this sentiment by establishing a religious affairs committee in the Arab Socialist Union and increasing religious programming on television and radio. He also released from prison over a thousand of the least threatening MB members in early 1968. However, the MB of the late 1960s lacked the organization and leadership needed to harness the public's renewed interest in Islam. Instead, isolated cells of MB sympathizers began operating autonomously. Members of these cells participated in the large student riots of February 1968 protesting the regime, but there is little evidence that they organized the riots or played a role in leading them. To the extent that the MB had a strategy in the late 1960s, it focused on public education. Zainab al-Ghazali, for example, writes of an extensive MB plan to spread its views through a network of schools, mosques, and prayer groups.[19]

The Brotherhood underwent a significant revival during the 1970s. Sadat released the leadership of the organization and many of its members in 1971, as part of a general amnesty designed to show the tolerance and openness of his new regime. He also encouraged the MB to organize on university campuses in order to offset the growing influence of leftist and Nasserist groups. The MB was happy to play this role. It was a principled opponent of Nasserism, and offered a clear Islamic rationale for dismantling much of the Nasser regime. Its efforts on university campuses included organizing "training programs" in which prominent members of the movement would explain their views and mobilize students. It also offered a variety of services for students, including providing cheap copies of expensive textbooks, financial aid for needy students, and Islamic

---

[18] One of the clearest statements of this sentiment is Muhammad al-Ghazali, *Hasad al-Ghurur* (Cairo: n.p., 1978).

[19] Zainab al-Ghazali, *Ayyam min Hayati* (Cairo: Dar al-Sharuq, n.d.).

dress for women. These grassroots efforts paid off. By 1977, the Brotherhood controlled the student associations at all thirteen of Egypt's universities. In 1978, it won control of the nationwide General Union of Egyptian Students.[20]

In 1975, Sadat further loosened the constraints on the Brotherhood and allowed it to undertake social and religious activities.[21] The MB jumped at the opportunity and began constructing schools, hospitals, and medical clinics.[22] The Brotherhood's journal, al-Da'wa, appeared in 1977 and reached a circulation of 80,000 by 1979. By 1981, the MB was sufficiently well-organized to mobilize 250,000 members to attend a prayer rally in Cairo's Abdin Square. It organized a comparable event in the stadium at Alexandria University.[23]

The most prominent MB ideologues of this period were 'Umar al-Tilmisani, Muhammad al-Ghazali, and Muhammad 'Amara. They called for the implementation of Islamic law, a reduction in political and cultural ties with the West, and the cessation of contacts with Israel. They opposed Sadat's economic opening to the West (infitah) on the grounds that participation in the global economy required adopting principles that were at odds with Islam (such as consumerism, materialism, and charging interest on loans). They also argued that the infitah benefited only a small elite while impoverishing most Egyptians. They further condemned the general moral decay, corruption, and spiritual vacuum in Egyptian society, and called for a deepening of the country's commitment to Islamic law and belief. They argued that the transition to a more Islamic order should be achieved without violence. Indeed, the General Guide of the Brotherhood, 'Umar al-Tilmisani, intervened on university campuses to dissuade students from using violence. They were told to "mind their own business, stay out of trouble, and worship God."[24]

Sadat was assassinated in 1981 by a member of Jihad, a militant Islamic group that had split off from the Brotherhood in the early 1970s. In the wake of the assassination, over four thousand members and supporters of the Brotherhood were arrested. However, most of them were soon released. The new regime of Husni Mubarak began a concerted strategy to win over the peaceful Islamic opposition and discredit the ideology of the radicals. The government sponsored conferences in which supporters of

[20] Rosefsky-Wickham, Mobilizing Islam, 116.

[21] Waterbury, The Egypt of Nasser and Sadat, 361. This step was partially due to pressure from the Saudi government, which became an important benefactor of Egypt after the 1973 war.

[22] These efforts were funded, in part, with assistance from Saudi donors and remittances from workers employed in the Gulf.

[23] Beattie, Egypt during the Sadat Years, 264. Also, Baker, Sadat and After, 270.

[24] "Hiwar ma'a 'Umar al-Tilmisani," al-Musawwar, January 22, 1982.

Islamic extremism expressed their views and were then critiqued by senior Islamic scholars from al-Azhar University and (on occasion) leaders of the Muslim Brotherhood.[25] Several of these exchanges were broadcast on television. In addition, imprisoned militants were invited to recant their violent beliefs. Those who agreed were released. They were often interviewed on television, where they admitted the error of their ways and warned other young people not to make the same mistake. The government also undertook a substantial media campaign to disseminate and strengthen a moderate conception of Islam. This included an increase in Islamic broadcasts on television and radio and the establishment of two new Islamic newspapers.

The leadership of the Brotherhood largely supported the government's efforts to weaken radical Islamic groups. The General Guide, 'Umar al-Tilmisani, expressed his support for Mubarak by stating that the new president had inaugurated a "promising era" and that all Muslims should "join hands with the President at this critical moment."[26] The regime reciprocated by allowing the MB to participate more fully in politics. The organization was not permitted to establish its own political party, due to an Egyptian law that bans the formation of parties based on religion. However, it was permitted to participate in electoral alliances with the New Wafd Party (in 1984) and the Socialist Labor Party and the Liberal Party (in 1987). It won eight seats in Parliament in 1984 and thirty-eight in 1987. These results constituted a small minority of the total Parliament of 454 seats. Nonetheless, they gave the MB a prominent public platform for disseminating its views and challenging public officials. The regime also allowed the MB to expand its influence on university campuses and in professional associations.

The social base of the MB's support lay primarily in the middle class, which expanded rapidly in the 1970s and 1980s. The growth of the middle class was due largely to reforms in the 1960s and 1970s that made university education available to virtually any citizen who wanted it. For the first time, the children of peasants and workers were able to attend university. After graduating, they expected white-collar jobs commensurate with their level of education. However, the Egyptian economy produced only a fraction of the jobs needed. In the 1970s and early 1980s, the government tried to cope with this problem by giving all university graduates jobs in either the bureaucracy or the public sector. However, by 1985, the financial burden of this policy was overwhelming and the regime had no choice but to end it. The universities, however, continued to produce

---

[25] 'Umar al-Tilmisani participated in some of these programs. See *al-Anba*, March 5, 1984.

[26] *al-Jumhuriyya*, December 25, 1981.

record numbers of lower-middle-class graduates, most of whom were unable to secure jobs in their fields. They grew to resent the "old boy" network that found jobs for upper-middle-class graduates regardless of their abilities. They were also deeply offended by the growing prosperity of less-educated persons in the private sector, whom they believed acquired their wealth through illicit dealings and personal connections rather than ability and hard work.[27]

The MB appealed to many of these lower-middle-class university graduates. Its emphasis on morality and honesty stood in sharp contrast to the growing corruption and cronyism within society. It also offered specific services to improve the lot of unemployed university graduates, including job training, apartments, health care, and emergency funds.[28] Significantly, the Brotherhood's popularity was not the result of widespread support for its ideology or its conception of Islamic government. Indeed, the Brotherhood remained vague regarding its specific political goals. Rather, young people were drawn by the organization's moral principles and its social service network.[29]

In the early 1990s, the regime became less tolerant of the Brotherhood and of political Islam in general. This was due, in large measure, to the Brotherhood's growing power and organization. By 1992, MB members were leading all the major professional associations (except that of the journalists) and all the university student unions. The MB also controlled a sophisticated network of social welfare services. As the government faced an ever-deepening economic crisis, it proved unable to provide even basic services in many areas. The MB filled this void by establishing schools, health clinics, and credit unions.[30] The capabilities of the MB became particularly clear in the wake of a serious earthquake in Cairo on October 12,

[27] Rosefsky-Wickham, *Mobilizing Islam*, 36–62. Davis argues that the MB's core base of support has always been in the middle class, even in the 1930s and 1940s. See Eric Davis, "Ideology, Social Classes, and Islamic Radicalism in Modern Egypt," in *From Nationalism to Revolutionary Islam*, ed. Said Arjomand (Albany: State University of New York Press, 1983), 140–43.

[28] This aspect of the MB's appeal was made clear at an Islamist student demonstration at Cairo University on October 24, 1995. The flyer distributed by the students focused almost entirely on practical considerations: overcrowded classes, poor-quality student housing, lack of adequate financial support for students, and lack of a good cafeteria on campus. I spoke with ten participants in the demonstration, each of whom emphasized these practical problems that students faced. None spoke of Islamist ideology. When questioned on this point, most said that they favored the implementation of *Shari'a* (although two were unwilling to assert even this view). None offered a more extensive discussion of Islamist political views.

[29] For further discussion of the origins of the Brotherhood's popular appeal, see Hala Mustafa, *al-Dawla wa-l-Haraka al-Islamiyya al-Ma'arada* (Cairo: al-Mahrusa, 1995); Rosefsky-Wickham, *Mobilizing Islam*, especially pp. 36–62; 93–118.

[30] For a valuable discussion of the activities of medical clinics tied to Islamist groups, see Clark, *Islam, Charity, and Activism*, especially pp. 42–81.

1992. The quake injured over 12,000 people and damaged over 50,000 buildings. Within hours, Islamic activists had set up first-aid centers and distributed food, medicine, and money. These efforts were mostly organized by the physicians' syndicate and the engineers' syndicate, which were under the control of the MB. The regime, in contrast, was slow and inefficient. Its programs to provide first aid and emergency housing were woefully inadequate. It promised 5,000 LE to each family member who lost a home or breadwinner, but it proved unable to follow through on even this meager financial assistance. On October 24, Mubarak tried to rein in the MB's humanitarian efforts by ordering that all aid must be provided through state agencies and that only licensed charitable organizations could disperse it.

In addition, the regime claimed that the Islamic opposition was engaged in a large and violent conspiracy to overthrow the government and transform Egyptian society. This specific charge was raised in a case involving a local computer company, Salsabil. Prosecutors alleged that the firm was a front for an elaborate plot to seize power. They claimed that both the Muslim Brotherhood and radical groups were involved, and that the plot had cells in the police, military, security services, and government.[31]

By the end of 1992, the government concluded that its efforts in the 1980s to engage the moderate Islamists had been misguided. The editor of *al-Ahram*, whose columns generally reflect the views of the government, wrote: "Egypt is not facing reckless youth who are doing harm because of their immature understanding of faith, life and everything in Egypt . . . we are facing organized forces with deep roots under the surface, organization, financing and resources. They have opted for a bloody and armed confrontation with the forces of the state, enlightenment, security, safety, and stability in our country."[32]

The interior minister echoed these views: "We must recognize that we are in a *de facto* state of war with a determined enemy. We must take all necessary measures to win."[33] The regime regarded all Islamic organizations that were not under state control as hostile, and stopped distinguishing between the MB and the militants. Mubarak declared: "They [the MB] assassinated two prime ministers and a finance minister before the [1952] revolution. Then they pretended to back the late President Jamal 'Abd al-Nasser but attempted to assassinate him in Alexandria. President Sadat did not act against them early in his tenure, having been preoccupied with restoring the occupied territories, and so they killed him. The

---

[31] Al-Sayyid Yasin, ed., *al-Taqrir al-Stratiji al-'Arabi, 1992*, 318–24.
[32] *Al-Ahram*, December 23, 1992.
[33] Middle East News Agency (Cairo), December 16, 1993.

Muslim Brothers, the Jihad, the Islamic Groups, and the rest of them, are all the same."[34]

This sentiment led to extensive suppression of Islamic groups of all types. In July 1992, the regime issued a new anti-terrorism law that empowered the security forces to arrest any person for up to three days without charge and stiffened prison sentences for those found guilty of "assisting or expressing sympathy for" terrorists. Under the new law, seven thousand persons were arrested in the wake of an attack on a German tour bus. The government destroyed the family homes of several suspects, and held the mother and grandmother of one suspect hostage in an effort to persuade the suspect to surrender.[35] In the first few months of 1994, the regime undertook a broad sweep that led to the arrest of 29,000 suspected Islamic militants.[36] This effort succeeded in pushing the militants out of the major cities. They fell back on their hideouts in southern Egypt (particularly Assiut and Minya), where the government laid siege to them and conducted periodic raids and mass arrests.

In 1993, the regime began using military courts to try suspected militants. The verdicts of these courts were handed down more quickly and were more severe than those of ordinary courts. Rules of evidence were lax (for example, the prosecutor was not required to present the source for evidence used in his case). There was also no opportunity for judicial appeal.[37] The regime initially used these courts only to try suspected violent militants. However, in 1995, it began using them to try nonviolent Islamists as well. Its most prominent case involved fifty-four leaders of the Muslim Brotherhood. The accused were acquitted of all the serious charges against them, but were found guilty of involvement in an illegal organization (the MB) and were sentenced to three- to five-year jail terms. The list of those convicted was a veritable who's who of the Brotherhood's younger stars who had led the organization's ascent within the

[34] Interview with Mubarak in *Le Monde*, November 17, 1995. See also his interview in *Der Spiegel*, May 16, 1994. He reiterated this view in 2004. When asked whether the MB should be permitted to form a political party, he responded, "No, the last thing our country needs is a group like the Muslim Brotherhood. They have a terrorist past, they killed a prime minister and others who did not agree with their political goals." "The Reform Buzz," *al-Ahram Weekly*, December 30, 2004–January 5, 2005.

[35] The government's abuses are documented in the annual reports of the Egyptian Organization for Human Rights for 1992, 1993, and 1994.

[36] The estimate is based on interior ministry sources, and is cited in *Economist Intelligence Unit, Egypt: Country Report, 1994*, number 2, p. 9.

[37] Trials before military courts are flawed in several other respects. For example, trials are often conducted en masse, with as many as 97 defendants being tried simultaneously. For a full discussion of the military courts, see *Military Courts in Egypt* (Cairo: Center for Human Rights Legal Aid, September 1995). Also, A. Seif El-Islam, "Exceptional Laws and Exceptional Courts," 372–75.

universities and the professional associations: 'Isam al-'Iryan, a former member of Parliament and assistant secretary general of the Doctor's syndicate; 'Abd al-Mon'am Abu al-Fatuh, secretary general of the Doctor's syndicate and secretary general of the Federation of Arab Doctors; Ibrahim al-Zafarani, another prominent doctor; Muhammad al-Sayyid Habib, a respected geologist and university professor; and Muhammad Khayrat al-Shatir, a leader in the engineers' syndicate.[38] The court also ordered the closure of the MB's headquarters in central Cairo, which had been open since 1972.

The government claimed on several occasions that the Brotherhood had direct ties to the militants, but it did not provide evidence of this link. It was unable to prove MB involvement in violent acts even in trials before the relatively sympathetic military courts.[39] Nonetheless, the regime made a systematic effort to harass and weaken the MB. In addition to imprisoning many key leaders in 1995, the interior ministry periodically summoned the General Guide for interrogation on the grounds that he was involved with an illegal organization. In the run-up to the October 1995 parliamentary elections, several hundred MB activists were detained until after the election and then released without explanation. This was a clear effort to disrupt the MB's plans for mobilizing its voters.[40] Only one member of the MB managed to win a seat in Parliament in 1995. The regime arrested him in December 1996 on the grounds that he used his office in Helwan for "subversive activity."[41] In October 1999, it carried out another wave of arrests and sentenced fifteen of the MB's younger leaders to prison terms.[42] The pattern continued in the 2000 parliamentary election. Several hundred Brotherhood activists were rounded up in the weeks preceding the election. Twenty of the Brotherhood's candidates were tried before a military court and sentenced to three- to five-year terms. Despite these attacks, the Brotherhood fielded seventy-five candidates who ran as independents. Seventeen of them were successful, making the Brotherhood the largest opposition bloc in Parliament. One of these members was later unseated on the grounds that his election had been tainted by procedural

[38] Mona El-Ghobashy, "The Metamorphosis of the Egyptian Muslim Brothers," *International Journal of Middle East Studies* 37 (2005): 384. Also, Rosefsky-Wickham, *Mobilizing Islam*, 215.

[39] According to al-Awadi, a former minister of interior has confirmed that the MB has no ties to violent Islamic groups. Hesham al-Awadi, *In Pursuit of Legitimacy: The Muslim Brothers and Mubarak, 1982–2000* (New York: Tauris, 2004), 179.

[40] *CHRLA's Final Report on the Legislative Elections in Egypt, 1995* (Cairo: Center for Human Rights Legal Aid, 1996), 31–32, 34–36.

[41] *Economist Intelligence Unit, Egypt: Country Report*, 1997, number 1, p. 15.

[42] Rosefsky-Wickham, *Mobilizing Islam*, 215.

irregularities.[43] Sixteen additional MB activists were sentenced to prison by military tribunals in 2002, and several dozen local leaders of the movement were detained and prosecuted in 2003. Brotherhood activists on university campuses also faced detention and arrest periodically, particularly in the run-up to student elections.

The Brotherhood's growing popularity and power in the 1980s and 1990s masked serious internal divisions. These divisions were the product of four factors:

Leadership disputes. Ever since Hasan al-Banna's death in 1949, the MB had difficulty selecting a leader who commanded the respect of the entire organization. Intense rivalries over leadership and tactics in the 1950s and 1960s severely weakened the organization. In the mid-1960s, the MB's senior members hoped to avoid future succession struggles by agreeing that the oldest member of the guidance council would become General Guide. This approach worked well with the appointment of 'Umar al-Tilmisani in 1977. He was a vigorous General Guide who commanded widespread respect in the organization as both a thinker and an activist. However, his successor, Hamid Abu al-Nasr, lacked Tilmisani's stature as a scholar of Islam and a leader of the movement. He also developed serious health problems that prevented him from effectively directing the MB. Without a strong and credible leader, the organization split into cliques centered upon prominent personalities—particularly Seif al-Din Hasan al-Banna (son of the organization's founder) and Ma'mun al-Hudeibi (son of the MB's second General Guide). A new generation of dynamic younger leaders created a third major bloc in the 1980s, centered around the lawyer Mukhtar Nuh and the physician 'Isam al-'Iryan. These three blocs were unable to reach consensus on the person best qualified to lead the organization. Indeed, in order to avoid a protracted clash among them, Hudeibi maneuvered behind the scenes to appoint Mustafa Mashur as the successor to Abu al-Nasr in 1996.

Generational differences. For most of the Brotherhood's history, leadership positions were assigned on the basis of seniority. As a consequence, the top leaders were usually over sixty years old. In contrast, most MB activists in the professional syndicates were in their thirties and forties. The activists on university campuses were generally under thirty years old. These younger activists grew increasingly impatient with the old guard's reluctance to share power. Many of the younger leaders, such as 'Isam al-'Iryan, openly criticized what they considered the old guard's overly cautious response to the regime's repression of the MB. The younger ac-

---

[43] The Brotherhood member involved was Jamal Hashmat. For details of the case, see el-Ghobashy, "Metamorphosis of the Eyptian Muslim Brothers," 388.

tivists also felt that their hard-won organizational and mobilizational skills—honed in the political trenches of student unions and professional syndicates—were underappreciated and underutilized by the older MB leadership.[44] In addition, the younger leaders favored modifying the Brotherhood's ideology to support greater cooperation with secular groups, expanded rights for women, and increased tolerance of Copts. The older leaders were generally less willing to make these adjustments. These tensions became so sharp that several younger leaders attempted to split off from the MB in 1996 and establish a new party, *al-Wasat*. Their party would include Christians, leftists, Nasserists, and MB members in a broad coalition of forces seeking to change the Egyptian political system. The regime denounced the group as a back-door effort to legalize the MB. It arrested eighteen of the group's leaders and denied the party's request for a license.[45] Intriguingly, the MB leadership also denounced it and demanded that the MB members return to the fold. The founders of *al-Wasat* responded by resigning from the MB in October 1996. Another round of resignations came in July 1998, when seven leading younger figures on the MB's *shura* council resigned in protest over the organization's policies and leadership style.[46]

The emergence of independent and well-funded Islamic activists. The oil boom of the 1970s and 1980s transformed Islamic politics in Egypt. It produced wealthy benefactors in Saudi Arabia and elsewhere who began to fund Egyptian clerics and their activities. It also provided well-paying jobs in the Gulf for many millions of Egyptians. These expatriate workers often earned substantial sums of money, which they used to support Islamic causes in Egypt. Wealthy investors from the Gulf also established Islamic investment companies, banks, publishing houses, and other enter-

---

[44] One MB activist who is now a lawyer told me that he engaged in a wide range of activities while an MB leader at Cairo University. He organized a dispensary for distributing medicine, disseminated MB newspapers and pamphlets, recruited new members, successfully debated with competing groups on campus, and negotiated with the regime. However, after he graduated, he found that the MB leadership "treated me like a child." They showed no appreciation of his hard-won skills and experience.

[45] The party's request was denied on May 15, 1996. Thirteen members of the party were put on trial in military court on June 15, 1996, charged with trying to "reactivate an illegal organization [the MB]." The verdict was reached August 15, 1996. Six of the accused were acquitted. The remainder received light sentences. For further discussion, see Augustus Richard Norton, "Thwarted Politics: The Case of Egypt's Hizb al-Wasat," in *Remaking Muslim Politics: Pluralism, Contestation, Democratization*, ed. Robert W. Hefner (Princeton, NJ: Princeton University Press, 2005), 133–60; Carrie Rosefsky-Wickham, "The Path to Moderation: Strategy and Learning in the Formation of Egypt's Wasat Party," *Comparative Politics* 36, no. 2 (2004): 205–28; Raymond William Baker, *Islam without Fear: Egypt and the New Islamists* (Cambridge, MA: Harvard University Press, 2003), 192–203.

[46] *Al-Hayat*, July 14, 1998.

prises that provided additional sources of revenue for Islamic clerics and charities. As a result of this influx of oil-related wealth, the MB no longer served as the only source of financing and organization for Islamic activists.[47] Any individual with a wealthy benefactor could establish a mosque, build a health clinic, or form a Qur'an school.[48] Many of the new Islamic activists were sympathetic to the MB and its objectives, but they felt no obligation to obey the MB leadership.[49] Thus, MB membership and organizational complexity grew in the 1970s and 1980s. However, the Brotherhood's leadership exerted progressively less influence over this far-flung web of activists. The MB increasingly became an umbrella organization for Islamists with widely varying views and objectives.

Government repression: The regime's campaign against the MB since 1992 aggravated all of these internal sources of fragmentation. The government harassed the MB's leaders, arrested thousands of its grassroots activists, and closed its headquarters. These measures worsened the leadership crisis by creating a heated internal debate over whether, and how, the MB should respond. They also weakened the MB's organizational structure and further reduced its capacity to influence the many autonomous Islamic activists that emerged in the 1970s and 1980s. In addition, the government's repression worsened the generational splits within the organization, as younger activists bore the brunt of the crackdown while the older leadership did little to protest their imprisonment. Thus, government repression was not the source of the MB's fragmentation, but it made the problem significantly worse.

THE CONSTRAINTS AND OPPORTUNITIES FACED BY THE BROTHERHOOD

As the Brotherhood entered the mid-1990s, the organization still lacked a clear set of political goals. The leadership asserted that "Islam is the

---

[47] An interesting indicator of the degree of external involvement in Egyptian Islamism lies in the distribution of Egypt's major Islamic newspaper, *Liwa al-Islam*. In the early 1990s, the newspaper printed 95,000 copies each month. Almost half of these copies were sold outside of Egypt. Rosefsky-Wickham, *Mobilizing Islam*, 101.

[48] Indeed, it has become increasingly common for these types of activities to be undertaken by a single individual acting with members of his family or village. Some of the more prominent Islamic entrepreneurs with Gulf funding are Sheikh Shara'awi, Sheikh Kishk, Sheikh Mahallawi, Wajdi Ghunim, and Ahmad al-Qatan.

[49] Rosefsky-Wickham's interviews with Islamic activists in the early 1990s found that relatively few of them were members of any Islamic organization. Most were simply local activists who worked with their local mosque to raise levels of religious consciousness and observance, and to forge "new kinds of communal solidarity based on Islamic principles of charity and self-help." Rosefsky-Wickham, *Mobilizing Islam*, 102.

solution" and that it supported the implementation of *Shari'a*. However, it was scrupulously vague regarding the practical meaning of these slogans. This haziness had a certain utility, in that it allowed the organization to appeal to a very large portion of the Egyptian public. In essence, anyone who was unhappy with the status quo and believed that a greater emphasis on Islam was desirable could find a home in the Brotherhood. In addition, this vagueness allowed the MB to avoid acrimonious internal debates over questions of policy that would have further aggravated the tensions within the organization.

However, this lack of clarity on basic issues of policy and doctrine also had negative repercussions. It dramatically complicated efforts to build long-term alliances with other actors in civil society. Potential allies— whether political parties, NGOs, or other groups—were reluctant to coop- erate with an organization whose goals were so unclear and whose mem- bership contained such disparate views. Alliances with the New Wafd Party, the Socialist Labor Party, and the Liberal Party eventually foun- dered over questions about the Brotherhood's true objectives and whether the organization was genuinely committed to long-term compromise and cooperation. In a political setting where the Brotherhood was illegal, this inability to form sustained alliances with legal parties was a major impedi- ment to broadening the organization's reach and influence.[50]

The Brotherhood's vagueness regarding its political goals also produced deep anxiety among secular Egyptians, who feared that the MB might try to create a strict Islamic order that would limit the rights of women and non-Muslims. As one prominent lawyer put it, "the models for Islamic government in our region are Sudan and Iran. If the Brotherhood wants to move us in that direction, I will fight them at every turn."[51] Faced with this prospect, many secular Egyptians threw their support behind the regime despite its long history of repression. The status quo, although it had many flaws, at least allowed them to practice their faith as they understood it. It also provided protection against the medieval political vision of the extremist Islamic groups. Thus, the Brotherhood's ideologi- cal vagueness alienated potential allies among secular Egyptians and inad- vertently strengthened support for the regime.

In addition to these self-inflicted wounds, the Brotherhood faced a wide range of constraints imposed by the regime. The MB was illegal, which enabled the government to arrest its leaders and activists at will. The re- gime could also invoke the ever-present emergency law to arrest MB mem-

---

[50] The Brotherhood's political bureau expressed this concern repeatedly. Political Bureau of the Muslim Brotherhood, "The Muslim Brotherhood and the Egyptian Regime," re- printed in al-Awadi, *In Pursuit of Legitimacy,* 205.

[51] Yahia al-Jamal, "A Glimpse at Egypt's Future," *al-'Arabi,* January 17, 1998.

bers without charge and hold them for long periods of time. In addition to these broad powers, the government had specific legal and extra-legal tools to limit the Brotherhood's influence in several areas of political life:

Elections. Although the Brotherhood was permitted to compete in elections, it faced numerous restrictions. The regime held the authority to determine which groups could form political parties. It used this authority to block the formation of any party tied to the Brotherhood. It manipulated voter lists to favor the government's candidates, and adjusted the boundaries of electoral districts to favor candidates from the ruling party. It also manipulated the counting of ballots to favor regime supporters and engaged in physical intimidation of Brotherhood voters at polling places. As if these impediments were not enough, it rounded up the MB's campaign organizers on the eve of elections in 1987, 1995, 2000, and 2005, thereby disrupting the Brotherhood's "get out the vote" efforts.[52]

Professional syndicates. As mentioned earlier, the Brotherhood's influence within the professional syndicates grew dramatically in the 1980s and 1990s. The MB won control of the governing board of the Doctors' syndicate in 1986, the Engineers' syndicate in 1987, the Pharmacists' in 1990, and the Lawyers' in 1992. The regime responded with two tactics. First, it encouraged lawsuits alleging that the Brotherhood-controlled boards had misused the syndicate's funds. The resulting legal wrangles led to sequestration of the syndicate's assets and judicial supervision of the syndicate's affairs. This tactic was used in the syndicates for doctors, engineers, and lawyers. Second, it passed law 100 of 1993, which altered the procedure for elections within the syndicates. The Brotherhood's success in the syndicates had been due largely to the apathy of most of the membership. For example, in the 1992 Lawyers' syndicate elections, only 10 percent of the syndicate's 150,000 members bothered to vote. The Brotherhood mobilized its core supporters with great skill, and won eighteen of twenty-four seats on the board. Law 100/1993 required that any syndicate election have a quorum of 50 percent of the membership. If this quorum was not achieved, a second round would occur in which a threshold of only 30 percent was required. If this was not met, a third round would be organized. If the 30 percent threshold was again not met, control of the syndicate would pass to a panel of judges. This measure effectively ended elections in the syndicates for the balance of the 1990s, and sharply reduced the Islamists' influence on syndicate affairs.[53]

[52] These tactics are summarized in Independent Committee for Elections Monitoring, "A Testimony for History: Monitoring the Egyptian 2005 Parliamentary Elections" (ICEM: Cairo, December 2005).

[53] Kienle, *A Grand Delusion*, 85–87. Also, Alashhab et al., *Clash in Egypt*.

Media: The law governing the press required that the government-controlled Supreme Press Council approve the establishment of newspapers or magazines except those produced by political parties, trade unions, or professional syndicates.[54] The law also empowered the government to approve the appointment of newspaper editors, and to monitor the factual accuracy of newspaper reporting. A paper whose reporting was deemed inaccurate or harmful to public order could have its license revoked. A journalist whose articles were deemed insulting to the president or to any public body could be fined and imprisoned.[55] Similarly, any journalist whose articles advocated "changing the basic principles of the Constitution or the basic system of the social structure" was subject to fine and imprisonment.[56] These legal restrictions enabled the government to block the MB's efforts to buy and control its own newspaper. They also placed sharp limits on what journalists supportive of the Brotherhood could write. The broad language used in several of the laws created considerable uncertainty as to where the threshold for criminality lay. This uncertainty served as an important deterrent to journalists writing articles that might be construed as advocating "substantial social change" or supporting the activities of an illegal organization such as the Brotherhood.

Grassroots organizing: The foundation of the Brotherhood's power lay in its network of social service and religious organizations at the local level. It had established hundreds of schools, medical clinics, private mosques, day-care centers, and job-training centers. These organizations were regulated by a web of laws and regulations, particularly the laws governing Non-Governmental Organizations. All NGOs were supervised by the Ministry of Social Affairs (MOSA). This ministry held the power to appoint the board of an NGO, oversee its elections, monitor its sources of funding, and regulate its activities. It could also disband any NGO that violated its myriad regulations or posed a threat to "the general order and proper behavior."[57] Beginning in 1996, the MB's private mosques faced similar restrictions. Law 238 of 1996 brought all private mosques under the control of the Ministry of Religious Endowments (*Wizarat al-Awqaf*). The ministry held the power to appoint the *imam* of the mosque, determine the content of the weekly sermon by the *imam*, and monitor the

---

[54] Newspapers produced by these three bodies are governed by separate laws. For a useful discussion of the press law, see K. el-Zoheiri and W. Rady, "Press Law," in *Egypt and Its Laws*, ed. Nathalie Bernard-Maugiron and Baudouin Dupret (New York: Kluwer Law International, 2002), 345–57. Also, Kienle, *A Grand Delusion*, 98–104.

[55] Public bodies include the Parliament, the army, the courts, and "other official bodies." Article 184, Law 96/1996.

[56] Article 174, Law 96/1996.

[57] The quote is taken from Law 32/1964, and is mentioned in Rosefsky-Wickham, *Mobilizing Islam*, 99.

mosque's funding. Furthermore, the Brotherhood also faced stringent restrictions on mobilizing its followers for political purposes. The law governing public assembly required that any public meeting involving more than seven people receive prior approval from the Ministry of Interior. In addition, any written material used to mobilize the MB's supporters (such as fliers or pamphlets) was subject to monitoring and suspension if it was deemed "threatening to public order" by the Ministry of Interior.

Thus, the Brotherhood of the mid-1990s faced internal impediments to its development as well as a formidable array of regulations and laws imposed by the regime. This combination of internal and external constraints created a strong incentive to end the ambiguities in MB doctrine and define the organization as tolerant, flexible, and pro-democracy. Interviews with MB leaders at the time,[58] as well as internal strategy documents from the Brotherhood,[59] indicate that the younger generation of activists believed that a clearly stated moderate doctrine would offer several rewards:

- It would provide increased opportunities for cooperation with other groups, particularly through alliances with legal political parties. These alliances were essential to "activat[ing] a political existence" for the MB that would convert its broad social support into effective political influence.[60] More specifically, strong alliances would provide several tactical advantages for the MB: the organization would have access to new media outlets (particularly party newspapers, which are exempt from the strict constraints of the press law); it would gain valuable opportunities to run candidates for Parliament and other offices; these electoral campaigns would provide many new chances to disseminate the MB's views and attract new recruits; and, if it won seats through these elections, it could challenge laws and government officials on the issues that concern the organization.
- It would help calm the fears of secular Egyptians. As noted earlier, many secular Egyptians regarded the Brotherhood with skepticism and trepidation. A sincere and convincing stance of moderation by the MB would address

[58] Personal interviews with: 'Isam al-'Iryan, January 2, 1995; and Mukhtar Nuh, December 10, 1995.

[59] Hesham al-Awadi acquired these documents from the director of the Brotherhood's political bureau, 'Abd al-Mon'am Salim Jabara. The documents are translated by al-Awadi and reprinted in the appendix to his book, *In Pursuit of Legitimacy*, pp. 198–232. Al-Awadi's acquisition of the documents is described on pp. 175–76. He presents four documents. Only the first of these carries a date (May 22, 1996). The other three documents discuss topics that are similar to the first one. The discussion below will draw only on the first document, which is clearly dated to the period of the mid-1990s when the Brotherhood was reformulating its political strategy.

[60] Political Bureau of the Muslim Brotherhood, "The Muslim Brotherhood and the Egyptian Regime," reprinted in al-Awadi, *In Pursuit of Legitimacy*, 205.

these worries. In the words of al-'Iryan, "It would dispel the fear that the Brotherhood supports violence or radicalism."[61] It would reduce the anxiety and suspicion that drove many secular Egyptians to support the regime as a bulwark against radical change. A convincing moderate posture would also enable the MB to more effectively tap the public's growing dissatisfaction with the political order and, possibly, broaden its base of support to include at least some of the secularists who were eager for change.

• It would reassure the government that the Brotherhood was not colluding with radical Islamists and was willing to cooperate with the existing political order. The Brotherhood was very eager to distance itself from all violent organizations. Any association with violent groups would provide the regime with the justification to "wage a serious war" that would decimate the organization.[62] Furthermore, if the Brotherhood were associated with violent tactics, the international community would rally around the regime and further empower it to eradicate the MB.[63] The Brotherhood's leaders also wanted to avoid a "zero-sum" conflict with the regime in which the Brotherhood's political gains could be achieved only through the regime's losses. In the view of the Brotherhood's political bureau, rhetorical claims that the MB was the main political force in the country and that it offered a comprehensive alternative to the existing order tended to reinforce the regime's sense of vulnerability. This led the regime to intensify its repression of the organization. The Brotherhood's younger leaders wanted to clarify the organization's political objectives in a manner that showed a willingness to work within existing political institutions to achieve change that was peaceful and incremental. This required showing that it was willing to compromise and "look for points of rapprochement" with the regime.[64]

• It would attract international support, particularly from Western governments that exercised some influence over the regime. The younger generation of MB leaders hoped that the European Union and the United States would pressure the Egyptian government to reduce the level of repression and allow the Brotherhood greater freedom to operate. Mukhtar Nuh believed that Turkey's experience was particularly relevant. In the early 1990s, the European Union pressured the Turkish government to allow greater political com-

---

[61] Personal interview with 'Isam al-'Iryan, January 2, 1995.

[62] Political Bureau of the Muslim Brotherhood, "The Muslim Brotherhood and the Egyptian Regime," reprinted in al-Awadi, *In Pursuit of Legitimacy*, 206. The Brotherhood has expressed opposition to acts of violence by Islamists at least since the early 1970s. However, it has often accompanied these denunciations with a statement suggesting that these attacks are inevitable in light of the degree of repression and injustice in contemporary Egypt. The regime claims that this caveat constitutes a de facto justification of violence.

[63] Political Bureau of the Muslim Brotherhood, "The Muslim Brotherhood and the Egyptian Regime," reprinted in al-Awadi, *In Pursuit of Legitimacy*, 206.

[64] Ibid., 207.

petition. The regime responded, and loosened the restrictions on the Islamist Welfare party. As a consequence, Welfare competed freely in the 1995 parliamentary elections and won a share of political power in the Turkish government. Nuh hoped that a clearly moderate political posture by the Brotherhood could achieve the same result in Egypt.[65]

The younger generation of Brotherhood leaders began to develop a strategy that responded to this set of constraints and opportunities. The most prominent figures in this effort were the activists who organized the Brotherhood's ascent in the professional syndicates, particularly the lawyer Mukhtar Nuh, the engineer Abu-l-'Ila Madi, and the physicians 'Isam al-'Iryan and Ibrahim al-Zafarani. There is little evidence that this group formulated a comprehensive plan and philosophy to enhance the MB's power. Rather, they began to articulate a moderate political doctrine in an ad hoc fashion in response to the constraints and opportunities that the MB confronted in the early- and mid-1990s.

Their efforts focused on the issues that caused the greatest degree of public anxiety about the Brotherhood—particularly its views on women, Copts, and political competition. The younger generation of leaders authored a series of pamphlets on these topics. They were released under the name of Ma'mun al-Hudeibi, the spokesman for the Brotherhood.[66] The first pamphlet appeared in early 1994, and dealt with the rights of women. It begins with a Qur'anic passage to the effect that men and women are morally equal in the eyes of God because he considers both to be "the offspring of Adam."[67] It endorses granting women full equality before the law, the right to vote, and the right to run for public office (except for the post of leader of the *umma*). It adds that a woman may become a judge, so long as her duties do not "compromise her honor."[68] Later in the same year, the Brotherhood published a pamphlet on the status of Copts. It invokes the Qur'anic passage, "Let there be no coercion in religion" (2:256), and describes the Copts as "partners and brothers in our long struggle to build the nation."[69] It adds that the presence of multiple faiths on earth is a product of God's will and a reflection of his divine

---

[65] Personal interview with Mukhtar Nuh, December 10, 1995.

[66] The pamphlets were later gathered together and published as a single document, Muhammad M. al-Hudeibi, *al-Islam wa-l-Siyasa* (Cairo: Dar al-Islam li-l Nashr, 1997). An English translation was also released under the title, Muhammad M. El-Hudeibi, *Politics in Islam* (Cairo: Islamic Home for Publishing and Distribution, 1997). In addition, a summary of the statements was published in *Ruwaq 'Arabi*, January 1997, 139–43. The quotations in the text are taken from the Arabic version, *al-Islam wa-l-Siyasa*.

[67] Ibid., 31.

[68] Ibid., 31–32.

[69] Ibid., 27.

plan.[70] It emphasizes that Copts enjoy "equal rights and duties" with Muslims, unrestricted freedom of worship, and the right to practice their own law in matters of personal status. In 1995, the Brotherhood issued a pamphlet on political pluralism. It asserts that the community (*umma*) is the source of political authority (*sulta*), and that the country's leaders should be chosen by the people through the "exercise of free choice" in "free and clean elections."[71] The system of government should be based upon the principle of *shura* (consultation) and should "derive its legitimacy from consulting the people."[72] The ruler is accountable to the *umma* and may be replaced if he does not fulfill his duties properly. The ruler's primary duty is to implement *Shari'a*, which includes issuing man-made laws that conform with *Shari'a*. The pamphlet also advocates a balance among the institutions of government so that "no institution overtakes or transgresses the others."[73] It particularly calls for a strong and independent judiciary.

These pamphlets show the MB's younger leadership attempting to delineate a political doctrine that emphasizes tolerance and moderation.[74] This was not a fully developed agenda or ideology. Indeed, none of the younger leaders involved were ideologues. Rather, they were activists who had gained popularity and influence by building a very effective network of social services within the universities and professional syndicates. They now sought a moderate political path that would enable the Brotherhood to gain greater public support and, eventually, political power. In essence, the constraints and opportunities of the Egyptian political scene pushed political entrepreneurs within the Brotherhood toward supporting the creation of a more liberal government based on Islamic principles.

In order to clarify this objective and lend it greater doctrinal legitimacy, they drew upon the ideas of the leading moderate Islamic thinkers in Egypt. Four thinkers, in particular, had developed the legal and doctrinal details of a liberal Islamic state in some depth: Yusuf al-Qaradawi, Tariq al-Bishri, Kamal Abu al-Majd, and Muhammad Salim al-'Awwa. These thinkers form a school of political and legal thought that can be termed "Islamic constitutionalism." As we will see below, there is almost a complete correspondence between the 1994/1995 pamphlets and the views of these thinkers. The Brotherhood's younger leaders have continued to

[70] Ibid., 27–29.

[71] Ibid., 24.

[72] Ibid., 24–25.

[73] Ibid., 25.

[74] The old guard did not fully agree with this direction. For example, the General Guide, Mustafa Mashur, gave an interview in 1997 that called for limiting the rights of Copts and charging them a special tax (*jizya*) in exchange for protection by the state. El-Ghobashy, "The Metamorphosis of the Egyptian Muslim Brothers," 386.

utilize the ideas of the Islamic constitutionalists, particularly in the organization's 2004 reform initiative and its 2005 campaign platform.[75] Al-'Iryan describes these thinkers as providing a "roadmap" that he and other younger leaders follow.[76] In order to understand the type of political order that the MB has come to support, we now turn to the works of these thinkers and, particularly, their view of an Islamic polity.

ISLAMIC CONSTITUTIONALISM: DEFINING AN ISLAMIC CONCEPTION OF LAW AND GOVERNMENT

For well over a century, Egypt has been an important center for legal thinkers seeking to adapt Islam to the challenges of contemporary governance. This effort began in the late nineteenth and early twentieth centuries with the works of Jamal al-Din al-Afghani, Muhammad 'Abduh, and Rashid Rida. It moved forward with 'Abd al-Razzaq al-Sanhuri's remarkable synthesis of Islamic and French law in the Egyptian civil code. It is continued today by the four thinkers just mentioned: Yusuf al-Qaradawi, Tariq al-Bishri, Kamal Abu al-Majd, and Muhammad Salim al-'Awwa.

These are certainly not the only Egyptian writers who publish on issues of Islam and governance. One could add to this list Tawfiq Shawi (a prominent legal scholar), Fahmi Huweidi (a prolific journalist), Muhammad 'Amara (a journalist and historian), and others. However, the scholars studied here have developed an Islamic conception of governance in much greater detail than any other contemporary figures in Egypt. As noted earlier, they also exert considerable influence over the younger generation of MB leaders.

These four writers have varied backgrounds. Al-Qaradawi received formal training in Islamic law at al-Azhar University in the 1950s and 1960s. He eventually earned a doctorate in 1973 with a thesis that examined the legal and social foundations of *zakat*. He worked briefly at the Egyptian Ministry of Religious Endowments before moving to Qatar, where he established the faculty of *Shari'a* and Islamic studies at the University of Qatar. He has written more than fifty books and is one of the most widely read contemporary Islamic thinkers in the Arab world. He also hosts a

---

[75] These documents will be discussed in chapter 4.

[76] Personal interview, January 2, 1995. Mukhtar Nuh expressed a similar view, stating that these thinkers provided the "intellectual framework (*itar*)" for efforts to expand the political role of Islam in Egypt. Personal interview, December 10, 1995. The influence of these thinkers was further confirmed through additional interviews in November 2005 with al-'Iryan, Nuh, and Muhammad Habib (another important figure among the younger generation of MB leaders).

weekly call-in show ("Islamic Law and Life") on the satellite channel *al-Jazeera,* which further broadens his reach and influence.[77] Tariq Al-Bishri's background is somewhat more eclectic. He was trained as a lawyer in the early 1950s, and began public life as a secular intellectual with leftist leanings. He embarked on a successful career in the judiciary, where he eventually rose to the post of first deputy president of the State Council, one of the most senior positions in the administrative judiciary. While pursuing these judicial duties, he also found time to write several highly regarded books on Egyptian history. His best known books deal with the emergence of Egyptian nationalism and the historical significance of the 1952 revolution.[78] These works return constantly to the themes of reviving Egypt's cultural identity, building national unity, and increasing the country's independence. Al-Bishri argues that strengthening the role of Islam in Egyptian society is essential to achieving each of these goals. Most of his scholarly works since the early 1990s have focused on this issue, with particular emphasis on the question of how to apply Islamic law to contemporary Egyptian society and politics.[79]

Abu al-Majd also has a strong legal background. He earned a Ph.D. in law from Cairo University and an M.A. in comparative law from the University of Michigan. He served as Minister of Youth and Minister of Information in the early 1970s, before moving to Kuwait to serve as legal advisor for the crown prince. He returned to Egypt in the late 1980s and entered private practice. He has been appointed to several prestigious public bodies, including the Institute of Islamic Research at Al-Azhar University and the government-sponsored Egyptian Society for Human Rights.[80] Al-'Awwa followed a similar path of advanced legal training in Egypt, supplemented by doctoral studies in comparative law at the University of London. He served as a law professor in Saudi Arabia from 1974 through 1985. He then returned to Egypt and joined the law faculty at Zagazig University. He is well known for his lengthy book on Islamic

---

[77] For further information on al-Qaradawi, see the websites that he helped to found, http://www.islamonline.net/arabic/ and http://www.qaradawi.net/. Also, see the entry about him in Philip Mattar, ed. *Encyclopedia of the Modern Middle East & North Africa.* 2nd ed. (Detroit: Macmillan Reference USA, 2004), 1870.

[78] Tariq al-Bishri, *al-Haraka al-Siyasiyya fi Misr, 1945–1952—al-Tab'aat al-Thaniyya* (Cairo: Dar al-Sharuq, 1983); Tariq al-Bishri, *al-Dimaqratiyya wa Nitham 23 Yuliyu, 1952–1970* (Cairo: Dar al-Hilal, 1991).

[79] For further detail on al-Bishri's background and views, see Ibrahim al-Bayumi Ghanim, ed., *Tariq al-Bishri: Al-Qadi, al-Mufakkir* (Cairo: Dar al-Sharuq, 1999).

[80] For further information, see the brief biography of Abu al-Majd at http://www.un.org/Dialogue/Aboulmagd.html. Also see the biography of him posted on the website of the Egyptian state information service at http://www.sis.gov.eg/. Both sites accessed June 27, 2007.

criminal law,[81] which established his reputation as one of the leading academic specialists on *Shari'a*. He has also been active in efforts to create a moderate Islamic political party in Egypt. Toward this end, he helped to build the *al-Wasat* party in the mid-1990s and remains one of its most important advocates.[82]

Nathan Brown observes that these four thinkers are part of an "emerging consensus" regarding the application of Islamic law and tradition to contemporary governance.[83] Raymond Baker argues that they constitute a coherent school of Islamic reformist thought that he calls the "New Islamists."[84] As noted below, these thinkers do not march in lock-step. However, their works are sufficiently similar that they collectively define a coherent view of Islamic constitutionalism.

In order to understand this view, the analysis will focus on these writers' treatment of the same four dimensions of constitutionalism discussed in the previous chapter: the rule of law; constraints on state power; protection of civil and political rights; and public participation in politics. This is certainly not an exhaustive list of issues relevant to a discussion of constitutionalism. However, it allows us to delineate the essential characteristics of Islamic constitutionalism and its philosophical foundations.

The Rule of Law

For students of Islamic thought, the views of the Islamic constitutionalists with regard to law are quite familiar. They largely reiterate the positions of Islamic reformers from the early twentieth century, particularly Muhammad 'Abduh and Rashid Rida. They stress that Islam is a religion built around the revelation and enforcement of law. Indeed, it is difficult to overemphasize the centrality of law to their conception of the polity. For these thinkers, "Religion is law in practice,"[85] and "The government of

[81] Muhammad Salim al-'Awwa, *Fi Usul al-Nitham al-Jin'i al-Islami* (Cairo: Dar al-Ma'arif, 1979).

[82] For further details on al-'Awwa's background, see his official website: http://www.el-awa. com/. Also see Baker, *Islam without Fear.* In addition, al-'Awwa was the driving force behind a new NGO, the Egyptian Society for Culture and Dialogue. The group has close ties with *al-Wasat* and aims to "support the culture of dialogue in a society in which violence prevails." See Rosefsky-Wickham, *Mobilizing Islam,* 220.

[83] Nathan J. Brown, *Constitutions in a Nonconstitutional World: Arab Basic Laws and the Prospects for Accountable Government* (Albany: State University of New York Press, 2002), 161–93.

[84] Baker, *Islam without Fear,* 1.

[85] Muhammad Salim al-'Awwa, *Religion and Political Structures: An Islamic Viewpoint,* Occasional Papers, No. 3 (Birmingham, UK: Center for the Study of Islam and Christian-Muslim Relations, 1999), 2.

Islam is the government of law."[86] God "sent his messengers and revealed his books so that the people may establish justice . . . the essence of justice is *Shari'a*."[87]

The theorists of Islamic constitutionalism agree that *Shari'a* has two sources. The first is the Qur'an, which is the literal word of God. It consists of roughly six thousand verses, approximately five hundred of which deal with matters of governance. The second is the sayings and actions of the Prophet (the *sunnah*). These must come from "trusted" and "reliable" sources.[88] The *Shari'a* delineates an ethical and spiritual path that guides each believer to a moral life and a fuller understanding of God's truth. Obedience to *Shari'a* is a religious obligation. The believer who obeys *Shari'a* will enjoy a righteous life and admittance to paradise.[89]

However, *Shari'a* is not simply a guide to personal conduct. It also provides the legal and moral foundations for a spiritual community (*umma*) under the "governance of Islam" (*hukm al-Islam*). By delineating a shared set of moral principles that all members of the community accept, it gives the community identity, purpose, and stability. It is the "source of the community's unity."[90] Furthermore, the creation of this spiritual community is fundamental to the life of a Muslim. Islam is not a faith that one practices alone. The challenge of living a devout life is a constant struggle that requires personal reflection, interaction with fellow Muslims, and interaction with divine law. Each of these can be achieved only within a community of Muslims. Indeed, "Muslims are sinners until they live within *hukm al-Islam*"[91] and must strive constantly to build this community through the application of *Shari'a*.[92] Within this framework, the purpose of the state is to bring the community into being through the enforcement of divine law. The state is created by believers in order to implement *Shari'a*. It is, in turn, constrained by the divine law.[93]

On those topics where the Qur'an and the *sunnah* are clear, there is no room for human interpretation or debate. Each Muslim must simply obey.

---

[86] Ibid., 6.

[87] Muhammad Salim al-'Awwa, *Fi-l-Nitham al-Siyasi li-l-Dawla al-Islamiyya* (Cairo: Dar al-Sharuq, 1989), 140.

[88] In practice, this means relying primarily on hadith from al-Bukhari and al-Imam Muslim.

[89] Yusuf al-Qaradawi, *Min Fiqh al-Dawla fi-l-Islam* (Cairo: Dar al-Sharuq, 1997), 18.

[90] Tariq al-Bishri, *Al-Wad'a al-Qanuni bayn al-Shari'a al-Islamiyya wa al-Qanun al-Wad'ai* (Cairo: Dar al-Sharuq, 2003), 38.

[91] Al-Qaradawi, *Min Fiqh al-Dawla*, 15.

[92] Ibid., 15, 17, 18.

[93] Al-'Awwa, *Fi-l-Nitham al-Siyasi*, 137. Abu al-Majd observes that one of the Prophet's most important acts in the early years of Islam was to create a state in Madina and, thereby, create the Islamic community. Ahmad Kamal Abu al-Majd, "Taqdim," in Ahmad Muham-

This applies to duties such as the performance of prayers five times a day, fasting, and the payment of the *zakat* (alms tax).[94] But on issues where the Qur'an and *sunnah* are unclear or silent, the theorists under discussion favor the creation of man-made laws that are compatible with *Shari'a*.[95] Man-made laws are possible on any topic where "devout Muslims can hold multiple opinions."[96]

Governance is a prime arena for the development of man-made law. The Qur'an and *sunnah* provide very little guidance on the specifics of running a state. The theorists emphasize that this is one of the strengths of Islam. God knew that Muslims would need to govern effectively in an enormous variety of political, cultural, and economic circumstances. The *Shari'a* presents only broad principles of law and governance, which Muslims can then adapt to the specific conditions of time and place. The central principles of *Shari'a* with regard to governance are: to establish justice; to rule through consultation (*shura*); to govern in a manner accountable to the citizenry; to derive laws from the Islamic *Shari'a*; and to respect the people's rights.[97]

The essence of governance is to give these abstract principles practical force and meaning through man-made law. *Ijtihad* is the key to this lawmaking process. Those who exercise *ijtihad* and draft laws should aim to serve the best interests of the community (*al-maslaha*) while not directly contradicting the *Shari'a*. If a given objective is deemed to be in the interests of the community, then all the laws adopted to achieve this objective are considered compatible with *Shari'a*. New laws should also respond to the needs of the community (*darura*) and the distinctive circumstances (*dhuruf*) of a particular moment in time.[98] The primary tools for conducting *ijtihad* are consensus (*ijm'a*) among believers over a matter of law or practice, analogy (*qiyas*) to legal principles clearly presented in the *Shari'a*, and the synthesis (*talfiq*) of ideas from multiple schools of law. The persons

mad Amin, *Al-Dawla al-Islamiyya wa-l-Mabad' al-Dusturiyya al-Haditha.* (Cairo: Maktabat al-Sharuq al-Dawliyya, 2005), 9.

[94] Al-Bishri provides a more detailed list. Al-Bishri, *al-Wad'a al-Qanuni*, 107. Also, see al-'Awwa, *Religion and Political Structures*, 4.

[95] Some of the theorists prefer to use the term "interpretation" to describe human application of the principles of *Shari'a*, rather than "law." In this view, law can be issued only by God. Humans are limited to interpreting and applying this law. However, in practice, this leads to political bodies issuing statutes that conform to the widely accepted understanding of the term "law." As a consequence, I will refer to man-made legislation as "law."

[96] Al-Qaradawi, *Min Fiqh al-Dawla*, 142. Also, Al-'Awwa, *Religion and Political Structures*, 4.

[97] Abu al-Majd, "Taqdim," 10.

[98] Ahmad Kamal Abu al-Majd, *Natharat Hawla al-Fiqh al-Dusturi fi-l-Islam* (Cairo: Matba'aat al-Azhar, 1962), 4.

drafting law should draw on whatever sources serve the best interests of the community. These include any of the four schools of *Sunni* law, as well as *Shi'a* thought.[99] In addition, Abu al-Majd and al-'Awwa call for utilizing those elements of non-Muslim law that do not contradict *Shari'a*.[100]

This process of reinterpreting *Shari'a* to meet the challenges of daily life is the science of *fiqh*. The theorists maintain a firm distinction between *Shari'a* and *fiqh*. *Shari'a* embodies the sublime principles of the faith that transcend time and place. *Fiqh*, in contrast, is the imperfect effort of humans to apply these broad principles to specific conditions. It is a product of incomplete human understanding of the divine text, as well as flawed human judgment. It is applicable only to the unique conditions of time and place that produced it. An infinite number of these "context-specific interpretations of *Shari'a*" are possible because Shari'a "applies to an infinite reality."[101] None of these interpretations is binding on other Muslims in a different time and place.[102]

Maintaining the distinction between *Shari'a* and *fiqh* is essential for strengthening Islam. Indeed, the theorists attribute the stagnation of Islamic law to an excessive reverence for *fiqh*. In Abu al-Majd's words, "Those who combine *Shari'a* and *fiqh* and call them 'Islamic legislation' that should be implemented to the letter commit a grave injury to Islam and the people. They introduce things in Islam that are not there originally. They stipulate restrictions and obligations that God did not decree."[103]

As one might expect, Islamic constitutionalist thinkers attribute the weakness of the Islamic world to flaws in the understanding and implementation of *Shari'a*. The solution to this problem lies in a "return to *Shari'a*." Part of this process entails improving each Muslim's understanding of divine law. This involves not only establishing more religious schools, improving teacher training, and increasing religious education in public schools.[104] It also entails utilizing all the tools of mass media to

[99] Al-Bishri, *al-Wad'a al-Qanuni*, 48.

[100] Abu al-Majd, *Natharat Hawla al-Fiqh*, 2,4; al-'Awwa, *Fi-l-Nitham Al-Siyasi*, 141.

[101] Al-Bishri, *al-Wad'a al-Qanuni*, 36. Al-'Awwa makes a similar point. Muhammad Salim al-'Awwa, *Al-Haqq fi-l-Ta'abir* (Cairo: Dar al-Sharuq, 1998), 67.

[102] Al-Qaradawi, *Min Fiqh al-Dawla*, 60–68; Ahmad Kamal Abu al-Majd, *Ru'ya Islamiyya Mu'asira* (Cairo: Dar al-Sharuq, 1991), 45; Ahmad Kamal Abu al-Majd, *Hiwar La Muwajaha* (Cairo: Dar al-Sharuq, 1988), 89–90.

[103] Abu al-Majd, *Hiwar La Muwajaha*, 89. Also, Al-Bishri, *al-Wad'a al-Qanuni*, 51, 54.

[104] Abu al-Majd places particular emphasis on the need to improve the training of religious scholars. Abu al-Majd, *Ru'ya Islamiyya Mu'asira*, 44. Al-'Awwa calls for improvements in the training of state officials who deal with religious issues, particularly officials at the Ministry of Awqaf (Religious Endowments). This ministry has the authority to regulate who may preach in mosques and what they may say. However, in al-'Awwa's view, the Ministry's officials often have an extremely poor understanding of Islam. Muhammad Salim al-'Awwa,

educate the public in the principles of the faith and how these principles should be applied to modern life. Of the theorists under discussion, al-Qaradawi has gone the furthest in this regard. His writings and opinions are available in every media form imaginable, including books, video, cassette, radio, and satellite TV. He also operates his own websites (http://www.islamonline.net and http://www.qaradawi.net). They distribute his speeches and other writings, and allow Muslims to submit their requests for advice. A response is generally posted within twenty-four hours.

However, the return to *Shari'a* consists of much more than simply education. As noted earlier, the state is seen as an essential actor within the *umma*. Its enforcement of Islamic law is the key to creating and sustaining an Islamic community. The decline of *Shari'a* is due, in part, to the decline of the state as a moral actor that implements and promotes divine law. This problem has deep historical roots. It began when non-Arabs (particularly Persians and Turks) assumed positions of leadership in the Islamic world, starting in the ninth century. These non-Arabs lacked sufficient knowledge of the Arabic language to fully understand the meaning of *Shari'a*. In some cases, they also lacked a moral and spiritual commitment to Islam. Instead of implementing *Shari'a*, they manipulated it to serve their personal ambitions for wealth and power. Their machinations led to the steady distortion and corruption of *Shari'a* over the course of Islamic history.

This problem was aggravated by the influx of European culture in the nineteenth century. Reformist leaders in Egypt and elsewhere tried to modernize their societies by emulating European institutions in fields such as education, medicine, and government. This process included a widespread effort to transfer European laws to Islamic countries, which had profound repercussions. As al-Qaradawi argues, the central feature of the European legal tradition is its strict separation between religious law and positive law. He emphasizes that this is a product of Europe's unique historical experience. It is alien to the Islamic world. Imposing European positive law on Egypt created a legal order divorced from the culture and history of the people.[105] Furthermore, it led the state to abandon its obligation to enforce *Shari'a*. As *Shari'a* receded from public life, the moral and spiritual bonds that held Egyptian society together weakened and collapsed. The result was a demoralized and fragmented society unable to resist the continued onslaughts of Europe. The emulation of European

---

Azmat al-Mu'ssasat al-Diniyya (Cairo: Dar al-Sharuq, 1997), 50–51. Also, Al-Bishri, *al-Wad'a al-Qanuni*, 75; Al-Qaradawi, *Min Fiqh al-Dawla*, 58.

[105] Al-Qaradawi, *Min Fiqh al-Dawla*, 13, 23, 76. Al-Bishri also makes this argument. Al-Bishri, *al-Wad'a al-Qanuni*, 32–35. Al-Qaradawi faults Attaturk for having borrowed Western legal institutions without adapting them to Islamic tradition. In his view, Turkey was "like the crow that tried to be an eagle. In the end, it could not be an eagle, and it could not go back to being a crow." Al-Qaradawi, *Min Fiqh al-Dawla*, 77.

laws also produced governments with very little legitimacy. It "drove a wedge between governments and their peoples" as citizens increasingly felt that the laws of the land failed to reflect their values and their sense of justice.[106]

At this point in the analysis, a seeming contradiction emerges. The Islamic constitutionalists argue at some length that the underlying cause of the crisis in the Islamic world is the declining role of *Shari'a* in politics and society. The key to solving this crisis, presumably, lies in revising the legal code to render it more compatible with the original precepts of divine law. However, the writers assert on numerous occasions that the large majority of existing laws are compatible with divine law and that a return to *Shari'a* would not require sweeping legal reform.[107] On closer reading, it is clear that the Islamic constitutionalists are not objecting to the details of most Westernized laws. They are ready to accept most of these laws, provided they are shown to be compatible with *Shari'a*. In practice, virtually all of Egypt's laws meet this requirement.

The central issue for these theorists is *how* law is developed and applied. The theorists reject the premise that Islamic law and tradition have little to offer and that Muslim countries have no choice but to imitate Western models. They believe that Islam offers a comprehensive moral and social order. As a consequence, there is no need to graft foreign ideas on to it. Rather, Muslims must reinterpret Islam to meet the challenges of modern life.[108] The final outcome may well resemble Western law in many respects, but the process of deriving it from Islamic sources reaffirms the dignity and relevance of the Islamic tradition. This focus on legal process, rather than outcome, suggests that calls to "implement *Shari'a*" are more about identity and pride than about the specifics of law. Indeed, as one reads through the works of these theorists, the moral and cultural importance of reasserting *Shari'a* often takes primacy over the legal details of what *Shari'a* would actually look like in the modern world. In the writings of these theorists, the phrase "return to *Shari'a*" is not a call to implement a particular legal code. Rather, it serves as shorthand for a broader effort to re-ground Egyptian society in its Islamic history, culture, and tradition.

Al-Bishri provides a valuable illustration of this point. He was asked by a student, "How do we know when *Shari'a* is being implemented by a government?" Al-Bishri responded that *Shari'a* is being implemented when four conditions are met: the people of the country express their commitment to Islam; the state and legislation are based upon *Shari'a*;

---

[106] Tariq al-Bishri, *Dirasat fi-l-Dimaqratiyya al-Misriyya* (Cairo: Dar al-Sharuq, 1987), 174–175; Al-Bishri, *al-Wad'a al-Qanuni*, 32–35.

[107] Al-Qaradawi, *Min Fiqh al-Dawla*, 65; Abu al-Majd, *Ru'ya Islamiyya Mu'asira*, 47.

[108] Abu al-Majd, *Natharat Hawla al-Fiqh*, 10.

all political actors—both government and opposition—base their policy positions upon *Shari'a*; and the people utilize the values of *Shari'a* as the basis for interacting with each other.[109] His emphasis lies entirely on the community and the state expressing their commitment to *Shari'a*. The specific legislation that they produce is not important, as long as it is the product of a community that makes a sincere effort to act in accordance with Islamic precepts. "Implementing *Shari'a*" invokes an approach to life and to law, not a specific legal code.

Abu al-Majd adopts a similar line of argument when he proposes that *Shari'a* is "not just a set of texts that the people worship."[110] It is fundamentally a set of sacred principles that guide the individual and the community. He argues that *Shari'a* is grounded upon protecting five principles: religion (*al-din*);[111] life (*al-nafs*); rationality (*al-'aql*); property (*al-'ard*); and wealth (*al-mal*).[112] He then proposes that the core ethical precepts of *Shari'a* are justice, fairness, and compassion. Any law that protects these principles or advances these ethical precepts is compatible with *Shari'a*.[113] Al-'Awwa agrees, concluding that "*Shari'a* is that which establishes justice."[114] Al-Qaradawi makes a similar point when he observes that Egypt's existing laws are largely compatible with *Shari'a* because they "try to advance the interests of the people and limit harm" within the specific context that the country faces.[115]

For the Islamic constitutionalists, the key to reviving the Islamic world is to reconceptualize law and governance according to these core principles and precepts of *Shari'a*. They carefully avoid providing the details of how a contemporary Islamic government should be structured. Rather, they focus on the *process* of generating new laws. This new *ijtihad* is the "only guarantee for the preservation of the *Shari'a* and the fulfillment of its purposes."[116] It will require careful and thorough analysis of the many problems facing Egypt, and the thoughtful weighing of different legal solutions to these problems in order to ensure that the principles of *Shari'a* are respected and the public's interests are served. It will not be a process dominated by individual leaders. The leader of the Islamic community has

[109] Al-Bishri, *al-Wad'a al-Qanuni*, 76.

[110] Abu al-Majd, "Taqdim," 8.

[111] The term that he uses is "*al-din*," not "*al-Islam*." This suggests that he is referring to the right to believe rather than belief in the specific faith of Islam.

[112] Abu al-Majd, "Taqdim," 9.

[113] Ibid.

[114] Al-'Awwa, *Al-Haqq fi-l- Ta'abir*, 67.

[115] Al-Qaradawi, *Min Fiqh al-Dawla*, 65. He later adds that the Egyptian Constitution is compatible with *Shari'a* because it contains a clause stating that *Shari'a* is the primary source of law. Al-Qaradawi, 141.

[116] Abu al-Majd, *Hiwar La Muwajaha*, 90.

no special relationship with God and, thus, no special capacity to interpret the *Shari'a* and issue law.[117] Religious scholars (*'ulama*) should play a role, but they should not be the primary drafters of law.[118]

Indeed, several of the theorists have serious reservations about the *'ulama*, due to their closeness to political power and their past willingness to legitimate autocratic rulers.[119] The *'ulama* have also failed to educate the people fully in Islam and, as a consequence, bear some responsibility for the weakness of the Islamic world.[120] In the view of the Islamic constitutionalists, no member of the *'ulama* should be empowered to issue rulings that are binding on all Muslims. Rather, different *'ulama* may issue different opinions. The people, or their representatives, are then free to follow whichever opinion they consider most sound.[121]

The process of drafting law should involve those with "the most relevant knowledge."[122] This may be a person with formal religious training. Or, depending on the topic, it may be a person with secular technical training who has the most relevant expertise regarding the issue at hand. If the law in question deals with public morality or the well-being of the entire community, the public as a whole should be involved.[123] This emphasis on the public's involvement in the formulation of law is one of the innovations of the Islamic constitutionalists. Al-Bishri argues that this public involvement is the "only way to ensure that law reflects social norms and is in harmony with them."[124] Without this broad public participation, "There will be a divergence between formal law and informal practice" which leads to an illegitimate legal system and social disorder.[125]

---

[117] Abu al-Majd, *Natharat Hawla al-Fiqh*, 7. He notes that the first Caliph, Abu Bakr, expressly rejected the title "Caliph of God" because it implied that he had a special relationship with the deity. Instead, he took the title, "Caliph of the Messenger of God." Ibid., 8. Also, Al-Qaradawi, *Min Fiqh al-Dawla*, 34.

[118] Abu al-Majd, *Natharat Hawla al-Fiqh*, 7–8.

[119] Al-Qaradawi describes the *'ulama* as "weak of body" because they have issued numerous fatwas that "serve their political masters" rather than Islam. Al-Qaradawi, *Min Fiqh al-Dawla*, 98. Al-'Awwa writes that the *'ulama* have "misused authentic religious texts and perverted them to serve the desires of despots." Al-'Awwa, *Religion and Political Structures*, 10.

[120] Al-Qaradawi, *Min Fiqh al-Dawla*, 98; Al-'Awwa, *Religion and Political Structures*, 10; al-'Awwa, *Azmat al-Mu'ssasat al-Diniyya*, 13–15.

[121] Al-'Awwa, *Azmat al-Mu'ssasat al-Diniyya*, 22. Al-'Awwa practices this view in his discussion of the Mufti's fatwa dealing with the controversial case of Nasr Hamid Abu Zayd. In his opinion, the Mufti's understanding of the Hanafi school of Islamic law is incorrect and, therefore, "should not be given any weight." Al-'Awwa, *Al-Haqq fi-l- Ta'abir*, 54.

[122] Al-Qaradawi, *Min Fiqh al-Dawla*, 146.

[123] Abu al-Majd, *Natharat Hawla al-Fiqh*, 20–21; Al-Bishri, *Dirasat fi al-Dimaqratiyya*, 154; al-Qaradawi, *Min Fiqh al-Dawla*, 38–39.

[124] Al-Bishri, *Dirasat fi-l-Dimaqratiyya*, 152.

[125] Ibid. He adds that broad public participation in the legislative process also ensures that laws will serve the interests of the entire community rather than just a small elite (154).

As this brief discussion suggests, the Islamic constitutionalists offer a conception of law that has several important repercussions for governance. They emphasize that the state is created by law and is constrained by it. They also argue that believers are not passive consumers of law and legal rulings. Rather, they actively participate in the drafting of man-made law. In addition, the theorists emphasize that the law applies equally to ruler and ruled. These principles provide the foundation for each of the three remaining dimensions of constitutionalism.

Constraints on State Power

As the preceding discussion indicates, Islamic constitutionalists emphasize a fundamental constraint on state power: the *Shari'a*. If the ruler violates *Shari'a*, citizens are free to disregard the ruler's edicts and, under certain conditions, remove him from office.[126] Abu al-Majd argues that *Shari'a* plays the same role in Islamic legal thought that natural law plays in the Western constitutional tradition. It defines the purposes of state power and delineates its boundaries.[127] A ruler who exceeds these boundaries should not be followed. Within these boundaries, rulers and citizens are free to develop specific laws that respond to the needs of their community.

The Islamic constitutionalists point to several other features of classical Islamic thought that constrain the power of the ruler. They make frequent reference to the concept of *'Aqd* (contract), which dates to the earliest days of Islamic government in the seventh century. This concept held that a leader could assume power only after reaching a firm understanding with the senior members of the *umma* regarding the style and goals of his leadership. Once this agreement was reached, the senior members of the *umma* swore an oath of allegiance—a *baya'a*—to the leader that was conditioned on the leader fulfilling the terms of the *'Aqd*. Abu al-Majd points out that these principles were used in the formation of the first Islamic state by Muhammad in Madina. The Prophet negotiated a "Constitution of Madina" that defined the relationship among the Muslims, the residents of Madina, and the non-Muslim communities in the area. It also specified the procedure for reconciling disputes among these groups. Abu al-Majd argues that this document constitutes "the first example in human history" of a political community being created through a contract.[128] The

---

[126] The theorists differ over when and how citizens should remove an unjust ruler. Al-Qaradawi is the most cautious, arguing that the ruler should be deposed only if his removal will not lead to civil disorder (*fitna*). Al-Qaradawi, *Min Fiqh al-Dawla*, 117.

[127] Abu al-Majd, *Natharat Hawla al-Fiqh*, 13–14. Also, al-Qaradawi, *Min Fiqh al-Dawla*, 38.

[128] Abu al-Majd, *Natharat Hawla al-Fiqh*, 14. Al-'Awwa makes a similar claim. Al-'Awwa, *Fi al-Nitham al-Siyasi*, 61.

Rashidun Caliphs continued this example of assuming power under the terms of a governing contract with the *umma*. This contract granted the ruler the power to manage the community's affairs on the condition that he abided by the wishes of the community. Al-Qaradawi adds that the concept of *baya'a* embodies the principle that believers join an Islamic state through a voluntary expression of allegiance. Their obedience to the state is conditioned on the ruler acting in accordance with the law and the community's will.[129] The institutional details of how these constraints on state power actually operate are left undefined in classical Islamic thought. However, the theorists argue that these ideas provide doctrinal support for the principle that the leader is chosen through the consent of the people and that he is accountable to them.

The theorists develop several additional arguments in support of governmental accountability. Their analysis begins from the premise that the ruler is neither divine nor infallible. He can make mistakes. The only way to avoid mistakes, and to correct them after they occur, is to draw on the knowledge and vigilance of the community. The key mechanism for seeking the advice of the community is *shura* (consultation). *Shura* is mentioned in the Qur'an and entails the leader consulting with senior members of the *umma* on issues of importance. The theorists argue that—unlike in the classical period—*shura* is an obligation (*fard*) of both the ruler and the ruled. They often quote the Qur'anic passages that call on Muhammad to consult with the community. They note that if a leader with the stature of the Prophet was required to consult with his followers, then the average Muslim ruler bears an even stronger obligation to do so. They also cite statements from the four rightly guided Caliphs that demonstrate the importance of consultation in Islamic governance. A quote from Abu Bakr is particularly common, to the effect that he would "gather the people together and consult them"[130] on any issue where the Qur'an and *sunnah* are unclear. He further stated that "I have been given authority over you, but I am not the best of you. If I do well, help me. If I do ill, put me right."[131] A quote from the Caliph 'Umar also appears quite often, stating that "all Muslims have the right to be consulted on matters that affect them."[132]

The concept of governmental accountability is also derived from the principle that "political authority (*sulta*) lies with the community (*umma*)."[133] The people create the state in order to implement the law,

[129] al-Qaradawi, *Min Fiqh al-Dawla*, 30–32.
[130] Abu al-Majd, *Natharat Hawla al-Fiqh*, 19. Al-Qaradawi, *Min Fiqh al-Dawla*, 34.
[131] Al-'Awwa, *Fi al-Nitham al-Siyasi*, 233. Al-Qaradawi, *Min Fiqh al-Dawla*, 34, 59.
[132] Abu al-Majd, *Natharat Hawla al-Fiqh*, 19.
[133] Al-Qaradawi, *Min Fiqh al-Dawla*, 62.

both divine and man-made. This state is accountable to them and serves them. Al-Qaradawi, for example, writes that the ruler is the "agent" (*wakil*) of the *umma*. The people hire him, and he has the same obligations toward the people as an employee toward his employer.[134] If a ruler becomes corrupt, the community may remove him. The preferred method is through legislative action. If this is ineffective, then the armed forces should intervene. If this is not possible, then the masses should be mobilized. If none of these options are available, the believers should wait, resist the leader by whatever means are available, and gradually build the broad public support needed to change the regime.[135]

In order to give the principle of accountability additional practical force, the theorists argue that Muslims have an obligation to monitor the behavior and policies of the ruler. They underscore this point by invoking the Prophet's claim that "the best *jihad* is speaking truth to an unjust ruler."[136] This obligation to monitor the ruler is derived from each Muslim's duty to "enjoin good and forbid evil" among all members of the community. As al-'Awwa puts it, "The principle of *shura,* and the obligation of each believer to enjoin good and forbid evil, together constitute a right by every member of the *umma* to question the head of state."[137]

The Islamic constitutionalists also support the concept of checks and balances. The centralization of power in a single institution "usurps power from the people" because the institution will "serve its interests rather than the interests of the public."[138] The theorists place particular emphasis on the importance of an independent judiciary, which is considered a fundamental and immutable feature of an Islamic political order. It is required by *Shari'a* and is essential for achieving justice. Although judges may be appointed by the executive, they are obligated to interpret the law in accordance with *Shari'a.* The *Shari'a,* in turn, is separate from the executive and cannot be altered by any human ruler. As a consequence, judges enjoy a

[134] Al-Qaradawi, *Min Fiqh al-Dawla*, 35. He stresses that the leader is not a delegate or representative of God (59).

[135] Al-Qaradawi stresses that mobilizing the masses is a last resort. They should be mobilized only if a consensus has been reached on the injustice or turpitude of the ruler. Ibid., 117.

[136] Ibid., 92.

[137] Al-'Awwa, *Fi al-Nitham al-Siyasi*, 232. Al-Qaradawi makes a similar point. Al-Qaradawi, *Min Fiqh al-Dawla*, 36. Al-'Awwa invokes additional evidence from the period of the Rashidun Caliphs to support this position. He observes that the Caliph sought the opinion of the people regarding the appointment and performance of provincial governors. If the people of a region were dissatisfied with their governor, the Caliph replaced him. This principle was soon extended to the Caliphate, and constituted the basis for some Muslims to demand the dismissal of the Caliph Othman for alleged corruption. In al-'Awwa's view, these examples show that the concept of the ruler's accountability to the people was present in the earliest decades of Islam. Al-'Awwa, *Fi al-Nitham al-Siyasi*, 87–88.

[138] Al-Bishri, *Dirasat fi-l-Dimaqratiyya*, 155.

structural separation from executive power that is divinely sanctioned and unchangeable.[139] Al-Bishri further observes that strong judicial institutions have existed throughout Islamic history. He pays particular attention to the "Council of Grievances," an institution common in Islamic monarchies that allowed citizens to air their criticisms of state officials and have them addressed. He argues that the modern-day administrative judiciary is a descendent of this Council.[140] He further adds that judges are more powerful under Islamic law than under Western law. For example, a judge under Islamic law may issue rulings and impose penalties without a specific case before him if he believes that such action will serve the public interest.[141]

Abu al-Majd argues that independent judicial institutions should be created in order to constrain the power of the legislative branch and ensure that its laws conform with the principles of *Shari'a*.[142] Al-Qaradawi agrees, and proposes that the Supreme Constitutional Court is the institution best-suited to fulfill this role.[143] Al-'Awwa shares this view, concluding that the judiciary has an obligation independent of the executive to enjoin good and forbid evil through its interpretation and application of law. In his view, the independence and integrity of the judiciary should be protected by both the state and the public. Public criticism of individual judges should be discouraged, and public debate over court decisions should be restrained and respectful. These steps are particularly important in the contemporary Middle East, where the judiciary serves as "the last defender of the rights of Arabs and Muslims."[144]

Several of the theorists observe that classical Islamic political thought does not include a legislature. Rather, it stresses that law comes from God and that the ruler implements it. However, throughout Islamic history, the *Shari'a* was interpreted by religious scholars (*mujtahidun*) who were often independent of the executive. Respected *mujtahidun* would often

---

[139] Tariq al-Bishri, *Minhaj al-Nithr fi al-Nuthum al-Siyasiyya al-Mu'asira li Buldan al-'Alam al-Islami* (Cairo: Dar al-Sharuq, 2005), 63–64; also, Al-Bishri, *Dirasat fi-l-Dimaqratiyya*, 166, 170, 184–90.

[140] Al-Bishri, *Minhaj al-Nithr*, 69. Al-Bishri laments the fact that Egypt has had difficulty creating a fully independent judiciary. In his view, an independent judiciary can flourish only when the executive and legislative branches enjoy roughly comparable power. The judiciary can then mediate between them and retain its independence by receiving support from each. In Egypt, the executive branch dwarfs the power of the legislature and, as a consequence, this essential balance of powers is absent. Al-Bishri, *Dirasat fi-l-Dimaqratiyya*, 170, 229.

[141] Al-Bishri, *Minhaj al-Nithr*, 64.

[142] Abu al-Majd, *Natharat Hawla al-Fiqh*, 26–27. He believes that an independent judiciary provides essential "practical protection for the rights of the community and its freedoms." Abu al-Majd, *Ru'ya Islamiyya Mu'asira*, 59.

[143] Al-Qaradawi, *Min Fiqh al-Dawla*, 31.

[144] Al-'Awwa, *Al-Haqq fi-l- Ta'abir*, 10, 35; Al-'Awwa, *Religion and Political Structures*, 7.

disagree over how to apply *Shari'a* to a given problem, and would issue different opinions. The influence of a given *mujtahid* and his opinions was determined by how many people attended his lectures and followed his instructions. Al-Bishri argues that this involvement of the public in determining which *mujtahid*'s views prevailed constituted a de facto legislative process.[145]

Several of the theorists also endorse the creation of civil society organizations that can constrain the state. Al-Qaradawi advocates a multi-party political system in which each party offers a different view regarding the best strategy for serving the interests of the *umma* and implementing *Shari'a*.[146] Al-Bishri calls for a rich network of social and professional groups. He observes that individual citizens lack the resources and power to challenge and constrain the state. This problem can be solved only by citizens banding together in professional associations, NGOs, and other groups that enable them to "confront the state" and limit its power.[147]

Protection of Civil and Political Rights

When discussing the issue of individual rights, the theorists begin by stressing the importance of justice in Islam. Exhortations to increase justice or eliminate injustice appear over three hundred times in the Qur'an. According to al-Qaradawi, this principle enabled Islam to assert the basic rights of individuals "1000 years before [these rights] appeared in the West."[148] The theorists identify several general principles that guide the granting of rights and freedoms in an Islamic political order. Al-Qaradawi speaks of a fundamental right to "security and sufficiency," which includes a guarantee that all members of the community enjoy a decent standard of living.[149] Abu al-Majd argues that every human being is entitled to "life, dignity, and property."[150] He observes that these rights were enumerated in the Prophet's last sermon. They were reiterated in the Caliph 'Umar's instructions to provincial governors before they assumed their posts.[151] Al-'Awwa identifies "consultation, justice, freedom, equality, and the accountability of the ruler" as the core principles of an Islamic government.[152] In

---

[145] Al-Bishri, *Minhaj al-Nithr*, 60–61.

[146] Al-Qaradawi, *Min Fiqh al-Dawla*, 151, 153. He stresses that these parties should not represent competing interests of individuals. Al-'Awwa holds a similar view. Al-'Awwa, *Religion and Political Structures*, 13–14.

[147] Al-Bishri, *Dirasat fi-l-Dimaqratiyya*, 229. Also, al-Bishri, *Minhaj al-Nithr*, 51–54.

[148] Al-Qaradawi, *Min Fiqh al-Dawla*, 37. Also, 49.

[149] Ibid., 49. This is ensured by the state gathering *zakat* and redistributing it to the poor.

[150] Abu al-Majd, *Natharat Hawla al-Fiqh*, 23.

[151] Ibid., 23.

[152] Al-'Awwa, *Fi al-Nitham al-Siyasi*, 179.

his view, they are commanded in the Qur'an and constitute "binding legal rules for the community and not mere ethical directives."[153] Whatever rights are needed to carry them out are, therefore, divinely ordained.

The Islamic constitutionalists also elaborate several specific liberties that are protected by Islam. Freedom of choice is considered particularly important. Al-'Awwa notes that the very first human being whom God created—Adam—was given the power to choose between obeying God and not obeying. In his view, this fact shows that freedom of choice is a fundamental feature of humanity and has been part of each human being's character since the dawn of creation. Furthermore, the Qur'an stresses that each believer must voluntarily choose to submit to the will of God. In order for this choice to have meaning, believers must also be free not to submit. Thus, choice is at the core of what defines an Islamic community.[154] However, al-'Awwa adds an important caveat: the freedom to leave the Islamic faith is restricted. The Qur'an clearly states that apostasy is a sin, although it does not specify a penalty.[155]

Al-'Awwa further argues that each Muslim is obligated to exercise *ijtihad*, which he defines as a personal struggle to understand the faith. This struggle requires reason, reflection, and dialogue with fellow believers. As a consequence, freedom of thought, inquiry, and speech are essential to the full expression of each Muslim's faith.[156] He reiterates the importance of reason on several occasions. In his view, "the lives of all the messengers of God were . . . a statement of evidence and argument that the mind accepts and to which it submits before the heart accepts it."[157] He adds that the Qur'an expressly calls on Muslims to use reason to persuade others to join the faith. Thus, the free exercise of reason is fundamental to practicing and spreading the faith.[158]

In addition, Al-'Awwa proposes that Muslims bear an obligation to "enjoin good and forbid evil" within the community. In order to fulfill this obligation, each Muslim must be free to criticize evil and corruption. Speaking out in this manner is a religious duty and, thus, freedom of speech is divinely sanctioned and mandated.[159] However, this freedom is

[153] Ibid., 26 (footnote 1).
[154] Al-'Awwa, *Fi al-Nitham al-Siyasi*, 211–12.
[155] Al-'Awwa, *Al-Haqq fi-l- Ta'abir*, 65–72.
[156] Al-'Awwa, *Fi al-Nitham al-Siyasi*, 210–25. He adds that "thinking about God's creations constitutes an obligatory duty ordained upon each person to enable him to discover the Creator." Ibid., 213. Also, al-Qaradawi, *Min Fiqh al-Dawla*, 49.
[157] Al-'Awwa, *Fi al-Nitham al-Siyasi*, 213.
[158] Ibid., 213–14.
[159] In al-'Awwa's view, "public declaration of opinion is obligatory and not simply permitted" because the Qur'an expressly calls on Muslims to "order what is good and forbid what

not absolute. Speech may be restricted if it compromises "the prevailing order and moral appropriateness."[160] This includes speech that may cloud another Muslim's understanding of Islam and lead him to stray from the faith.[161] Al-'Awwa concludes that freedom of speech and thought within these limits are "commandments in Islam . . . [they are] inviolable basic rights of man."[162] Al-Qaradawi holds a similar view. He observes that Islam has a long history of multiple schools of law, jurisprudence, and interpretation. Dialogue and debate among them are essential to the functioning of a devout Muslim community.[163]

Each of the theorists also addresses women's rights. Al-Qaradawi offers a detailed discussion of this topic. He observes that women "can be smarter and wiser than many men."[164] They have the same public duties as men, and they play an important role in the life of the community. Trying to exclude them from public life "is like trying to breathe with one lung or fly with one wing."[165] Women should be allowed to vote and run for office. They should also be permitted to hold positions of authority, including the posts of judge and head of state.[166] They have the same obligation as men to enjoin good and forbid evil, and to monitor the ruler and offer him constructive advice.[167] However, these rights are bounded by a traditional view of a woman's role in society. A woman's first duty is child rearing. She should embark on public life only if she has no children, or her children are grown.[168] Also, al-Qaradawi makes no effort to challenge the discrimination against women found in the Qur'an and the *sunnah*, which includes assigning less importance to a woman's testimony in

is bad." al-'Awwa, *Religion and Political Structures*, 11. Also, al-Qaradawi, *Min Fiqh al-Dawla*, 49; Al-Bishri, *Minhaj al-Nithr*, 72.

[160] Al-'Awwa, *Al-Haqq fi-l- Ta'abir*, 25.

[161] Ibid., 69. Al-'Awwa makes this point in the context of discussing the crime of *ridda* (apostasy) in the case of Nasr Hamid Abu Zayd, a prominent Egyptian intellectual. Al-'Awwa claims that there are two types of *ridda*. One is entirely personal and entails an individual Muslim choosing to renounce Islam in his own mind. So long as this renunciation is limited to the individual who chooses to do it, there is no punishment. However, if the individual tries to persuade other Muslims to follow his path and leave the faith, this form of speech may be restricted in the interest of protecting the Islamic community. Ibid., 71–72.

[162] Al-'Awwa, *Fi al-Nitham al-Siyasi*, 211, 213.

[163] Al-Qaradawi, *Min Fiqh al-Dawla*, 49–50, 151–54.

[164] Ibid., 169.

[165] Ibid., 82. Abu al-Majd expresses a similar view. Abu al-Majd, *Ru'ya Islamiyya Mu'asira*, 62.

[166] Al-Qaradawi, *Min Fiqh al-Dawla*, 165–66, 175–76. However, a female judge is not permitted to rule on matters of vengeance (*qasas*) or cases involving the *hudud* punishments. Al-Qaradawi, *Min Fiqh al-Dawla*, 166. Also, Al-'Awwa, *Religion and Political Structures*, 7.

[167] Al-Qaradawi, *Min Fiqh al-Dawla*, 166–67.

[168] Ibid., 173.

court, granting women less right to inherit than men, and prohibiting women from leading prayer or leading the *umma*.[169]

The theorists also advocate protecting the rights of non-Muslims. They argue that differences in religion were created by God and, as such, should be respected and protected. Al-Bishri pays particular attention to this topic in a lengthy book that examines the relationship between Copts and Muslims in Egypt.[170] He argues that Egypt's unique historical experience has produced a national identity that embraces both Muslims and Copts. Islam is part of this Egyptian identity, but does not dominate it and does not define Copts as second-class citizens.[171] A strengthening of Islam's role in society need not threaten Copts, so long as the country's shared Egyptian identity is preserved. Copts are further protected by the Qur'an's respect for religious difference and its commandment that there is "no compulsion in religion" (2:256).[172] Al-'Awwa makes essentially the same argument, and proposes that sectarian strife has risen in recent years primarily because of political opportunism by troublemakers on both sides. These tensions are not a reflection of any fundamental incompatibility between Muslims and Copts, and can be resolved through "dialog and popular action."[173] Al-Qaradawi holds a similar view. He writes that Muslims and Copts constitute a shared "national brotherhood" that is grounded in respect and tolerance. He argues that Copts are equal to Muslims before the law on civil matters, and that they are entitled to practice their own laws on matters of creed, worship, and personal status. Copts may also hold senior positions in government, serve in the bureaucracy, and participate in Parliament. However, the post of president must always be held by a Muslim in order to ensure that the polity remains an Islamic state. For the same reason, Muslims must also hold a majority in Parliament.[174]

---

[169] Ibid., 161–63. However, in al-Qaradawi's view, a woman's testimony on matters related to child rearing should carry the same weight as a man's, and a woman is permitted to serve as head of state of a country. Women are only prohibited from leading the entire religious community of Muslims (the *umma*). In essence, they are prohibited from assuming the post of Caliph. As the Caliphate no longer exists, al-Qaradawi considers this restriction to have little practical meaning. Al-Qaradawi, *Min Fiqh al-Dawla*, 175.

[170] Tariq al-Bishri, *Al-Muslimun wa-l-Aqbat fi Itar al-Jama'aa al-Wataniyya* (Cairo: Dar al-Sharuq, 2004).

[171] Al-Bishri writes that many Copts in the past have embraced the Islamic tradition as part of their Egyptian identity. He notes with particular approval a prominent scholar of *Shari'a*, Dr. Shafiq Shahata, who was a Copt. Al-Bishri, *al-Wad'a al-Qanuni*, 47.

[172] Al-Bishri, *Al-Muslimun wa-l-Aqbat*, especially pp. 161–92 and 803–86. Abu al-Majd adds that these protections should be supplemented with constitutional guarantees that protect the basic rights of religious minorities from infringement by the majority. Abu al-Majd, *Ru'ya Islamiyya Mu'asira*, 57.

[173] Muhammad Salim al-'Awwa, *Al-Aqbat wa-l-Islam* (Cairo: Dar al-Sharuq, 1987), 62.

[174] Al-Qaradawi, *Min Fiqh al-Dawla*, 32, 195. Al-'Awwa echoes these views. Al-'Awwa, *Religion and Political Structures*, 6–7.

Public Participation in Politics

The theorists of Islamic constitutionalism emphasize that political authority lies with the people. In their view, the Qur'an, the *sunnah*, and the historical experiences of the Rashidun Caliphs all confirm that the people are entitled to select their ruler. Al-Qaradawi argues that this idea lies at the foundation of the faith. It is most clearly captured in the Prophet's statement that Muslims are empowered to choose who will lead them in prayer.[175] Al-'Awwa writes that the public's right to choose the ruler can be traced back to the selection of Abu Bakr as the first successor to Muhammad. The history of this event states that Abu Bakr ascended to power through the following process: two prominent members of the community ('Umar and Abu 'Ubayda) showed their support for him by expressing an oath of loyalty (*baya'a*); then, the community showed its support through its expression of *baya'a*. Al-'Awwa argues that the first *baya'a* constituted a nomination, while the second was a referendum.[176] He concludes that "one of the most significant results of this event was the decision that a ruler can be chosen only through consultation with the community of Muslims."[177] This principle was upheld by the Rashidun Caliphs, and serves as the foundation for Islamic government.[178]

The theorists further propose that the public should participate in day-to-day governance. One of the central purposes of an Islamic state is to "serve the interests (*masalih*) of the governed."[179] These interests can be ascertained only through consultation (*shura*) with the community.[180] As noted earlier, the concept of *shura* has clear doctrinal support in both the Qur'an and the *sunnah*. However, the texts are not clear regarding *which* members of the community should be consulted. Abu al-Majd observes that the classical texts sometimes refer to the group involved in consultation as "the people of consultation" (*ahl al-shura*), which is understood to mean those members of the community with knowledge relevant to the issue at hand. At other times, the texts refer to the "people who loose and

---

[175] Al-Qaradawi, *Min Fiqh al-Dawla*, 132.

[176] Al-'Awwa, *Fi al-Nitham al-Siyasi*, 71.

[177] Ibid., 79. Also, p. 71. Abu al-Majd makes a similar point in his analysis of the selection of 'Umar as the successor to Abu Bakr. Abu al-Majd, *Natharat Hawla al-Fiqh*, 15, 18.

[178] Al-'Awwa quotes the Caliph 'Umar as proclaiming to one of his followers, "You are free to kill anyone who claims leadership without consulting the Muslims." Al-'Awwa, *Fi al-Nitham al-Siyasi*, 80.

[179] The other central purpose of the state is to "establish the faith." Al-'Awwa, *Fi-l-Nitham al-Siyasi*, 138.

[180] Abu al-Majd observes that the obligation to consult is not limited to the ruler. All officials involved in making decisions that affect the well-being of the *umma* are obliged to engage in *shura*. Abu al-Majd, *Hiwar La Muwajaha*, 112.

bind" (*ahl al-hal wa-l 'aqd*), who are understood to be the most respected and influential members of the community.[181]

The Islamic constitutionalists argue that the circle of persons involved in *shura* should expand to include the entire *umma*. Abu al-Majd develops this point by invoking an event from the *hadith*. The passage describes the Prophet consulting with his followers over how to treat prisoners captured in a recent battle. The Prophet not only consulted with the believers who were present; he also told them to travel to their homes, consult with their relatives, and then return to inform him of their opinions. Abu al-Majd argues that this is proof that *shura* was conceptualized from the earliest days of Islam to include the entire community.[182] He believes that this conception of *shura* should be revived today. Al-'Awwa agrees, concluding that "*Shura* will have no meaning if the view of the majority [of the *umma*] is not adhered to."[183]

The theorists further note that the classical texts do not specify the procedure for conducting *shura*. Al-'Awwa observes that neither the Qur'an nor the *sunnah*, nor the experiences of the Rashidun Caliphs, offer "any specific method for conducting this consultation or any fixed system for its application."[184] Muslims are free to develop the specific mechanisms that are best suited to their time and circumstances. The Islamic constitutionalists then proceed to argue that the most effective mechanism for *shura* under modern conditions is an elected Parliament. The deliberations of Parliament constitute a collective *ijtihad* that adapts the principles of *Shari'a* to the challenges of daily governance. These deliberations are also described as a form of *ijm'a*, or consensus building, in which the community gradually reaches agreement over the course of action that conforms with *Shari'a* and best serves the interests of the community.[185]

The Parliament may legislate in any area where *Shari'a* is unclear or silent. The range of topics is vast: from traffic laws to taxation to the decision to wage war. The laws produced by these deliberations will command public support because they are the product of careful reflection by respected members of the community in accordance with *Shari'a* and the juridical principles of *ijm'a* and *shura*.[186]

In this view, members of Parliament assume the role of the "people who loose and bind." These individuals are selected through free and fair elections. Elections provide a transparent and reliable means for identi-

---

[181] Ibid., 117–18. Abu al-Majd also mentions the "people of *ijtihad*" (*ahl al-ijtihad*). However, they appear to be identical to the *ahl al-shura*. Ibid., 118.

[182] Abu al-Majd, *Natharat Hawla al-Fiqh*, 20–22.

[183] Al-'Awwa, *Fi-l-Nitham al-Siyasi*, 199.

[184] Ibid., 80.

[185] Al-Qaradawi, *Min Fiqh al-Dawla*, 38–39.

[186] Ibid., 37–39; Al-'Awwa, *Fi al-Nitham al-Siyasi*, 186.

fying those citizens who command the public's respect and, thus, can be entrusted with the responsibility of exercising *ijtihad* on behalf of the community. In order for elections to work effectively, every citizen must participate fully and seriously. Al-Qaradawi makes a detailed case on this point. He writes that voting is analogous to testifying in a court of law, since it entails expressing one's personal witness to the moral and professional suitability of a candidate. He then cites a Qur'anic passage to the effect that each believer is obligated to testify in court if he has information relevant to a case. Thus, by analogy, each citizen has a religious obligation (*fard*) to vote, since he has a religious duty to convey his knowledge of the candidate for office.[187] Al-'Awwa holds a similar view, and invokes the Qur'anic proclamation, "Do not conceal testimony, for he who conceals it has a sinful heart."[188]

In order to facilitate electoral competition and public debate, the theorists support a political system with multiple political parties. For al-Qaradawi, they resemble the multiple schools of law within Islam that reflect different perspectives on understanding and implementing the Qur'an and the *sunnah*.[189] He assumes that all political parties share the goals of deepening the religiosity of the community and interpreting *Shari'a* to serve the community. Their different perspectives help to ensure that the community will achieve these goals.[190] Multiple parties also provide an additional means to monitor the ruler, hold him accountable, and prevent the emergence of tyranny. For al-Qaradawi, parties do not reflect competing interests. Rather, they reflect honest differences of opinion among sincere and selfless believers who aim to serve the *umma*. Members of differing parties should "argue honorably" and exhibit patience, wisdom, and compassion. Their interaction leads to better governance and ensures that any errors by the ruler are quickly identified and corrected.[191] Al-Bishri holds a somewhat less idealistic view of parties. For him, multiple parties reflect the varied interests that naturally emerge in society. Social

[187] Al-Qaradawi, *Min Fiqh al-Dawla*, 138.

[188] Al-'Awwa, *Fi al-Nitham al-Siyasi*, 209. Also, Abu al-Majd, *Natharat Hawla al-Fiqh*, 20–21.

[189] Al-Qaradawi notes that the founder of the Muslim Brotherhood, Hasan al-Banna, opposed political parties. Al-Qaradawi writes that this position was the product of the specific moment in history when al-Banna lived. At that time (in the 1930s and 1940s), political parties reflected the personal ambitions of their leaders. Their competition tended to heighten social tensions and fragment society. Al-Qaradawi argues that the situation has now changed and, if al-Banna were alive, he would support multiple political parties. Al-Qaradawi, *Min Fiqh al-Dawla*, 157.

[190] Ibid., 142–43, 151. He adds that all parties must acknowledge Islam and work to strengthen it. He would not allow areligious or atheistic parties, or parties that "contradict Islam." Ibid., 154.

[191] Ibid., 149, 151, 153–54.

order and harmony require that these interests be given expression through parties, in order to ensure that competing concerns are recognized and reconciled peacefully.[192] Al-'Awwa also accepts that multiple parties reflect the presence of competing interests and dissenting voices. He argues that tolerance of dissent has been central to Islam since its earliest years, and notes that the Caliph 'Ali tolerated the Kharijites despite their sharp differences with him.[193] He proposes that God intentionally created differences of opinion and perspective, and that these differences are also a result of mankind's imperfect and incomplete understanding of God's message. Peaceful interaction among differing views is necessary to determine God's true intent and to better serve his will.[194] Al-'Awwa concludes, "The existence of political parties . . . is necessary for the advancement [of society] and for freedom of opinion within [it], and to ensure the absence of oppression."[195]

The theorists note that institutions such as Parliament, elections, and political parties are borrowed from Western democracies. However, each stresses that this borrowing is conducted in a highly selective manner. Al-Qaradawi's view is typical when he writes that the Islamic world must "take the best elements of democracy without seeking to duplicate it."[196] The primary goals of an Islamic state are to enhance justice and oppose tyranny. At this moment in history, democratic institutions are the best means for achieving these goals and, thus, democracy "is the form of government that is closest to Islam."[197] It is "the best way to fight tyranny and trim the claws of totalitarianism."[198] Because democracy serves this desirable end, Islam supports whatever institutions are needed to make it function. These include elections, referenda, multiple political parties, freedom of speech, and judicial independence.

However, democracy must operate within predefined ethical boundaries. The fundamental shortcoming of Western democracy lies in its "lack of restraint and discipline."[199] As a result, it can cater to the basest instincts of a ruler or a community. Unconstrained democracy can legalize vice, perpetuate injustice, and strengthen tyranny. All of these outcomes are at

---

[192] Al-Bishri, *Dirasat fi-l-Dimaqratiyya*, 225–26.

[193] Al-'Awwa, *Fi al-Nitham al-Siyasi*, 105–6. Abu al-Majd makes the same point. Abu al-Majd, *Natharat Hawla al-Fiqh*, 24.

[194] Al-'Awwa, *Religion and Political Structures* , 9, 13–14. Also, al-Qaradawi, *Min Fiqh al-Dawla*, 153–54.

[195] Al-'Awwa, *Religion and Political Structures* , 14.

[196] Al-Qaradawi, *Min Fiqh al-Dawla*, 36.

[197] Ibid., 9.

[198] Ibid., 131. Al-Qaradawi adds that the struggle for freedom "is the primary battle for Islamic *da'wa* and Islamic revival . . . in our era." Ibid., 145.

[199] Ibid., 36.

odds with Islam. In order to avoid them, an Islamic democracy requires that man-made law conform to the moral precepts of *Shari'a*. No law may violate *Shari'a* and allow what is forbidden in Islam (such as adultery or alcohol consumption) or prohibit what is required (such as prayer, *zakat*, or pilgrimage). In al-Qaradawi's words, "We take from democracy its structures (*asalib*)[200] . . . and its guarantees that are beneficial to us, while retaining the right to amend them. But, we do not take its philosophy in which it is possible to permit what is forbidden, forbid what is allowed, and abandon what is required of Muslims."[201]

In practice, this means that the representatives of the people who draft man-made laws must have substantial knowledge of Islam. They need not be *'ulama*, but they should be willing to consult with specialists on religious law when the topic under discussion requires it. They should draw on the principles of *Shari'a* to ensure that legislation remains within the moral parameters of Islam and that the rights of those with minority opinions are protected from the tyranny of the majority.[202] In this regard, the theorists argue (once again) that *Shari'a* plays a role comparable to that of natural law in Western democracies. Abu al-Majd notes that the term "natural law" does not appear in Islamic jurisprudence. However, he proposes that "Islam itself is natural law."[203] God created Islam as "eternal and divine," and this revelation included the principle that people are born free with fundamental rights and religious duties. Each legislator is required to draw upon this principle to ensure that legislation remains within the ethical parameters of Islam while serving the interests of the community.

THE UNIQUENESS OF ISLAMIC CONSTITUTIONALISM: THE STATE AND SOCIAL TRANSFORMATION

These theorists define a view of Islamic constitutionalism that shares many characteristics with classical liberalism.[204] They support the rule of law,

---

[200] *Asalib* can also be translated as "styles" or "mechanisms."

[201] Al-Qaradawi, *Min Fiqh al-Dawla*, 138.

[202] Ibid., 38.

[203] Abu al-Majd, *Natharat Hawla al-Fiqh*, 13.

[204] It should be noted that these thinkers do not describe their ideas as "liberal." In contemporary Egyptian discourse, this term is associated with Western political thought and, particularly, with the British colonial presence in the interwar period. It is also associated with the relatively lax moral standards of the West. The Islamic constitutionalists emphasize that their ideas are derived entirely from Islamic sources and are not drawn from any Western inspiration. Nonetheless, the specific institutional reforms that they advocate can be usefully described as "liberal" in the sense that they incorporate the key features of classical liberalism. These key features include a clear and unbiased legal code, the separation of powers, checks

constraints on state power, and the protection of many civil and political rights. They also advocate broad public participation in politics. However, their views diverge from classical liberalism in several important respects. This divergence is most obvious in their frequent calls to transform the character of individual Muslims. Al-Bishri, for example, writes that the weakness of the Islamic world is not simply a product of colonialism or political corruption. Rather, it is also a result of individual Muslims losing sight of the core principles of the faith. This problem can be addressed only through a "transformation that revives the spiritual character of every Muslim."[205] This does not simply entail self-reflection and deeper personal spirituality. The theorists believe that an individual's character is shaped by the community in which he lives. In order to transform the individual, one must transform every dimension of society—from "ideas, concepts, values and ethics" to "customs, organizations, and legislation."[206]

Furthermore, the state plays the central role in this process of transformation. Indeed, the theorists' emphasis on the state as a moral actor is one of the distinctive features of Islamic constitutionalism. For example, Al-Qaradawi argues that the state in Islam is "not simply a state that maintains order."[207] Rather, it is "an intellectual creedal state"—a state based on a creed that it promotes by "creating an atmosphere that converts the teachings of Islam into tangible reality."[208] In his view, the state "represents the justice of God on earth."[209] Its actions "deepen the Islamic character of the people and spread Islam."[210] It also ensures that people abide by worship and adhere to good manners and good dealings.[211]

Abu al-Majd holds a similar view. He argues that the central moral imperative of Islam is to enhance justice. This can be achieved only through implementation of *Shari'a*, which creates the moral and ethical framework that makes justice possible. This implementation of divine law, in turn, requires the establishment of a strong and effective state.[212] Al-'Awwa adds that the state creates the Islamic community by enforcing Islamic law.[213]

---

and balances among these powers, an independent judiciary, and the protection of many civil and political rights. This point will be discussed further in chapters 4 and 6.

[205] Al-Bishri, *al-Wad'a al-Qanuni*, 84.

[206] Al-Qaradawi, *Min Fiqh al-Dawla*, 127.

[207] Ibid., 19–20.

[208] Ibid. Abu al-Majd uses similar language, describing the Islamic state as an "intellectual state"—*al-dawla al-fikriyya*. Abu al-Majd, *Natharat Hawla al-Fiqh*, 26.

[209] Al-Qaradawi, *Min Fiqh al-Dawla*, 51.

[210] Ibid., 41.

[211] Ibid., 20.

[212] Abu al-Majd, "Taqdim," 9–10.

[213] Al-'Awwa points out that, after Muhammad's death, his companions moved to choose a successor even before they had buried the Prophet. Al-'Awwa interprets this as evidence that a ruler and the state institutions that he leads are essential to the well-being of the

It gives the abstract moral precepts of Islam practical substance that shapes the lives of individual Muslims and deepens their conviction to the faith. By doing so, it "establishes the faith" and enables each Muslim to live a more devout life.[214]

This conception of the state as a moral actor receives its clearest statement in the theorists' call for reviving the doctrine of *hisba*. This is an ancient principle in Islam that dates back to the earliest days of the faith.[215] It mandates that each individual has a duty to strengthen the religiosity of his fellow Muslims and thereby build a stronger and more pious community. As Michael Cook points out, the obligation of *hisba* quickly became grafted on to the duties of the state. The ruler assumed the obligation to "enjoin good and forbid evil" in each member of the community.[216] From the earliest years of Islam, the state had a duty to shape the moral character of its citizens in a systematic manner. This involved not only the obvious task of enforcing a wide range of laws governing personal behavior. It also included designing the education system, selecting judges, and appointing officials at all levels of society with the goal of enhancing the piety of the community.

Al-Bishri writes at some length about *hisba* as an "obligation of the entire community."[217] However, each person is permitted to delegate this obligation to another. In practice, it has been delegated to the state.[218] Al-Bishri adds that many rulers created a specific post—the *muhtassib*—to carry out this duty.[219] This person had broad powers to monitor and improve public morality, but he was also obligated to show restraint. Drawing on the writings of the medieval philosopher Ibn Taymiyya, al-Bishri stresses that the person carrying out *hisba* must exercise his powers with

community. He quotes one of the companions of the Prophet, who asserted that they moved quickly to choose a successor because "we disliked spending even part of the day without being in a community." Al-'Awwa, *Fi-l-Nitham al-Siyasi*, 81.

[214] The full quotation from al-'Awwa on this point is: "The establishment of faith is the fundamental goal of the Islamic state. Indeed, it is the justification for its existence and the intangible quality that distinguishes it from other states." Ibid., 137–38.

[215] The obligation to enjoin good and forbid evil appears in eight Qur'anic verses: 3:104; 3:110; 3:114; 7:157; 9:71; 9:112; 22:41; and 31:17. However, the use of the term *hisba* to describe this obligation was adopted only in the eleventh century. Al-Ghazzali was the first to utilize it. Michael Cook, *Commanding Right and Forbidding Wrong in Islamic Thought* (New York: Cambridge University Press, 2000), 13, 449. For a useful summary of al-Ghazzali's conception of *hisba*, see Cook, 428–59.

[216] Ibid., 470–79. Also, Michael Cook, *Forbidding Wrong in Islam: An Introduction* (New York: Cambridge University Press, 2003), 65–72.

[217] Al-Bishri, *Minhaj al-Nithr*, 72.

[218] Ibid., 74.

[219] Ibid. Cook translates *muhtassib* as "official censor." Cook, *Commanding Right and Forbidding Wrong*, 448. The root meaning is derived from the term for keeping an account—in this case, an account of the moral shortcomings of one's fellow Muslims.

"kindness, patience, self-discipline, and perseverance."[220] Abu Al-Majd holds a similar view, and suggests that the state's assumption of the duty of *hisba* is both necessary and desirable. If the obligation of *hisba* remained in the hands of every believer, groups of moral vigilantes might try to impose their view of morality. When the state exercises the duties of *hisba*, it can do so in a manner that is balanced, fair, and consistent.[221]

Al-Qaradawi also discusses the concept of *hisba*. He argues that each Muslim is required by his faith to care for the physical and spiritual well-being of others. If he sees wrongdoing, he must confront it by whatever means are available—by deed and word, if possible. If these are not possible, then he must hold a sincere commitment in his heart to oppose the wrongdoing.[222] This responsibility is also a central feature of the duties of the ruler. However, the ruler must exercise this power with great care. He must invoke it only when the moral principle involved is widely shared by the community and supported by a consensus among jurists.[223]

Al-'Awwa develops the concept, as well. He writes at some length about the nature of the Prophet's leadership in the early years of Islam, when the faith was attracting its first followers. The Prophet sought to "correct the concepts and ideas of those around him in order to purify their souls, clarify their minds, and eliminate remnants of the habits of *jahiliyya*[224] from their hearts."[225] In al-'Awwa's view, the modern ruler assumes this same obligation and must ensure that each individual remains on the path to deeper piety. This responsibility is an integral part of the ruler's duties and is the equivalent of "supporting God himself."[226] In al-'Awwa's view, this obligation applies to "every conceivable matter related to the public life of the *umma*."[227]

The fact that the theorists place the concept of *hisba* alongside all the institutions of constitutionalism is quite striking. In essence, they make a long and detailed case for creating institutions that are normally associated with constraining and limiting state power. Then, in the next breath, they invoke the concept of *hisba* and its dramatic expansion of the state's power to interfere in the private lives of citizens.

[220] Al-Bishri, *Minhaj al-Nithr*, 71.

[221] Abu al-Majd, *Ru'ya Islamiyya Mu'asira*, 10. Also, al-'Awwa, *Al-Haqq fi-l- Ta'abir*, 72.

[222] Al-Qaradawi, *Min Fiqh al-Dawla*, 94. Al-'Awwa makes the same point, and cites a hadith to this effect. Al-'Awwa, *Fi-l-Nitham al-Siyasi*, 147.

[223] Al-Qaradawi, *Min Fiqh al-Dawla*, 121.

[224] *Jahiliyya* is the polytheistic order that existed in Arabia prior to the arrival of Islam.

[225] Al-'Awwa, *Fi al-Nitham al-Siyasi*, 42.

[226] Ibid., 148. Also, 138.

[227] Ibid., 218. Al-'Awwa further argues that many institutions of the modern Egyptian state—such as the State Council and the Supreme Constitutional Court—are modern-day manifestations of the concept of *hisba*. Al-'Awwa, *Al-Haqq fi-l- Ta'abir*, 23.

How can we explain this juxtaposition of seemingly contradictory ideas? One possibility is that the theorists are trying to deceive their audience. They invoke the rhetoric of liberal institutions and procedures, perhaps to calm the fears of domestic and international critics. But, at heart, they are actually committed to an autocratic form of rule based on a powerful state that enjoys divine sanction and few constraints on its power. If this is their strategy, it is executed with remarkable clumsiness. The theorists make no secret of their goal of transforming individual Muslims and Islamic society. It is stated clearly and repeatedly in each of their works.

There is a certain inconsistency to the claim that the liberal rhetoric of Islamists is merely a smokescreen for an underlying autocratic agenda. On the one hand, it implies considerable intelligence and skill among Islamist leaders. They present well-developed arguments—complete with numerous Qur'anic citations and references from the hadith—that articulate a plausible case for liberal government derived from Islamic sources. They repeat this case consistently in many different settings, with minor adjustments to address the concerns of specific audiences. This conceptual sophistication and coherence suggests that the leaders of the movement are smart, disciplined, and well-organized. And yet, if the "smokescreen" theory is correct, these same individuals are also capable of remarkable ineptness. They reveal their supposedly secret agenda of transforming individuals and society in every public forum available to them. They also openly make the case for a powerful state that guides this process. In order to conclude that the Islamists discussed above are engaged in an elaborate charade, one must believe that they are capable of great cleverness and great stupidity at the same time. This is certainly possible. However, it is unlikely. We need to look for a more plausible explanation.

The other possibility is that the institutions of constitutionalism play a different role in the thinking of these theorists than they do in classical liberalism. In liberal thought, constitutionalism begins from the assumption that the state is a threatening institution. Its control over vast resources and personnel gives it enormous potential to trespass on the rights and liberties of citizens. The purpose of constitutionalism is to create institutions that place clear limits on state power in order to protect individual rights, private property, and the private sphere.[228]

For the theorists of Islamic constitutionalism, the nature of the state is fundamentally different. From their standpoint, the state is a good institution. Through its enforcement of *Shari'a*, it brings the Islamic community

---

[228] For a useful summary of the liberal conception of constitutionalism and its role in democracy, see Walter F. Murphy, "Constitutions, Constitutionalism, and Democracy," in *Constitutionalism and Democracy: Transitions in the Contemporary World*, ed. Douglas Greenberg et al. (New York: Oxford University Press, 1993), 3–25.

into being and ensures that this community remains pious. Through its implementation of the doctrine of *hisba*, it strengthens the morality and spirituality of individual Muslims. Its institutions perform functions fundamental to Islam such as the collection of *zakat*, the reconciling of tensions within the community, the protection of the *umma* from external threats, and the spreading of the faith. From this perspective, constraints on state power play a different role than they do in liberalism. The institutions of constitutionalism are not intended to erect a barrier that prevents the state from interfering in the private lives of citizens. Rather, their purpose is to direct state power toward the goal of transforming individual Muslims and society.

Phrased differently, the metaphor for liberal constitutionalism is a wall built around the state. This wall constrains the state, limits its power, and protects citizens from unwelcome intrusions into their private lives. In contrast, the metaphor for Islamic constitutionalism is a carefully maintained path that directs state power toward the transformation of individual Muslims and the creation of a more pious community. Within this framework, the institutions of constitutionalism ensure that the state stays on this path and fully achieves its potential to change individuals and society.

If the Islamic constitutionalism described above were fully implemented, it would have many of the institutional features of liberalism such as an independent judiciary, a Parliament with considerable power and autonomy, and an executive accountable to at least part of the citizenry. However, the net result of these constitutional features would be a state that is far more invasive than that found in Western liberal regimes. The purpose of law, police, and courts would not be to simply maintain order. They would also be tasked with monitoring and changing the moral character of the community. The state would play an active role in shaping educational curricula to convey a specific set of moral and religious values. It would also monitor publications, scholarship, the arts, and other forms of expression that shape the morality of the community. In addition, there would be less protection of civil and political rights in some areas. For example, freedom of speech with regard to religious and moral matters would be constrained. Freedom of religious choice would also be limited, in that Muslims would not be allowed to choose a different faith. Non-Muslims would probably face some discrimination in economic life and in politics. In addition, women would probably enjoy fewer rights than men.

It should be noted that Islamic constitutionalism is not a doctrine that supports a totalitarian conception of the state. It does not assert that the state holds a monopoly on truth and that it imposes this truth on the citizenry. Rather, this conception of constitutionalism is based on a collaborative relationship between state and society. It is grounded in the premise that both state and society seek to create a pious community. Individual citizens, as well as the state, carry the obligation to improve the moral character of the community. As a consequence, society constrains and monitors the state in order to ensure that it plays its role as effectively as possible and stays "on the true path of Islam."[229] The resulting regime is participatory and bound by law. But, it serves different objectives than in the West.

Furthermore, it would not be accurate to conceptualize this moral role for the state as simply the "unification of church and state." The Islamic constitutionalists argue that their goal is a "civil state governed by Islam."[230] To a reader grounded in Western political thought, this phrase is self-contradictory. However, the Islamic constitutionalists use this formulation to emphasize that their goal is not a religious state in the Western sense of the term. They do not call for the state to act on behalf of a religious body or class, nor do they support empowering the state to implement the conception of religious law adopted by the ruler.[231] Rather, they advocate a "civil state" in the sense that it is created by citizens to serve their goals and is accountable to them. The state is not divine, nor does it exercise divine power. However, its fundamental goal is to implement *Shari'a* and, thereby, create a more pious community. Thus, it serves a religious purpose. A state with a religious purpose is not a divine state that is beyond criticism and constraint. To the contrary, the fact that the state has a religious mission in which society also participates means that the state faces two fundamental constraints: the religious law that it is created to enforce; and the public's understanding of this law, which is ascertained through the mechanism of *shura* (consultation). The institutions that create this form of government are spelled out in broad terms: an executive elected through popular vote; an elected Parliament that issues legislation; and an independent judiciary that monitors whether man-made law conforms to the prevailing understanding of the Qur'an and the *sunnah*.

An obvious question to consider is whether Islamic constitutionalism can support democracy. If democracy is a set of institutions that constrain the state, enforce law, and allow public participation in politics, then Islamic constitutionalism is fully compatible with democracy. However, if one views democracy as the adoption and promotion of a set of values—such as individual liberty, freedom of choice, popular sovereignty, and a minimalist state—then the conclusion with regard to Islamic constitutionalism is more ambiguous. The Islamic thinkers discussed above place

[229] Al-Qaradawi, *Min Fiqh al-Dawla*, 30.

[230] Ibid.

[231] Al-Qaradawi argues that secular observers of the Islamic world often have this misperception. It is due to their misunderstanding of the term *al-hakimiyya al-Islamiyya*. He emphasizes that this term does not mean the rule of God. Rather, it means rule in accordance with God's law. This law constrains the ruler as well as the subject. Ibid., 61–62.

less emphasis on individual rights than one finds in the West. The individual is not at the center of the political and legal universe. Rather, the focus is on building a pious community. In pursuit of this goal, the state assumes an invasive role in the lives of its citizens. The purpose of the institutions of constitutionalism is to enhance and refine this invasive role, rather than to limit it.

The Persistent Vagueness of Islamic Constitutionalism

In addition to these important conceptual differences with classical liberalism, the theorists discussed above are less precise than their liberal counterparts regarding the specific institutions they hope to create. For example, they answer the question "who is sovereign in an Islamic state" by proposing that God is sovereign, but that authority (and thus some lawmaking power) resides with the *umma* and its representatives.[232] This approach provides a clear doctrinal foundation for man-made law. However, it does not specify who holds the power to determine which areas are subject to man-made legislation. Similarly, they accept that laws should be written by an elected Parliament. But, they are unclear on the specific procedures for electing MPs, how long these MPs serve, and the extent of their power. The theorists also do not spell out the institutional relationships that create an effective balance of power among the branches of government. In addition, they frequently write that laws should serve "the best interests of the community." However, they provide no criteria or procedures for determining how the community's interests should be ascertained. Furthermore, they write that the ruler is accountable to the people and that an unjust ruler should be dismissed, without specifying how this accountability occurs or the procedures for removing a ruler.[233]

Several of the theorists acknowledge that their work is unclear regarding these details of governance. They consider this vagueness unavoidable and argue that the institutional characteristics of Islamic governance will vary depending on the specific features of each Islamic polity. Al-Qaradawi's view is typical. He writes that Islam provides the essential principles of

---

[232] Abu al-Majd uses a slightly different formulation. He makes a distinction between the source of legislation (which is divine) and the political authority to interpret and apply this legislation (which is human and fallible). Abu al-Majd, "Taqdim," 11–12.

[233] Al-Qaradawi writes that if a ruler acts improperly, the "people who loose and bind" should meet, discuss the matter, and issue their opinion. The ruler should then heed their opinion. He provides no further detail on who convenes the "people who loose and bind," how their deliberations unfold, or how their opinion is enforced if the ruler refuses to comply. Al-Qaradawi, *Min Fiqh al-Dawla*, 66.

governance, but it leaves the details of how it will work "to the *ijtihad* of Muslims . . . to be worked out according to time and place, and determined by the conditions of mankind at that moment."[234] Al-'Awwa agrees: "The Prophet left the matter of choosing the ruler and determining the system of government to Muslims to decide according to their interests and the requirements of time, place, and circumstance . . . nothing decreed is binding on them, except the general rules of Islamic law with regard to consultation, justice, equality, and the high moral values that the Prophet exhibited during the Madinan period."[235]

In essence, one cannot gain a clear understanding of contemporary Islamic constitutionalism by simply reading the works of theorists. One must examine how these ideas are given substance by Islamic political actors in a specific context.

The Muslim Brotherhood's younger generation of leaders began this process in an ad hoc and tentative fashion in the mid-1990s. Their pamphlets on Copts and women asserted specific rights for each of these groups. More importantly, their pamphlet on political pluralism delineated several specific institutions—a Parliament, an independent judiciary, and a more rigorous and transparent electoral procedure—that began to flesh out the institutional details of Islamic constitutionalism in an Egyptian setting.

In the mid-1990s, the Muslim Brotherhood became the de facto advocate of Islamic constitutionalism. This was not the result of the Brotherhood's leadership formally adopting a comprehensive program based on Islamic constitutionalism. Nor was it a natural outgrowth of the Brotherhood's earlier ideology and doctrine, which had been scrupulously vague regarding the political order that it hoped to create. Rather, the Brotherhood came to advocate Islamic constitutionalism after a series of incremental steps by political entrepreneurs who sought to maximize the organization's influence within the political constraints of the mid-1990s. The theorists discussed above provided a rich reservoir of ideas and doctrine to support a liberal conception of Islamic political order. The Brotherhood's younger generation of leaders tapped this resource to lend intellectual weight and doctrinal credibility to their plans for moderate political reform. By basing their political posture on the ideas of Egypt's most prominent moderate Islamic thinkers, the MB's reformers could demonstrate that their moderation was tied to a long and respected tradition in Islamic thought and was not simply an opportunistic political maneuver. The fact that they borrowed ideas from a former minister (Abu al-Majd) and a

[234] Ibid., 137.
[235] Al-'Awwa, *Fi al-Nitham al-Siyasi*, 67. For a similar view, see Abu al-Majd, "Taqdim," 10.

respected judge (al-Bishri) lent even greater credibility to their claim that they were committed to pursuing peaceful change in cooperation with leaders of the existing order.

This process was cut short by the regime's imprisonment of the most dynamic younger leaders in the mid-1990s (particularly 'Isam al-'Iryan, 'Abd al-Mon'am Abu al-Fatuh, and Mukhtar Nuh). With the release of these younger activists in the early 2000s, the effort to give institutional specificity to Islamic constitutionalism resumed. The younger leaders returned to their previous posts in the MB almost without skipping a beat. They also enjoyed the enhanced stature of having endured substantial prison terms on behalf of the Brotherhood's cause. As we shall see in the next chapter, this younger generation of MB leaders began to spell out the institutional details of Islamic constitutionalism with unprecedented clarity during the 2005 parliamentary campaign.

CHAPTER FOUR

The Decline of Statism and the Convergence of Political Alternatives

As THE PRECEDING two chapters suggest, Egypt's rich intellectual history has produced both liberal and Islamic conceptions of constitutionalism. However, they were on the periphery of political life for much of the 1960s, 1970s, and 1980s. Throughout this period, the prevailing ideology was a sweeping conception of statism that created a vast and pervasive state apparatus. A series of economic crises in the late 1980s and early 1990s weakened this statist order. Its decline created an opportunity for liberal constitutionalism and Islamic constitutionalism to broaden their public appeal and expand their influence over political and legal debates. As these debates unfolded, these alternatives began to converge around advocacy of constraints on state power, improvements in the rule of law, and protection of basic civil and political rights.

EGYPT'S STATIST TRADITION

When the Free Officers assumed power in 1952, their political goals were unclear. Nasser initially indicated that he sought to "cleanse" the party system and then return the country to a democratic path.[1] He also hinted that the regime might have an Islamic character, and that Islamic organizations (including the Muslim Brotherhood) would play an important role.[2] However, as the Free Officers settled into power, they became less willing to share authority with other groups or individuals. This tendency toward concentrating power may have been part of Nasser's character from the start: military officers often dislike the inefficiency and squabbling of open political debate. Nasser seemed particularly concerned that open debate would allow the leaders of the *ancien régime* to organize more effectively and frustrate his plans for social and economic reform.[3] Or, the autocratic

---

[1] Beattie estimates that of the 90 individuals at the core of the Free Officers in 1952, 60 supported some form of reformed democratic order. He bases this estimate on extensive interviewing of the surviving Free Officers in the 1980s. Beattie, *Egypt during the Nasser Years*, 44, 68. Also, Gordon, *Nasser's Blessed Movement*, 58–59.

[2] Gordon, *Nasser's Blessed Movement*, 100–101.

[3] Beattie, *Egypt during the Nasser Years*, 77–79.

direction of the regime may have been a response to the practical experiences of the Free Officers during their first decade in power. One of their central goals was to confront the threats posed by Britain and Israel. Indeed, preparing the country for an imminent war with Israel became a pillar of the regime's ideology. Some Free Officers argued that open democratic debate would aggravate the country's internal divisions and slow its preparations for battle. In this view, autocracy would help to preserve national unity on the eve of war.[4] The democratic cause was further weakened by a hasty arms deal with Czechoslovakia in 1955, which moved Egypt into the Soviet camp at the height of the Cold War. This step made it even more difficult for any members of the regime to support democratic reforms that were associated with the West.[5] A war with France and Britain in 1956 continued this trajectory. It was awkward—to say the least—for democrats to promote a Western conception of political reform at a time when two major Western powers had just attempted to re-occupy Egypt. The country's movement toward autocracy was further reinforced by an ill-fated experiment in political unity with Syria (the United Arab Republic) that came to an abrupt end in 1961. Nasser attributed the failure of this effort to middle-class merchants in Damascus who plotted against his plans to lead the country. He assumed that the Egyptian middle class harbored the same hostility and moved quickly to squash them through widespread nationalizations in 1961. These nationalizations dramatically weakened the middle-class merchants and professionals who were the natural supporters of a more open political order.

Regardless of the motivation, Nasser chose to create a highly centralized statist regime that controlled the economy, polity, and society. Rival political parties were outlawed. All political participation was channeled through a single mass party controlled by the government.[6] Independent associations for workers and professionals were also prohibited. They were replaced with a vast corporatist network of state-controlled unions and professional associations.[7] The state also took control of radio, television, and newspapers.

[4] For a clear statement of this view, see Nasser's speech before the Liberation Rally, October 17, 1954. Reprinted in Jamal 'Abd al-Nasser, *Awraq 'Abd al-Nasser* (Cairo: Maktabat Madbuli, 1988), 42–48.
[5] This movement leftward in foreign policy was reinforced by Nasser's attendance at the Non-Aligned Conference in Bandung in 1955, when he assumed the mantle of leader of the Arab world and co-leader of the Third World's struggle against imperialism.
[6] The party was initially called the Liberation Rally, which was formed in 1953. It was succeeded by the National Union, then by the Arab Socialist Union.
[7] For a valuable analysis of this corporatist order, see Bianchi, *Unruly Corporatism.*

Three institutions were particularly important for maintaining and extending the state's control over society: the public sector, the subsidy system, and the bureaucracy.

Public sector. With the sweeping nationalization of private firms in the early 1960s, the regime brought virtually all of the country's productive enterprises under state control. The public sector became the driving force of the economy. It served three fundamental purposes. It enabled the state to seize the commanding heights of the economy and direct investment toward those economic enterprises that state officials preferred and that they could control. It also produced a large volume of goods at affordable, state-controlled prices. Although the quality of these goods was often poor, they nonetheless enabled many Egyptians to enjoy a higher standard of living. Finally, the public sector provided employment for many thousands of Egyptians. It became the employer of last resort for much of the burgeoning urban population. As a consequence, it played a key role in maintaining political and social stability.[8] The rate of growth of the public sector under Nasser is striking. By 1965, investment by the public sector made up 95 percent of gross domestic fixed investment.[9] This figure remained above 75 percent well into the 1980s.[10] The percentage of GDP originating in the public sector increased from roughly 13 percent in 1952 to about 40 percent by the early 1970s.[11] Public-sector employment rose from 450,000 in 1960 to 780,000 in 1970.[12]

Subsidies. One of the cornerstones of the Free Officers' revolution was their pledge to improve social justice and reduce inequality. At the heart of this effort was an extensive system of subsidies designed to ensure that Egyptians enjoyed a decent standard of living. The state provided food, electricity, gasoline, public transportation, education, medical care, and a host of other services either free or at heavily subsidized prices. As international prices for key commodities such as wheat rose, subsidies consumed an ever greater piece of the government budget. In 1975, subsidies cost the government 622 million LE. By 1990, they cost 4.6 billion LE.[13] Over

[8] Waterbury, *The Egypt of Nasser and Sadat*, 66–82.

[9] Khalid Ikram, *The Egyptian Economy, 1952–2000: Performance, Policies, and Issues* (New York: Routledge, 2006), 92.

[10] Ibid.

[11] Ibid., 155.

[12] Nader Fergany, "A Characterization of the Employment Problem in Egypt," in *Employment and Structural Adjustment: Egypt in the 1990s*, ed. Heba Handoussa and Gillian Potter (Cairo: American University in Cairo Press, 1991), 38. Waterbury reports that public-sector employment in 1970 may have been as high as 965,000. Waterbury, *The Egypt of Nasser and Sadat*, 243. See also Nazih N. Ayubi, *The State and Public Policies in Egypt since Sadat* (Reading, U.K.: Ithaca Press, 1991), 94.

[13] Ikram, *The Egyptian Economy*, 160.

the period 1965 to 1990, subsidies absorbed 18 percent of total government expenditure.[14] In certain years, the figure could be much higher. For example, from 1975 to 1981, subsidies consumed 22 percent of total government expenditure.[15]

Bureaucracy. Nasserist ideology stressed that the state embodied the will and aspirations of the people. The knowledge and expertise of government officials—combined with their selfless commitment to the public good—enabled public agencies to make the best choices for guiding national development.[16] The state not only made all key decisions for the country. It also implemented these decisions and monitored their effectiveness. The regime built a vast bureaucracy to carry out these many complex tasks. In addition to performing these practical functions, the bureaucracy also became a key source of employment. Indeed, as its efficiency in performing its core tasks steadily declined, the bureaucracy's primary contribution lay in buttressing social and political stability by providing large numbers of secure jobs. At the time of the coup in 1952, about 350,000 persons were employed in the civilian public bureaucracy.[17] By 1970, the figure was 1.2 million.[18] From 1962 to 1972, the bureaucracy grew at a rate of 7.5 percent per year, well in excess of the 2.2 percent annual growth rate in the national work force.[19] The number of government agencies and ministries doubled from fifteen to thirty between 1952 and 1970.[20] The number of "public organizations"—separate administrative structures that report directly to the cabinet—grew from 1 to 46.[21]

These three institutions were essential to the Nasser regime. They allowed the government to control a citizen's employment opportunities, the salary he would earn, the consumer goods that he could purchase, the price he paid for these goods, and most of the activities that he could engage in. They enabled the state to exercise decisive influence over both the standard of living and the quality of life that most citizens enjoyed. The state's dominance of the economy also gave it the resources needed to develop a large and effective intelligence service that further extended its control over society.[22]

[14] Ibid., 171.
[15] Ibid., 172.
[16] For a valuable analysis of this bureaucratic ethos, see Nazih Ayubi, *Bureaucracy and Politics in Contemporary Egypt* (London: Ithaca Press, 1980), 157–87.
[17] Ibid., 243.
[18] Ibid., 243.
[19] Waterbury, *The Egypt of Nasser and Sadat*, 242. Ayubi estimates that the total Egyptian labor force grew by approximately 20 percent from 1962 to 1970. During this same period, posts in the bureaucracy grew by 70 percent. Ayubi, *The State and Public Policies*, 94.
[20] Waterbury, *The Egypt of Nasser and Sadat*, 243.
[21] Ayubi, *The State and Public Policies*, 108.
[22] Waterbury, *The Egypt of Nasser and Sadat*, 338–42.

From its earliest days, this statist order contained several fundamental contradictions. The most basic lay in the regime's effort to create a comprehensive welfare state that provided good jobs and extensive subsidies while, simultaneously, trying to achieve rapid economic growth. There simply was not sufficient money available to achieve both goals. The political stability of the regime came to rely upon sustaining the key features of the welfare state. However, maintaining these services drained capital that was essential for investment and economic development. At the same time, the country's population increased steadily by about 2.8 percent per year. More Egyptians meant even greater public demand for the generous welfare services provided by the regime.

As the population expanded, and as economic growth remained modest at best, the viability of the statist system came into question. Its underlying weaknesses were made even more apparent after the 1967 war and the ensuing reconstruction of the military, which diverted vast amounts of capital from productive economic investment. Furthermore, the country's foreign policy placed it at odds with the West. This stand reduced its access to concessionary loans as well as modern technology.

Anwar Sadat inherited these problems when he came to power in 1970. They were aggravated by the expense of another war with Israel in 1973 and a sharp increase in the cost of imported food in 1974. However, in Sadat's view, the underlying challenges facing the economy were not structural. He believed the country merely faced a short-term fiscal shortfall that could be solved by attracting capital from the wealthy countries of the Gulf as well as from Egyptian expatriates. In an effort to tap these sources of capital, Sadat issued the October White paper in 1974. The paper announced a series of reforms designed to make Egypt more attractive to foreign investment, particularly from the petro states of the Gulf. This effort to open Egypt to foreign investment—the *infitah*—was not a sweeping restructuring of the economy. Instead, as Ikram concludes, it was "principally an opportunistic tactic intended to facilitate the inflow of Arab funds."[23] In the decade following the *infitah*, the Egyptian economy performed surprisingly well. GDP growth averaged 9 percent per year in real terms. Real per capita income increased an average of 6 percent per year. The investment rate doubled from 13.7 percent of GDP in 1973 to 28.7 percent in 1985.[24] However, most economists do not attribute this performance to economic changes brought about by the *infitah*. Rather, the country enjoyed a fortuitous inflow of resources from several sources. Oil production increased sharply after the end of the 1973 war as Egypt regained control over oil fields in the Sinai Peninsula and the Gulf of Suez.

[23] Ikram, *The Egyptian Economy*, 19.
[24] Ibid., 24.

The end of the 1973 war also allowed Egypt to reopen the Suez Canal and reap a sharp increase in earnings from Canal tolls. Rapid economic growth in the Gulf states following the rise in oil prices in 1973 created an enormous demand for Egyptian expatriate workers, who sent much of their salaries home and provided yet another source of foreign exchange. Tourism receipts also rose, as did foreign economic and military aid. This influx of funds alleviated the economic crisis that Sadat had inherited and eliminated the pressure for structural reform.[25] Indeed, each of the three pillars of regime control grew during the Sadat years. Public-sector employment rose from 780,000 in 1970 to 1.1 million in 1980.[26] The percentage of GDP originating in the public sector rose from 40 percent in 1973 to 50 percent in 1981.[27] Total subsidies rose from less than 2 percent of GDP in 1971 to 13 percent in 1980.[28] The size of the bureaucracy grew from 1.2 million employees in 1970 to 1.9 million in 1978.[29]

The flow of external rents began to ebb in the mid-1980s, primarily due to a drop in oil prices that started in 1983. Oil revenues fell from $2.7 billion in 1983–84 to $900 million in 1986–87, a decline of 66 percent. This decline alone reduced Egypt's import capacity by 12 percent—a serious consideration when the country imported most of its food.[30] Falling oil prices also led to a recession in the Gulf, which reduced opportunities for overseas employment for Egyptians. The number of Egyptians working in the Gulf fell from roughly 3 million in the early 1980s to less than 1 million in 1987. In addition to a decline in remittance income, these lost jobs meant that many Egyptians in the Gulf returned home and joined the ranks of the unemployed.[31] Tourism revenue—the country's third largest source of foreign exchange—was also down due to a series of terrorist incidents in the region. The government attempted to cope with this financial crisis through a dramatic increase in foreign borrowing.[32] Interest

---

[25] Ibid., 25–26.

[26] Fergany, "A Characterization of the Employment Problem in Egypt," 38. Despite the increase in private-sector investment resulting from the *infitah*, the public sector's share of total investment remained high throughout the Sadat period. At the start of Sadat's rule in 1970, public investment as a percentage of Gross Domestic Fixed Investment stood at 90 percent. By 1980, it had only fallen to 75 percent. Ikram, *The Egyptian Economy*, 92.

[27] Ibid., 155.

[28] The figure for 1971 is taken from ibid., 158. The figure for 1980 is taken from Mourad M. Wahba, *The Role of the State in the Egyptian Economy, 1945–1981* (Reading: Ithaca Press, 1994), 149. From 1974 to 1980, subsidies as a percentage of total government expenditure rose from 43.2 percent to 58.7 percent. Ibid.

[29] Ayubi, *Bureaucracy and Politics*, 243; Ayubi, *The State and Public Policies*, 94.

[30] Ikram, *The Egyptian Economy*, 55.

[31] Galal Amin, *Egypt's Economic Predicament: A Study in the Interaction of External Pressure, Political Folly, and Social Tension in Egypt, 1960–1990* (Leiden: E. J. Brill, 1995), 46–52.

[32] Ibid., 17–18. Also, David Butter, "Debt and Egypt's Financial Policies," in *Egypt Under Mubarak*, ed. Charles Tripp and Roger Owen (London: Routledge, 1989), 123–29.

payments on external debt tripled between 1982 and 1987.[33] Total debt outstanding exceeded $40 billion by June 1987, equivalent to 112 percent of GDP. This last figure is calculated using the official exchange rate. If calculated using the free market rate, Egypt's debts were equivalent to 184 percent of GDP, which made it the most heavily indebted major debtor country in the world.[34] Egypt became caught in a classic debt trap, taking on new loans to acquire the resources needed to service the existing debt. By 1987, new loans were not sufficient to cover the payments falling due. Egypt dealt with this immediate crisis by rescheduling some of its outstanding private debt through the Paris Club in May 1987. However, the bulk of the debt remained. Egypt continued to spend roughly 36 percent of its foreign-exchange receipts on servicing it. This figure was well beyond the ratio of 25 percent at which the World Bank becomes concerned about a country's creditworthiness.[35]

This precarious economic situation tipped into crisis in 1990. The economy had grown "little, if at all, in the previous two years";[36] unemployment was estimated at 20 percent; inflation was 20 percent annually; and external debt had continued to grow and now represented 115 percent of GDP.[37] GDP per capita had fallen from $750 in 1985–86 to $640 in 1989–90.[38] Mubarak openly acknowledged the need for fundamental reform, particularly in the public sector. In his May Day speech for 1990, he noted that the public-sector wage bill had grown from 1.9 billion Egyptian pounds in 1981–82 to an estimated 13 billion LE in 1990—a sum that consumed one-third of all state revenues.[39]

The Gulf War, which began with Iraq's invasion of Kuwait in August 1990, only worsened this situation. Over 400,000 Egyptian workers returned from jobs in Iraq and Kuwait, dramatically reducing foreign remittances and aggravating unemployment in Egypt.[40] Tourism receipts fell sharply due to the war, as did Suez Canal revenues.

However, Egypt's willingness to assume a leadership role in opposing the Iraqi invasion produced a bonanza of economic rewards. The United States forgave $6.7 billion in military debt, and the Gulf countries wrote

[33] Ikram, *The Egyptian Economy*, 56.
[34] Ibid.
[35] Ibid., 58.
[36] *Foreign Economic Trends and their Implications for the United States: Report for the Arab Republic of Egypt, June 1990* (Cairo: United States Embassy, June 1990).
[37] *Economist Intelligence Unit, Egypt: Country Report*, 1990, number 2, 8–11.
[38] Hans Lofgren, "Economic Policy in Egypt: A Breakdown in Reform Resistance?" *International Journal of Middle East Studies* 25 (1993): 410.
[39] *Al-Ahram*, May 2, 1990.
[40] According to World Bank statistics, Egypt received $3.5 billion in income from remittances in 1988–89. As much as 30 percent of income in Egypt's rural areas came from remittances. *World Development Indicators*, 2007

off another $6.6 billion in loans. The Paris Club of private creditors agreed to write off another $10 billion in debt, and to reschedule and cut interest rates on the remaining $10 billion that it administered.[41] In total, roughly 50 percent of Egypt's foreign debt was forgiven in the years following the Gulf War. At the same time, the Gulf, Europe, the United States, Japan, South Korea, the World Bank, and the International Monetary Fund (IMF) combined to provide a dramatic increase in economic aid.[42] The country received $7 billion in emergency assistance during the Gulf War, in order to ease the economic strains of the conflict. It received another $8 billion after the war.[43]

Much of this debt forgiveness and aid was conditioned on significant economic reforms. The Paris Club, in particular, insisted that Egypt comply with the terms of an IMF restructuring program. Egypt entered into intensive negotiations with the IMF, and reached an agreement in May 1991. This agreement aimed to transform Egypt into a competitive market economy that was fully integrated into the global economic system. It had three core components: an ambitious program to reduce the government's chronic budget deficits by cutting government services; liberalization of interest rates and the exchange rate, which meant that the government could no longer manipulate these rates to maintain political and social stability;[44] and a substantial privatization program that concentrated on public firms involved in services and industrial production.

These commitments led to important structural changes. The government cut public investment from 11.5 percent of GDP in 1992 to 5.4 percent in 1997.[45] It also cut subsidies from 5.2 percent of GDP in 1992 to 1.6 percent in 1997. This meant drastically reducing the number of items subsidized—from eighteen to four (bread, wheat flour, sugar, and cooking oil).[46] The government also embarked on an extensive privatiza-

---

[41] Lofgren, "Economic Policy in Egypt," 411.

[42] The United States reportedly intervened at the IMF to secure balance-of-payments assistance for Egypt with less rigid conditionality than usual. Tony Walker, "Baker in Pledge on Egypt Aid," *Financial Times*, March 12, 1991.

[43] For a thorough discussion of these aid and debt relief programs, see *Foreign Economic Trends and their Implications for the United States: Report for the Arab Republic of Egypt, June 1991* (Cairo: United States Embassy, June 1991).

[44] After a series of reforms, the exchange rate was pegged to the U.S. dollar and effectively devalued by 25 percent. The government also allowed an increase in interest rates to over 20 percent in order to make them positive in real terms. Ikram, *The Egyptian Economy*, 64.

[45] Ibid., 67.

[46] Ibid. Despite this reduction in the number of items subsidized, the total subsidy bill began to rise in 2002. A decline in the value of the pound raised the cost of imported wheat. As a consequence, the total cost of subsidies reached 18 billion LE in 2004—14 percent of total government expenditure and 2.2 percent of GDP. Omneia Helmy, *The Efficiency and Equity of Subsidy Policy in Egypt* (Cairo: The Egyptian Center for Economic Studies, 2005).

tion program. As Ikram observes, "privatization on the scale proposed was not simply a financial exercise, but rather the abandonment of a model of development that had shaped Egyptian society for a generation."[47] In the early 1990s, public enterprises produced around 10 percent of GDP and employed about 6 percent of the labor force. They operated in virtually every sector of the economy from industrial raw materials (iron, steel, cement, phosphates) to consumer goods (refrigerators, soap, beer) to services (hotels, movies). They also dominated the banking and insurance sectors. In July 1991, the government began to privatize 314 of these public-sector enterprises. By June 2000, it had sold a controlling interest in 118 enterprises with a sale value of about 12.3 billion LE. It had sold a minority interest in another sixteen companies, with a sale value of about 1.8 billion LE. In 1998, the IMF concluded that Egypt's program of privatization was the fourth most successful in the world.[48]

By the mid-1990s, the implementation of the structural adjustment program had produced dramatic improvements in Egypt's macroeconomic situation. The contrast between 1990 and 1996 could not be sharper: GDP growth went from negative 2 percent to positive 5 percent; inflation fell from over 20 percent to 7 percent; the government budget deficit fell from 20 percent of GDP to 2 percent; savings rose from 8 percent of GDP to 19 percent; the current account deficit disappeared; and the country's foreign-exchange reserves rose from $3 billion to $17 billion. New laws governing labor relations, property rights, formation of companies, capital markets, and banking began to shift Egypt toward a more competitive and market-oriented economy. Egypt joined the World Trade Organization and announced plans to participate in the Euro-Mediterranean free-trade zone.

In essence, the Nasserist system was based on an unsustainable mix of a generous welfare state, a large and inefficient public sector, low domestic savings rates, and a high degree of insulation from the global economy. The regime was able to limp along largely by relying on external rents of various types: Suez Canal tolls, oil revenues, expatriates' earnings, and foreign aid. These windfalls delayed the day of reckoning, but they could not postpone it indefinitely. The system reached the point of collapse in the early 1990s. Regime elites concluded that the only way to retain power and preserve social stability was to discard the core economic features of the statist order. As noted above, this included taking significant steps

---

[47] Ikram, *The Egyptian Economy*, 78.

[48] The metric for making this assessment was privatization receipts per year as a share of GDP. Egypt was surpassed only by Hungary, Malaysia, and the Czech Republic. Howard Handy, *Egypt: Beyond Stabilization: Toward a Dynamic Market Economy* (Washington, DC: International Monetary Fund, 1998), 52.

toward dismantling the public sector and the subsidy system.[49] By taking these steps, the government effectively abandoned the Nasserist doctrine of state-guided economic development that included state provision of education and health care as well as subsidized food, transportation, clothing, and energy.[50] In an important sense, the regime became hollow. It had effectively renounced the ideology on which it was based and the principles that gave it legitimacy. This development did not, in itself, constitute an immediate threat to regime stability. Indeed, the improved economic performance resulting from the reforms of the 1990s probably enhanced the regime's strength. However, by abandoning any pretense of upholding the basic premises of statism, the regime created an opportunity for alternative conceptions of the polity to develop and gain broader support. The two alternatives discussed earlier—liberal constitutionalism and Islamic constitutionalism—moved into this vacuum. They were advocated by, respectively, the Judges' Club and the Muslim Brotherhood.

ADVOCATING LIBERAL CONSTITUTIONALISM: THE JUDGES' CLUB AND EGYPTIAN POLITICS

As the analysis in chapter 2 shows, the judiciary has developed a robust and distinctive conception of liberal constitutionalism through the jurisprudence of the Supreme Constitutional Court, the administrative courts, and the ordinary courts. However, many judges believe that their obligation to promote liberal principles is not limited to the courtroom. They argue that judges also have a duty to participate directly in legal and political debates. Advocates of this view use the Judges' Club (*Nadi al-Quda*) as a forum for articulating their agenda for liberal reform. They also use the Club to engage in negotiations with the regime and to shape the development of law.[51]

---

[49] The regime did not attempt to shrink the bureaucracy, which grew to over 5 million workers by 2000. As its size grew, its efficiency steadily declined to the point where it failed to implement most government policies effectively or consistently. Ikram, *The Egyptian Economy*, 292–98.

[50] For further discussion of the changing character of the state in Egypt and the Middle East, see Hakimian and Moshaver, eds., *The State and Global Change*; also, Heba Handoussa and Noha El-Mikawy, "Conclusion: Redefining the Role of the State," in *Institutional Reform and Economic Development in Egypt*, ed. Heba Handoussa and Noha El-Mikawy (Cairo: American University in Cairo Press, 2002), 165–71.

[51] The Judges' Club is not formally registered as a professional association (*niqaba*). The judges have avoided this step because it would place the Club under the jurisdiction of the Ministry of Social Affairs, which would limit its independence. However, the Club functions as a de facto representative of the judiciary in its interaction with the regime. It also manages several social services normally associated with professional syndicates, such as medical care and housing assistance.

The Judges' Club was founded in 1939 primarily as a social club. It provided a setting in which members of the very insular judicial profession could meet and exchange views. It began to evolve into a more political organization when the Nasser regime adopted a conception of law and governance at odds with the liberal traditions of the judiciary. Nasser and his supporters referred to this new approach as "socialist legality." In this view, the purpose of law was to advance the goals of the state and aid its efforts to transform society. The purpose of courts was to interpret and apply the law using a "revolutionary spirit," and to facilitate the regime's effort to dismantle laws from the *ancien regime* that blocked Nasser's revolutionary ambitions. The judiciary never accepted this conception of law.[52] It issued numerous rulings that frustrated the regime's reform agenda, as well as public statements (through the Judges' Club) that criticized the regime's disregard for law and the courts.[53] These tensions came to a head in August 1969, when the regime adopted several laws designed to end the judiciary's independence. Law 84/1969 dissolved the board of the Judges' Club and declared that its officers would be appointed by the president. Law 82/1969 altered the procedure for appointing and promoting judges and effectively gave the executive greater influence over these decisions through its control of a new agency, the Supreme Council of Judicial Bodies. Law 83/1969 held that, since the procedure for appointing judges had changed due to Law 82/1969, all current judges must be reappointed. During this process, over two hundred judges were not "reappointed" and were effectively dismissed. The victims included the entire board of the Judges' Club, the president and many members of the Court of Cassation, numerous lower court judges, and members of the public prosecutor's office. The judiciary quickly labeled these steps the "massacre of the judges" and immediately brought suit in the Court of Cassation to reverse them.[54]

With Nasser's death in 1970, Anwar Sadat ascended to power and sought to quickly differentiate his regime from Nasser's. In his first speech

[52] In essence, this was a disagreement over whether Egypt would develop the "rule of law" (in which the law is applied equally to ruler and ruled) or "rule by law" (in which law is an instrument of state power). For a valuable discussion of this distinction, see Geoffrey de Q. Walker, *The Rule of Law: Foundation of Constitutional Democracy* (Carlton, Victoria: Melbourne University Press, 1988).

[53] For further detail on the tension between the judiciary and the regime in the 1960s, see: Brown, *The Rule of Law in the Arab World*, 84–92; Muhammad Kamil 'Ubayd, *Istiqlal al-Qada'* (Cairo: Maktabat Rijal al-Qada', 1991); 'Abd Allah Imam, *Mathbahat al-Qada'* (Cairo: Madbuli, 1976); Mumtaz Nasaar, *Ma'arakat al-'Adala fi Misr* (Cairo: Dar al-Sharuq, 1974).

[54] The Club's legal efforts to challenge the laws were led by Yahia al-Rif'ai. He recounts the legal battle in great detail, and reprints many of the relevant documents, in Yahia al-Rifa'i, *Sha'un Rijal al-Qada'* (Cairo: Maktabat Rijal al-Qada', 1990–91), 3–136.

to Parliament as president, he stated that his policies would be based on the ideals of the relatively liberal March 30 declaration of 1968.[55] He released political prisoners, reinstated civil servants dismissed by Nasser, and returned property sequestered for political reasons.[56] He also expressed a strong interest in the rule of law. In a speech to the Judges' Club on January 12, 1971, he said, "I shall discuss with the Minister of Justice all problems that interest you, as judges, and facilitate your work with a view toward creating a legal framework for the Revolution that ensures the supremacy of law . . . the judiciary is sacrosanct, surrounded by an aura of sanctity and respect that is an asset to the entire people."[57]

Sadat further pledged to reinstate the judges dismissed during the "massacre of the judges." They were reappointed in 1973.[58] The Judges' Club regained its autonomy in 1975, and was again allowed to elect its governing board. Beginning in 1975, it held a series of seminars on international human rights law. It also issued statements in 1977 and 1979 calling for greater respect for human rights, improved implementation of court decisions, and greater commitment by the regime to the rule of law.[59]

The Judges' Club adopted an aggressive stance on issues of judicial reform. Prior to Nasser's "massacre of the judges" in 1969, judicial appointments and promotions had been controlled by the Supreme Judicial Council (SJC)—a body made up entirely of senior judges. The massacre disbanded this body and replaced it with a new agency, the Supreme Council of Judicial Bodies, which was chaired by the president and included the minister of justice. This step gave the executive substantial influence over judicial appointments. The Judges' Club criticized the dissolution of the SJC throughout the 1970s, and initiated many long and detailed lawsuits to reverse this decree.[60] When the Ministry of Justice proposed a law that would restore only part of the SJC's authority, the Judges' Club issued a sharp and extensive criticism of its failure to restore full judicial control over appointments and judicial administration.[61] The

---

[55] *Al-Ahram*, November 20, 1970. Sadat argued that the March 30 declaration was the most appropriate guide for government for two reasons: it was the last integrated program that Nasser proposed; and, it had been approved by the people in a referendum.

[56] Waterbury, *The Egypt of Nasser and Sadat*, 352. Baker, *Sadat and After*, 58.

[57] "The President with the Men of the Judiciary," *al-Ahram*, January 13, 1971.

[58] President Sadat issued decree 43 in 1973 that reinstated the judges, effectively preempting a decision by the Court of Cassation. For the text of the decree, see Yahia al-Rif'ai, *Tashriat al-Sulta al-Qada'iyya* (Cairo: Maktabat Rijal al-Qada', 1991), 630–34.

[59] Yahia al-Rifa'i, *Sha'un Rijal al- Qada'*, 142–51.

[60] These efforts were led by Yahia al-Rif'ai. For a detailed discussion of these legal battles, including the text of the Judges' Club's legal petitions regarding the SJC and the SCJB, see al-Rif'ai, *Tashriat al-Sulta al-Qada'iyya*, 642–93.

[61] Ibid., 645–50.

Club's efforts finally came to fruition in 1984, when the regime adopted several amendments to the Judicial Authority law that reestablished the Supreme Judicial Council and restored most of its authority. The Supreme Council of Judicial Bodies continued to exist, largely because it is mentioned in the 1971 Constitution and could be disbanded only by changing the constitution. However, the 1984 amendments transferred its powers of appointment and administrative control to the SJC.[62]

The Judges' Club built on this success by formulating a broad agenda for reform of the laws governing the judiciary. It defined and promoted this agenda by organizing the first National Conference on Justice in 1986.[63] The conference was divided into working groups that addressed legislation, civil procedures, criminal procedures, judicial affairs, and administrative support for the judiciary. Its concluding recommendations placed significant emphasis on judicial structure and procedure.[64] They focus on four themes:

Unification of the court system: The Judges' Club was a long-standing critic of the proliferation of specialized courts that trespass on important areas of jurisdiction normally held by the ordinary courts. The recommendations of the conference criticize these courts on three grounds: they are often staffed by nonjudicial personnel with little legal training; they often lack the procedural guarantees regarding evidence and appeals that are the norm in ordinary courts; and they violate the constitutional provision that all citizens are entitled to a trial before their "natural judge," which the conference members interpreted to mean the ordinary judiciary. The Club specifically called for disbanding the Court of Values, the State Security Courts, the Court of Sequestration, and the Socialist Public Prosecutor. It also criticized the clause of the military courts' law that allows the transfer of civilian cases to military tribunals.

Enhancement of judicial independence: The report notes that the judiciary still had not achieved complete independence. It lacked full control over its budget, the Ministry of Justice retained the authority to investigate and penalize judges, and the public prosecutor was still appointed by the executive and remained subject to political pressure. These measures needed to be addressed quickly and decisively in order to "preserve and deepen the independence of the judiciary."[65]

Increased administrative efficiency and professionalism of courts: The final statement notes that the work of the judiciary was hampered by lack of

---

[62] Law 35/1984 and law 136/1984.

[63] The conference occurred April 20–24, 1986.

[64] *Mu'tamar al-'Adala al-Awal 1986: Al-Watha'iq al-Asasiyya* (Cairo: Nadi al-Quda, 1986), 27–54. The following discussion is taken from these documents. Also see Brown, *The Rule of Law in the Arab World*, 117–18.

[65] Ibid., 47.

office space, inadequate professional resources (such as libraries and computers), and a shortage of administrative support staff. In order to address these problems, it calls for more resources and improved training for both judges and their staff.[66]

Greater respect for law and the courts by the regime: The Club's statement rose to particular eloquence on this point. It posits that the "legitimacy of all regimes lies in their respect for law." Law "springs from the people" and reflects their collective values and aspirations. It also organizes the state and ensures that it serves the needs and interests of the people. A regime that undermines the law and the judiciary is "weakening the very foundations of society." The statement particularly criticizes the regime's continued reliance on the emergency law, which "undermines the public's trust in the law and in the political system."[67]

Interestingly, the report avoids any detailed statement on civil or political rights. It makes a general reference to the importance of human rights for "social peace and national unity."[68] However, the substantive question of which specific rights should be protected by law receives little attention. There is no effort to assert that the protection of individual rights is inherently desirable. The Judges' Club's approach to rights is a faithful reflection of the judicial philosophy discussed in chapter 2. In this view, the well-being of the nation and the community is paramount. Individual rights are protected to the extent that they contribute to this goal.

The Judges' Club developed these recommendations into a specific set of legal proposals in 1991, when it put forward a draft law to restructure the judiciary.[69] The law codified each of the main conclusions of the Conference on Justice. Its central objective was to enhance the judiciary's independence by reducing the role of the Ministry of Justice in judicial affairs. It called for complete budgetary autonomy for the judiciary. It also proposed that the Supreme Judicial Council (SJC) hold full authority over all judicial appointments, promotions, and administration. Responsibility for training and disciplining of judges should also be transferred to the SJC. Control over judges' pensions and health benefits should be shifted to a new entity supervised by the SJC, not by the Ministry of Justice. Furthermore, judges should no longer be delegated to serve as advisors to ministries within the executive branch (this practice was widely seen as compromising judicial independence). Judges should still be permitted to work on temporary assignment overseas, particularly in the Gulf states. How-

---

[66] Ibid., 52–53.

[67] Ibid., 13–19, 27–31.

[68] Ibid., 28.

[69] The text of the proposed law is printed in al-Rif'ai, *Tashriat al-Sulta al-Qada'iyya*, 705–16.

ever, selection for these lucrative positions should be based on objective criteria and should be controlled by the SJC, not the Ministry of Justice. The draft law also called for making the SJC more responsive to the community of judges. The SJC is led by the president of the Court of Cassation, who is appointed by the president of the country. The law proposed that he be elected by his fellow judges.[70] The law also proposed that the Judges' Club be granted two seats on the SJC, and that these representatives be elected by the entire membership of the Club. The draft law received the formal endorsement of the entire membership of the Judges' Club in January 1991. The chairman of the Club, Yahia al-Rif'ai, then submitted it to the Ministry of Justice. Leading members of the Club called for adoption of the law in interviews and op-ed newspaper articles. Implementation of this draft law became the centerpiece of the judiciary's demands for legal reform. However, the government dragged its feet. More than eleven years passed before the Ministry of Justice formed an internal committee to begin studying it.

While the goal of enhancing judicial independence was widely shared within the Club, some judges were uncomfortable with the overt public lobbying adopted by al-Rif'ai and his supporters. The Club became divided between a group of activists (led by al-Rif'ai) and a more quiescent group that supported a less confrontational approach (led by Muqbil Shakir). This split has its roots in Egyptian judicial philosophy. As noted in chapter 2, this philosophy emphasizes the importance of preserving a strong and effective state, which is essential for maintaining public order and creating conditions that allow for the practice of personal liberty. However, judges disagree over the best judicial strategy for building this powerful state. The activist camp argues that it can be created only through the efforts of a vigilant and aggressive judiciary that constantly reins in the state and keeps it focused on serving the public interest. The more quiescent judges fear that this aggressive posture may damage the public interest by weakening the state and undermining its popular legitimacy.

In the debate surrounding the 1991 draft law, the activist camp argued that the executive had abused its power by interfering in the operations of the judiciary and compromising its independence. This could be reversed only through a vigorous defense of judicial autonomy. Members of the activist camp also argued that judges are enmeshed in a broader legal, political, and cultural order. In order for judicial independence to become well-rooted, its principles must be deeply grounded in all of the institutions of society and the values of every citizen. Thus, judges must actively

---

[70] The Court of Cassation has a general assembly, which consists of all the judges serving in that court. The proposed law called for allowing the general assembly to elect the president of the Court of Cassation.

seek to shape this broader institutional and cultural environment. The promotion of a new judicial law was part of this effort. The effort also included advocating other reforms that "enhance respect for the law and build a more just and law-abiding society."[71] It further entailed building the expectation among citizens that they are "entitled to look to law and the courts for justice."[72] The judges who promoted this view stressed that they were not involved in politics, in the sense that they were not endorsing specific political parties or candidates. However, they recognized that their approach required shaping the political environment in the country. One of the most prominent activists, Ahmad Makki, wrote that judges have a "duty to enforce the law and increase respect for the law" and to "draw attention to infringements of the law by any body or agency."[73] This inevitably led judges to take an interest in the broad direction of political change and the conduct of the state in order to "defend the interests of the nation and protect our constitution and laws."[74]

The more quiescent camp accepted the goal of strengthening judicial independence, but it rejected involvement in any activity that could be construed as political. Indeed, they argued that advocates of a prominent public role for judges were hypocrites: they called for judicial independence, but then adopted public positions that effectively entangled the judiciary in political debates. For the more quiescent judges, judicial independence required total disengagement from all public controversies. In this view, the cloistered character of the judiciary was essential to maintaining its objectivity, independence, and stature. This does not mean that the judiciary should refrain from defending its rights and prerogatives. However, it should pursue these goals through quiet consultation with the relevant branches of government, rather than public lobbying.[75]

Some supporters of this quiescent view also emphasized the importance of maintaining public order. Public order is the "foundation of social peace, the basis for prosperity, and essential for the true enjoyment of rights and freedoms."[76] In this view, the foundation of order is a strong and capable state that enjoys the respect of the people. Involving the

---

[71] "Kalimat Quda Misr fi Iftah al-Mu'tamar li-l Mustishar Yahia al-Rif'ai," reprinted in *Mu'tamar al-'Adala al-Awal 1986: Al-Watha'iq al-Asasiyya* (Cairo: Nadi al-Quda, 1986), 16.

[72] Ibid., 17.

[73] Ahmad Makki, "Kalimat al-Mustishar Ahmad Makki—al-Amin al-'Amma—fi al-Jalasa al-Khitamiyya li-l Mu'tamar," reprinted in *Mu'tamar al-'Adala al-Awal 1986: Al-Watha'iq al-Asasiyya* (Cairo: Nadi al-Quda, 1986), 23–24.

[74] Ibid., 25.

[75] See Muqbil Shakir, "The Role of Judges." *al-'Arabi*, January 22, 1992. Also see the interview with him in *Uktubir*, December 1, 1991. For a more recent statement of this view, see the interview with Shakir in *al-Misri al-Youm*, March 13, 2007.

[76] See Mustafa al-Rabi'a, "The Duty of the Judges." *al-'Arabi*, February 5, 1991.

Judges' Club in direct confrontations with public officials and agencies undermined the effectiveness and stature of the state. It also eroded the public's respect for the state and thereby made governance more difficult.[77] Advocates of this view are sometimes described as "pro-government." In some cases, this appellation may be appropriate, as on the rare occasions when some judges respond to government requests out of a sense of obedience to state authority.[78] However, this label can be misleading if it is applied to all judges who advocate a quiescent posture. In many cases, the judges who adopt this view are not the errand boys of state officials. Rather, they see themselves as acting in a responsible manner that upholds their obligation to preserve public order. These judges are conservative in the sense that they value the preservation of institutions and harbor deep reservations about the instability and uncertainty associated with mass-based politics, which may be unleashed by judicial appeals for mass support. This quiescent view gained momentum within the Judges' Club in the early 1990s.

The Judges' Club elections of 1992 pitted the activists (led by Yahia al-Rif'ai) against advocates of the quiescent view (led by Muqbil Shakir). Shakir and his followers won, and took control of the Judges' Club board. This group held power for the next nine years and, as a consequence, the Judges' Club discontinued its public advocacy of legal and political change. The Club shifted to quiet lobbying on bread-and-butter issues related to judicial autonomy. During his tenure in office, Muqbil Shakir managed to win a substantial increase in the flow of resources to the judiciary. Court facilities were remodeled and upgraded, salaries increased several fold, and judges enjoyed substantial annual bonuses.[79]

The pension scheme for judges was also overhauled. This was an issue that attracted particular attention during Shakir's tenure. The underlying concern was that the base salary of judges constituted only about one-third of their annual income. The remainder came from bonuses tied to the number of cases a judge heard, the quality of his work, and the additional duties and responsibilities that he performed. However, when a

---

[77] Ibid.

[78] For example, two judges initiated a lawsuit in 1990 to place the Judges' Club under the jurisdiction of the Ministry of Social Affairs. This was a clear effort to enhance the government's control over the judiciary. Another example occurred more recently. In April 2006, eight senior judges in the Courts of Appeal issued a public statement claiming that the leadership of the Judges' Club had damaged the reputation of the judiciary and should resign. The statement was widely interpreted as part of a government campaign to discredit the Judges' Club's leadership. See Mona al-Nahhas, "Nothing Will Stop Us," *al-Ahram Weekly*, April 6–12, 2006.

[79] These achievements are documented in the issues of the Judges' Club's magazine, *al-Quda*, from 1993 through 2000.

judge retired, his pension income was calculated using only his base salary. As a consequence, judges routinely saw a 60 percent drop in their income upon retirement. In order to cope with this problem, it became standard practice for retired judges to seek "advisory posts" in state agencies or public-sector firms. These positions would assure them of additional income with minimal work. However, this practice posed an obvious threat to judicial independence, as judges would be loath to issue rulings that might anger the government and threaten their appointment to lucrative posts after retirement. The Judges' Club under Shakir managed to win guarantees of larger pensions and better health benefits for retirees. It also expanded the SJC's power to control the allocation of these benefits, and reduced the Ministry of Justice's role in this process. Thus, the more quiescent camp within the Judges' Club achieved meaningful improvements in judicial independence, but it did so in a less confrontational manner than the camp led by activists such as al-Rif'ai.[80]

The strength of the more quiescent group of judges began to wane in 2000. This was due, in part, to the group's inability to win further salary and benefits increases from the government. There were also allegations that the Shakir leadership had focused too much attention on benefits for the most senior judges, while neglecting the needs of more junior judges who make up the bulk of the Club's membership.[81] These concerns were compounded by a dramatic change in the political role of the Club. This new role was the product of a landmark decision by the Supreme Constitutional Court regarding the judiciary's power to supervise elections and referenda. Article 88 of the 1971 Constitution specified that referenda and parliamentary elections must take place "under the supervision of members of a judicial body."[82] However, it did not indicate how this supervision should occur. Prior to 2000, the government argued that Egypt had only five thousand or so judges, and that this number was insufficient to monitor the more than fifty thousand voting sites spread across the country. As a consequence, the role of judges was limited to supervising the casting of ballots at a small percentage of polling booths. All other aspects of the election, including the actual counting of ballots and the announcement of results, were handled by the Ministry of Interior. The

[80] These issues were raised repeatedly in the journal of the Judges' Club, *al-Quda*, throughout the 1990s. For a summary of progress made on issues of salary, pensions, and health benefits, see *al-Quda*, January–June 1998, 10–14.

[81] These observations were made in personal interviews with two judges who participated in the 2001 Judges' Club election.

[82] This article was amended in 2007 to reduce the judiciary's role in supervising elections. It now specifies that elections are supervised by a "supreme commission" whose composition is defined by the legislature. According to the amendment, judges will play a role in supervising elections but they will not exercise control over the process.

SCC decision in July 2000 pronounced this system unconstitutional and called for full judicial supervision of all balloting sites as well as full judicial control over the counting of ballots. The regime responded with a law that spread balloting across several days, which allowed judges to move around the country in order to supervise every polling place. It also empowered the personnel of two quasi-judicial agencies (the administrative prosecution and the state cases organization) to monitor the elections. Some critics observed that these personnel were employees of the executive branch and, thus, lacked sufficient independence to monitor the elections objectively.[83] This criticism would resurface in the 2005 elections.

However, a more fundamental criticism of the elections emerged as the voting unfolded. Judges were empowered to supervise only the balloting and counting. All other aspects of the election were beyond their control. Opposition leaders and election observers reported a host of tactics employed by regime supporters to slant the vote in their favor, including: using public buses to transport public-sector employees to the polls; manipulating the voter registration lists to include the same person multiple times, or to include dead people; blocking opposition supporters from reaching the polls; and, in some cases, attacking opposition candidates and their supporters. So long as these transgressions took place outside the voting station, judges were powerless to stop them. Many opposition candidates filed petitions with the Court of Cassation protesting the pervasiveness of fraud. The Court dutifully investigated the allegations, and often found in favor of the plaintiff. However, the Parliament ignored the Court's findings and allowed the beneficiaries of fraud to remain in office. Similar findings by administrative courts were also ignored by the Parliament.[84] The Speaker of Parliament argued that the Constitution grants Parliament, alone, the authority to evaluate disputes regarding its membership. Granting this power to the judiciary would violate the separation of powers.

For the regime, the 2000 elections were business-as-usual. Electoral fraud was a common tactic for the ruling NDP and its supporters, and had been used widely in all of Egypt's prior elections at least since the reemergence of multiparty politics in the mid-1970s. However, this was the first occasion when the judiciary was directly implicated in legitimatizing these abuses. To many judges, it cast a profound stain on their dignity

---

[83] For discussion of the debate over the judicial status of these bodies, see: al-Rif'ai, *Tashriat al-Sulta al-Qada'iyya*, 642–93; Moustafa, *The Struggle for Constitutional Power*, 208.

[84] Ahmad Sabr 'Abd Allah, "Al-Ta'un al-Intikhabiyya," in Hala Mustafa (ed.), *Intikhabat Majlis as-Sha'ab 2000* (Cairo:Markaz al-Dirasat al-Siyasiyya wa-l-Istratijiyya bi-l-Ahram, 2001) 37–56. Also, Ahmad Munisi, "Al-'Anf fi al-Intikhabat," in Hala Mustafa (ed.), *Intikhabat Majlis as-Sha'ab 2000*, 209–26.

and professionalism. For example, a prominent member of the activist camp within the Club, Ahmad Sabr, wrote that judges were never given the proper tools to genuinely supervise the election. As a consequence, they should renounce any connection to the election and call for revisions to the electoral law that would ensure a free and fair ballot.[85]

The leadership of the Judges' Club, under Muqbil Shakir, took no public action to protest the handling of the elections.[86] Its behind-the-scenes efforts to improve the administration of the elections produced no meaningful response from the regime. Shakir's seeming inability to defend the dignity of the judiciary raised serious doubts about the desirability of the quietest approach. Furthermore, the government's electoral abuses and disregard for court decisions in electoral disputes seemed to reflect a broader disrespect for the rule of law and the courts. These concerns sparked the resurgence of the activist camp within the Club, led by Zakariyya 'Abd al-'Aziz. 'Abd al-'Aziz and his allies entered the 2001 elections for the Club's board with a platform that stressed their commitment to "restoring the dignity of the judges" and resuming the battle for full judicial independence.[87] They argued that judges could pursue these goals while also addressing their material concerns. Their appeal to both pragmatism and idealism proved a powerful combination. They won control over the Club's entire board, and promptly moved to revive its activist tradition.[88]

'Abd al-'Aziz did not lose sight of the bread-and-butter issues that contributed to his election. The pages of the Club's magazine, al-Quda, continued to report at length on salaries, pensions, and benefits throughout 2002 and 2003. The magazine also drew attention to a host of special services arranged for members by the Club's board, including special discounts on mobile phone service, apartments, and vacations. However, the president's editorial at the beginning of each issue adopted a markedly different tone from the era of Muqbil Shakir. 'Abd al-'Aziz's first editorial as president spoke of the continuing struggle to increase judicial independence, and encouraged the Club to revive the proposed judicial law that it drafted in 1991. He also called for preserving the independence of the

[85] Ahmad Sabr, "The Men of the Judiciary and the Election," al-'Arabi, December 15, 2000.

[86] In public, Shakir claimed that the election was clean and that the role of the judges in the election was "admired by the world." See the interview with Shakir in al-Khamis, May 3, 2001.

[87] "Counselor Zakariyya 'Abd al-'Aziz to al-Ahali," al-Ahali, June 27, 2001.

[88] The clash within the Judges' Club was covered well in the reporting of al-Wafd newspaper. In particular, see the issues for June 2001. For 'Abd al-'Aziz's statement of his goals for the Club, see "Counselor Zakariyya 'Abd al-'Aziz to al-Ahali," al-Ahali, June 27, 2001.

Judges' Club by ensuring that it was not categorized as an NGO and, thus, not subject to the NGO law.[89]

'Abd al-'Aziz's views were reinforced by a new line of argument adopted by some of the leading judges in the activist camp, such as Ahmad Makki, Ahmad Sabr, and Hisham Bastawisi. These officials argued that Egypt was entering a "period of transformation." By adopting wide-ranging economic reforms in the early 1990s, Egypt had moved decisively away from the socialist legacy of the Nasser era toward a more market-oriented and democratic future. As Egypt moved in this new direction, the judiciary had an obligation "to advocate the cause of law, respect for rights, and autonomy for the judiciary."[90] In Ahmad Makki's words, "We are now embarking on building true democracy. The judiciary has a central role to play in this transformation. It must shape the development of law and courts in a manner that holds true to Egypt's long tradition of respecting law and protecting judicial independence."[91] Makki added that many judges felt an obligation to return Egypt to the path of legal development that it pursued prior to the Nasser period. In this view, Egypt laid the foundations for liberal democracy and the rule of law in the interwar period. Nasser suppressed this path of development, and sought to take Egypt in the direction of "socialist legality" that was at odds with the legal traditions of the country. Sadat failed to fully expunge this legacy, as had Mubarak during his first decade of rule. However, as the 1990s progressed, the government steadily dismantled the central institutions of Nasserism such as rent controls, housing laws, restrictions on property ownership, and the public sector. Rethinking the legal code was a logical extension of this process. As the country's foremost specialists on law and its staunchest defenders of liberalism, the judiciary had an obligation to contribute to this process. The activist judges saw themselves as reviving a liberal vision of law and politics that had been marginalized for more than forty years.[92]

Despite these ambitious plans, the regime showed little interest in allowing the judges to play a more prominent role in legal affairs. It did not even make a serious attempt to review and comment on the Club's

---

[89] If the Judges' Club was considered an NGO, it would fall under the administrative authority of the Ministry of Social Affairs. The judges were loath to allow a nonjudicial body to hold sway over the only elected representative of the judiciary. *al-Quda*, July–December 2001, 1–2.

[90] Ahmad Makki, "The Judiciary and Reform in Egypt," *al-'Arabi*, July 12, 2002.

[91] Ibid.

[92] Ibid. Also, personal interview with Ahmad Makki, March 14, 2005; personal interview with Hisham Bastawisi, March 20, 2005. For further detail on this view, see the interview with Hisham Janaina in *al-Misa'iyya al-Misriyya*, May 12, 2007; and, the interview with Mahmud al-Khadiri in *al-Ahali*, December 28, 2005.

proposed law for judicial reform. The Club responded by re-issuing the proposed law in 2004.[93] It forwarded the law to the Ministry of Justice and requested its quick referral to the Supreme Judicial Council and to Parliament. The government delayed, and the Judges' Club grew increasingly frustrated at the regime's seeming indifference to its long-standing concerns. Events took an unexpected turn in April 2005. During the course of a trial, a member of the Alexandria branch of the Judges' Club was pressured to alter a ruling under threat of physical violence from several lawyers. The response to this incident by the local police was tepid and ineffectual. The Alexandria Judges' Club called an urgent meeting, and concluded that the police's indifference to the plight of this judge was symptomatic of the regime's general disrespect for the judiciary. Discussion soon shifted to the regime's disregard of the judges' carefully drafted law for judicial reform, and members decided that the time had come to take more decisive action. The judges noted that a presidential election was scheduled for September and a parliamentary election for November/December, and that the judiciary had the responsibility to oversee these elections. The Alexandria judges then made a bold proposition: they would refuse to oversee the elections until the government agreed to adopt their proposed law and to grant them full supervisory powers over the electoral process. The proposition was adopted by the Alexandria judges by acclamation. It was then taken to the national Judges' Club in Cairo, which called an emergency meeting of all its members on May 13. The national club endorsed the boycott proposal in a voice vote. With this step, the Judges' Club inserted itself into the heart of the debate over electoral reform and suddenly became the most powerful challenger of executive authority in the country.

In response to this decision, the president of the Club appointed a committee to draft an action plan for achieving the Club's goals. This committee included some of the most prominent advocates of an activist role for the Club, including Ahmad Makki (who chaired the committee), Muhammad Naji Darbala, Hisham Janaina, and Ahmad Sabr. The committee issued its report on August 22, 2005.[94] It provides the clearest statement of the Judges' Club's political and legal objectives since the 1986 National Conference on Justice. In this report, the judges spell out two key goals:

1. *Full judicial control of the upcoming elections.* The judges call for amending both the electoral law and the law of political rights to ensure

[93] The draft law is summarized in "Completion of Amendments to the Law on Judicial Power," *al-Wafd*, May 31, 2004. Also, see "The Most Important Features of the Proposal to Amend the Law on Judicial Power," *al-Wafd*, June 3, 2004. The full text of the draft law is reprinted in *al-Quda*, September 2003–August 2004, 192–206.

[94] *Taqrir Lajna Tafʾil Qararat al-Jamʾaiyya al-ʿAmma li Quda Misr al-Maʾaquda bi Tarikh 13/5/2005* (Cairo: Nadi al-Quda, 2005).

that judges exercise "true and effective supervision over the Presidential and Parliamentary elections."[95] They add that judges should supervise the electoral process "from the nomination of candidates through the announcement of results."[96] They call for several specific changes in the procedures for the election, including: drawing up new and accurate voter registration rolls; adopting stronger penalties for electoral crimes, especially crimes that interfere with voters or with judges in the performance of their duties; easing the procedure for filing lawsuits that allege electoral fraud; forming judicial committees to supervise the election that enjoy "absolute neutrality";[97] ensuring that the decisions of these electoral committees may be contested, and that the challenge be heard within twenty-four hours; and, if the plaintiff is unhappy with the results of the challenge, guaranteeing that he may appeal to an administrative court. In the view of the judges, adoption of these measures is the only means for "ensuring free and fair elections."[98] Furthermore, the judges argue that strengthening the electoral process is essential to the security of the nation and the struggle against terrorism. If elections function smoothly and fairly, peaceful change will be within the reach of every citizen and the path of violence espoused by terrorists will be discredited.[99]

2. *Adoption of the new draft judicial law that the Club re-issued in December 2004.* Beyond a general call for implementing the draft law, the judges focus on several key features of the law that hold particular importance for the Club: complete budgetary independence for the judiciary; full independence for the Judges' Club, from both the Ministry of Justice and the Supreme Judicial Council; unifying the judiciary by abolishing the Supreme Council of Judicial Bodies as well as all exceptional courts (especially the Court of Values and the Socialist Public Prosecutor); separating the power to prosecute from the power to investigate, thereby ensuring that prosecutions are more objective and professional; and ensuring that the heads of courts (including the Court of Cassation) are selected through elections involving all the judges who serve in the court. In order to reiterate the continuity of the Judges' Club's recommendations, the

[95] Ibid., 3.

[96] Ibid., 4.

[97] This specific phrasing was widely seen as a criticism of the Presidential Election Committee. This Committee was headed by the president of the Supreme Constitutional Court, who is appointed by the president of the republic. The Judges' Club wanted to ensure that it had full control over the electoral committees.

[98] The judges argued that, without these steps, the upcoming presidential and parliamentary elections would be marred by the same level of fraud that tainted the May referendum on amending the constitution. In their view, the referendum was "a disgrace by any measure." *Taqrir Lajna Tafʿail*, 10.

[99] Ibid., 12.

Club's report includes an appendix that reprints the final recommendations of the National Conference of Justice in 1986.[100] The authors of the
report clearly saw their work as the logical extension, and culmination, of
this earlier effort at judicial reform.

The report issued in 2005 also offers an impassioned statement of the
Club's obligation to engage in public debates over Egypt's legal and political development. It describes the Club as "an elite . . . that respects the law
and loves justice."[101] Furthermore, the Club "enjoys the public's trust"[102]
because it acts in the interests of the nation and its stability. The people
consider the judiciary "their hope for justice and freedom" because it is
the only actor in public life that "is not motivated by self-interest."[103] This
unique position gives it an obligation to engage in political discussions,
including a "wise and noble dialog" with other institutions such as the
Ministry of Justice, the Supreme Judicial Council, the People's Assembly,
the *Shura* Council, and the Presidential Election Committee.[104] The report concludes that: "The most important guarantee of judicial independence is not in the texts. Rather, it is in the unity and conviction of the
people. The mission of the Judges' Club is to reinforce the bonds that
connect the people and not allow them to be torn asunder. The mission
of the Club is to serve the interests of the people."[105]

Toward the end of the report, the authors add that "the only objective
of the judiciary is strengthening the system of government and ensuring
its continuity, as well as comprehensively improving justice."[106] A deeper
respect for law and justice would lead not only to a more stable and prosperous society. It would also eliminate one of the primary justifications
for foreign intervention in Egypt and in the region as a whole. In the
committee's view, autocratic and unaccountable governments in the Arab
world have led to instability and violence that create opportunities for
foreign intervention. The formation of more just and law-abiding regimes
would eliminate this instability and allow the region to grow stronger and
more independent.[107]

In addition, the report addresses the question of whether the judges
should boycott their supervisory role in the upcoming elections if their
demands were not met. The tone of the document suggests that support
for a boycott was not deeply rooted, and that the authors of the report

[100] Ibid., 15–17.
[101] Ibid., 5.
[102] Ibid.
[103] Ibid., 10.
[104] Ibid., 5.
[105] Ibid., 11.
[106] Ibid., 12.
[107] Ibid., 10.

were laying the groundwork for backing away from this threat. The report notes that the judges' obligation to supervise the elections is specified in the Constitution and, thus, they have a legal duty to comply. Failure to conform with the law would "open the door to government based upon self-interest and chaos" and would "weaken the state at a critical moment."[108] If individual judges are unhappy with the way the law is currently drafted and executed, they should seek to amend it. Furthermore, the judiciary is "the conscience of the nation" and, as such, has a duty to objectively monitor the elections and report fully and openly on any transgressions that it observes. These objective reports on the election, in turn, will "spark the public's conscience" and motivate citizens to seek electoral reform and other political reforms.[109] The nation "would not forgive the judges" if they failed to perform their legal duty.[110] The report concludes that any decision to boycott the elections should be supported by a majority of the entire membership of the Club—not just the members who attend the meeting at which the issue is discussed.[111]

The report offers few expressions of support for individual rights. There is discussion of revising the law of political rights, but with the sole objective of improving electoral procedure.[112] The report also calls for "supporting the rights of citizens" and "improving guarantees of human rights," as well as an end to the emergency law. These steps are described as "entitlements of the Egyptian people."[113] Failing to act on them is "unjust."[114] However, it provides no detail on which rights should be promoted and what new laws should be adopted. This vagueness on individual rights is particularly striking in light of the specificity of the report's recommendations regarding electoral procedure and the institutional relationship among the judiciary, the executive, the Judges' Club, and the Supreme Judicial Council. In this regard, the report is true to the judiciary's conception of liberalism discussed in chapter 2. The Club places a high priority on issues of procedure and institutional structure, with the goal of ensuring the separation of powers, enhancing the independence of the judiciary, and strengthening constraints on the executive. It also emphasizes the importance of respect for the law and unbiased implementation of the law, particularly with regard to the elections. But it says relatively little about

---

[108] Ibid., 11.

[109] The report notes that this was the line of argument used by the Supreme Constitutional Court in its ruling of 2000, which dramatically expanded the role of judges in monitoring elections. Ibid., 11.

[110] Ibid.

[111] Ibid., 13.

[112] Ibid., 5–6.

[113] Ibid., 9.

[114] Ibid.

individual rights. The emphasis is on collective well-being and the institutional structures that ensure it, rather than individual liberty.

Similarly, the report includes little discussion of the principle of free elections, the right of citizens to vote, or the need to deepen public participation in politics. These substantive questions of democratization are not the Club's concern. Indeed, it never called for independent monitoring of the elections by local NGOs in order to enhance their fairness, and remained a staunch opponent of international monitoring. It resisted any temptation to broaden its mandate and become a principled advocate of democratization.

With this report in place, the Judges had effectively defined their bargaining position vis-à-vis the regime. Although a boycott of the elections was never a likely possibility, the Judges still retained considerable leverage over the regime through their assessment of the honesty and fairness of the elections. In essence, the judges would determine whether the elections were perceived as legitimate or illegitimate by the Egyptian public. This was a formidable power. If they concluded that the presidential election was invalid, Mubarak's claim to be a democratic reformer would ring hollow and the legitimacy of his leadership would be called into question. While it is unlikely that this would pose a mortal threat to Mubarak's regime, it would be a source of considerable embarrassment—particularly at a time when Egypt's primary foreign supporter, the United States, was emphasizing the importance of democratic reform in the Arab world. If the judges concluded that the parliamentary elections were invalid, the regime would face similar embarrassment. In addition, it might face a practical challenge to its economic reform program. According to his campaign platform, Mubarak planned to pass a series of laws that would create a more market-oriented economy. If the legitimacy of the Parliament were called into question, the reforms it adopted would also be tainted and would be subject to legal challenges on the grounds that they were issued by an unsound legislature. Thus, the Club's reports on the elections provided the judges with considerable power. Indeed, the judges used these reports as a lever for pressuring the regime to adopt its draft judicial law.

The Club recognized the political risk involved in challenging Mubarak directly and, as a consequence, issued a vague but positive report on the September 7 presidential election. It pointed to several areas of concern such as flawed voter registration lists, individuals casting multiple ballots, and some voters being permitted to vote without having registered.[115] It also objected to the procedure for selecting which judges would supervise

---

[115] Nadi al-Quda, *Taqrir Lajna Taqassa al-Haqa'iq 'an Ishraf al-Quda 'ala al-Intikhabat al-Ra'isiyya bi Tarikh 7/9/2005* (Cairo: Nadi al-Quda, 2005).

polling places.[116] However, it concluded that these problems were not sufficiently widespread to affect the outcome of the election. Mubarak was
pronounced the winner. The report is a clever balance of carrot and stick.
It shows the judges' willingness to document electoral abuses clearly and
bluntly. But, it also shows their willingness to exercise discretion and reach
a final decision that conforms with the regime's interests. In the words of
a senior judge involved in preparing the Club's report, the judges were
not seeking to embarrass the regime for purposes of political posturing.
They were prepared to be reasonable and responsible, if the regime responded to their concerns.[117]

As the parliamentary elections approached, the judges reiterated their
demands for greater control over voting sites and the vote-counting process. As noted earlier, the elections were held in three separate rounds
spread over three weeks in November and December in order to ensure
that judges could move around the country and supervise most (if not
all) of the polling sites. The Club chose not to issue formal reports on each
round of the election. Rather, it would issue a single report, and it would
delay issuing the report until the middle of 2006. This long delay was
ostensibly to enable the report to include a discussion of the court challenges filed by candidates who believed they were victims of fraud. However, it also gave the Club time to negotiate with the regime over the
new judicial law while it "prepared the report" and decided what tone it
would adopt. The tone could be adjusted to reflect the pace and character
of the negotiations.[118]

Instead of issuing formal reports as the election unfolded, senior judges
from the Club made extensive use of the press to convey their concerns
over the electoral process and make clear to the regime how much damage
they could inflict if their demands for a new judicial law were not met.[119]
A prominent member of the State Council, Samir Yusuf al-Bahi, claimed

[116] The Presidential Election Committee was responsible for selecting which judges would
supervise the election. It chose to exclude several hundred judges, without offering an explanation. Many of the excluded judges had expressed support for the activist posture within
the Judges' Club, and thus their exclusion was interpreted as a form of punishment and
intimidation. However, some of the excluded judges were not from the activist camp. There
appeared to be no clear pattern regarding which judges were excluded.

[117] Personal interview with Ahmad Makki, November 10, 2005.

[118] Ibid.

[119] Some of the articles written by judges include: Hisham al-Bastawisi, "Judge Hisham
al-Bastawisi Challenges any Opponents to the Judges' Work," al- 'Arabi, December 4, 2005;
Zakariyya 'Abd al-'Aziz, "The Judges Say to Government: Speaking on Politics is Part of the
Right of Citizenship," Sawt al-Umma, December 19, 2005; 'Adil 'Aid, "I Pay the Price for
My Opinions . . . and My Sorrow is Great for the Fate of this Country," al-Ahali, November
30, 2005; Ashraf al-Barudi, "Judges are the Carriers of the Burden of Freedom," al-Ghad,
December 28, 2005.

that the ruling NDP had hired thugs to attack voters and judges, and that the police and security services had done nothing to stop this intimidation. He called for the judges from the State Council to boycott the third round of the elections, on the grounds that judges were unable to effectively combat the pervasive fraud employed by the regime.[120]

Ahmad Makki made the same claim about government-initiated violence against judges and voters. He took the extraordinary step of calling for the military to intervene and provide protection, because the civilian security services had been "pressured into a lack of neutrality."[121] The minister of justice and the minister of interior released statements indicating that they would improve the security of voting sites for the final round of voting. However, the promises were empty and the level of violence actually increased during the final round of voting.

Other judges also used the media to publicize abuses. The most dramatic accusation came from Nuha al-Zaini, a member of the administrative prosecution who was responsible for supervising the election in the Damanhour constituency. The contest pitted a prominent figure in the ruling NDP (Mustafa al-Fiqi) against a leader of the Muslim Brotherhood (Jamal Hashmat). Al-Zaini wrote a letter to an independent newspaper, *al-Misri al-Youm*, stating that her tally of the votes indicated that Hashmat had won by a substantial margin. She reported this result to the parliamentary election committee. However, al-Fiqi was pronounced the winner in what she called a "falsification of the results."[122] Al-Zaini faced harsh criticism in the government press.[123] The fact that she wears a *hijab* led some to claim that she harbored sympathies for the Muslim Brotherhood. Prominent members of the Judges' Club stood behind her, despite her affiliation with a quasi-judicial body (the administrative prosecution) that the Club did not regard as qualified to supervise the election. Nonetheless, the government persisted and awarded the seat to al-Fiqi.

One of the strongest condemnations of the elections came from Yahia al-Rif'ai, the former president of the Judges' Club. Al-Rif'ai had presided over the Club during its periods of greatest activism, including the 1986 National Conference of Justice and its drafting of a new judicial law in 1991. His conclusions with regard to the parliamentary elections were

---

[120] Samir Yusuf al-Bahi, "Disregarding Rulings of the State Council Occurs Only in a Police State," *al-Ahali*, November 30, 2005.

[121] See the interview with Makki in Hamada Imam, "Why Do We Request Protection from the Army?" *Al- 'Arabi*, November 27, 2005.

[122] *Al-Misri al-Youm*, November 24, 2005.

[123] However, she received considerable support in the opposition press. For example, see: Yahia al-Wajdi, "Justice Will Not Be Lost in a Country where Nuha al-Zaini Is Judge," *Sawt al-Umma*, November 28, 2005; 'Azizi 'Ali 'Azizi, "The Government Falls and Nuha al-Zaini Lives," *al-Usbu'a*, November 28, 2005.

scathing. They were a "universal scandal" which effectively "closed the door on any hope of true reform. They showed a lack of commitment to reform at the highest level." Furthermore, they demonstrated that Egypt is not a state of institutions, but rather "a state of thuggery" in which the Ministry of Interior effectively governs the country.[124]

In the midst of these growing tensions, the Judges' Club held its regularly scheduled elections to select a new governing board in mid-December 2005. The government quietly backed an alternative leadership within the Club that challenged the activist camp. The elections were widely seen as a referendum on the activist posture adopted by the current president, Zakariyya 'Abd al-'Aziz. 'Abd al-'Aziz and his supporters won in a landslide: 'Abd al-'Aziz won 3,680 votes for president, while his pro-government challenger won only 930.[125] 'Abd al-'Aziz's victory further emboldened the activists. At the Club's General Assembly meeting that followed, the judges agreed that they would not supervise future elections unless the procedural reforms they had requested were adopted fully. They also denounced acts of violence against judges during the election. The meeting included extensive testimony from judges who had been victims of attacks by thugs believed to have ties to the ruling NDP. The General Assembly called for the public prosecutor to thoroughly investigate all incidents of violence against judges. If the investigations were not quick and thorough, 'Abd al-'Aziz threatened to invite international agencies (presumably, the United Nations) to investigate. He also denounced efforts by the Supreme Judicial Council to limit the Club's discussion of political matters. He described these efforts as "intellectual terrorism" and noted that judges would not be intimidated because "they fear only God."[126]

Another layer of complexity was brought to the Club's activities by tensions within the judiciary itself. As noted earlier, the new judicial law proposed by the Club called for altering the structure and role of the Supreme Judicial Council (SJC). It proposed that the judges on the Council be elected by their respective courts, rather than being appointed by the president or by seniority. It also called for recognizing the Judges' Club as the sole representative of the judges, which directly challenged the SJC's

[124] Yahia al-Rif'ai, "What Occurred in the Recent Elections Is a Universal Scandal," *Al-Misri al-Youm*, December 31, 2005.

[125] "Judges Give a Powerful Slap to the Government," *al-Wafd*, December 18, 2005; "Victory of Counselor 'Abd al-'Aziz and His List is a Victory for All of Egypt," *Sawt al-Umma*, December 19, 2005.

[126] Ahmad Rabi'a, "The Judges Announce their Boycott of Any Future Elections Unless their Conditions for Supervision Are Met Completely," *Nahdat Misr*, December 18, 2005. Also see Tariq Amin, "Unprecedented Turnout for the Judges' Club Elections," *Al-Misri al-Youm*, December 17, 2005.

traditional position as the spokesman for the judiciary.[127] Several judges on the SJC were advocates of the quietist approach to relations with the regime, and disagreed sharply with the activist posture adopted by the Judges' Club's leadership.[128] Their views led the SJC to suspend the immunity of several prominent activist judges and begin disciplinary proceedings against them, on the grounds that they had violated the stipulation in the judicial law that prohibits judges from involvement in politics. Two of the judges—Ahmad Makki and Hisham Bastawisi—were also charged with having "sullied the reputation of the judiciary" by suggesting that some judges may have cooperated with the regime in its efforts to rig the parliamentary election. Although these steps were rooted in the institutional rivalry between the SJC and the Judges' Club, they were widely seen by the Judges' Club and the public as an effort by the government to intimidate judges who criticized it. A large group of judges held demonstrations at the Club to protest the hearings, and several judges went on a hunger strike to protest the issue. Some even raised the possibility of a work stoppage by judges and threatened to "sue the government before international courts."[129] The disciplinary hearings against Makki and Bastawisi also became a focus for opposition groups. Secular critics of the regime (such as the *Kifaya* movement) as well as the Muslim Brotherhood participated in demonstrations to protest the treatment of Makki and Bastawisi. These demonstrations met with swift and brutal repression by the regime. Makki was ultimately exonerated. Bastawisi received a reprimand, which meant that his next promotion would be delayed. However, this punishment had no practical meaning, as he had already achieved the highest rank available (vice president of the Court of Cassation) without direct presidential appointment.[130]

[127] The Club argued that the SJC was only an administrative body that handled management of the judiciary. It could not claim to represent the judiciary as a whole because its leadership was not elected. The Judges' Club, in contrast, had an elected leadership that represented the will and interests of all judges. See the interview with Ahmad Makki in Hamada Imam, "Why Do We Request Protection from the Army?" *Al- 'Arabi*, November 27, 2005. Also, Naji Darbala, "Electing Members of the Supreme Council as a Means to Judicial Independence," *al-Misri al-Youm*, May 2, 2006.

[128] For a helpful discussion of the tensions between the SJC and the Judges' Club, see Nathan J. Brown and Hesham Nasr, "Egypt's Judges Step Forward: The Judicial Election Boycott and Egyptian Reform" (Washington, DC: Carnegie Endowment for International Peace, May 2005).

[129] This proposal was made by Mahmoud Makki. It is unclear which international court he had in mind. Mona el-Nahhas, "Judicial Stand-Off," *al-Ahram Weekly*, February 23–March 1, 2006.

[130] For coverage of the demonstrations, see the issues of *al-Wafd* from April 24 through May 24, 2006.

The government sought to assuage at least some of the Club's concerns by adopting a new Judicial Authority law in June 2006. The Judges' Club complained that it had not been formally involved in the drafting process for the law. Indeed, it had not even been shown a copy of the draft law. Nonetheless, its views were clearly known to the government through the Club's numerous meetings with the minister of justice and other senior officials. The final law responded to several of the judges' concerns. It granted the judiciary budgetary independence from the executive branch. It also separated the office of the public prosecutor from the Ministry of Justice, making it an autonomous entity (although the chief prosecutor is still appointed by the president of the republic). However, the judges were disappointed on several fronts. The new law did not respond to their demand that members of the Supreme Judicial Council be elected by the members of their courts. It also did not end the policy of seconding judges to executive agencies as "advisors," which the Club believed compromises their independence. In addition, it did not recognize the Judges' Club as the official representative of Egypt's judges (the Supreme Judicial Council continues to play this role). 'Abd al-'Aziz announced in a public statement, "Without doubt, there have been issues that we have demanded that have been achieved. We can't argue about this."[131] Nonetheless, the Club announced its plans to continue pushing for further revisions in the law.[132]

Although the Club enjoyed only partial success in reforming the judicial law, its clash with the regime over this law and the procedures for conducting the elections established the Club as the country's strongest advocate for liberal reforms. Its conception of liberalism arises from a rich and wide-ranging jurisprudence, which has been distilled into a coherent set of political and legal objectives through several specific documents: the final statement of the National Conference on Justice; the proposed law for reform of the judiciary, first drafted in 1991 and then reissued in 2004; and the reports issued by the Club as it prepared to supervise the presidential and parliamentary elections. These documents call for the creation of a balance of powers, with particular emphasis on judicial independence. They also advocate strengthening the rule of law, with particular stress on the principles that exceptional courts should be abolished and that the regime must act in accordance with the law and judicial rulings. They also refer to civil and political rights as an entitlement of the people and a

---

[131] "Head of the Judges Comments on the New Law," al-'Arabi, June 19, 2006.

[132] "President of the Judges to al-Ahali: The Law Does Not Achieve True Independence for the Judges," al-Ahali, June 28, 2006. Also see the interview with Hisham Janaina in al-Jumhuri al-Hurr, April 30, 2007.

fundamental element of justice, although the doctrine of rights is not well developed or detailed.

This is a conception of liberalism that focuses on institutional relationships, procedural fairness, and respect for the dignity of the judicial profession. It supports the creation of a strong and effective state, but this state is constrained by the law and accountable to it. These constraints ensure that state power is not abused to serve the interests of a narrow elite. Intriguingly, this is not a conception of the polity that stresses popular rule. It places little emphasis on popular sovereignty, the right of citizens to participate in government, or the need to broaden public involvement in political life. It supports civil and political rights, but there is little discussion of innate individual rights or liberties. In this conception of liberalism, the best guarantor of individual rights is a well-regulated state. The focus remains on strengthening the institutions that constrain and monitor the state, rather than empowering the individual to challenge it.

Nathan Brown has written that this conception of liberalism is largely compatible with the regime's objectives and, for this reason, the regime has allowed it to develop and grow. He writes that it "has never been worse than annoying to the country's political leadership; far more often . . . it serves their ends."[133] The analysis above suggests that this perspective may neglect important differences between statism and liberalism in contemporary Egypt. The statist perspective that lies at the heart of the regime's power is grounded in a highly instrumental conception of law. The mentality of "socialist legality" persists, even though the term may be out of fashion. For many in the executive branch, law is a tool of state power. Its purpose is to facilitate the goals and policies of government. Court rulings should also serve these ends.

The conception of law and courts articulated by the judiciary is qualitatively different from this view. Its approach to liberalism is fully compatible with a strong and effective state, which it regards as essential for preserving public order and enhancing collective well-being. But, the judiciary is not the positivistic and bureaucratic institution that Brown suggests. The judges advocate a conception of the polity grounded in the rule of law. Its fundamental premises are classically liberal: law applies equally to ruler and ruled; a central purpose of law is to constrain state power and ensure its just application; and law exists, in part, to protect citizens from the arbitrary actions of the state. Courts are the pivotal institution in this legal order. They are the guarantor that law is applied equally. They are the protector of citizens from a whimsical and sometimes predatory state.

[133] Brown, *The Rule of Law in the Arab World*, 128.

This conception of law and the polity is not compatible with the statism of the regime. The regime has been able to coexist with it only by building institutions that circumvent it, such as extraordinary courts and an emergency law. As the ideological justification for these statist institutions erodes, and as the public's tolerance of them declines, clashes between the liberal conception of the polity articulated by the judges and the statism of the regime are likely to intensify. If the events of 2005 and 2006 are any indication, the liberal alternative is likely to attract meaningful public support. The judges are a natural rallying point for groups in society that seek gradual reform of the political order. They offer a viable alternative to the arbitrary power of statist rule, and their alternative is tempered by the judgment, experience, and dignity that accrue to the judicial profession. Furthermore, their appeal for constraints on state power and improvements in the rule of law is reinforced by developments elsewhere in the polity. It is particularly strengthened by the emergence of a new generation of leadership within the Muslim Brotherhood that articulates a conception of Islamic constitutionalism that shares many features with the liberalism advocated by the Judges' Club.

The Islamic Alternative:
The Muslim Brotherhood and Islamic Constitutionalism

As noted in chapter 3, the Muslim Brotherhood refrained from stating a clear set of political objectives for most of its history. This began to change in the early and mid-1990s, as the Brotherhood adapted to the constraints and opportunities of the Egyptian political environment. The younger generation of Brotherhood leaders—particularly 'Isam al-'Iryan, Mukhtar Nuh, and 'Abd al-Mon'am Abu al-Fatuh—began to articulate a moderate political agenda in an effort to broaden the appeal and effectiveness of the MB. However, the regime began imprisoning these leaders in 1995. As a consequence, the effort to develop a Brotherhood political platform effectively ceased for the remainder of the 1990s. It began to reemerge after 2000, when several of the younger leaders finished their prison terms and returned to their posts in the Brotherhood. This effort was made easier by the waning of the old guard. The General Guide, Mustafa Mashur, died in 2002 at the age of eighty-one. His successor, Ma'mun al-Hudeibi, died after only two years in office at the age of eighty-four. While the younger generation was not permitted to take the top spot, two of its most respected leaders—Muhammad Habib and Khayrat al-Shatir—were promoted to the post of Deputy General Guide. The new General Guide,

Muhammad 'Akif, publicly endorsed the moderate political views promoted by the younger generation.[134]

As the younger generation of MB activists assumed positions of leadership, they began to refine and develop a moderate political agenda. One of the clearest statements of this agenda was a book by 'Isam al-'Iryan, *al-Haraka al-Islamiyya wa-l-Intiqal al-Dimaqrati: al-Tajriba al-Misriyya fi rob'a Qarn (The Islamic Movement and Democratic Transition: The Egyptian Experience over the Past Quarter Century)*, published in 2004.[135] Despite his long career of activism, this was the first book-length work by al-'Iryan. It provides a detailed discussion of the doctrinal foundations for a moderate conception of Islamic governance. These doctrinal arguments appear to draw heavily on the four theorists discussed in chapter 3 (al-Qaradawi, al-Bishri, al-'Awwa, and Abu al-Majd), although these authors are not formally cited.

The book asserts that "the procedures and structures of democracy . . . are fully compatible with Islamic *Shari'a* . . . and the attainment of the public interest of the Islamic *umma*." [136] Indeed, al-'Iryan proposes that the conception of Islamic governance developed by the Brotherhood can be deemed "Islamic democracy."[137] It is grounded in constitutional governance based on the following principles:

- Personal freedom in all its forms;
- Consultation, and the principle that political authority is derived from the *umma*;
- Accountability of the ruler to the people;
- The balance of powers among the institutions of the state.[138]

He concludes that "the Muslim Brotherhood considers constitutional governance (*al-hukm al-dusturi*) the form of government . . . that is closest to Islam."[139] He affirms the importance of political pluralism "in Mus-

---

[134] Some of the younger generation of moderate Islamists chose to break away from the MB in the mid-1990s and form a new organization, *Hizb al-Wasat*. This group sought to create a moderate Islamic party that would include non-Muslims and would advocate democracy, equality, and greater respect for civil and political rights. The regime has consistently blocked its efforts to form a political party. The MB, particularly in the late 1990s, saw the *Hizb al-Wasat* as a potential challenge to its political power and denounced its members. For further detail and analysis, see: Norton, "Thwarted Politics: The Case of Egypt's Hizb al-Wasat," 133–60; Baker, *Islam without Fear*, 192–211; Rosefsky-Wickham, "The Path to Moderation," 205–28.

[135] 'Isam al-'Iryan, *Al-Haraka al-Islamiyya wa-l-Intiqal al-Dimaqrati: al-Tajriba al-Misriyya fi rob'a Qarn* (Al-Mansura: Dar al-Kalima, 2004).

[136] Ibid., 17–18.

[137] Ibid., 18.

[138] Ibid.

[139] Ibid.

lim society and in the Islamic system [of government]"; the granting of political rights to women, including the right to run for office, because the full exercise of these rights is part of each woman's obligation to "enjoin good and forbid evil"; and the maintenance of good relations with religious minorities in Egypt in accordance with the *Shari'a* principle that they enjoy the same rights and duties as Muslims.[140] He writes that the Brotherhood has tried and failed to cooperate with the regime, and that it has tried to build strong political alliances with parties and other political forces. Succeeding in these areas is a high priority for the organization and the topic of "many studies and discussions."[141]

The book contains separate chapters dealing with the rights of women and the importance of political pluralism. Al-'Iryan writes that these topics deal with the "most important fundamental principles that the Muslim Brotherhood has decided."[142] In his discussion of women's rights, he utilizes several quotations from the Qur'an to substantiate his view that women are "equal in the eyes of God" and are "entitled to the same legal rights."[143] They have the right to vote, to run for seats in the representative assembly, and to hold public office.[144] To further substantiate this position, he cites a passage from the Qur'an which he interprets to mean that women were allowed to participate in selecting "the people who loose and bind."[145] He explicitly addresses the sections of the Qur'an and *hadith* that limit the rights of women, and argues in each case for the narrowest possible interpretation of these limits. For example, he notes that a passage in the *hadith* states that women have weaker intellects than men. Al-'Iryan interprets this to mean only that they have less capacity to testify in court on specific matters of religious law (such as the *hudud* punishments and when they should be applied).[146] Although feminists may find this position unsatisfactory, it is a significant advancement among Islamic thinkers in the Brotherhood. Al-'Iryan is taking a step that, for example, al-Qaradawi has not. He has not attempted to renounce the passages of the Qur'an that are hostile toward women, but has sought to interpret them so narrowly that they have no practical application in contemporary society. He also goes to some lengths to refute several popular prejudices against women participating in public life. He addresses the common assertions that women lack relevant experience and judgment; that their child-

---

[140] He adds that a Copt ran successfully on the Islamic alliance's electoral list in Assiut in the 1987 Parliamentary elections. Ibid., 37–38.

[141] Ibid., 38.

[142] Ibid., 39.

[143] Ibid., 45.

[144] Ibid., 53.

[145] Ibid.

[146] Ibid., 47.

rearing duties consume so much time that they could not hold public office effectively; and that participation in public life would compromise a woman's honor. In each case, he argues that analogous arguments can be made for excluding men from public life, and reiterates that none of these views has a sound foundation in the Qur'an.[147] There are, however, limits to his progressiveness. He concludes the chapter by returning to a traditional view of women. He writes that "bearing and raising children are the primary roles for women."[148] He also adds an intriguing caveat. He argues that while, in principle, women enjoy the full range of rights that he describes, women's capacity to actually practice these rights is limited by "the traditions and conditions of society."[149] This suggests that even the most progressive of Brotherhood thinkers is not prepared to work aggressively to broaden the role of women in Egyptian society.

Al-'Iryan's discussion of political pluralism draws heavily on the four theorists discussed in chapter 3. He writes, as do these theorists, that the *umma* is the source of political authority. *Shura* (consultation) is the only approach to governance supported by the Qur'an. It is "essential to the establishment of justice and to implementing the governance of God and serving the interests of Muslims."[150] Like al-'Awwa, he cites the historical example of Abu Bakr's ascension to power as evidence that all Muslims should participate in the selection of the ruler.[151] Like al-'Awwa, he concludes that "the leader may be selected only through the choice of Muslims."[152] He quotes the same passage from the *hadith* as al-Qaradawi, to the effect that each member of the *umma* is entitled to correct the ruler if he makes a mistake.[153]

He adds:

> The people have the right to exercise choice with regard to their religion, their security, and their work. The people are also entitled to constrain the powers of the state. . . . The Qur'an and the Sunnah are the titular constitution (*al-dustur al-ismi*) for the governance of the Muslims, and nothing they do may contradict it. Also, the *umma* must produce a written constitution . . . that draws on the principles of *Shari'a*, achieves a balance among the institutions of the state, and

[147] Ibid., 54–56.

[148] However, he is not arguing that women should be passive and subservient. Indeed, within the confines of the home, she is "lord and queen." Ibid., 50.

[149] Ibid., 56.

[150] Ibid., 59.

[151] Ibid. He also notes that Abu Bakr's successor, 'Umar, was chosen by representatives of the *umma*. As noted in chapter 3, Abu al-Majd also makes this point when discussing the method for selecting a leader.

[152] Ibid., 60.

[153] Ibid.

ensures that one institution is not allowed to dominate the others . . . [the constitution] should protect the public and private freedoms of all people, both Muslim and non-Muslim . . . governance should be based upon constant consultation with the *umma* and the institutions of government should be constrained by the people and be accountable to them and corrected by them.[154]

He further advocates that legislation should be drafted by a council of representatives that is chosen through free elections. The president should also be chosen through elections, and he serves as the "agent" (*wakil*) of the people. He should hold office for a limited term, which can be renewed only for a clearly specified period in order "to avoid tyranny."[155] Public debate and discussion should be encouraged because they "reveal the truth, facilitate reform, and serve the public interest."[156] A wide variety of civil society groups—"intellectual, scientific, legal, and cultural"—are essential for "constraining power" and "ensuring social peace."[157] Furthermore, "power should rotate among political groups and parties by means of regular elections."[158]

Just as the Brotherhood was moving in this more moderate direction, it encountered a fortuitous development within the regime. Since 2001, Mubarak's government had come under increasing pressure from the United States to adopt meaningful democratic reforms. The Bush administration was convinced that the persistence of autocracy in the Arab world contributed to the anger and hopelessness that fueled radical Islam. In this view, democratization would provide a peaceful avenue for venting this anger and lead to more stable and legitimate governments in the region.[159] In pursuit of this goal, the United States called repeatedly for the Mubarak regime to allow increased political competition and demonstrate greater respect for human rights.[160] Mubarak responded by stating that he would allow free parliamentary elections in the fall of 2005.[161] Egypt came under increasing scrutiny from the U.S. Congress to deliver on this promise. Although the regime would eventually retreat from this commitment

[154] Ibid., 61–62.
[155] Ibid., 62.
[156] Ibid.
[157] Ibid., 63.
[158] Ibid.
[159] The clearest statement of this view is *The National Security Strategy of the United States of America* (Washington, DC: The White House, 2006), 1–4.
[160] The most overt example of this call for reform in Egypt was President Bush's State of the Union address for 2005. He stated, "The great and proud nation of Egypt, which showed the way toward peace in the Middle East, can now show the way toward democracy in the Middle East." The address was delivered on February 2, 2005.
[161] Transcript of Mubarak's interview with Charlie Rose, January 14, 2005. He later agreed to allow multi-candidate presidential elections in September 2005.

as the balloting process unfolded,[162] it permitted the campaigning phase of the election to occur with remarkably little interference. The Brotherhood was allowed to compete openly using its own name and to support a group of independent candidates. It was able to publish a "Reform Initiative" (in March 2004), issue a campaign platform (in October 2005), publicize its agenda through pamphlets and newspaper articles (particularly in its de facto newspaper, *Afaq 'Arabiyya*), and explain its views in numerous interviews to the media. These documents demonstrate the ascendancy of the younger generation of moderates within the organization's leadership. They also show how the Brotherhood interprets and applies the general principles of Islamic constitutionalism discussed in chapter 3. Through its preparations to compete in these elections, the Brotherhood defined a coherent Islamic alternative to the existing political order.

The Brotherhood's Reform Initiative states that the organization seeks to create a "republican system of government that is democratic, constitutional, and parliamentary and that conforms with Islamic principles."[163] In pursuit of this goal, the Brotherhood specifies the institutional changes needed to achieve each of the features of Islamic constitutionalism discussed in chapter 3:

The rule of law: Like the theorists discussed earlier, the Brotherhood's campaign documents stress the centrality of law to the political order that they hope to create. Law applies equally to ruler and ruled, and is the primary means for achieving a more just society. These campaign documents also call for Parliament to adopt laws that are compatible with *Shari'a*. Significantly, the MB's literature makes relatively little use of the phrase "implementing *Shari'a*." Rather, it stresses that man-made law should play a prominent role in the day-to-day affairs of the community, and that it should be formulated "within the framework (*itar*) of Islamic *Shari'a*."[164] This framework is to be delineated by elected representatives of the people. These representatives may consult with religious scholars (*'ulama*), but the *'ulama* have no authority to issue legislation or to declare legislation invalid. The only body with the authority to oversee laws

---

[162] The parliamentary election consisted of three rounds in November and December 2005. The first round was relatively clean. The subsequent rounds suffered from substantial violence and vote-rigging. When the dust settled, the Brotherhood had won eighty-eight seats—roughly 20 percent of the total. See Independent Committee for Elections Monitoring, "A Testimony for History: Monitoring the Egyptian 2005 Parliamentary Elections" (Cairo: ICEM, December 2005).

[163] *Mubadirat al-Ikhwan al-Muslimin hawwal Mabad' al-Islah fi Misr* (Cairo: Dar al-Manara, 2004), 12–13.

[164] Mahmud Ghazlan, "Five Reasons that Led to the Success of Our Candidates in Most Districts," *Afaq 'Arabiyya*, December 10, 2005, p. 5. Ghazlan is a prominent member of the Brotherhood's governing body, the Guidance Office (*Maktab al-Irshad*).

is the Supreme Constitutional Court, which evaluates laws based on their conformity with the Constitution.[165]

The MB argues that Parliament may not adopt legislation that "sanctions what is prohibited (*haram*) or prohibits what is permissible (*halal*)."[166] As examples, the MB specifies that Parliament may not issue laws that allow adultery, or which interfere with prayer or with the performance of the Haj.[167] Beyond the stipulation that man-made law may not directly contradict the *Shari'a*, the Brotherhood has adopted the broad conception of Islamic legality advocated by the theorists in chapter 3. The purpose of law is to "promote justice and to serve the best interests of the community."[168] "Implementing *Shari'a*" means that legislators pursue these two objectives. It does not entail adherence to a specific set of codes. While drafting laws, legislators may draw on a wide range of legal sources, including non-Muslim law.[169] In this regard, the Brotherhood has adopted a posture that is well-suited to the polyglot character of Egyptian law. Egyptian law is a mix of the French civil code, Islamic law, and some remnants of British law. The Brotherhood's conception of *Shari'a* suggests that it is fully prepared to accept most of this diverse legal tradition so long as it does not directly contradict *Shari'a*. It goes to considerable lengths to stress that its conceptualization of legal reform is compatible with the existing legal code, and would not require a dramatic change from it. *Shari'a* will be given practical effect "through constitutional and statutory law" drafted by representative institutions.[170] Conformity with *Shari'a* is defined in terms of *process* (it is drafted by elected legislators who draw on the advice of religious scholars, when appropriate) and *intent* (a genuine desire to serve justice and the public interest).

The extent of state power and constraints upon it. The MB's campaign documents conceptualize the state in the same terms as the theorists dis-

---

[165] Ibid., 5.

[166] Muhammad Mahdi 'Akif, "In a Comprehensive Dialog: The General Guide of the Muslim Brotherhood," *Afaq 'Arabiyya*, December 22, 2005.

[167] The Brotherhood's General Guide expressly states that the organization will not seek the adoption of strict Islamic criminal punishments (*hudud*). Ibid.

[168] *Al-Birnamij al-Intikhabi li-l Ikhwan al-Muslimin* (Cairo: n.p., issued October 15, 2005).

[169] Ibid. See also 'Isam al-'Iryan, "The Brotherhood, Parliament, and the Future . . . Egypt in a State of Transformation," *Afaq 'Arabiyya*, December 1, 2005.

[170] *Mubadirat al-Ikhwan al-Muslimin*, 4. Several Brotherhood leaders return to this theme of the organization's willingness to work with the existing regime and its institutions. For example, 'Isam al-'Iryan writes that the Brotherhood was prepared to run 250 candidates in the election. It ultimately chose to run only 161 in order to "not appear as if we were trying to monopolize the political competition, or that we were trying to overwhelm the regime." Al-'Iryan argues that this self-restraint shows the Brotherhood's willingness to compromise its own political ambitions in order to create a better climate for cooperation

cussed earlier. They view the state as an essential force for transforming both the individual and society. It is the mechanism for ensuring that people "worship, practice good manners, and act honorably."[171] It protects the rich and the poor,[172] distributes *zakat* (alms), guides industrial development, and initiates the revival of the country's agricultural sector.[173] Through these efforts, it "guards the economic system" and ensures the country's prosperity.[174] It strengthens the morality of individual Muslims by "purging the media of material that runs counter to the rules of Islam and the values that it instills."[175] It also shields believers from "alienation and disorientation" at the hands of salacious television programs and films.[176] It achieves "godliness and religiosity in society" by "constructing an individual with Islamic principles and values that are deeply rooted in his character"[177] and by "protecting values, ethics, and manners."[178] It builds and supervises an educational system that "deepens religious values, moral principles, and loyalty to the nation."[179] It also publishes books, holds conferences, develops television programs, and produces films that strengthen the ethical and moral foundations of society.[180]

This conception of the state as a moral actor is also reflected in the Brotherhood's call for reviving the doctrine of *hisba*, which empowers the state to "enjoin good and forbid evil" in individual Muslims.[181] It is an integral part of the Brotherhood's broader project of reforming society

with the regime. 'Isam al-'Iryan, "After the Election, Anxiety and Fear Will Soon Be Dispelled," *Afaq 'Arabiyya*, December 8, 2005.

[171] *Mubadirat al-Ikhwan al-Muslimin*, 12.

[172] The services that the state should provide to the poor include decent housing, clean water, electricity, balanced nutrition, clothing, health care, education, and medicine. These essentials should be made available at "affordable prices." The subsidies needed to pay for these services should be paid for by funds the state collects through *zakat*. *Mubadirat al-Ikhwan al-Muslimin*, 32–33.

[173] *Al-Birnamij al-Intikhabi*.

[174] *Mubadirat al-Ikhwan al-Muslimin*, 22. The MB views this role for the state as compatible with a strong private sector. It supports both private property and private enterprise, provided the owners pay the alms tax (*zakat*) required by Islamic law. *Mubadirat al-Ikhwan al-Muslimin*, 20. It advocates public ownership only in those areas of the economy that are essential for the nation's well-being, such as military production. Ghazlan, "Five Reasons that Led to the Success of Our Candidates," 5.

[175] *Al-Birnamij al-Intikhabi*.

[176] *Mubadirat al-Ikhwan al-Muslimin*, 38; private ownership of media outlets is allowed, but the state must monitor them in accordance with a "code of honor." *Al-Birnamij al-Intikhabi*.

[177] *Mubadirat al-Ikhwan al-Muslimin*, 34, 38.

[178] 'Akif, "In a Comprehensive Dialog."

[179] *Mubadirat al-Ikhwan al-Muslimin*, 27.

[180] Ibid., 38–39.

[181] This call is present in the Reform Initiative (Ibid., 34) as well as in the Brotherhood's campaign platform (*Al-Birnamij al-Intikhabi*).

through "returning to our faith."[182] Indeed, the state's active transformation of the character of individual Egyptians is the foundation for meaningful and sustained reform. In the Brotherhood's view, the morality of Egyptians has been steadily eroded by "selfishness and materialism."[183] The starting point for reform lies in rebuilding the character of each Egyptian based upon "faith, integrity, and sound ethical principles." Without this transformation in personal character, the process of reform will lack a firm foundation and resemble merely "ploughing the sea or building in the air."[184]

The Brotherhood clearly accepts the theorists' argument that a strong and invasive state is necessary for building pious individuals and a pious community. However, it also accepts the principle that this state must be monitored and constrained in order to ensure that it plays its transformative role effectively. The Brotherhood's campaign platform states that Egypt should "draw on the experience of modern civilizations" in order to reform its government and political life, as long as these examples do not contradict *Shari'a*.[185] It specifically calls for borrowing the principles of separation of powers, multiple political parties, and the peaceful rotation of power through free elections. The Brotherhood's campaign documents further state that governments are formed through a "social contract" (*al-'aqd al-ijtim'ai*) between ruler and ruled that is "established by the *umma* and carried out by the civil institutions of the state."[186] The *umma* controls the government and has the right to exercise authority over it. The ruler functions as an agent (*wakil*) of the people.[187] The MB provides no details on how this contract is drafted under current conditions, or whether the current Constitution is considered a contract.

The Brotherhood places particular emphasis on limiting the power of the president. It calls for converting the presidency into a largely ceremonial post with no executive power, in order to ensure that the president is "a symbol for all Egyptians and not the head of any political party."[188] It proposes that the president be chosen through multi-candidate elections,

---

[182] *Mubadirat al-Ikhwan al-Muslimin*, 8.

[183] Ibid., 11.

[184] All quotations are from *Mubadirat al-Ikhwan al-Muslimin*, 11. These themes are reiterated in newspaper editorials by several MB leaders during the parliamentary campaign. For example, Muhammad Mahdi 'Akif, "Intellectuals and Scholars Know Nothing About the Policy of the Muslim Brotherhood." *Al-Ghad*, December 7, 2005; 'Isam al-'Iryan, "What If the Muslim Brotherhood Ruled?" *Afaq 'Arabiyya*, December 15, 2005.

[185] *Al-Birnamij al-Intikhabi*.

[186] Ibid.

[187] Ibid.; Ghazlan, "Five Reasons that Led to the Success of Our Candidates," 5. Also, Muhammad Mahdi 'Akif, "The Muslim Brotherhood Will Not Rest until the Ruler Serves the People," *Afaq 'Arabiyya*, December 22, 2005.

[188] *Mubadirat al-Ikhwan al-Muslimin*, 16.

and that he be prohibited from serving consecutive terms.[189] The MB also calls for replacing the current emergency law with a new law that places sharp restrictions on the executive. In the MB's view, a state of emergency should be declared only in response to an active war or a natural disaster. The period of emergency should be limited and its renewal should be subject to clearly specified and stringent conditions. The law should prohibit the president from suspending the Constitution during an emergency and from compromising the basic rights of citizens.[190]

The MB also seeks to restructure the executive branch in order to further limit its power. For example, it advocates an end to state involvement in the operations of al-Azhar University. It notes that al-Azhar has historically been an essential force for "confronting tyrants and supporting the weak."[191] However, its capacity to check state power declined when it was nationalized by the Nasser regime in the 1960s. In order to restore al-Azhar to its historical role, the Sheikh of al-Azhar should no longer be appointed by the president. Rather, he should be elected by senior clerics. Revenue from religious endowments (*awqaf*) should no longer be channeled through the state budget, but should pass directly to al-Azhar. And, the executive should cease its practice of telling imams and preachers what they should say to their followers.[192] The MB also insists that the military remain uninvolved in politics, and that the minister of defense (as well as all other ministers) be civilians. Similarly, it stresses that the police and the internal security forces should be civilian and that they "not be used by the government to secure its stay in power or suppress the opposition."[193] These agencies should be "barred from intervening in public activities and elections."[194]

In addition, the MB makes several proposals for increasing the accountability of state officials. It calls for amending the Constitution to ensure that government ministers are held legally accountable for misdeeds con-

---

[189] Ibid. The Brotherhood's stand regarding restrictions on the president's term in office varies. 'Akif and Ghazlan say that he should be limited to two, four-year terms. 'Akif, "In a Comprehensive Dialog"; Ghazlan, "Five Reasons that Led to the Success of Our Candidates," 5.

[190] Ghazlan, "Five Reasons that Led to the Success of Our Candidates," 5.

[191] *Mubadirat al-Ikhwan al-Muslimin*, 30.

[192] Ibid., 31–32.

[193] Ibid., 16.

[194] Ibid. The General Guide of the MB argues that the regime systematically uses these government agencies to manipulate elections and suppress its opponents. See Muhammad Mahdi 'Akif, "NDP Uses Despicable Methods to Forge the Elections," *Afaq 'Arabiyya*, November 17, 2005; Muhammad Mahdi 'Akif, "No Hope in Mubarak, His Son, or NDP," *al-Dustur*, December 14, 2005.

ducted in office.[195] It also calls for decentralizing power by granting provincial governments the authority to impose taxes and to make local policy decisions.[196] This measure should be accompanied by reforms that grant municipal councils the authority to monitor officials appointed by the state, investigate charges of wrong-doing against them, and dismiss officials who abuse their power.[197]

The MB places considerable emphasis on strengthening the autonomy of the judiciary. In its view, the judiciary is the "safety valve" that allows for the resolution of disputes before they lead to violence or social disorder. The judiciary must be independent in order to play this role effectively. The MB supports the new judicial law proposed by the Judges' Club in 1991 and reissued in 2004, which substantially strengthens the judiciary's budgetary independence and gives it complete control over the hiring and promotion of judges. In the words of the General Guide, this proposed law will "give these noble men their independence so they can perform their duty to defend justice, truth, and honor."[198] In addition, the Brotherhood calls for abolishing exceptional courts and limiting the jurisdiction of military courts to disputes involving military personnel. It supports two reforms long advocated by the Judges' Club: a firm guarantee that citizens will be tried before their "natural judge," which effectively means an end to the use of exceptional courts and military courts to try civilians; and a clear separation between the office of the prosecutor (*niyaba*) and the Ministry of Justice, in order to ensure that the prosecutorial process is not tainted by political considerations.[199]

In addition to these measures, the Brotherhood seeks to strengthen the Parliament and make it a more effective check on executive power. The MB supports increasing the Parliament's budget and staffing, as well as expanding its power to initiate laws, review the state's budget, and investigate the decisions and conduct of ministers.[200] The Brotherhood also calls for dramatic expansion of civil society, which it considers a "strategic partner" in its efforts to achieve reform and an essential force for balancing state power.[201] In pursuit of this goal, it advocates repealing laws that interfere with the formation, funding, and operation of civil society groups. It singles out the current law governing professional syndicates (Law 100/

---

[195] *Al-Birnamij al-Intikhabi.*
[196] Ibid.
[197] Ibid.
[198] 'Akif, "In a Comprehensive Dialog."
[199] *Mubadirat al-Ikhwan al-Muslimin,* 18.
[200] 'Akif, "In a Comprehensive Dialog ."
[201] *Al-Birnamij al-Intikhabi.*

1993) and the laws governing labor unions as particularly severe infringements on civil society that need immediate reform.[202]

Civil and political rights: Mahmud Ghazlan, one of the Brotherhood's most senior members, wrote during the parliamentary campaign that the organization "supports public freedoms within the framework of the Constitution, the prevailing system (*nitham*), and public custom."[203] The organization supports freedom of speech "within the limits of public order, social decorum, and society's constants."[204] The freedom to own and use different forms of media is also advocated. The freedom to own and use property is backed so long as it "plays its social function" and advances the interests of the community.[205] Freedom of assembly is supported "within the limits of the safety of society and public security."[206] The MB further advocates canceling all laws that "restrict freedom and have caused stagnation in the political life of Egypt." More specifically, it calls for annulling the emergency law and the laws dealing with political parties, the socialist public prosecutor, political rights, the press, and professional syndicates.[207] It proposes that all past verdicts issued by military courts and exceptional courts should be reviewed and, where necessary, new trials should be held before ordinary tribunals. It also supports the release of all political prisoners and a firm ban on torture. Toward this end, it advocates reducing the role of the state security forces (*al-amn al-markazi*) in maintaining public order, and expanding the role of the police.[208]

The Brotherhood's campaign literature discusses the rights of women in considerable depth. It stresses that men and women hold the same spiritual and moral value in the eyes of God, and cites the Qur'anic passages that proclaim that God "honors all the children of Adam" and that "heaven is at the feet of mothers."[209] Women should be treated equally in criminal, civil, and financial matters. They can make financial decisions without the approval of a male relative, and they may participate fully in Parliament and other elected institutions.[210] They can be appointed to all public posts except that of Grand Imam or president of the state, as long as the post does not compromise a woman's "chastity, morality, or honor."[211] The prohibition on a woman becoming president is not abso-

---

[202] Ibid.
[203] Ghazlan, "Five Reasons that Led to the Success of Our Candidates," 5.
[204] *Mubadirat al-Ikhwan al-Muslimin*, 14.
[205] Ibid., 20; Ghazlan, "Five Reasons that Led to the Success of Our Candidates," 5.
[206] *Mubadirat al-Ikhwan al-Muslimin*, 14.
[207] Ibid., 16–17. Also, *Al-Birnamij al-Intikhabi*.
[208] *Mubadirat al-Ikhwan al-Muslimin*, 16–17.
[209] *Mubadirat al-Ikhwan al-Muslimin*, 35.
[210] Ibid., 35–37; *Al-Birnamij al-Intikhabi*.
[211] *Mubadirat al-Ikhwan al-Muslimin*, 36.

lute. It holds only "under our current circumstances" due to the prevailing sentiments in society toward women assuming positions of political leadership.[212] The MB also calls for improving women's education, but it again stresses that these reforms should conform to prevailing social attitudes. It states that women's education should be "in accordance with the nature, role, and needs of women."[213] When traveling or working, women should be assured that they will be physically safe and respected.[214]

In addition, the General Guide claims that the Brotherhood wanted to run twenty-five female candidates in the 2005 parliamentary elections. However, he asserts that the security forces mistreated female candidates in the past. As a consequence, the husbands of these potential candidates would not allow their wives to enter the elections for fear they might be injured or insulted.[215]

The MB's campaign literature shows a similar degree of attention to the rights of Copts. The Reform Initiative states that Copts are an integral part of the social fabric and "partners in the nation (al-watan)."[216] In its discussion of Copts, the Brotherhood introduces—for the first time—the term "citizenship" into its discourse. Its electoral program states that the MB considers all Egyptians to be equal as citizens, regardless of religion.[217] As a consequence, Copts have the same rights and duties as Muslims. They have full freedom of belief and worship, and may utilize their own religious law in matters related to personal status. They are also permitted to engage in conduct that is forbidden to Muslims, such as consuming alcohol and pork.[218] This level of tolerance is essential for "preserving the spirit of brotherhood that has prevailed over the centuries among all the children of Egypt . . . and discouraging any activity that leads to sectarianism

[212] Ibid.

[213] Ibid., 37.

[214] Ibid.

[215] 'Akif, "In a Comprehensive Dialog." The Brotherhood ultimately ran only one female candidate in the election. She was not successful.

[216] *Mubadirat al-Ikhwan al-Muslimin*, 37.

[217] *Al-Birnamij al-Intikhabi*. One of the members of the Brotherhood's Guidance Office, 'Abd al-Mon'am Abu al-Fatuh, wrote after the election that "the citizen is considered the foundation of society, regardless of religion or color." He adds that the *jizya* (tax on non-Muslims) and the concept of *dhimmi* (separate legal status assigned to non-Muslims) are "historical terms only, which have been replaced by the concept of citizenship-based democracy in a nation of justice and law." 'Abd al-Mon'am Abu al-Fatuh, "Reformist Islam: How Gray Are the Gray Zones?" *Arab Reform Bulletin*. 4:6 (July 2006).

[218] Ghazlan, "Five Reasons that Led to the Success of Our Candidates," 5. Also, Muhammad Habib, "No Reason for Copts to Be Afraid of Us . . . They Are Citizens and They Have Rights as Well as Responsibilities," *Al-Ghad*, December 28, 2005; 'Abd al-Mon'am Abu al-Fatuh, "Letter from the Muslim Brotherhood to the Copts," *Afaq 'Arabiyya*, December 15, 2005.

or fanaticism among Egyptians."[219] The Brotherhood's electoral platform also cites a passage from the Qur'an that reaffirms freedom of religious belief.[220] During the campaign, MB candidates stressed that their organization sought to represent the entire nation and that the Brotherhood would provide services to all citizens—both Muslim and Coptic.[221] The General Guide of the MB called for a formal dialog with Coptic leaders to address their concerns.[222] Brotherhood leaders have also supported the formation of a Coptic political party that would defend and promote the interests of Copts.[223] Some Coptic leaders are skeptical of these promises.[224] However, the Brotherhood's campaign documents went to considerable lengths to reassure the Coptic community that the MB respects their rights.

It should be noted that the Brotherhood's tolerance of freedom of belief is limited to the "heavenly religions"—that is, Christianity and Judaism. The holy books in each of these faiths are considered divine revelations and, as a consequence, the followers of these faiths deserve respect and protection. However, the MB is not equally open-minded toward other religions. For example, it supported the government's efforts to deny official recognition to Bahaism and to prevent Baha'is from listing their faith on their identity cards.[225]

Public participation in politics: In this arena, the MB reiterates the broad themes mentioned by the theorists in chapter 3. The MB's electoral program states that "*Shura* is a fundamental concept in Islam, and democracy is its most appropriate mechanism within the modern state."[226] It entails allowing citizens to "select their representatives to all legislative institutions, as well as the leaders of the executive branch, professional syndicates,

[219] *Mubadirat al-Ikhwan al-Muslimin*, 37–38.

[220] *Al-Birnamij al-Intikhabi.*

[221] This theme appears repeatedly in the coverage of the MB's campaign by its de facto weekly newspaper, *Afaq 'Arabiyya.* See the issues from November 10 through December 29, 2005.

[222] "The Muslim Brotherhood's Guide Invites the Copts to a Political Dialog, and Copts Respond with Skepticism," *al-Sharq al-Awsat,* November 28, 2005.

[223] Personal interview with 'Isam al-'Iryan, December 21, 2005.

[224] See, for example, Milad Hanna, "If the Muslim Brotherhood Gains Power the Copts Will Leave Egypt," *al-'Arabi,* November 20, 2005; Majdi Khalil, "The Brotherhood in Parliament," *al-Watani,* December 4, 2005; Majdi Khalil, "The Muslim Brotherhood and the Copts," *al-Watani,* January 1, 2006.

[225] Mahmud Matwalli, "Alliance of the Brotherhood and Independent Deputies Warn Against Abolishing the Religion Blank in National Identity Card," *Nahdat Misr,* September 21, 2006; "The Brotherhood Protests the [Human] Rights Proposal to Change the Religion Blank on Official Papers," *al-Hayat,* September 12, 2007. For further information about restrictions on religious freedom in Egypt, see *Egypt—Prohibited Identities: State Interference with Religious Freedom* (New York: Human Rights Watch, November 2007).

[226] *Al-Birnamij al-Intikhabi.*

and private associations."[227] This broad public participation in political life is the only way to "carry forward the campaign for the nation."[228]

In addition, the people are the source of political authority. The MB's reform initiative proclaims, "No individual or party or association or body may style itself as the sole source of power, nor may it exercise power, without being chosen through the free expression of the people's will."[229] The representatives of the people must be chosen through fair elections and serve a limited term.[230] Furthermore, leaders at all levels of society are required to consult with the people or their representatives in order to ensure that public policy truly serves the public interest. Leaders are "civil leaders in every respect," without religious authority, and thus are fully accountable to the people.[231] Citizens can dismiss a ruler if he disregards their wishes or if his policies fail to serve the interests of the community.[232] These principles of participation and accountability are "core principles in Islam."[233] They are not open to change. The only thing that may vary is the specific institutions used to achieve them. Thus, there may be variations among countries over the type of democratic system (presidential or parliamentary), whether Parliament is bicameral or unicameral, the structure of the electoral system (proportional representation, first-past-the-post, or another alternative), and the length of the term served by members of Parliament and the president.[234]

In contemporary Egypt, the MB argues that public participation is best achieved through a parliamentary system in which the party winning the most votes in a free election is empowered to form a government.[235] These elections must be organized by a neutral organization or agency.[236] Each citizen has a right to vote and to run for office. Beyond these broad principles, the Brotherhood calls for specific reforms that will render elections more free and fair. Security agencies and the Ministry of Justice should be barred from any involvement in elections. The judiciary should supervise the entire electoral process—from drawing up voter lists through bal-

---

[227] Ibid.

[228] Ibid. See also 'Abd al-Mon'am Abu al-Fatuh, "We Will Dissolve the Brotherhood After We Become a Political Party," *al- 'Arabi*, November 27, 2005.

[229] *Mubadirat al-Ikhwan al-Muslimin*, 13.

[230] Ibid., 15.

[231] *Al-Birnamij al-Intikhabi*.

[232] *Mubadirat al-Ikhwan al-Muslimin*, 12–17; *Al-Birnamij al-Intikhabi*; Ghazlan, "Five Reasons that Led to the Success of Our Candidates," 5.

[233] Ghazlan, "Five Reasons that Led to the Success of Our Candidates," 5. Also, Muhammad Mahdi 'Akif, "No Hope in Mubarak, His Son, or NDP," *al-Dustur*, December 14, 2005.

[234] Ghazlan, "Five Reasons that Led to the Success of Our Candidates," 5.

[235] *Mubadirat al-Ikhwan al-Muslimin*, 15.

[236] Ibid.

loting, counting the ballots, and declaring the results. And, there should be no restrictions on campaigning. Candidates should be free to hold rallies, distribute leaflets, and hang posters without interference.[237]

The MB also advocates greater use of elections within al-Azhar, including the creation of a "senior clerics council" whose members would be elected by all clerics. This council would, in turn, elect the Sheikh of al-Azhar from among its members. The Brotherhood further calls for reducing the power of senior clerics at al-Azhar and granting greater freedom to imams and preachers to explain the principles and values of Islam.[238]

Finally, the MB seeks to strengthen political parties by removing impediments to the formation of parties and ending government interference in their operation. It expressly calls for an end to the political parties committee of the *Shura* council, which currently exercises veto power over the formation of parties. It advocates empowering the administrative judiciary to resolve all disputes regarding the establishment of parties.[239] However, the Brotherhood is divided over whether to create its own political party.[240] The General Guide states that the organization should wait until all the existing laws that interfere with the operation of parties are repealed. The Brotherhood's spokesman, 'Isam al-'Iryan, wants the Brotherhood to move more quickly to establish a political party with a "civil character" that would be open to membership by all citizens (including Copts). This type of party would mobilize more citizens into the political process, build trust between Muslims and Copts, and strengthen national unity.[241]

• • •

As this discussion suggests, the Brotherhood's political agenda in 2005 incorporated many of the principles of Islamic constitutionalism. The organization articulated this moderate view with remarkable consistency

[237] Ibid., 19–20. See also 'Isam al-'Iryan, "The Muslim Brotherhood and the Challenges of the Future," *Afaq 'Arabiyya*, January 5, 2006.

[238] *Mubadirat al-Ikhwan al-Muslimin*, 30–32.

[239] Personal interview with 'Isam al-'Iryan, December 21, 2005.

[240] For further discussion of the debate within the MB over forming a political party, see Nathan J. Brown and Amr Hamzawy, *The Draft Platform of the Egyptian Muslim Brotherhood: Foray into Political Integration or Retreat into Old Positions?* (Washington, DC: Carnegie Endowment for International Peace, January 2008), 10–15.

[241] Personal interview with 'Isam al-'Iryan, December 21, 2005. Al-'Iryan wants the Brotherhood to separate its religious and political activities. Its religious (*da'wa*) activity should focus on education and seek to spread the faith, in cooperation with al-Azhar University's *da'wa* programs. The political party would pursue a conservative social agenda that would appeal to both Muslims and Copts. Al-'Iryan argues that the party should be modeled on similar Islamic parties that have emerged in Jordan, Morocco, Pakistan, Malaysia, and Indonesia. 'Isam al-'Iryan, "After the Election, Anxiety and Fear Will Soon Be Dispelled," *Afaq 'Arabiyya*, December 8, 2005. For a similar view, see Khayrat al-Shatir, "We Will Become a Political Party at the Appropriate Time without Licensing from the Committee on Party Affairs," *al-'Arabi*, December 11, 2005.

throughout the 2005 campaign. It was stated clearly in the official campaign documents that were approved by the MB's governing body (the Guidance Office—*Maktab al-Irshad*). It was also presented in myriad interviews and editorials by the organization's leaders. The MB maintained a similarly united front during the May 2007 *Shura* Council elections. Although the regime worked vigorously to exclude the Brotherhood from these elections, the MB still issued a campaign platform that reiterated almost word-for-word the documents from the 2005 parliamentary campaign.[242] Observers sometimes wondered whether this moderate posture reflected the views of the entire organization. However, if there was dissent, the Brotherhood's leadership concealed it from public view.

The first evidence of internal disagreements within the MB emerged in the summer and fall of 2007. The Guidance Office formed a committee to draft a preliminary party platform, in preparation for formally declaring an MB political party. The large majority of this 128-page document was a faithful restatement of the positions put forward in the 2005 campaign materials. It expressed the MB's support for the rule of law, constraints on state power, and protection of basic civil and political rights. In many areas, it used language identical to that employed in the 2005 documents.[243] However, it contained several passages that reflect the reservations of some Brotherhood leaders toward unrestricted democracy. For example, the Brotherhood's documents from 2005 spoke in general terms about members of Parliament consulting with religious scholars in order to ensure that legislation did not violate the principles of *Shari'a*. The 2007 draft party platform gave this concept greater specificity by proposing the establishment of a "council of senior religious scholars."[244] Members of this council would be selected by their fellow *'ulama* in "free and direct elections."[245] The council would study proposed legislation and offer opinions on whether it conformed to *Shari'a*. However, the draft platform was vague about the degree of influence that these opinions would carry. It suggested that the council's views would be binding on legislators in those areas where the meaning of *Shari'a* is "certain and

[242] *Al-Birnamij al-Intikhabi li-l-Ikhwan al-Muslimin fi Majlis as-Shura*, issued May 14, 2007.

[243] This is particularly the case for the portion of the document that discusses political institutions. *Birnamij Hizb al-Ikhwan al-Muslimin: al-Isdar al-Awal*, August 25, 2007, 11–24.

[244] The precise phrase is *hay't min kubar 'ulama*. As noted earlier, a council of religious scholars was mentioned in the 2004 Reform Initiative in the context of reforming al-Azhar. In this earlier document, the council was to be selected by a vote among all the *'ulama*. It would then be responsible for choosing the Sheikh of al-Azhar from among its members. *Mubadirat al-Ikhwan al-Muslimin . . .*, 31.

[245] *Birnamij Hizb al-Ikhwan al-Muslimin: al-Isdar al-Awal*, 10. The Parliament would define the general qualifications for participation on the council. It would also determine the council's precise responsibilities.

unchanging."²⁴⁶ These areas were not spelled out.²⁴⁷ On all other topics (i.e., those where devout Muslims can disagree), the council's opinions would be nonbinding. The legislature would be required to consider the council's views, but it would be free to reach its own decision based on a majority vote. The clause's imprecision regarding the scope of the council's powers provoked a sharp response within the Brotherhood and in Egyptian society as a whole. There was particular concern that the council would be empowered to veto legislation that it deemed incompatible with Islam. In subsequent interviews, the presumed author of the passage—Muhammad Habib, the Deputy General Guide of the MB²⁴⁸—emphasized that the council's powers would be only advisory.²⁴⁹ It would provide "expert advice" on issues of Islamic law, which legislators could then utilize during their deliberations. This view was shared by the General Guide, Muhammad 'Akif, who stated that the council of religious scholars would only issue advisory opinions to the Parliament. He further stressed that the Parliament should have unrestricted power to draft and adopt legislation.²⁵⁰

The issue at stake here is quite fundamental: how will the principles of *Shari'a* be translated into specific legislation? The Islamic constitutionalists discussed in chapter 3 argue that this is accomplished through the deliberations of an elected Parliament that functions as the modern-day counterpart to the "people who loose and bind" in classical thought. The Brotherhood adopted this view in its 2005 campaign documents. It reiter-

---

²⁴⁶ Ibid., 10.

²⁴⁷ The idea that *Shari'a* contains core principles whose meaning cannot be disputed by devout Muslims is mentioned in the 2004 Reform Initiative. In that document, the five pillars of Islam are identified as definitive components of *Shari'a* (the statement of witness, prayer five times per day, alms giving [*zakat*], participation in the pilgrimage [*haj*], and fasting during Ramadan). An Islamic government could not take any action that restricted a Muslim's capacity to perform these duties. In addition, an Islamic government could not adopt legislation that allowed Muslims to consume alcohol or engage in adultery. The draft party platform does not explicitly state any additional definitive features of *Shari'a*. However, subsequent discussion of the platform indicated that some of the Brotherhood's members believe there is at least one other issue where *Shari'a* is definitive: women and non-Muslims may not hold the most senior political posts in an Islamic state.

²⁴⁸ Brown and Hamzawy, *The Draft Party Platform of the Egyptian Muslim Brotherhood*, 7. Other MB leaders who supported this passage include Muhammad Mursi and Mahmud 'Izzat.

²⁴⁹ 'Abdo Zina, "Brotherhood of Egypt Admit Mistake in their Platform for a Political Party Regarding the Suggested Council of Scholars," *al-Sharq al-Awsat*, October 16, 2007; "Text of Dr. Muhammad Habib's Conversation with Ikhwan Web," http://www.ikhwanonline.com/, November 11, 2007; "Text of Dialogue with Dr. Muhammad Habib," http://www.ikhwanonline.com/, December 6, 2007.

²⁵⁰ "Interview with the Guide of the Muslim Brotherhood, Muhammad Mahdi 'Akif, *al-Misri al-Youm*, November 24, 2007.

ated this view in the portion of the draft platform that deals with political institutions, in a discussion that runs over thirteen pages.[251] However, the passage inserted by Habib (which consists of only four lines at the beginning of the document) demonstrates that some Brotherhood leaders are not entirely comfortable with this formulation. This brief passage clearly was not an effort to reject the lengthy and detailed support for an elected Parliament that appears later in the draft platform, and which is emphasized in subsequent interviews with senior MB leaders. However, the passage reflects an underlying concern about democracy that persists within parts of the leadership and the rank-and-file. They fear that elected representatives may adopt legislation that is at odds with the core principles of the faith. As noted in chapter 3, this concern was also expressed by some of the theorists of Islamic constitutionalism (particularly, al-Qaradawi and Abu al-Majd). The council of religious scholars would provide expertise and advice that addresses this concern.

The draft platform contains another feature that further demonstrates the reservations of some Brotherhood leaders toward unrestricted democracy. While the draft platform reiterates the MB's long-standing view that Copts enjoy "full rights and duties" as citizens, it adds an important caveat: a non-Muslim should not hold the post of president or prime minister.[252] It explains this position by arguing that the country's most senior political leaders play an important role in ensuring the Islamic character of the state and society. A non-Muslim lacks the religious knowledge and personal convictions needed to perform this role effectively. This issue is discussed by some of the theorists of Islamic constitutionalism analyzed in chapter 3. Al-Qaradawi, for example, writes that the president should be Muslim and that the majority of Parliament should be Muslim.[253] How-

---

[251] *Birnamij Hizb al-Ikhwan al-Muslimin: al-Isdar al-Awal*, 11–24.

[252] Ibid., 15. The draft platform does not propose the adoption of legislation that prohibits Copts from holding these posts. Rather, it simply expresses the MB's view that only Muslims should hold these positions. Habib and other Brotherhood leaders indicated in subsequent interviews that, while they would not support a Copt for these posts, they would accept this outcome if it was the result of a free election. Ahmad al-Khatib, "The Brotherhood Leans toward Agreeing on Nominating a Copt to Presidency in the Final Draft of the Platform of the Party," *al-Misri al-Youm*, October 23, 2007; "Interview with the Guide of the Muslim Brotherhood, Mahdi 'Akif, *al-Misri al-Youm*, November 24, 2007; Islam 'Abd al-'Aziz, "The Brothers: No Firing of al-'Iryan and We Settled the Ruling of a Copt," http://www.islamonline.net/, November 7, 2007; 'Adil al-Darjali, "Heated Hour . . . Abu al-Fatuh: Impossible for Christian to Be President . . . and the Brotherhood Group Settles on the Right of the Citizen," *al-Misri al-Youm*, August 22, 2007; "Representatives of the Brotherhood: We Agree to the Candidacy of a Copt for the Presidency of the Republic So Long as He Fulfills the [Constitutional] Requirements," *al-Misri al-Youm*, September 13, 2006.

[253] Al-Qaradawi, *Min Fiqh al-Dawla*, 32, 195.

ever, this view had not appeared previously in the MB's political documents. In a like vein, the draft platform reiterates that women have full legal equality and the right to vote and to run for office. However, it adds a similar caveat: a woman should not serve as president.[254] This position is justified through reference to a woman's primary role as mother and wife, which renders her unsuited for the demanding responsibilities of the presidency. Significantly, this is a deviation from the views of the theorists discussed earlier. Al-Qaradawi, in particular, emphasizes that women are prohibited only from serving as head of the *umma* (the entire community of Muslims). He argues that an individual nation-state is only a small subset of the *umma*, and therefore the prohibition on women serving as leader of the *umma* does not apply.[255] Despite al-Qaradawi's view, the Brotherhood expressed its opposition to women holding the presidency in the 2004 reform initiative. While some MB members claimed that this position was required by *Shari'a*, most of the leadership explained that it reflected the values that prevail in contemporary Egypt.[256] Patriarchy is a well-entrenched norm in Egypt, particularly among the socially conservative segments of society that support the Brotherhood. The MB's leaders were responding to this sentiment among the rank-and-file.

It should be noted that this draft platform was not endorsed by the leadership body of the MB (the Guidance Office).[257] It also was not endorsed by the General Guide, Muhammad 'Akif, who emphasized that the draft platform was only a means to air ideas and to gain feedback from intellectuals and others on the best political direction for the organization.[258] Furthermore, the draft platform clearly was not a renunciation of the moderate views articulated in the 2005 campaign documents. Indeed, one of the striking features of the draft platform is the extent to which it incorporates these earlier documents. Rather, the three controversial

---

[254] *Birnamij Hizb al-Ikhwan al-Muslimin: al-Isdar al-Awal*, 103.

[255] Al-Qaradawi, *Min Fiqh al-Dawla*, 165, 175–76.

[256] "Text of Dialogue with Dr. Muhammad Habib," http://www.ikhwanonline.com/, December 6, 2007; Muhammad Gharib, "Al-'Iryan: The Reality Does Not Allow More than Three Women and Four Christians in Parliament," *al-Misri al-Youm*, October 29, 2007. Also, Khalil al-'Anani, "Internal Differences Stir Predictions about the Future of the Group: The Brotherhood of Egypt and the Story of 'Rule of Women and Copts,'" *al-Hayat*, November 7, 2007.

[257] The leader of the Brotherhood stated that the organization will analyze the many comments on the draft party platform and then issue a final platform that reflects the official views of the Guidance Office. "Interview with the Guide of the Muslim Brotherhood, Mahdi 'Akif." However, as of March 2008 (when this manuscript went to press), the final version of the platform had not been issued.

[258] "Dialogue with the Guide of the Muslim Brotherhood, Mahdi 'Akif," *al-Misri al-Youm*, November 24, 2007; Islam 'Abd al-'Aziz, "The Brothers: No Firing of al-'Iryan and We Settled Ruling of Copt," http://www.islamonline.net/, November 7, 2007.

positions mentioned above were adopted in order to affirm that a democratic political order would still respect and defend the core principles of *Shari'a*. These positions were also designed to demonstrate that the Brotherhood's leadership still shares the conservative social values held by many of the organization's members, particularly with regard to the role of women in society.

The debate over the Brotherhood's draft party platform raises an important question: does the moderate path presented in the Brotherhood's official documents enjoy broad support within the organization? There are several points of evidence which suggest that the moderate view articulated in the 2005 campaign documents commands substantial backing. As mentioned earlier, the 2007 draft party platform incorporates all of the key features of the 2005 campaign documents. There is no indication that the conservative wing of the leadership attempted to remove these moderate passages, despite having the opportunity to do so. The most that it attempted was to temper this moderate position with modifications that placed limits on the scope of unrestricted democracy, particularly by granting religious scholars an explicit role in advising the legislature and by limiting the opportunities for women and Copts to hold the most senior positions of political power. While these are important limits, they are also quite narrow: they must be weighted against what appears to be broad agreement within the leadership over the moderate character of the large majority of the 128-page draft party platform.

Another indicator of the extent of internal support for this moderate posture lies in the Brotherhood's conduct in Parliament. As mentioned earlier, the MB won roughly 20 percent of the seats contested in the 2005 election. Its subsequent performance in Parliament provides an opportunity to determine which political goals the organization pursues when it has a share (however small) of political power. Furthermore, this political power is held by Brotherhood MPs with direct accountability to the organization's electoral base. As a consequence, it is reasonable to assume that the positions adopted by the Brotherhood's parliamentary delegation are calculated, at least in part, to respond to the wishes of the organization's grassroots supporters.

The following discussion of the MB's conduct in Parliament is based on analysis of relevant articles that appeared in the newspaper *al-Misri al-Youm* from December 2005 (when the Parliament convened) through March 2008. According to this reporting, the Brotherhood was active in the following areas:

Corruption: This topic consumed more of the MB delegation's attention than any other. MB members of Parliament called for investigations into several alleged abuses of executive power, including: the government bribing MPs to vote in favor of the emergency law; NDP officials using their positions to gain preferential access to government land and other resources; granting of pilgrimage (*haj*) visas to NDP members at reduced cost, and providing them with government funds to offset the expenses of the pilgrimage; selling pilgrimage visas on the black market; and selling government land to Israeli investors in exchange for bribes.

Judicial reform: The MB voiced strong backing for the Judges' Club's proposed amendments to the law of the judiciary. It also expressed support for two prominent judges (Ahmad Makki and Hisham Bastawisi) who were subjected to disciplinary proceedings for reporting widespread fraud during the 2005 parliamentary elections. In addition, the MB criticized the judicial reform law put forward by the government and proclaimed that it failed to adequately protect judicial independence. Finally, the MB sharply criticized the law of the military judiciary and stressed that military courts should not be used to try civilians.

Renewal of the emergency law: The emergency law came up for renewal in April 2006. The MB delegation declared the law an abandonment of the Constitution and boycotted Parliament on the day when the vote was taken. It also organized public demonstrations in front of the Parliament building to protest the law. It further called for a recorded vote, in order to enable the public to see precisely which MPs supported the measure.

The power of the Ministry of Interior: Within the first month of taking their seats in Parliament, the MB delegation called for an investigation into the Ministry of Interior's role in allegedly manipulating the 2005 parliamentary elections. It also initiated several formal inquiries regarding cases of alleged torture by members of the security services. In addition, it called on the Ministry to clearly state the legal grounds for detaining several hundred citizens whom the MB described as political prisoners. The MB also made repeated calls to reduce the extent of the Ministry of Interior's influence over the administration of mosques. It alleged that the Ministry effectively determines who will be appointed as the imam of a mosque, and that it also dictates what the imam can say during his weekly sermon.

The Constitutional Amendments of March 2007: The MB delegation criticized the amendments sharply, asserting that they "abandon any hope of democracy." It particularly criticized the amendment to article 179, which substantially expands the authority of the security services to monitor and detain citizens with little judicial oversight. It described these clauses as a "return to a police state" and "thoroughly at odds with the goal of political reform."[259]

---

[259] "The Opposition, the MB, and the Independents: the Constitutional Amendments Are a 'Crime,'" *al-Misri al-Youm*, March 13, 2007; "102 Deputies Walk Out on the Constitutional Changes Session . . . and Most Say It Is the Day of Judgment," *al-Misri al-Youm*, March 19, 2007.

Accountability of state institutions during national crises: Three domestic crises occurred during the period under review: an overloaded ferry capsized in the Red Sea, killing most of its occupants; a train caught fire in upper Egypt, which led to the death of more than one hundred passengers; and there was evidence that an epidemic of bird flu may have spread to Egypt. On each occasion, the MB's delegation alleged that the government had failed to respond to the crisis adequately. It also called for full investigations of the government's performance.

Economic and budgetary policy: The MB delegation did not challenge the government's goal of privatizing public assets. However, it sharply criticized the conduct of the privatization process. It alleged that public-sector assets were being sold at a fraction of their actual value. It also argued that "strategic assets," such as public-sector banks (Banque du Caire), should be sold only to Egyptian investors. In addition, the MB advocated on several occasions for an increase in the budget for education. It called for hiring more teachers for public schools, and for increasing the salaries and pensions for teachers. It also called for greater financial support for public universities. Finally, it criticized a government proposal to grant large loans to support several state-controlled banks on the grounds that the loans were not a sound use of public funds.

Parliamentary procedure: The MB delegation made repeated efforts to modify the internal procedures of Parliament to allow the opposition a stronger voice, particularly in parliamentary committees. It also proposed that the executive branch be required to respond more quickly to questions from MPs (this position arose after the executive ignored several questions raised by members of the MB delegation). The MB delegation also insisted that the Parliament publish written minutes of its sessions within 140 days, as required by law.

Women's rights/the hijab: In November 2006, the Minister of Culture (Faruq Husni) stated that he considered the *hijab* a symbol of backwardness. The MB delegation in Parliament denounced this claim. It further asserted that wearing the *hijab* is a sign of devoutness that is required by Islam, and called for Husni to either withdraw his statement or resign.[260] He did neither.

---

[260] The MB's demand for Husni's resignation was framed in legalistic terms. It argued that the Constitution proclaims that Islam is the religion of the state, and that Islam requires women to wear the *hijab*. Therefore, Husni's hostility toward the *hijab* was at odds with the Constitution and should be grounds for dismissal. See Mahmud Muslim and Muna Yasin, "Ikhwan Demand President of the Republic Dismiss Faruq Husni." *al-Misri al-Youm*, November 18, 2006. It should be noted that the MB's General Guide, Muhammad 'Akif, stated that the MB does not advocate the adoption of a law that requires women to wear the *hijab*. Rather, it believes that women should be encouraged to wear the *hijab* and that the government should take no action that discourages them from doing so. He also asserted that the debate over the *hijab* is a relatively minor issue and should not be allowed to distract

In early 2008, the ruling National Democratic Party proposed several laws to improve women's rights. This legislation called for full equality between men and women in business transactions,[261] an increase in the minimum marriage age for women (from sixteen to eighteen), and a ban on female circumcision (female genital mutilation). Although the MB delegation as a whole did not take a stand on this legislation, individual members of the delegation opposed these laws on the grounds that they were at odds with *Shari'a* and weakened Egypt's traditional values and culture. They asked that deliberations on the proposed laws be postponed until religious scholars from al-Azhar could provide authoritative interpretations of *Shari'a* on the matters at issue.[262]

Israel: In March 2007, a documentary shown in Israel alleged that Israeli troops had executed 250 Egyptian POWs during the 1967 war. The MB delegation demanded a full investigation. However, even prior to the investigation, it called for expelling the Israeli ambassador to Egypt and withdrawing the Egyptian ambassador to Israel. The MB also took a firm stand against Israeli military incursions in Lebanon (in the summer of 2006) and Gaza (in February 2008). On each occasion, the MB delegation staged a sit-in at the Parliament and participated in demonstrations against the Israeli action. It also called on Parliament to suspend diplomatic relations with Israel and to increase economic assistance to Lebanon and Palestine. However, the MB's parliamentary delegation did not call for terminating diplomatic ties with Israel or cancelling the Camp David accords.[263]

This pattern of conduct indicates that the MB used its position in Parliament to advance many of the goals spelled out in the 2005 campaign materials. It sought to increase constraints on executive power, strengthen the rule of law, and improve protection of some civil and political rights.

---

the public's attention from more important matters such as government corruption. Majdi 'Abd al-Rasul, "Guide of the Brotherhood: The Crisis of the *Hijab* Is a Fog and the Minister of Culture has his Views." *al-'Arabi al-Nasiri*, November 26, 2006.

[261] The point at issue was the number of women needed to witness a business transaction. Currently, the law requires two women, whereas one male witness is acceptable.

[262] Muhammad Abu Zayd, "People's Assembly Representative Requests that a Woman's Testimony be Equal to that of a Man's . . . and the Brotherhood Refuses," *al-Misri al-Youm*, March 11, 2008; Huda Rashwan, "The Child's Law Reaches the Shura Council and will be Discussed in the People's Assembly after 20 Days," *al-Misri al-Youm*, March 6, 2008.

[263] The parliamentary delegation's position was more moderate than that of some other MB leaders. For example, the Brotherhood's General Guide called for mobilizing 10,000 volunteers and sending them to fight alongside Hizballah. See Muhammad Salah, "Guide of the Muslim Brotherhood: We Are Prepared to Send 10,000 Fighters to Lebanon," *al-Hayat*, August 4, 2006. For further discussion of the Brotherhood's response to the Lebanon war, see Amr Hamzawy and Dina Bishara, *Islamist Movements in the Arab World and the 2006 Lebanon War* (Washington, DC: Carnegie Endowment for International Peace, November 2006).

However, it opposed a broadening of women's rights. In this regard, the conservative views of women that surfaced during the debate over the party platform prevailed over the more progressive positions articulated in the 2005 campaign documents.

The Brotherhood's record as a constructive member of the parliamentary opposition was not perfect. It engaged in some rhetorical posturing, particularly during the debates over women's rights and relations with Israel. However, even on these high-profile issues that appeal to the Brotherhood's political base, its actions were restrained. It did not withdraw from Parliament over these disputes, nor did it demand the abandonment of the Camp David accords. Rather, it called for ministerial accountability, consultation with religious scholars at al-Azhar, and diplomatic retaliation against Israel for alleged violations of international law. When it was unsuccessful in these areas, it allowed the issues to pass and moved on to other matters. In addition, the MB delegation in Parliament did not attempt to advance any of the controversial features of the proposed Brotherhood party platform mentioned above. Indeed, the head of the MB's parliamentary delegation—Sa'ad al-Katatni—publicly criticized these ideas. He also objected to the fact that the parliamentary delegation's views were not considered during the drafting of these passages.[264]

Furthermore, the Brotherhood has maintained this moderate policy agenda in the face of a steady increase in repression by the regime. Since the 2005 elections, dozens of the organization's leaders and activists have been arrested and imprisoned. The regime also adopted a constitutional amendment in 2007 that expressly prohibited any organization with a "religious foundation" (*marja'iyya*) from participating in political life. These steps have made clear that a moderate posture by the Brotherhood is unlikely to produce any meaningful political payoff in the foreseeable future. The Brotherhood's persistent backing of a moderate policy agenda, despite the absence of any clear rewards for doing so, suggests that this agenda enjoys substantial support within the organization.

Some skeptics still argue that the Brotherhood advocates this moderate agenda merely to gain a short-term political advantage, and that it will retreat from this posture as soon as its political situation improves. There are two considerations that make such a change of direction difficult. In order to develop the doctrinal foundations for its moderate posture, the MB's leaders have drawn extensively on the works of the country's most respected Islamic thinkers. Indeed, they have linked their reform agenda very tightly to the ideas and stature of these thinkers. This link enables

---

[264] Interview with Sa'ad al-Katatni on http://www.ikhwanonline.com/, November 8, 2007; also, Ahmad al-Khatib, "Sa'ad al-Katatni in London: Program of the Party of the Brotherhood Is Open to Amendment," *al-Misri al-Youm*, October 28, 2007.

the MB to demonstrate a credible commitment to moderation that can assuage the concerns of mainstream Muslims, secularists, and Copts. It shows these groups that the MB's support for a constrained state, the rule of law, and stronger civil and political rights is sincere and doctrinally sound. The central tactical goal of this strategy is to build bonds of trust and confidence with other political groups which, in turn, can help the Brotherhood to achieve greater power. Abandoning this moderate path would mean discarding over a decade of work and foregoing all of the opportunities for power that it may yield. It would also thoroughly poison the waters for future cooperation and, as a consequence, preclude any possibility of working with other groups in the foreseeable future. Such a step would be remarkably self-destructive. Indeed, the storm of criticism generated by the controversial features of the 2007 draft party platform reminded many MB leaders just how much they have to lose by retreating from this moderate posture even slightly.[265] With each passing day, the Brotherhood has more to gain from remaining on a moderate path than from diverging from it.

Another consideration lies in the simple politics of power. The fact that the Brotherhood has moved in a moderate direction due to self-interested political calculations does not make its commitment to moderation less durable. Indeed, one could argue that this motive is preferable to a sweeping shift of ideological views which, presumably, could shift in the opposite direction just as quickly. As long as the path to power rewards moderation, the Brotherhood will have strong incentives to remain moderate. Furthermore, the longer the Brotherhood remains on this moderate path, the more likely it will continue to make ideological changes that internalize and deepen the organization's commitment to moderation. Similarly, the longer it is on this path, the more likely the MB will appoint leaders at the middle and lower levels of the organization that support moderation and who spread the doctrinal arguments for it among the membership. Moderation motivated by self-interest is not necessarily weak or insincere. Indeed, if a moderate path enables the Brotherhood to move toward its goal of strengthening the role of Islam in law and society, its commitment to moderation is likely to deepen with time.

This analysis indicates that the Brotherhood has developed a firm commitment to the moderate agenda defined during the 2005 parliamentary campaign. This agenda has three core features: effective constraints on

---

[265] "Dr. Jamal Hashmat Comments on the Program of the Party of the Brotherhood," *al-Dustur*, October 5, 2007; Hisham 'Umar 'Abd al-Halim, "Brotherhood Differences during Secret Meeting in London Regarding the Program of the Party of the Organization," *al-Misri al-Youm*, October 29, 2007; "Al-'Iryan Criticizes the Program of the Brotherhood," *al-Hayat*, October 13, 2007.

state power; improvements in the rule of law, with a particular emphasis on judicial independence; and greater protection of basic civil and political rights. This agenda shares important features with classical liberalism. It incorporates the principle that state power should be constrained and accountable to the citizenry. It also supports each of the key institutions of a liberal order, including: a clear and unbiased legal code; the separation of powers; checks and balances among these powers; an independent judiciary; and effective institutions for implementing the law. In these respects, the Brotherhood's views can be usefully described as "liberal" and, as noted below, share important similarities with the liberal constitutionalism articulated by the judiciary. However, the Brotherhood's views differ from classical liberalism in three important respects:

Rights of religious minorities (Copts and Baha'is): The Brotherhood has not embraced a universal conception of citizenship in which Muslims and non-Muslims are equal in every respect. Rather, it has limited itself to statements that assert the formal equality of Christians and Muslims before the law with equal rights and duties. These statements have not allayed the deeply rooted fears of the Coptic community.[266] As noted earlier, there is also support within the organization for opposing the appointment of Copts to senior positions of political leadership (particularly, the presidency and the premiership). Furthermore, the Brotherhood shares the government's view that Baha'is are not entitled to religious freedom and legal equality.

Rights of women: The Brotherhood sends a mixed message in this area. Its political documents advocate a wide range of women's rights, including the right to vote, to hold public office, and to be treated equally in legal and financial matters. There are several members of the MB's leadership (such as 'Isam al-'Iryan and 'Abd al-Mon'am Abu al-Fatuh) who hold progressive views on the role of women in society. However, a conservative view of women is also well-entrenched within the leadership and the rank-and-file. As a consequence, the Brotherhood's progressive statements are always tempered with the assertion that changes in women's rights should "conform to the traditions and conditions of society." As a result, the Brotherhood is unlikely to take any substantive action to improve the status of women. Indeed, some of its members of Parliament have resisted efforts to strengthen women's rights. The organization also opposes allowing a woman to hold the presidency.

The role of the state: The MB advocates a prominent role for the state in shaping the morality of individual Muslims. This view is likely to lead to

---

[266] For a recent statement of this view, see "Al-Ghazali Harb: Many Copts Support the Totalitarian Regime Due to Fear of the Brotherhood," *al-Misri al-Youm*, February 21, 2007.

some state involvement in the personal lives of citizens in order to strengthen their piety. This degree of state invasiveness is at odds with liberalism's emphasis on minimizing the state's intervention in the private lives of citizens.

Thus, the Brotherhood is an imperfect advocate of liberalism. However, it should be noted that the term "liberal" is frequently applied to individuals and movements that are not comprehensively liberal in every respect. For example, the framers of the American Constitution are often referred to as liberal despite the fact that many of them owned slaves and believed that slavery was morally acceptable—a position that is clearly at odds with liberalism's emphasis on individual liberty. It is appropriate to use the term "liberal" to describe a group if the preponderance of the group's views conform to the three core features of classical liberalism: constraints on state power; the rule of law; and protection of basic rights. Despite its shortcomings, the Brotherhood meets this threshold.[267]

The Convergence of Liberal Constitutionalism and Islamic Constitutionalism

At first glance, one would not expect the liberal constitutionalism advocated by the Judges' Club to have much in common with the Islamic constitutionalism promoted by the MB. Liberal constitutionalism is the product of a secular outlook that emphasizes reason and works to protect the individual from a predatory state. Islamic constitutionalism is grounded in divine revelation, stresses the importance of faith, and focuses on creating a pious community through the state's enforcement of *Shari'a*. The two approaches diverge over basic principles of law and governance, such as the source of law's legitimacy, the foundations of sovereignty, the public's role in politics, and the place of religious law. They seem to be polar opposites that engage in a zero-sum battle for influence in Egyptian political and legal life. A gain for liberalism and its secular vision must, by definition, be a defeat for Islamic constitutionalists.

---

[267] It is also noteworthy that the Brotherhood does not describe itself as "liberal." This term has several negative connotations in contemporary Egyptian discourse. It is associated with Western political thought and, in some circles, with Western imperialism. It is also associated with the relatively lax moral code that the Brotherhood and many other Egyptians attribute to the West. When I describe the Brotherhood's position as "liberal," I am not suggesting that the organization has adopted Western cultural or moral norms. Rather, as indicated in the text, I am observing that the Brotherhood has demonstrated sustained support for the core institutions of classical liberalism and for the principles of constraining state power and rendering it accountable to the citizenry.

However, these differences are sharper in principle than in practice. As the previous discussion suggests, there are important areas of similarity in the agendas for reform advocated by the Judges' Club and the Muslim Brotherhood. More specifically, they converge in three important areas:

The Need for a Powerful State That Is Constrained and Accountable

For the judges, a powerful state protects citizens' rights, builds the economy, and maintains order. It is essential for both liberty and national prosperity. For the Brotherhood, a powerful state is the key to creating a more devout community. Its enforcement of law (both divine and man-made) creates the *umma*. Its efforts to enjoin good and forbid evil help to transform the moral character of individual Muslims and build a community grounded in the faith.

However, both the judges and the MB are acutely aware of the risks posed by an unconstrained state. The judges speak at length of a state that has the duty to serve the public, but which is continually at risk of being captured by a small elite that serves its narrow self-interest. The only protection against this danger is an effective balance of powers and, particularly, a strong and independent judiciary. The judiciary not only constrains the state through its vigorous and principled application of the law. It also strengthens other institutions, particularly Parliament and civil society groups, that can provide further checks on an abusive state.

The Brotherhood shares this emphasis on the need to constrain the state. As noted above, it advocates each of the institutions supported by the judges: clear and effective laws that delineate executive power and its relationship to other institutions; a strong and independent judiciary that applies these laws consistently; an autonomous Parliament with meaningful power to monitor the executive and hold it accountable; and a vibrant civil society that also monitors the state and insists on the state's responsiveness to its demands. However, as noted in chapter 3, the MB and the theorists of Islamic constitutionalism have a fundamentally positive view of state power. It is the key institution for transforming the morality of individual Muslims and for building the Islamic community. As a consequence, the purpose of these constraints is different from that of the judges. Their goal is to guide and direct state power toward the transformation of individuals and society.

Thus, the judges and the MB have different motives for supporting constraints on the state. Nonetheless, they agree on both the principle of constraining the state and the institutions that achieve it.

Strengthening the Rule of Law

For the judges, law is "the defining feature of civilization. It is the tool that creates civilized societies."[268] It must be written to serve the best interest of the community and interpreted with this goal in mind. They are very aware of the possibility that political leaders will manipulate the law to extend and strengthen state power. For the judges, this is not an abstract threat. They retain a vivid collective memory of the "socialist legality" of the Nasser era, in which initially well-intentioned efforts to use law as a means for revolutionary change led to a systematic disrespect for both law and courts. It also produced a generation of political leaders who saw themselves as above the law and entitled to twist jurisprudence to serve their goals. The judiciary believes it has a moral and professional duty to protect against this erosion of law into a mere plaything of the powerful.

The MB holds a similar commitment to the centrality of law. The enforcement of law—both divine and man-made—brings the Islamic community into being. It also protects and strengthens its moral character. In addition, the MB shares the judges' suspicion of political leaders who may manipulate and corrupt the law to serve their personal ends. There is, of course, an important difference between the judges and the MB regarding the source of legitimacy of law. The judges hold a procedural conception of legality: law is legitimate when it is drafted by representatives of the people in conformity with the procedures specified in the Constitution. The MB, in contrast, explicitly invokes a normative element when assessing the legitimacy of law: law is valid only if it conforms to the principles of *Shari'a*. However, in practice, this difference is less sharp than it seems. The MB and other moderate Islamists have adopted a highly elastic conception of *Shari'a*. In essence, they argue that whatever advances justice and the best interests of the community (*maslaha*) is compatible with divine law. This conception of legality finds important echoes in the rulings of the Egyptian judiciary. As noted in chapter 2, judges often invoke the principle that "serving the public interest" is the fundamental purpose of law. Indeed, the Supreme Constitutional Court has willfully misinterpreted the Constitution on key issues (such as privatization) in order to advance the best interests of the nation. Thus, both the judiciary and the MB share a conception of law that focuses on advancing the community's well-being, rather than simply applying legal codes in a mechanistic fashion.

---

[268] "Kalimat Quda Misr fi Iftah al-Mu'tamar li-l Mustishar Yahia al-Rif'ai," reprinted in *Mu'tamar al-'Adala al-Awal 1986: Al-Watha'iq al-Asasiyya* (Cairo: Nadi al-Quda, 1986), 16.

In practical terms, this area of convergence between liberal constitutionalism and Islamic constitutionalism leads to their shared support for several important institutional changes: reform of the legal code to render it clearer, more consistent, and more explicit in the limits that it places on state power; strengthening the independence and professionalism of the judiciary; and ending the proliferation of specialized and exceptional courts that erode the judiciary's independence and weaken the public's respect for it.

In the view of both the judges and the MB, effective and impartial implementation of the law is the foundation of just government. The two groups agree, as well, on the inverse of this proposition: that the absence of the rule of law is the primary cause of poor government and flawed public policy. The Judges' Club made this assertion as early as 1968, when it argued that Egypt's lack of preparedness in the 1967 war was due to the Nasser regime's disregard for law and the institutions that defended it. In a statement in March 1968, the Club asserted that "the absence of respect for law was the root cause of the corruption and the mistakes that led to our defeat in the field."[269] It offered a similar view as recently as 2003 in a statement regarding the U.S.-led invasion of Iraq. As one might expect, it denounced the invasion as an act of aggression that violated international law. However, the statement also criticized the persistence of regimes in the Arab world that "rig elections and rule with despotic and extraordinary laws."[270] In the opinion of the Judges' Club, these abuses have produced weak regimes that lack legitimacy and popular support. This weakness renders them easy prey for ambitious outside powers that manipulate the region's affairs.[271] The MB expressed a similar opinion in the wake of Israel's invasion of Lebanon in the summer of 2006. The General Guide of the Brotherhood proclaimed that the ease with which Israel could attack an Arab country was a direct result of the repressiveness and illegitimacy of the regimes in the region.[272]

Protection of Basic Civil and Political Rights

The Judges' Club asserts repeatedly its support for the broad principle of human rights. It also advocates specific rights, including private property,

[269] "Bayan wa Qararat Nadi al-Quda, March 28, 1968," *al-Quda*, 1:2 (special issue), 1–5.

[270] The statement was issued on March 24, 2003. It is reprinted in *al-Ahram Weekly*, April 3–9, 2003. It continues, "The most fundamental reason behind the ongoing calamity is the debility of the [Arab] nation. There can be no dignity or freedom for a nation that fails to protect the freedom and dignity of its citizens."

[271] Ibid.

[272] "Interview with the General Guide," *Afaq 'Arabiyya*, August 2, 2006.

speech, and assembly. As one might expect, it is particularly vociferous about matters related to judicial procedure such as the right to due process, a fair trial, trial before one's "natural judge," and the right of appeal. Similarly, as noted earlier, the MB also endorses the broad principle of human rights. It enumerates several specific rights, including freedom of speech, assembly, property, and political participation. In addition, it calls for protection of many rights for Copts and women, although it advocates denying them the opportunity to serve in senior political posts. Its support for women's rights is constrained by its commitment to defending a conservative view of Egyptian values and culture.

While both groups express strong and consistent support for many rights, they also share a clear preference for emphasizing the well-being of the community over that of the individual. The Judges' Club frames its support for individual rights in terms of the contribution they will make to building a "stable and harmonious society." In the body of jurisprudence discussed in chapter 2, there is a clear and consistent philosophical commitment to the premise that a stable society is the best guarantor of prosperity and freedom. Thus, building a strong society and protecting it from division and fragmentation are the highest priorities. The MB adopts a similar view, and supplements it with a strong emphasis on building a pious community. Indeed, the creation and strengthening of this community is the fundamental purpose of law and the state. Individual rights, while important, are clearly subordinate to this collective goal. Thus, both the judges and the MB advocate individual rights, but this advocacy is tempered by concern for the well-being of the community.

It is noteworthy that both the Judges' Club and the MB exhibit reservations regarding broad public participation in government. The judges stress that citizens have a right to free elections and a right to vote. However, this position is always advanced in highly positivistic terms: citizens have these rights because they are granted to them in the law and the Constitution. There were numerous occasions during the debate over supervising the 2005 elections when the Judges' Club could have asserted a normative argument about the fundamental right of citizens to participate in their own governance. However, it refrained from doing so. The judges clearly prefer a process of legal and political decision making that relies on highly educated specialists to interpret and apply the law. They seem to harbor—particularly in their jurisprudence discussed in chapter 2—an underlying suspicion of mass politics and a persistent fear that unrestrained popular rule can lead to disorder and injustice. This fear does not make them hostile to democratic procedure. However, they tend to emphasize the "procedure" component of this term. They value the institutions that channel and discipline public participation such as responsible civil society groups, effective political parties, fair elections, and orderly parliamentary deliberations. They remain nervous about the disorder latent in unrestrained democracy. As noted earlier, the MB is also ambivalent about democracy. It argues that *shura* is the fundamental principle of Islamic governance and that every citizen is entitled to participate in deliberations over public policy and the choice of a leader. Furthermore, it concludes that this principle is implemented most fully in the modern era through the institutions of democracy. However, as the 2007 draft of the MB party platform shows, some leaders of the organization remain fearful that unrestricted democracy could lead to laws that violate the core principles of *Shari'a* or which contradict prevailing traditional values. As a consequence, some MB leaders have called for a council of religious scholars that advises legislators and provides a partial check on their power. Some members of the organization also advocate excluding some groups in society (women and Copts) from holding the most senior elected offices.

• • •

Both liberal constitutionalism and Islamic constitutionalism are, in part, products of the crisis of statism. Nasser's statist order was grounded upon the regime's control of several key institutions, particularly the public sector, the subsidy system, and the bureaucracy. These institutions have weakened to the point where they no longer provide the minimal standard of living needed to sustain public support for the statist order. Indeed, even leading figures in the regime—including the president—have concluded that the ideology and institutions of statism no longer serve the country well. They have become reluctant supporters of market-oriented economic reforms that move the regime away from its statist roots.

Liberal constitutionalism (LC) and Islamic constitutionalism (IC) provide the most coherent alternatives to statism in contemporary Egypt. They each seek a state that is accountable to the people and guided by them. Their views of how to achieve this goal converge around the creation of institutions that constrain executive power, strengthen the rule of law, and protect some civil and political rights. In institutional terms, this convergence can be termed "liberal," in the sense that it aims to create a more accountable and limited state through the institutions associated with classical liberalism—a clear and unbiased legal code, the separation of powers, checks and balances among these powers, an independent judiciary, and effective institutions for implementing the law. However, as noted above, both liberal constitutionalism and Islamic constitutionalism are derived from philosophical premises that are not entirely in harmony with liberalism. Both the Judges' Club and the MB place less emphasis on the protection of the individual than is common in liberal thought. The individual is not at the center of discussions over political and legal institutions. Rather, the building of an orderly and just community (for the judges) and a pious community (for the MB) are the fundamental goals. In addition, the MB advocates a role for the state in the personal lives of citizens that is more invasive than that found in liberal thought.

It is noteworthy that this convergence of views is not the product of active coordination between advocates of LC and IC.[273] It is not the result of leaders from each group negotiating a shared view. Nor is it the result of advocates of LC and IC interacting within an organization (such as the professional syndicates) and gradually arriving at a common position. This fact makes their convergence of views all the more striking. It also renders this convergence potentially quite durable. It is not contingent upon an agreement among individuals, which could be weakened if one of the individuals lost power or died. It is not the result of intense interaction within a syndicate or a political party, which could be easily suppressed by the regime. Rather, it is the product of leaders from each group calculating that support for the institutions of liberalism is both compatible with their deeply held beliefs and a sound tactical response to the political conditions prevailing in contemporary Egypt.

Both liberal constitutionalism and Islamic constitutionalism support reforms that yield a more constrained, law-abiding, and accountable state. The next questions to consider are: has this agenda of liberal institutional reform attracted significant support elsewhere in society? And, if so, what does it mean for the future of democracy in Egypt?

---

[273] Rosefsky-Wickham argues that increased interaction between Islamists and secular liberals led to the development of a moderate ideology among some Islamists, particularly within the *al-Wasat* party. Rosefsky-Wickham, "The Path to Moderation," 205–28. However, this process does not appear to be under way within the Brotherhood or between the Brotherhood and other groups.

CHAPTER FIVE

Economic Restructuring and the Rise
of Market Liberalism

THE CONVERGENCE of political alternatives offered by liberal constitutionalism and Islamic constitutionalism will not, alone, determine the future of Egyptian politics. Political decisions remain in the hands of a small elite that has few ties to the judges or the Muslim Brotherhood leaders discussed in the previous chapter. However, Egypt's market-oriented economic policies since the early 1990s have created new constituencies in the private sector and the ruling party that favor liberal reforms. They are powerful and durable advocates of the same institutional changes supported by the judges and the Brotherhood.

As noted in chapter 4, the economic foundations of the Nasserist state were precarious from the start. The regime made sweeping commitments to create a welfare state grounded upon a large public sector, an extensive network of subsidies, and a vast bureaucracy that employed upwards of 20 percent of the work force by the mid-1980s. Even with robust rates of economic growth, this welfare state would have proven difficult to sustain in the face of Egypt's steady population growth. However, high economic growth was not forthcoming, partly because of the economic inefficiency and low rates of investment engendered by this state-dominated economic structure.[1] By 1990, the underlying contradictions of Egypt's economy had proven too fundamental to overcome. International donors and lending agencies were willing to help the Egyptian government through the crisis, but only on condition that it undertake extensive economic restructuring under the supervision of the International Monetary Fund (IMF). Egypt agreed and entered into an IMF-sponsored Economic Reform and Structural Adjustment Plan (ERSAP) in 1991.[2]

In order to comply with the terms of this agreement, the regime initiated a series of legal reforms in the 1990s that aimed to expand the role of the private sector and improve competition. These reforms included

[1] For a thoughtful analysis of this period, see Amin, *Egypt's Economic Predicament*. Also see Ikram, *The Egyptian Economy*.

[2] For a good summary of the reform program, see Arvind Subramanian, "Egypt: Poised for Sustained Growth?" *Finance & Development* 34 (1997): 44–45. Subramanian was the IMF's representative in Cairo during part of the reform process.

several laws that began to alter the role of the state in the economy. At the heart of this legislation was the much-celebrated privatization law of 1991. By June 2000, the government had sold a controlling interest in roughly one-third of the enterprises that it owned, with a sale value of about 12.3 billion LE. Total labor in public enterprises dropped from just over 1 million in 1993 to under 600,000 by the middle of 2000.[3] Not surprisingly, this process had its share of critics. Some analysts argued that the government retained de facto control over at least some of the privatized firms by remaining the largest shareholder.[4] Others pointed out that important parts of the public sector were excluded from the privatization program, including utilities, the Suez Canal, the national oil company, social and health insurance, and the General Authority for Supply (which manages the import and distribution of subsidized commodities).[5] However, these flaws should not draw our attention away from the political and economic significance of the privatization program. The state discarded any ambition to reform the public sector and retain it as the cornerstone of the economy. Indeed, government officials at the highest levels publicly argued that Egypt's future lay in shifting economic production to the private sector and empowering it to compete in global markets. While the privatization process is incomplete, and will probably fall short of thoroughly removing the government from the economy, the regime has clearly signaled a shift in direction. The state will no longer be the driving force in economic development.

Other measures taken in response to IMF and World Bank pressure include: a new investment law (Law 8/1997) that lifted price controls on all products produced by companies formed under the law and sharply reduced the number of government permits needed to operate a business;[6] a new companies law (Law 3/1998) that allowed companies to form without receiving a license from the government;[7] unification of the exchange rate and, eventually, allowing the exchange rate to move toward a "managed float" in January 2003; a new arbitration law (Law 27/1994) that allowed businesses to resolve their disputes in accordance with international arbitration procedures, with minimal involvement by the Egyptian

---

[3] Ikram, *The Egyptian Economy*, 81.

[4] For an interesting discussion of the flaws in the privatization process, see John Sfakianakis, "The Whales of the Nile: Networks, Businessmen, and Bureaucrats During the Era of Privatization in Egypt," in *Networks of Privilege in the Middle East*, ed. Steven Heydemann (New York: Palgrave Macmillan, 2004), 77–100.

[5] Ikram, *The Egyptian Economy*, 79–80.

[6] Tarek F. Riad, "The Legal Environment for Investment in Egypt in the New Millennium," *Arab Law Quarterly* 15, no. 2 (2000): 117–19.

[7] Under the new law, companies are required merely to inform the government, after the fact, of their formation. Ibid., 122.

state; a new telecommunications law (Law 10/2003), which allowed private firms to operate cellular phone concessions and thereby end the state's dominance of the telecom sector; the establishment of a more vibrant stock market (Law 95/1993), which granted private firms access to entirely new sources of capital that were not linked to government banks or agencies; and an export promotion law (Law 155/2002) that eliminated most of the government permits and licenses previously required for exporting goods. Collectively, these new laws curtailed the state's role in economic production and in the provision of jobs and services. They also reduced its ability to control key features of the economy such as prices, interest rates, the formation of companies, and access to capital.

These changes in the state's economic role were reinforced by the country's increased integration into the global economy. The cornerstone of this effort was membership in the World Trade Organization (WTO). By joining the WTO in 1995, Egypt gained increased access to world markets on condition that it modify its laws and regulations to conform with global norms. In practice, this meant further shrinking the state and altering its role in the economy.

The underlying goal of the WTO is to increase world trade by reducing tariff and nontariff barriers. In the words of a senior WTO official, the primary means for achieving this goal is to tie each country to "a system of rules and procedures that together bring rule of law . . . replacing rule of the jungle . . . to international commercial relations."[8] Furthermore, when a country accepts the WTO's free-trade rules, it also demonstrates its commitment to a market-oriented path of economic development. Indeed, it has embedded this commitment within a formal, explicit, and legally binding set of agreements with the world's preeminent trade regulator. This step lends credibility to the country's reform plans. It also significantly raises the cost of retreating from these plans. Thus, WTO membership helps to reassure investors (particularly foreign investors) that the country's market reform policies are sincere and irreversible. Conforming to these international rules and regulations clearly limits a country's policy discretion and impinges on its sovereignty. But, in the view of the WTO, "the reduction in policy sovereignty is more than compensated by the increased predictability of trading partners' policies and more secure access to foreign markets."[9]

When Egypt joined the WTO in 1995, it agreed to gradually liberalize its trade laws over the next ten years. These changes had important reper-

---

[8] Richard Blackhurst, "World Trade Organization (WTO) Agreements: Benefits to Egypt," in *Institutional and Policy Challenges Facing the Egyptian Economy*, ed. Heba Nassar and Ahmad Ghoneim (Cairo: Center for Economics and Financial Research and Studies, 2003), 267. Blackhurst is the former director of economic research at the WTO.

[9] Ibid., 261.

cussions for each of the aspects of constitutionalism discussed earlier in this study, particularly the role of the state, the rule of law, and the protection of basic rights (especially property rights).

Reducing the State's Capacity to Protect Specific Industries and Favor Specific Firms

The state created by Nasser adopted an import substitution development strategy. Its goal was to expand local production in order to replace foreign imports and thereby improve the country's economic independence. The state pursued this objective by protecting major industries from foreign competition through tariff and nontariff barriers. Within a given industry, it also favored specific producers (particularly, public-sector producers over private-sector producers) by granting them concessionary loans, subsidized inputs, and government contracts without competitive bidding. If a firm engaged in trade, it could do so only with countries and companies approved by the government.[10]

WTO membership led to a fundamental change in this economic role for the state. Perhaps the clearest illustration of this change lies in the textile sector. This sector has been one of the primary beneficiaries of government protection and support. In 2000, it employed over 100,000 people and generated about $1.25 billion in export revenue.[11] The state has played a key role in protecting Egyptian textile producers by blocking textile imports, particularly from low-cost producers in Asia. Prior to 2000, the government simply banned all textiles from Asia. It then adopted a very high tariff (40 percent) on Asian textiles. However, the country's WTO commitments require this tariff to be steadily lowered and eventually eliminated. It reached 12.5 percent in 2005, and must be completely removed by 2015. Thus, WTO membership has eliminated the state's capacity to protect a key industry from competition and ensure employment for its workers.

The state was also pivotal to the textile sector's export development. On several occasions, Egypt's leaders used the country's strategic importance as a lever for gaining increased access to key markets. For example, the Egyptian government negotiated several textile quota agreements with European nations, Canada, and the United States in the late 1970s. The governments of these countries granted the quotas as part of a broader effort to reward Egypt for its dramatic progress toward peace with Israel, and to offset the sharp decline in trade and aid from Arab states that

---

[10] Waterbury, *The Egypt of Nasser and Sadat*, 59–66.

[11] Samiha Fawzy and Nada Massoud, *The Future of Egypt's Textile and Clothing Exports in Light of New Trade Rules* (Cairo: Egyptian Center for Economic Studies, 2003).

occurred following the Camp David accords. The quotas assured Egyptian textile producers the opportunity to export a fixed amount of products (worth $1.2 billion in 2000) to these markets each year. The products were admitted without any tariffs, which enabled them to compete successfully against local producers and foreign competitors. These quota agreements also empowered the Egyptian government to determine which firms would be permitted to export to these countries and, thereby, gain the opportunity to establish a foothold in these prime markets and earn foreign exchange. As a result of WTO membership, these quotas were phased out and finally eliminated in 2005. The Egyptian state has lost its power to create politically driven opportunities for trade. In addition, as a result of WTO rules, it can no longer determine which firms and individuals will benefit from trade.

These developments do not mean that the state has ceased to play a role in trade. However, its role is much narrower. It is now limited to enforcing WTO rules on fair trade and equal access, and to providing job re-training for workers displaced by increased foreign competition. It must carry out this role in accordance with the WTO's regulations. Its performance is subject to regular evaluations by the WTO in the form of an annual Trade Policy Review. If the country fails to comply with the WTO's requirements, it is subject to fines and to restrictions on its exports.

Improving the Rule of Law

As one might expect, WTO rules led to greater clarity in Egyptian tariff regulations. They also required Egypt to record with much greater precision the specific sums collected from tariffs on each type of product.[12]

However, WTO commitments had an important impact beyond the narrow arena of tariffs. They also required the Egyptian state to operate with substantially greater transparency. The clearest illustration of this development lies in the telecommunications sector. Egypt agreed to integrate its plans for liberalizing this sector into the GATS (General Agreement on Trade in Services) that it negotiated with the WTO. This step formally obligated Egypt to implement its stated reform plans in telecommunications according to a specific timetable, or it would be in violation of its WTO agreements. This decision was designed to reassure investors that the government's commitment to telecom reform was sincere and credible. It hoped that this demonstration of seriousness would help to attract foreign investors to this sector and encourage the transfer of essential technology (particularly technology for cellular telephone networks).[13]

---

[12] Howard Stovall, "Doubts Persist," *Middle East Economic Digest* 44, no. 13 (2000): 31.
[13] Blackhurst, "WTO Agreements," 264.

In addition, Egypt was obligated to conduct its telecoms policy in accordance with WTO rules. This had a particularly important impact on the auctions for allocating bandwidth for cellular telephone networks. These auctions proceeded with a degree of openness unprecedented in the Egyptian economy—the auctions were announced globally; the technical requirements for the bids were stated clearly and in a fashion that did not favor a specific bidder; the review of bids was conducted by an independent technical office within the ministry of telecommunications; and the reasons for selecting the winner were provided in writing and in considerable detail. WTO rules led to a significant improvement in both the accountability and transparency of government policy in telecommunications. Furthermore, this experience demonstrated that exercising the state's power in this manner produced good economic results. The bandwidth auctions generated over $1 billion in revenue for the government. The telecom sector has attracted another $3 billion in foreign direct investment and has enjoyed extensive technology transfer, including the latest GSM (Global System for Mobile communications) cellular networking equipment.[14]

Protecting Property Rights

WTO membership had a substantial effect on Egypt's protection of intellectual property rights. Egypt had long been criticized for its inadequate respect for the patents of foreign firms, particularly in the pharmaceutical sector. In the 1990s, Egypt's laws granted patent protection for only fifteen years rather than the international norm of twenty years. Furthermore, firms that violated patent rules faced mild penalties that were often not enforced. These conditions enabled Egyptian pharmaceutical companies to become leading producers of generic versions of major drugs that were still under patent protection in the developed world. This was a lucrative business with profit margins in excess of 25 percent.[15]

As part of its agreement with the WTO, Egypt signed the TRIPS (Trade-Related Aspects of Intellectual Property Rights) accord. This accord requires each signatory to modify its intellectual property laws to conform to the standards in developed countries. Egypt did so by adopting law 82 in 2002. This legislation substantially strengthened and clarified Egypt's laws governing patents, trademarks, and copyrights. It also led to substantial improvements in the state's capacity for patent assess-

---

[14] Paul Budde Communications, *Egypt—Mobile Communications and Broadcasting*. London, May 23, 2004.

[15] Daniel Pearl, "Big Drug Makers Push Egypt, Other Nations to End their 'Piracy'," *Wall Street Journal*, December 13, 1996.

ment and enforcement. The government established a new regulatory body to approve patents and investigate allegations of patent violation. It also increased the number of staff persons involved in patent evaluation and protection, and improved their training and equipment.

In addition to joining the WTO, Egypt became a member of the Euro-Mediterranean Partnership (EMP) in 1995. The EMP consists of the European Union and ten states of the southern and eastern Mediterranean (Algeria, Egypt, Israel, Jordan, Lebanon, Morocco, the Palestinian Authority, Syria, Tunisia, and Turkey). Its charter proclaims the goal of creating a "comprehensive partnership" that seeks democratization, coordination of security policies, economic and financial cooperation, and cultural exchanges.[16] It supports economic reform in the region through a series of bilateral "association agreements" between the EU and each of the ten Mediterranean partners. These agreements aim to create a free-trade zone among all the participants in the EMP by 2010.[17]

The EU and Egypt finalized an association agreement in 2001, which came into force on June 1, 2004.[18] The agreement improved Egypt's access to the European market by sharply cutting tariffs on Egyptian textiles and agricultural goods,[19] and by completely eliminating tariffs on industrial products. In return, Egypt agreed to eliminate its tariffs on raw materials, industrial components, and machinery within four years. It also agreed to abolish tariffs on finished industrial goods within twelve years. Like the WTO commitments, the EMP association agreement limits the government's capacity to use tariffs to protect specific industries. It also prevents the government from using subsidies to support specific firms. It further embeds Egypt within a network of international legal and regulatory obligations that limit the discretionary power of the state. It also raises the cost of deviating from these constraints. If Egypt fails to meet its commitments to liberalize trade, it not only faces sanctions from the WTO. It also

[16] The text of the document, known as the Barcelona Declaration, is available at http://ec.europa.eu/comm/external_relations/euromed/bd.htm, accessed July 12, 2007. For an overview of the EMP and its development, see Haizam Amirah Fernandez and Richard Youngs, eds., *The Euro-Mediterranean Partnership: Assessing the First Decade* (Madrid: Real Instituto Elcano de Estudios Internacionales y Estrategicos, 2005). Also, Samir Radwan and Jean Louis Reiffers, *The Euro-Mediterranean Partnership: Ten Years After Barcelona, Achievements and Perspectives* (Cairo: FEMISE and The Economic Research Forum, 2005).

[17] The participants will probably miss this deadline due to the slow pace of negotiating some of the trade liberalization agreements and the difficulties of increasing intra-Arab trade. Most observers believe the free-trade area is unlikely to emerge before 2020, if then.

[18] The three-year delay in implementation was due to the fact that each of the fifteen EU governments, as well as Egypt's government, had to ratify the agreement before it could come in to force.

[19] However, the agreement imposed restrictions on the quantity of textiles and agricultural goods that Egypt could export to the EU each year.

damages its relations with the EU and faces a reduction in EU economic aid. In essence, these international obligations create additional pressure to reform the Egyptian state along liberal lines.

DEVELOPING CONSTITUENCIES FOR MARKET LIBERALISM: THE RISE OF THE PRIVATE SECTOR

At the heart of Egypt's market reform strategy in the 1990s lay a fundamental premise: as the state withdrew from economic activity, the private sector would expand and fill the investment void. According to the World Bank's analysis, Egypt's private businessmen had ample investment funds available.[20] The government expected businessmen to deploy these funds once the state reduced its role in economic production and adopted tax incentives to encourage private investment. Indeed, the government's five-year economic plan called for private-sector investment to grow from 15 percent of GDP in 1993 to 45 percent in 1997.[21]

In fact, private-sector investment stayed virtually unchanged—it reached only 15.7 percent of GDP by 1997. This was cause for serious concern. The government had cut its total investment in the economy from 12 percent of GDP in 1987 to 6 percent in 1994[22]—in nominal terms, this was a decline of roughly 5.6 billion LE. At the same time, the country needed to create 600,000 new jobs annually in order to absorb new entrants into the labor force and hold unemployment at its current levels.[23] The government urgently needed private investors to create new firms and generate both jobs and income. This situation gave the private sector considerable leverage, which it used to call for more rapid and extensive market reforms. One prominent investor, Muhammad Wahba, captured the spirit of the moment when he told his fellow businessmen, "Egypt is in flux. You could not pick a better time for influencing it."[24]

---

[20] Ikram, *The Egyptian Economy*, 74.

[21] Heba Handoussa, "A Balance Sheet of Reform in Two Decades," in *Institutional Reform and Economic Development in Egypt*, ed. Noha El-Mikawy and Heba Handoussa (Cairo: American University in Cairo Press, 2002), 95. These targets were stated in the 1993/1997 five-year plan. Also, Ikram, *The Egyptian Economy*, 82.

[22] Ikram, *The Egyptian Economy*, 82.

[23] Samir Radwan, "Employment and Unemployment in Egypt: Conventional Problems, Unconventional Remedies" (Cairo: Egyptian Center for Economic Studies, August 2002), 2–3. According to Radwan, the economy generated only 435,000 jobs annually during the 1990s.

[24] Wahba made the statement in an address to the Egyptian-American Businessmen Association. It is quoted in Caryle Murphy, "The Business of Political Change in Egypt," *Current History*, January 1995, p. 22.

The private sector advocated reform through several avenues. Among the most important were the two major private business associations: the Egyptian Businessmen's Association (EBA) and the American Chamber of Commerce in Egypt (AMCHAM).[25] The EBA is the older of the two, formed in 1975 by a small group of wealthy businessmen.[26] The EBA's membership includes the largest and most powerful private business enterprises in Egypt.[27] In 2005, the EBA had only 450 members and showed no interest in increasing its size. The chairman, Jamal al-Nazar, explained that this relatively small number of members "allows us to be much more effective. We are a small group of the most prominent businessmen. We are the leaders of the private sector. When we meet with government officials, they can be certain that the views we express are an accurate reflection of what is actually happening in the private sector. We are the businessmen who make the private sector work."[28] According to the EBA, its members represent companies with a combined value of 22 billion LE in 2004 and 300,000 employees.[29]

AMCHAM has a substantially larger membership—over 1000 members as of 2005. It was the first American chamber of commerce in the Middle East, and remains the largest and most active business association in the

[25] There are several other business organizations in Egypt that aspire to represent both private- and public-sector companies. The two largest are the Federation of Egyptian Industries (with roughly 7,300 members) and the Confederation of Chambers of Commerce (with over 3 million members). Both of these institutions are products of Nasser-era corporatism and, as a consequence, remain under the tight control of the regime. See Bianchi, *Unruly Corporatism*, 165–72; Eric Gobe, *Les Hommes d'affaires Égyptiens: Démocratisation et Secteur Privé dans l'Égypte de l'infitâh* (Paris: Karthala, 1999), 117–25; Mustafa Kamil al-Sayyid, *Al-Mujtam'a wa al-Siyasa fi Misr: Dur Jam'aat al-Masalah fi-l-Nitham al-Siyasi al-Misri (1952–1981)* (Cairo: Dar al-Mustaqbal al-'Arabi, 1983), 53–86.

[26] The official website of the EBA (http://www.eba.org.eg/) indicates that it was "founded in 1975 and ratified in 1979 under the law 32/1964"; accessed July 15, 2007. Its bylaws state that membership is limited to owners, chief executive officers, board members, managing directors, and others who hold "final decision-making power." See "La'ithat al-Nitham al-Asasi li-l-Jama'aiyya," which was submitted by the EBA to the Ministry of Social Affairs in 1986.

[27] In 1986, the EBA accepted, in principle, that it would allow representatives of public-sector firms to join the organization. However, in practice, less than 10 percent of the membership is from public-sector firms. Personal interview with Jamal al-Nazar, March 17, 2005.

[28] Ibid. The EBA's lobbying efforts are often quite direct. For example, members of the EBA have been invited to sit on committees that draft economic legislation as "representatives of the private sector."

[29] Egyptian Businessmen's Association, "Twenty-Five Years of Achievements" (Cairo: New Almass Press, 2004), 3. One-third of the member firms are concentrated in traditional areas of manufacturing such as food processing, textiles, and construction materials. The remaining firms are involved primarily in metal products, chemicals, petroleum, tourism, consulting, finance, investment, and information technology. *'Udwiyya Jam'aiyya Rijal al-'Amal al-Misriyyin*, CD-ROM: Cairo, Egyptian Businessmen's Association, 2005.

region. It was founded in 1981 through an order of President Mubarak, whose intervention allowed the organization to avoid the constraints of operating under the country's restrictive NGO law (law 32/1964).[30] As of 2004, roughly 75 percent of the Chamber's members were Egyptian.[31] AMCHAM represents the largest and most profitable firms in Egypt. According to its president, the companies in AMCHAM accounted for approximately 20 percent of Egypt's GDP in 2004.[32]

The most comprehensive statement of each group's reform objectives came in October 1994, when they participated in the first Private Sector Development Conference. This event provided leaders of the private sector with direct access to senior government officials as well as to prominent figures in the public sector. The conference occurred before Egypt joined the WTO or the EMP, and while the government was still formulating its long-term plans for market reform. It was the private sector's best chance to shape the direction of reform. Both AMCHAM and EBA took advantage of the opportunity. They prepared detailed statements of their views on the role of government and private business in the Egyptian economy.[33] These statements focused on three topics: redefining the role of the state, strengthening the rule of law, and improving protection of some economic rights.

The role of the state: It comes as no surprise that the EBA and AMCHAM strongly opposed the interventionist state created during the Nasser era. The EBA proclaimed that reform should create a new economic order in which "the government rules, but does not own; organizes, but does not manage."[34] AMCHAM struck the same theme, arguing that Egypt's un-

---

[30] President Sadat agreed to allow the formation of AMCHAM during his visit to Washington in 1981. However, Sadat was assassinated on October 6, 1981. Mubarak followed through on his commitment a few months later. The organization was formally inaugurated in October 1982. Ninette S. Fahmy, *The Politics of Egypt: State-Society Relationship* (New York: RoutledgeCurzon, 2002), 173; Also, *Annual Report, 2003* (Cairo: AMCHAM, 2003), 3.

[31] AMCHAM's constitution limits general membership to: American companies with branches, agents, or representative offices in Egypt; Egyptian companies with American equity; Egyptian companies or individuals who have significant business relationships with the United States or are registered agents of American companies; and U.S. citizens residing in Egypt who have significant business relationships with the United States. See Article 3 of AMCHAM's Constitution, which is reprinted in the 2003 AMCHAM Annual Report, 27. Also, *Directory of Membership: 2004/2005* (Cairo: American Chamber of Commerce in Egypt, 2004), 38.

[32] Taher S. Helmy, "Letter from the AMCHAM President," *Directory of Membership: 2004/2005* (Cairo: American Chamber of Commerce in Egypt, 2004), 16.

[33] The statements are reprinted in Marcelo M. Giugale and Hamed Mobarak, eds., *Private Sector Development in Egypt* (Cairo: American University in Cairo Press, 1996).

[34] Egyptian Businessmen's Association, "The Role of the Government," in *Private Sector Development in Egypt*, ed. Giugale and Mobarak, 17.

derdevelopment was due largely to the "inability of interventionist institutions to substitute for market forces in allocating resources among participants, fostering the accumulation of human capital, and effecting technological advancement."[35] In its view, "the main thrust of reform in the upcoming stage should be to divest the government from its central planning and interventionist public sector culture."[36] The first practical step in this effort was to privatize most of the public sector and to end state policies that gave it an advantage over private firms.[37] Both organizations also called for the immediate repeal of Nasser-era laws that micromanage the operation of firms, particularly in the areas of labor relations and research and development.[38] They also advocated ending the state's dominance of the financial sector.[39]

Strengthening the rule of law: AMCHAM argued that the key to private-sector development was a macroeconomic environment characterized by "stability, transparency, and sustainability."[40] Clear laws, enforced consistently, are the foundation of this order. Both the EBA and AMCHAM emphasized that the Egyptian legal code fell well short of these ideals. It was "very complex," "often contradictory," and "designed for an era of centrally-directed economic policy."[41] They called for a comprehensive review of laws and regulations in order to create a competitive market environment without favoritism to either public or private firms. However, they reserved their harshest words for the Egyptian bureaucracy. It suffered from "scarcity of information, obsolete data management facilities, and poor working conditions. This is compounded by declining quality of skills of civil servants . . . and by the pronounced mismatch of skills and jobs (a result of the past policy of guaranteed public employment for graduates)."[42] These problems produced an administrative apparatus that was unable to implement laws with consistency, fairness, and speed. In-

[35] American Chamber of Commerce in Egypt, "The Role of the Private Sector," in *Private Sector Development in Egypt*, ed. Giugale and Mobarak, 37–38.

[36] Ibid., 38.

[37] American Chamber of Commerce in Egypt, "Recommendations to Eliminate Impediments to Investment and Doing Business in Egypt" (Cairo: AMCHAM, 1996), 1. Also, Egyptian Businessmen's Association, "Policy Brief: The Relationship between the Public Sector and the Private Sector" (Cairo: EBA, 1995), 3.

[38] Nasser-era laws empowered the government to regulate and monitor all research projects and to approve all efforts to import foreign technology. As a consequence, firms faced strong disincentives to adopt new technology or develop their own innovations.

[39] AMCHAM, "Recommendations to Eliminate Impediments to Investment and Doing Business in Egypt," 9.

[40] AMCHAM, "The Role of the Private Sector," 31.

[41] Ibid., 38, 40; Egyptian Businessmen's Association, "Policy Brief: The Relationship between the Public Sector and the Private Sector," 7.

[42] AMCHAM, "The Role of the Private Sector," 38.

deed, civil servants were "more likely to delay and obstruct transactions than to expedite them."[43] As a consequence, "most proprietors . . . dedicate up to 30 percent of their time to problem solving with the government bureaucracy."[44]

This concern over the consistent enforcement of laws and regulations also extended to the judicial system. AMCHAM wrote that the court system suffers from a lack of staff, poorly trained judges, and unreliable enforcement of rulings. In addition, procedural laws allow for a plaintiff to delay proceedings for months and even years by continually extending the discovery process. AMCHAM concluded that the current judicial system failed to protect consumers or private property rights, and provided inadequate dispute resolution and contract enforcement.[45]

Protection of rights. Both AMCHAM and the EBA complained about insufficient protection of property rights. Their criticism focused on the laws governing land ownership, rent, and tenancy. In the 1990s, rents were often fixed by law at rates that were set decades earlier. Owners were prohibited from raising the rent without explicit government approval, which was rarely granted. Evicting a tenant was "virtually impossible and leads to long and costly court proceedings which end up, in the best of cases, only in forcing the tenant to pay a rent."[46] These laws effectively prevented the owner of a building or a plot of land from exercising meaningful control over his property. Indeed, legal claim to land had become so tenuous that many banks would not accept land as collateral for loans.[47]

These EBA and AMCHAM documents from the mid-1990s provide a clear accounting of the private sector's major complaints about the existing order. They also present, in broad terms, the type of liberal reforms that businessmen support. Their stated goal is an economic and legal system that creates a "predictable and contestable business environment."[48] This includes the creation of a more constrained and accountable state. Some observers are skeptical of their sincerity. Advocates of this critical view argue that the private sector benefits from the powerful and unconstrained state that emerged in the 1960s and 1970s.[49] This state kept firm control over Egypt's labor movement, thereby ensuring economic

[43] Ibid., 39.

[44] Ibid., 40.

[45] Ibid.

[46] Ibid., 35.

[47] Ibid. Also, Egyptian Businessmen's Association, "The Law Governing Agricultural Land" (Cairo: EBA, 1996). And, Egyptian Businessmen's Association, "The Law Governing the Rental of Apartments" (Cairo: EBA, 1997).

[48] AMCHAM, "The Role of the Private Sector," 35.

[49] For an interesting discussion of how private businessmen have developed ties with government to protect their interests, see Sfakianakis, "The Whales of the Nile," 77–100. Also, Yahya M. Sadowski, *Political Vegetables? Businessman and Bureaucrat in the Development of Egyptian Agriculture* (Washington, DC: Brookings Institution, 1991).

stability and profits. It also maintained public order and social peace, even during periods of economic crisis. Furthermore, and perhaps most importantly, it was a mother lode of economic opportunities for the well-connected businessman.[50]

This critical view of the private sector suggests that businessmen have a substantial stake in the political and economic status quo. In principle, this should be particularly true for the wealthy and powerful businessmen who make up the membership of the EBA and AMCHAM. These "fat cats" are precisely the individuals who benefited most from the comfortable collusion of state and business that emerged under the *infitah*. Why would they call for restructuring the state and reducing its role in the economy? Part of the explanation lies in the changing character of the private sector. When Mubarak succeeded Sadat in 1981, he removed some of the regulatory impediments to forming private industrial enterprises in an effort to stimulate job growth and exports. As a consequence, large private firms with a more entrepreneurial bent began to emerge in areas such as chemicals, metallurgy, and high-quality textiles.[51] Leaders of some of these firms became important figures in the EBA and AMCHAM. However, the more fundamental explanation lies in the private sector's ambiguous and tension-ridden relationship with the state from the very beginning of the *infitah*. As noted above, this relationship produced many profitable opportunities for businessmen. However, it also placed stringent limits on private-sector growth. Centralized state control over the flow of information and resources made it difficult to reach sound business decisions and to respond quickly to business opportunities. These problems were aggravated by the vast web of regulations on everything from labor management and factory design to product pricing and marketing. These regulations were constantly changing and were enforced inconsistently, which made long-term strategic planning virtually impossible. In addition, the bureaucracy that implemented these regulations was cumbersome and slow. Power to make key decisions was centralized in the hands of a few ill-trained bureaucrats who reached unpredictable, and often hostile, decisions. Furthermore, these officials sometimes insisted on bribes or other favors.[52]

---

[50] For a more detailed statement of this argument, see Malak Zaalouk, *Power, Class, and Foreign Capital in Egypt: The Rise of the New Bourgeoisie* (London: Zed Books, 1989), especially 144–54. Some scholars have argued that an economic "power elite" emerged during the *infitah* that manipulated state resources and institutions to serve their interests. The empirical support for this argument is thin. Nonetheless, this view is influential among the Egyptian Left. See Samia Sa'id Imam, *Man Yamluk Misr?* (Cairo: Dar al-Mustaqbal al-'Arabi, 1986).

[51] Waterbury, *The Egypt of Nasser and Sadat*, 188.

[52] These observations were made in personal interviews with the following senior members of AMCHAM in October and November 1994: Shafiq Jabr, Ahmad Shawki, Ismail Osman, and Ihab Shalabi.

Businessmen had tolerated these myriad irritants and obstacles for decades. In many cases, they managed to thrive despite them. However, their attitude changed as Egypt began to integrate into the global economy. The ERSAP, WTO, and EMP agreements were particularly important in this regard. They required substantial structural changes in the state's economic role that sharply reduced its capacity to serve as the "cash cow" for private enterprise. The private sector could no longer turn to the state to provide it with subsidized capital, cheap raw materials, and generous contracts. In addition, these agreements steadily lowered the tariffs that protected Egyptian firms from foreign competition. In order to succeed in this new environment, Egyptian businessmen had to build companies that could compete in regional and global markets. The sclerotic bureaucracy and byzantine regulatory code that were annoyances in the past now became major threats to the survival of businesses. As one prominent member of the EBA and AMCHAM put it, "Internationalization is inevitable. Egypt simply has no choice but to open its market to global forces. My challenge, as a businessman, is to figure out how to compete in this environment. Frankly, the old system just isn't going to work when we have to compete on the global stage. We need to move toward international business practices."[53]

A former president of AMCHAM held a similar view: "The real business opportunities going forward are regional, not national. We need to think in terms of combining labor and capital across Arab countries, with an eye toward exporting to Europe. You just can't do that under the current regulatory and customs regime, which treats each country as if it were an economic island. We need to rethink the role of government and try to harmonize that role across the countries of the region."[54]

Furthermore, businessmen had grown extremely frustrated with the old economic order. The bureaucracy had become so vast and unpredictable that even well-connected businessmen were no longer assured of an outcome in their favor. In the words of a prominent lawyer who advises the EBA, "We've given up on trying to maneuver the state to our advantage. It's simply too large, too inefficient, and too unreliable. We need to rein it in, shrink it, and dramatically reduce both the size and nature of its role in the economy."[55]

Egypt's most powerful businessmen had concluded that the Nasserist state was a fundamental threat to their prosperity, particularly as the country opened to foreign competition. The key to business' future lay in redefining the role of the state in a manner that facilitated the private sector's development by providing a clearer legal code, more predictable enforce-

[53] Personal interview with Ismail Osman, October 21, 1994.
[54] Personal interview with Shafiq Jabr, October 28, 1994.
[55] Personal interview with Yahia al-Jamal, November 11, 1994.

ment of laws, and a sharp reduction in the regulatory power of the bureau-cracy. These changes would produce a state that was more predictable, accountable, and responsive.

As the 1990s progressed, the EBA and AMCHAM articulated these views with increasing urgency. However, they did not have the resources or the expertise to develop specific policy proposals for reform. Several powerful businessmen addressed this gap by establishing a think tank, the Egyptian Center for Economic Studies (ECES), in the mid-1990s.[56] Its board included many of the most prominent figures from AMCHAM and the EBA.[57] They hired a full-time, professional research staff that issued research papers, policy recommendations, and books. The ECES's publi-cations sought to document the problems encountered by private busi-nessmen and to propose specific policy recommendations. These recom-mendations drew extensively on the prevailing neoliberal approach to development advocated by the World Bank.[58] The ECES became the pri-mary institution for translating the broad principles of neoliberal reform into specific policy proposals that suited Egypt's situation. Egypt's leading businessmen had essentially concluded that neoliberal reform served their long-term interests, and were prepared to lend their stature and financial support to a think tank that applied this economic philosophy to Egypt's development challenges. Through the efforts of the ECES, the private sector's aspirations for change were converted into a coherent policy agenda.[59] This agenda presented a comprehensive and well-argued case for

[56] USAID assisted with the start-up funding for the ECES. See the ECES's website: http://www.eces.org.eg/. Accessed July 12, 2007.

[57] The list of board members appeared in the ECES's first "Policy Viewpoint" statement, which was released in October 1997. The board members were: Moustafa Khalil, Taher Helmy, Galal El Zorba, Mohamed Lotfy Mansour, Hazem Hassan, Mounir Abdel Nour, Assaad S. Assaad, Ahmad Bahgat, Shafik Boghdady, Moataz El Alfi, Farouk El Baz, Mostafa El Beleidy, Mohamed El Erian, Ahmad Ezz, Adel El Labban, Ahmad El Maghraby, Magdi Iskander, Ibrahim Kamel, Mohamed Farid Khamis, Ayman Laz, 'Umar Mohanna, Hatem Niazi Moustafa, Jamal Mubarak, Mohammed Sheta, and Raed H. Yehia.

[58] Indeed, the first executive director and head of research at the ECES (Ahmad Galal) was a former World Bank economist.

[59] The ECES's efforts were reinforced by the work of another think tank that emerged at about the same time, the Economic Research Forum for the Arab Countries, Iran, and Turkey (ERF). The ERF is a product of direct funding from several international agencies, including the Arab Fund for Economic and Social Development, the Ford Foundation, the UNDP, and the World Bank. Its headquarters is in Cairo. It produces research papers and books that seek to apply the most current thinking in development economics to the MENA region. A few of its reports deal specifically with Egypt, and reinforce the arguments being made by the ECES. Indeed, several authors commissioned to write papers for the ECES also write for the ERF, including Heba Handoussa, Mahmud Mohieldin, Ahmad Ghoneim, and Hanaa Kheir El Din. These writers also produce research for another influential market-oriented think tank, the Center for Economic and Financial Research and Studies (CEFRS). The CEFRS is based in the Department of Economics and Political Science at Cairo University.

creating a more liberal state. It would later play a key role in shaping the direction of the government's reform policy.

The ECES issued detailed reports and research papers in each of the three areas of private-sector concern identified by the EBA and AM-CHAM. With regard to redefining the role of the state, the ECES reiterated the broad view put forward by EBA and AMCHAM. In the ECES's first working paper (issued in 1996), its executive director wrote that "the Egyptian economy is overregulated, contract enforcement is relatively weak and costly, and investors view government commitment to reform to be less credible than in other countries. Overregulation of inputs (labor, capital, other inputs), outputs (especially exports) and tax administration, together with uncertainty about policy predictability and weak enforcement of contracts, increase the transaction costs of investment and operation of firms."[60]

In order to develop practical solutions to these problems, the ECES began conducting detailed research studies. One of its most ambitious studies attempted to evaluate the economic impact of the government's industrial policy from 1980 through 2000. Through this policy, the government attempted to use tariffs, subsidies, barriers to entry, and price controls to aid specific sectors of the economy. The ECES's project evaluated the effectiveness of these measures by creating a large database on factor productivity and firm diversification in each of Egypt's major economic sectors. After extensive quantitative analysis, it concludes that the Egyptian government's efforts to guide the development of Egyptian industry produced no meaningful diversification of Egyptian firms and no improvement in productivity (indeed, it led to a decline in productivity in some sectors). It further observes that "industries that received greater protection and subsidies performed less well than industries that did not."[61] For most observers of the Egyptian economy, this conclusion was not surprising. The contribution of the ECES's research lay in providing rigorous empirical evidence of this widely held view and an appreciation for the extent of its effect on the economy. Intriguingly, the paper does not call for an end to state efforts to guide economic development. Rather, it suggests that industrial policy be rendered more focused, efficient, and accountable by following the example of the East Asian "tigers."[62]

---

[60] Ahmad Galal, *Which Institutions Constrain Economic Growth in Egypt the Most?* (Cairo: Egyptian Center for Economic Studies, 1996), 8.

[61] Ahmad Galal and Nihal El-Megharbel, *Do Governments Pick Winners or Losers? An Assessment of Industrial Policy in Egypt* (Cairo: Egyptian Center for Economic Studies, 2005), 13.

[62] More specifically, it calls for a new industrial policy with four characteristics: a focus on creating new areas of economic activity rather than protecting old enterprises; tying state

The ECES issued numerous other papers that analyzed the shortcomings of the Egyptian state, documented their negative impact on the economy, and proposed changes. The papers include: an extensive analysis of the financial sector that offered wide-ranging recommendations for reform;[63] a study demonstrating that the current trajectory of public expenditure on subsidies and civil service salaries is not financially sustainable;[64] several studies that evaluate the privatization process and offer suggestions for improvement based on the experiences of Latin America and Central Europe;[65] an assessment of the flaws in existing tax laws and their repercussions for investment and growth;[66] an analysis of state investment policy and why it produced inadequate economic and job growth;[67] and a study of how public investment in non-infrastructure activities crowds out private-sector investment and slows economic growth.[68]

Through these research papers, the ECES presents copious evidence of the inefficiencies produced by the state's role in the Egyptian economy. It calls for dramatic reduction in the size of government. Indeed, the ECES's director estimates that a decline in government spending from 30 percent of GDP to 20 percent would add almost 1 percent to the country's annual growth rate.[69] The ECES also advocates restructuring the state in order to disperse power more fully among the three branches of government. This step would strengthen checks and balances and make policy reversals

support to the achievement of specific and measurable goals; providing assistance for a limited time period; and supporting activities (such as technical training, subsidized credit, and research and development) rather than specific sectors of the economy. Ibid., 15–19.

[63] Mohamed El-Erian and Mahmud Mohieldin, eds., *Financial Development in Emerging Markets: The Egyptian Experience* (San Francisco: Egyptian Center for Economic Studies and International Center for Economic Growth, 1998).

[64] Pedro Alba, Sherine Al-Shawarby, and Farrukh Iqbal, *Fiscal and Public Debt Sustainability* (Cairo: Egyptian Center for Economic Studies, 2004).

[65] Mokhtar Khattab, *Constraints to Privatization: The Egyptian Experience* (Cairo: Egyptian Center for Economic Studies, 1999); Ahmad Galal, *Savings and Privatization* (Cairo: Egyptian Center for Economic Studies, 1996); Alan R. Roe, *The Egyptian Banking System: Liberalization, Competition, and Privatization* (Cairo: Egyptian Center for Economic Studies, 1998). The executive director of the ECES, Ahmad Galal, was a specialist in privatization. He led a World Bank study of this topic in the early 1990s, which was eventually published as Ahmad Galal, *Welfare Consequences of Selling Public Enterprises: An Empirical Analysis* (New York: Oxford University Press, 1994).

[66] Hanaa Kheir-El-Din, Samiha Fawzy, and Amal Rafaat, *Marginal Effective Tax Rates and Investment Decisions in Egypt* (Cairo: Egyptian Center for Economic Studies, 2000).

[67] Samiha Fawzy, *Investment Policies and the Unemployment Problem in Egypt* (Cairo: Egyptian Center for Economic Studies, 2002).

[68] Samiha Fawzy, *Public and Private Investment in Egypt: Crowding-Out or Crowding-In?* (Cairo: Egyptian Center for Economic Studies, 2004).

[69] Egyptian Center for Economic Studies, *Policy Viewpoint: Priorities for Rapid and Shared Economic Growth in Egypt* (Cairo: Egyptian Center for Economic Studies, 1998), 2.

more difficult.[70] However, the ECES also presents a neo-institutionalist argument for strengthening the state in specific areas. In its view, the state must be sufficiently powerful to regulate the market, collect taxes, monitor the financial and insurance industries, enforce contracts, protect private property, restrain monopoly behavior, and resolve commercial disputes quickly and consistently. In the words of the ECES's principal economist, "private sector development is only one element of Egypt's growth. The emergence of a viable private sector also hinges on a major sustained effort to develop competent, capable government."[71]

In order to create this type of state, the ECES calls for reforms modeled primarily on the experiences of East Asia. A central theme is the establishment of strong and independent regulatory agencies for the banking sector, the stock market, the insurance industry, and telecommunications.[72] The ECES also supports several other types of government involvement in the economy, including government programs to restructure the textile industry in order to make it more competitive;[73] government regulation of competition in order to guard against the possibility of monopolies;[74] and government tax incentives that encourage export-oriented firms, labor-intensive investment, and small and medium-sized businesses.[75] The ECES also advocates dramatic strengthening of the state's role in providing education.[76]

---

[70] Galal, *Which Institutions Constrain Economic Growth in Egypt the Most?* A more recent ECES working paper reaches the same conclusion. Mustafa K. Nabli and others, *The Political Economy of Industrial Policy in the Middle East and North Africa* (Cairo: Egyptian Center for Economic Studies, 2006).

[71] Samiha Fawzy, *The Business Environment in Egypt* (Cairo: Egyptian Center for Economic Studies, 1998), 1.

[72] Ziad A. Bahaa Eldin and Mahmud Mohieldin, "On Prudential Regulation in Egypt," in *Financial Development in Emerging Markets,* ed. Mohamed El-Erian and Mahmud Mohieldin (Cairo: Egyptian Center for Economic Studies, 1998), 111–40; Mahmud Fahmy, "The Legal and Regulatory Framework of the Capital Market in Egypt," in *Financial Development in Emerging Markets: The Egyptian Experience,* ed. Mohamed El-Erian and Mahmud Mohieldin (Cairo: Egyptian Center for Economic Studies, 1998), 167–84; Samiha Fawzy, *Assessment of Corporate Governance in Egypt* (Cairo: Egyptian Center for Economic Studies, 2003); Egyptian Center for Economic Studies, *Policy Viewpoint: Towards More Efficient Telecommunication Services in Egypt* (Cairo: Egyptian Center for Economic Studies, 1998).

[73] Miria Pigato and Ahmad Ghoneim, *Egypt After the End of the Multi-Fiber Agreement: A Comparative Regional Analysis* (Cairo: Egyptian Center for Economic Studies, 2006).

[74] Bahaa Ali El Dean and Mahmud Mohieldin, *On the Formulation and Enforcement of Competition Law in Emerging Economies: The Case of Egypt* (Cairo: Egyptian Center for Economic Studies, 2001).

[75] Egyptian Center for Economic Studies, *Policy Viewpoint: Egypt's Export Puzzle* (Cairo: Egyptian Center for Economic Studies, 2001); Sanjay Lall, *Strengthening SMEs for International Competitiveness* (Cairo: Egyptian Center for Economic Studies, 2000).

[76] Egyptian Center for Economic Studies, *Policy Viewpoint: Priorities for Rapid and Shared Economic Growth in Egypt.* The ECES estimates that improving education to the level

In addition, the ECES calls for a sharp increase in public expenditure on basic social services such as health care, unemployment insurance, and pensions. In the ECES's view, the decline of basic social services has important repercussions for labor mobility and economic development. Under the current system, any worker who loses his job faces immediate hardship and poverty due to the absence of unemployment insurance. Consequently, workers gravitate toward jobs that are extremely secure. For most Egyptians, this means working for the state even if the salary is low. Workers are also very reluctant to run the risk of changing jobs, even if a better salary and professional opportunities are available, because the downside risk of possible unemployment is so immense. Strengthening the state's provision of social services is essential for addressing these fears and enabling Egyptian workers to move easily from public-sector jobs to private-sector positions, and to move among positions in the private sector in response to changing economic conditions. In order to expand the state's capabilities in this area, the ECES calls for increasing government expenditure on basic social services from the current level of 0.5 percent of GDP to 2.0 percent.[77]

The ECES analysis of Egypt's economic situation also includes considerable discussion of the rule of law. The ECES's research pays particular attention to the complexity of the bureaucracy and its deleterious effect on the implementation of law. An ECES survey of 154 businesses found that the tax bureaucracy is particularly onerous, due to the arbitrariness of tax officials and the inefficiency of the dispute-settlement system.[78] The customs bureaucracy suffers from similar problems, and is considered a major impediment to the expansion of exports and the opening of the

---

found in fast-growing LDCs would increase economic growth by 1.06 percent annually. Another ECES paper observes that one of the most significant differences between East Asia and the Middle East lies in the quality of its education systems. Marcus Noland and Howard Pack, *The East Asian Industrial Policy Experience: Implications for the Middle East* (Cairo: Egyptian Center for Economic Studies, 2005).

[77] Heba Handoussa and Nivine El Oraby, *Civil Service Wages and Reform: The Case of Egypt* (Cairo: Egyptian Center for Economic Studies, 2004). The ECES also calls for substantial changes in how social services are provided. Drawing on the experiences of Chile and Bangladesh, it recommends a dramatic improvement in the accountability of the agencies that provide these services, the development of quantitative measures of their performance, and increased involvement of citizens in deciding how services are designed and provided. Omneia Helmy, *Pension System Reform in Egypt* (Cairo: Egyptian Center for Economic Studies, 2004). Also, Ahmad Galal, *Social Expenditure and the Poor in Egypt* (Cairo: Egyptian Center for Economic Studies, 2003); Heba Handoussa, *Employment, Budget Priorities and Microenterprises* (Cairo: Egyptian Center for Economic Studies, 2002). Also, Heba Handoussa, *The Role of the State: The Case of Egypt* (Cairo: Economic Research Forum, 1994).

[78] Sahar Tohamy, *Tax Administration and Transaction Costs in Egypt* (Cairo: Egyptian Center for Economic Studies, 1998), 12–24.

economy to new technologies.[79] The ECES offers several proposals for reform based on the experience of other developing countries. Some of its
suggestions are obvious, such as increasing the salaries of civil servants,
improving their training, basing promotions on merit rather than seniority, and reducing the total number of civil servants (through a hiring
freeze, outsourcing of some functions, and early retirement schemes).[80]
Other proposals are more innovative, including: decentralizing some government services to municipal and local authorities; developing a detailed
database on personnel, their training, and performance that can be accessed across ministries; facilitating movement of civil servants across ministries in response to changing needs; and expanding micro-credit programs that enable former civil servants to start their own businesses or
expand existing businesses.[81]

The ECES also makes a strong case that integration into the global
economy will lead to dramatic improvements in the rule of law. In its view,
increased involvement in global trade leads to a steady harmonization of
Egyptian laws and procedures with those of advanced industrialized countries. These institutional changes have a ripple effect throughout the economy. They not only lead to increased trade. They also produce clearer and
more consistent laws, effective regulatory institutions modeled on those
of Egypt's main trading partners, a modern capital market that can attract
funds from both domestic and international investors, and a more capable
judicial system that can resolve disputes quickly and consistently. Thus,
the ECES's advocacy of trade liberalization goes beyond the traditional
claims about the virtues of comparative advantage. It views globalization
as a catalyst for institutional changes that build the rule of law. These
institutional changes, in turn, are the most fundamental component of
sustained market development.[82]

In addition, the ECES has argued long and hard for improving the
protection of property rights. It sponsored a major research project on

---

[79] Omneia Helmy, *Reforming Customs Administration* (Cairo: Egyptian Center for Economic Studies, 2003).

[80] Laila El Baradei, *Do Parallel Structures Resolve the Problems of the Egyptian Government
Bureaucracy?* (Cairo: Egyptian Center for Economic Studies, 2006), 31; Handoussa and
Oraby, *Civil Service Wages and Reform: The Case of Egypt*, 10.

[81] Handoussa and Oraby, *Civil Service Wages and Reform: The Case of Egypt*, 10–23.

[82] Mohamed A. El-Erian, *Globalization and the Arab Economies: From Marginalization to
Integration* (Cairo: Egyptian Center for Economic Studies, 1997); Ahmad Galal and Sahar
Tohamy, "Toward an Egypt-U.S. Free Trade Agreement: An Egyptian Perspective," in
Building Bridges: An Egypt-U.S. Free Trade Agreement, ed. Ahmad Galal and Robert Z. Law-
rence (Washington, DC: Brookings Institution Press, 1998), 13–36. Mahmud Mohieldin,
"The Egypt-EU Partnership Agreement and Liberalization of Services," in *Regional Part-
ners in Global Markets: Limits and Possibilities of the Euro-Med Agreements*, ed. Ahmad Galal
and Bernard Hoekman (Cairo: Egyptian Center for Economic Studies, 1997), 238–56.

this topic by a well-known Peruvian economist, Hernando DeSoto. De-Soto first gained notoriety among development economists by document-ing the impact of weak protection of property rights on economic growth in Peru. ECES supported DeSoto's research on the same issue in Egypt. Over several years, DeSoto and his team documented the number of dwell-ings in Egypt with unclear legal title and estimated their value. The total figure is stunning: over 90 percent of urban dwellings, and 80 percent of rural homes, lack clear title. Their total value is estimated at $240 billion, roughly three times Egypt's annual GDP. Because the title on this prop-erty is unclear, small businessmen who effectively "own" it cannot use it as collateral to acquire loans for growing their businesses. Lack of clear title also means that the owners have difficulty accessing state-subsidized infrastructure services such as electricity, water, sewage, and roads. These facts have profound repercussions for Egypt's economic development. Small and medium-sized enterprises (SMEs) with fewer than ten employ-ees make up 95 percent of the firms in Egypt's private sector. They also employ over 60 percent of the nonagricultural private labor force. The Egyptian government is counting on them to create at least 325,000 jobs per year (out of the total of 600,000 new positions needed annually).[83] However, without access to capital and basic services, these SMEs stand little chance of playing this role. DeSoto and the ECES make a well-docu-mented case that the key to unlocking the potential of this sector lies in more effective protection of property rights, particularly rights to land and the buildings on it. This can be achieved by dramatically simplifying the laws for purchasing property;[84] creating clearer procedures for gaining formal title to property that citizens have used informally for years;[85] re-ducing the taxes imposed on registered land; simplifying the procedure for acquiring a permit to build; and clarifying the laws allowing a property owner to pass his property to a designated heir.[86]

In some respects, the reforms that the ECES advocates are classically liberal. It calls for a more efficient, accountable, and constrained state. It supports a strengthening of the rule of law, and it advocates an expansion

[83] *Egypt in the 21st Century* (Cairo: Government of Egypt, 1999), 12.

[84] DeSoto's research found that a citizen had to carry out at least seventy-seven bureau-cratic procedures in thirty-one public and private entities in order to purchase and register a piece of property. The process was estimated to take between five and fourteen years. Her-nando DeSoto, *Dead Capital and the Poor: Appendices* (Cairo: Egyptian Center for Eco-nomic Studies, 1997), 16.

[85] DeSoto estimated that the procedures needed to regularize ownership of an informal dwelling required between six and eleven years to complete. Ibid., 20.

[86] Hernando DeSoto, *Dead Capital and the Poor in Egypt* (Cairo: Egyptian Center for Economic Studies, 1997), 27–35. DeSoto also discusses his findings in Hernando DeSoto, *The Mystery of Capital* (New York: Basic Books, 2000). This book studies the phenomenon of dead capital in Egypt, the Philippines, Peru, and Haiti.

of some rights (particularly property rights). Yet, it goes a step beyond this classical view by calling for a strong state that intervenes in the economy to achieve specific goals such as subsidizing key economic activities and sectors, improving education, strengthening social services, and regulating the market. This is a muscular liberalism that requires a powerful and invasive state. But, this invasiveness is targeted and constrained.

BROADENING THE POLITICAL BASE FOR MARKET LIBERALISM: THE "NEW THINKING" OF THE NDP

With each new research paper, the ECES added another plank to its increasingly sophisticated platform of reforms for the Egyptian state and economy. Just as the ECES was developing this precise path of reform, the ruling National Democratic Party (NDP) was headed in the opposite direction. Its troubles first became apparent in the 1995 parliamentary elections, when it managed to avoid an embarrassing defeat only by extensive use of graft and violence. Indeed, the 1995 elections—during which fifty people were killed, over eight hundred were wounded, and several thousand were arrested—were the most disorderly and chaotic in Egyptian history.[87] A half-hearted attempt at internal party reform and reorganization in 1998 had little effect. The party entered the 2000 parliamentary election with no coherent platform and sharp divisions within its leadership over what the party stood for and who should represent it in the elections. Its organizational structure had grown weak and unreliable, as local NDP officials hijacked the party's structures to bolster their local patronage networks with little regard for the ideas or objectives of the national leadership. These internal weaknesses led to an abysmal performance in the 2000 parliamentary elections. Despite widespread fraud and violence, only 32 percent of NDP candidates managed to win their contests. The NDP was able to retain a majority in Parliament only by wooing back NDP defectors who had run as independents. While this measure allowed the NDP to remain formally in control of Parliament, it only aggravated the internal incoherence of the party as the newly empowered NDP-independents confronted the old guard leadership for control of the party's key institutions.[88]

---

[87] Kienle, *A Grand Delusion: Democracy and Economic Reform in Egypt*, 56–62; al-Awadi, *In Pursuit of Legitimacy*, 171; also, Sandrine Gamblin, *Contours et Détours du Politique en Egypte: Les élections législatives de 1995* (Paris: Harmattan, 1997).

[88] Hala Mustafa, "Intikhabat 2000 Mu'shirat 'Amma," in *Initkhabat Majlis as-Sha'ab 2000*, ed. Hala Mustafa (Cairo: Markaz al-Dirasat al-Siyasiyya wa-l-Istratijiyya bi-l-Ahram, 2001), 7–14; 'Amru al-Shubki, "Al-Mustaqilun wa al-Intikhabat," in *Intikhabat Majlis as-Sha'ab 2000*, ed. Hala Mustafa (Cairo:Markaz al-Dirasat al-Siyasiyya wa-l-Istratijiyya bi-l-Ahram, 2001), 85–102.

In an effort to reinvigorate the party, its top leaders—led by Husni Mubarak, the party's chairman—called for "new ideas" and "new blood."[89] The figure chosen to lead this effort was the president's son, Jamal Mubarak.[90] By choosing his son, Mubarak was demonstrating his personal commitment to this new direction while also ensuring that he maintained control over it. The younger Mubarak was appointed to the NDP's governing body (the 25-member General Secretariat) in February 2000, despite having played no previous role in party affairs. His subsequent rise within the party was meteoric. He was appointed to the twelve-member Guidance Committee of the General Secretariat in December 2001. In September 2002, he was appointed the third-ranking official in the NDP as well as the chair of the newly created Policies Secretariat. This new secretariat was described by the secretary general of the NDP (Safwat al-Sharif) as "the party's throbbing heart and its tool for turning new thoughts into reality and crystallizing a clear political vision on all national issues."[91] It effectively made Jamal Mubarak one of the primary architects of policy reform for both the party and the regime.[92]

Jamal has both a pro-Western and pro-business background. A graduate of the American University in Cairo, he worked for six years as an investment banker with Bank of America's office in London. He then established his own investment advisory firm, Med Invest Partners, which became one of the leading intermediaries for Western investors seeking to purchase stocks and companies in Egypt. He was also one of the driving forces behind the formation and development of the ECES. He has served on the board of the ECES since its founding. As Jamal's influence in the NDP grew, he began to appoint businessmen and researchers associated with the ECES to positions of influence within the party. Ahmad Ezz, owner of Egypt's largest steel company and a founding member of the ECES, was made chairman of the Parliament's Budget and Planning committee. He was also appointed to the General Secretariat of the NDP and put in charge of "membership," which meant that he selected the NDP

[89] Husni Mubarak, "Address to the General Assembly of the National Democratic Party," Cairo, September 2002.

[90] Jamal Mubarak had explored the possibility of establishing a new party—*Hizb al-Mustaqbal*—in the 1990s. It was intended to revive the party system and serve as an advocate of market-oriented reform. However, Jamal was persuaded by his father and other advisors to pursue his agenda for reform from within the NDP.

[91] Quoted in Jamal Essam El-Din, "NDP Congress' Aftershocks," *al-Ahram Weekly*, September 26–October 2, 2002. Kamal al-Shazli, the second most senior leader in the party, described the policies secretariat as "entrusted with forging the party's vision on all national issues and passing it on to the government for implementation." Ibid.

[92] This discussion of Jamal Mubarak's background draws upon Jihad 'Auda, *Jamal Mubarak: Tajdid al-Libraliyya al-Wataniyya* (Cairo: Dar al-Huriyya, 2004), especially pp. 173–206.

members who would run in municipal and parliamentary elections. Hussam Badrawi, an active participant in ECES events and a former vice president of AMCHAM, was appointed chairman of the Parliament's Education and Scientific Research committee. He was also assigned to head up the NDP's Business Secretariat, which served as the liaison between the party and the business community and aimed to "raise awareness within the business community, increase their participation in political life, and encourage them to join the Party."[93] Mahmud Mohieldin, a prominent economist who played a central role in developing the ECES's proposals for reform of the financial system, was made chairman of the NDP's economic affairs committee. He was also elevated to the twenty-five-member General Secretariat of the Party.[94]

Each of these figures—Ezz, Badrawi, and Mohieldin—were also members of the Policies Secretariat of the NDP, which served as Jamal's vehicle for advocating reform within the party and the government. They were joined on this secretariat by another key ECES figure, Taher Helmy. Helmy was a prominent, American-trained lawyer who established one of the most successful law firms in Egypt.[95] He was also a co-founder of the ECES and was chairman of its board. In addition, he held the presidency of AMCHAM, where he was a frequent and eloquent advocate of reform along the lines proposed by the ECES.[96]

As the influence of Jamal and his allies grew within the NDP, they began to chart a new course for the party's policy and ideology. This process started at the NDP's General Assembly in September 2002.[97] This Assembly saw the appointment of Ezz, Badrawi, Mohieldin, and Helmy to the party posts mentioned above. The reformers had their first opportunity to present a statement of their policy plans at the annual meeting of the NDP the following year.[98] The documents from these two events help to clarify

[93] *Internal Regulations of the National Democratic Party*, Article 56.

[94] Mohieldin was an associate professor in the department of economics and political science at Cairo University. He holds a Ph.D. in economics from Warwick University in Britain, where he specialized in the study of financial markets in the developing world. He co-edited the ECES volume on reform of the financial sector: El-Erian and Mahmud Mohieldin (eds.), *Financial Development in Emerging Markets: The Egyptian Experience*. As noted below, he would later join the government as minister of investment in July 2004.

[95] The firm is Helmy and Hamza. For further information, see "Legal Eagles," *Business Today*, May 2004. For a profile of Helmy, see Niveen Wahish, "Taher Helmi: Feats of Circumstance," *al-Ahram Weekly*, March 17–23, 2005.

[96] See, for example, his "Viewpoint" in each issue of AMCHAM's monthly magazine, *Business Monthly*, beginning in July 2003.

[97] The General Assembly occurs every five years and brings together leaders from all levels of the Party—a total of roughly 6,000 persons in 2002. The NDP claims a total national membership of 2 million.

[98] The annual meeting of the NDP is a smaller event than the General Assembly. It is intended to follow up on the action recommendations of the General Assembly and evaluate whether the government has implemented them effectively.

both the magnitude of the reformers' break with the NDP's ideological past, and the extent to which their new path drew on the conception of market liberalism developed by the ECES.

Jamal Mubarak's speech at the 2002 NDP General Assembly declared that "Egypt has undergone radical changes in all aspects of life. The ruling party should cope with these changes by reconsidering some of its founding principles and outlining a new vision for the future."[99] Under the banner of "New Thinking" for the party, he concluded that Egypt must strengthen its efforts at social and economic development "through the perfect application of free-market principles . . . to achieve the best distribution and manipulation of the national wealth."[100] The subsequent policy papers presented at the 2003 conference fleshed out the details of this strategy. These documents echo many of the themes of the ECES's research. They call for a dramatic increase in the private sector's role in the economy, since "the economy needs 800,000 jobs annually. The private sector must generate 80 percent of these."[101] The NDP supports privatization of public-sector firms, even in the pharmaceutical sector, in order to "improve efficiency and quality." It also backs increased private-sector involvement in the provision of services and infrastructure projects, particularly utilities.[102] It calls for the development of a new national health insurance scheme that would include a prominent role for the private sector, and which would limit publicly subsidized insurance to only the most needy citizens.[103] The private-sector role in education should also expand, particularly at the university level, and fees for high school and university education "should be discussed."[104] It further advocates "rationalizing" subsidies through the use of surveys that identify which members of the community genuinely need assistance, with the eventual goal of eliminating subsidies for most Egyptians and replacing them with job-training programs. In addition, the tax laws should be overhauled and unified into a single tax code, which will be administered by a better-equipped and better-trained tax authority.[105] Trade liberalization also receives considerable attention. The NDP's policy documents call for lowering tariffs, sim-

[99] Jamal Mubarak, "Manthar ila Mustaqbal Misr." Speech delivered at the 2002 General Assembly of the National Democratic Party.

[100] Ibid.

[101] Al-Hizb al-Watani al-Dimaqrati, *Taqrir 'an al-Siyasa al-Iqtisadiyya* (Cairo: Al-Hizb al-Watani al-Dimaqrati, 2003), 12.

[102] Ibid., 24–25.

[103] Al-Hizb al-Watani al-Dimaqrati, *Taqrir 'an Mustaqbal al-Siyasa al-Sihhatiyya* (Cairo: Al-Hizb al-Watani al-Dimaqrati, 2003), 15.

[104] Al-Hizb al-Watani al-Dimaqrati, *Mustaqbal al-Ta'alim fi Misr* (Cairo: Al-Hizb al-Watani al-Dimaqrati, 2003), 24.

[105] Al-Hizb al-Watani al-Dimaqrati, *Taqrir 'an al-Siyasa al-Iqtisadiyya* (Cairo: Al-Hizb al-Watani al-Dimaqrati, 2003), 42.

plifying the customs law, modernizing the country's ports, and improving the training of customs officials.[106]

The NDP also advocates strengthening state capabilities in many of the same areas mentioned by the ECES. It supports a sharp expansion of the state's capacity to regulate monopolistic behavior and corruption. It recommends that the "competition protection and anti-trust bill be submitted to Parliament in the very near future."[107] In its view, the state also plays an essential role in ensuring that citizens are not injured by an unfettered market economy. It should provide job retraining, micro-loans, and unemployment insurance to help workers adjust to the dislocations caused by economic reform. The NDP also calls for the "complete independence" of the Egyptian Central Bank, an expansion of its regulatory power over the banking industry, and an increase in its staff and resources. It further advocates an active state policy to promote small- and medium-sized enterprises by providing soft loans, marketing assistance, and training in new production techniques.[108] Similar support should be extended to export-oriented businesses.[109] In addition, it endorses the creation of independent agencies to monitor the quality of publicly provided services in education and health care in order to "increase the accountability of public service providers."[110]

These NDP documents do not address all of the ECES's concerns. There is a noticeable absence of any discussion of civil service reform. There is a similar lack of attention to the pension system, property rights, and the need to formalize the informal sector (despite the ECES's extensive research on this topic). Thus, it would be inaccurate to suggest that the ECES's agenda for reform was transferred wholesale to the NDP. However, the extent of overlap is striking. Interviews with several of the persons involved suggest that this overlap reflects a commonality of goals and fortuitous timing. Mahmud Mohieldin, the chair of the NDP's economic committee, recalled:

> There was a decision at the highest levels of government to move away from the Nasserist institutions and develop a more market-based economy. ECES was simply in the right place at the right time. It had a set of proposals already on hand that harmonized with where the government wanted to go. The fact that many of these proposals were developed by people who would later join the leadership of the NDP made it even more likely that they would become party and government policy.[111]

[106] Ibid., 62–63.
[107] Ibid., 2.
[108] Ibid., 8.
[109] Ibid.
[110] Ibid., 4.
[111] Personal interview with Mahmud Mohieldin, March 22, 2005.

Thus, by 2003, the market liberalism developed within the ECES in the 1990s had largely displaced the statist ideology of the NDP. It had been integrated into the core policy documents of the party. It was also the guiding light for the most influential reformers in the regime. Policy statements, however, can often amount to little more than rhetoric in the Egyptian system. Many observers still wondered whether the regime would take meaningful steps to implement the new policies. This question was answered in July 2004, when Mubarak appointed Ahmad Nazif as prime minister. Nazif had been the minister of telecommunications in the previous government, where he developed a reputation as a dedicated market reformer. He led the government's efforts to deregulate the telecommunications sector and presided over the sale of two mobile phone licenses to private-sector firms. These steps created the first meaningful competition for the state-owned Telecom Egypt. When he was invited to form a new cabinet, he gave several key portfolios to prominent businessmen. Rachid Muhammad Rachid, a senior executive at the Unilever corporation and a board member of the ECES, was made minister of foreign trade and industry. Ahmad al-Maghrabi, the chief executive of a major hotel chain and another board member of the ECES, was appointed minister of tourism. Mahmud Mohieldin, the ECES researcher mentioned above, was put in charge of an entirely new portfolio—the Ministry of Investment—whose primary mission was to revive the privatization process.[112] When Nazif was invited to form his second government in January 2006, the trend in business-oriented appointments continued. Each of the businessmen in the earlier cabinet remained.[113] They were joined by Muhammad Mansur, CEO of a major industrial equipment company and another ECES board member, who became minister of transportation.

Nazif acted quickly to implement both the letter and the spirit of the market-oriented reforms approved by the NDP. One of his central goals was to "redefine the role of what the government should do and what it should leave to the private sector."[114] At the heart of this effort was an aggressive plan to accelerate the pace of privatization. In the year prior to Nazif assuming power (2003), Egypt privatized nine firms with a total value of $17.5 million.[115] In 2005–2006, the state sold fifty-nine firms worth $2.6 billion.[116] It also announced plans to sell another forty-five

---

[112] This ministry combined the Public Enterprise Ministry, the General Authority for Investment and Free Zones (GAFI), and the Capital Market Authority.

[113] Ahmad al-Maghrabi, Minister of Tourism in the first Nazif government, was assigned to the housing portfolio in the second government.

[114] "Transcript of Interview with Egypt's Ahmad Nazif," *Wall Street Journal*, February 2, 2005.

[115] *Economist Intelligence Unit, Egypt: Country Report*, November 2004, 23.

[116] Ibid., August 2006, 20.

firms, as well as its share of an additional fifty-eight joint ventures. The list of firms on the block included some of the state's most prosperous enterprises, including Alexandria Mineral Oils Company and Sidi Krir Petrochemicals. Even a portion of the national airline, EgyptAir, will be privatized through a listing on the stock exchange.

The government implemented several other policies that expand the contribution of the private sector and shrink the role of the state in the economy. The highlights include: privatizing one of the four public-sector banks (Bank of Alexandria); expanding private investment in infrastructure, particularly railroads and telecommunications; dramatically simplifying the customs code and the tax code; establishing a commercial court to resolve business disputes more quickly; promulgating a new anti-trust law; simplifying the procedures for registering title to property; and forming a high-level committee to undertake a comprehensive review of all legislation regarding the economy.[117]

OPPOSITION TO MARKET LIBERALISM: THE RISE OF AN INDEPENDENT LABOR MOVEMENT

The changes Nazif's government adopted were not welcomed by all Egyptians. The decision to further shrink the public sector was particularly controversial. Egypt's public sector had deep roots in the statist ideology of the Nasser era. As noted earlier, this ideology waned as the Nasserist regime declined and Arab nationalism faded from both national and regional politics. The collapse of socialist and communist regimes in the former Eastern bloc further eroded the appeal of state-led economic development.[118] Nonetheless, some intellectuals on the Left continued to assert the importance of the public sector and its central role in building national strength and unity. They remain principled opponents of a market-based economy, which they believe places Egypt in a subservient role in the international economic system and leads to widespread exploitation of Egypt's workers and resources. They express these views primarily through the major leftist party (*al-Tajamu'*) and its newspaper (*al-Ahali*). However,

[117] For further detail on these reforms, see *Economist Intelligence Unit, Egypt: Country Report* from July 2004 through November 2007. These reform policies will be discussed further in chapter 6.

[118] For additional discussion of the history of the Left in Egypt, see: Joel Beinin and Zachary Lockman, *Workers on the Nile: Nationalism, Communism, Islam, and the Egyptian Working Class* (Princeton, NJ: Princeton University Press, 1987); Selma Botman, *The Rise of Egyptian Communism, 1939–1970* (Syracuse: Syracuse University Press, 1988); Tareq Y. Ismael and Rifa'at El-Sa'id, *The Communist Movement in Egypt, 1920–1988* (Syracuse, NY: Syracuse University Press, 1990).

their views have gained relatively little public support. *Al- Tajamu'* won only two seats in the 2005 parliamentary elections (out of 454). The demand for issues of *Al-Ahali* has declined to the point where it is published only once per week.[119] Its articles and editorials have little impact on public debate. Indeed, it has been largely displaced by a new wave of independent newspapers (such as *al-Misri al-Youm* and *al-Dustur*) that offer more vigorous and credible reporting. The Left also suffers from sharp internal divisions based on ideological disagreements and personality clashes among leaders.[120] In addition, the regime has worked to keep the Left weak, divided, and lacking any national organizational structure.[121] All of these pressures have combined to render the Left a largely ineffectual force in Egyptian political life. It does not offer a coherent ideological alternative to market liberalism, nor does it command sufficient organizational resources to mount a sustained challenge to market reform.

As the Left's political influence declined, a new center of opposition to market reform emerged: the independent labor movement, which has grown dramatically in the past decade. This movement arose from workers' frustration and disappointment with the official institutions for representing labor. By law, Egyptian laborers are organized into labor federations that represent workers in each of the major sectors of the economy.[122] All public-sector workers are required to join the relevant federation.[123] These federations, in turn, report to a single national body—The General

---

[119] In 1997, *al-Ahali* published 80,000 copies weekly and distributed 50,000. By 2007, these figures had fallen to 25,000 and 10,000. Personal interview with 'Adil Bakr, distribution director for *al-Ahali*. The interview was conducted by Naseema Noor, February 21, 2008.

[120] For example, there have been serious disagreements over how to respond to the rise of political Islam. Rif'at Sa'id, a senior leader of *al-Tajamu'*, has supported the regime's crackdown on Islamists of all stripes. In contrast, many other leaders and members of *al-Tajamu'* have objected to the scope and brutality of the crackdown, as well as other restrictions on the rights and political activities of peaceful Islamists.

[121] For a discussion of the decline of the Left and the reasons for its weakness, see Rif'at Sa'id, *al-Yasar, al-Dimaqratiyya, wa-l-Ta'salam* (Cairo: Mu'ssasat al-Ahali, 1998); also, Marsha Pripstein Posusney, "Egyptian Privatization: New Challenges for the Left," *Middle East Report* 29, no. 1 (1999): 38–40.

[122] There are currently twenty-three labor federations. Each federation contains both regional and local "labor committees."

[123] Private-sector workers are largely un-unionized. According to the 2003 labor law, they are permitted to form factory committees that can petition to join the relevant labor federation. In practice, activists who attempt to form labor committees at private firms are usually fired. The Land Center for Human Rights, an NGO that follows labor matters, estimated that 90 percent of private-sector workers have been unable to unionize. See Ahmed Namatalla, "Card-Carrying Members," *Business Today* (January 2006), 67–73. Also, Joel Beinin and Hossam el-Hamalawy, "Egyptian Textile Workers Confront the New Economic Order," *Middle East Report Online*, March 25, 2007.

Federation of Trade Unions (GFTU).[124] The federations and the GFTU are the sole legitimate representatives of labor in Egypt. They are responsible for conveying all of labor's concerns to the regime, and for negotiating wages, benefits, and working conditions. However, elections within the federations have been carefully managed to ensure that only regime supporters rise to positions of leadership. As a result, the official organs for representing workers have evolved into tools of regime control over labor rather than effective advocates of labor's interests.[125]

As the privatization plans discussed above unfolded, many workers grew fearful. Most public-sector firms were severely overstaffed. Many analysts expected privatization to produce job losses, salary cuts, and reduced benefits.[126] Indeed, the firms sold in the first fifteen years of the privatization process (1991–2006) experienced precisely these results.[127] However, the GFTU proved remarkably ineffective at reversing these effects. It had a few formal victories—for example, its efforts led to a clause in the 1991 privatization law that prohibited mass layoffs in newly privatized firms. The GFTU also managed to negotiate a clause in the 2003 labor law that ensured the preservation of workers' pensions and guaranteed that any worker who was harmed by privatization would receive "adequate compensation."[128] However, these clauses were often evaded. It was common for firms on the verge of being sold to evade the ban on mass layoffs by undertaking a dramatic downsizing of staff immediately prior to the sale. This usually took the form of "early retirement" of thousands of workers. Under these plans, each worker received a lump-sum payment, combined

---

[124] Marsha Pripstein Posusney, *Labor and the State in Egypt: Workers, Unions, and Economic Restructuring* (New York: Columbia University Press, 1997), 88; Bianchi, *Unruly Corporatism*, 126–30.

[125] For the history of regime efforts to control the GFTU, see Bianchi, *Unruly Corporatism*, 126–44. For a valuable discussion of how regime control of the GFTU was consolidated during the Mubarak era, see Pripstein Posusney, *Labor and the State in Egypt*, 113–26. Also see Nicola Pratt, "Maintaining the Moral Economy: Egyptian State-Labor Relations in an Era of Economic Liberalization," *Arab Studies Journal* 8–9, no. 1–2 (Fall 2000/Spring 2001): 117–18.

[126] In 1996, the Ministry of Public Enterprise estimated that roughly one-third of the employees in the public sector (300,000 workers) were redundant. Ikram, *The Egyptian Economy*, 81.

[127] This was particularly the case in the textile sector. For example, the government hoped to sell the ESCO textile mill in Qalyub. In pursuit of this goal, it undertook an aggressive strategy of reducing the number of employees in order to make the firm more attractive to private buyers. Through a combination of attrition, a hiring freeze, and early retirements, the number of staff was reduced from 24,000 to 3,500. Joel Beinin, "Popular Social Movements and the Future of Egyptian Politics," *Middle East Report Online*, March 10, 2005.

[128] Agnieszka Paczynska, "Globalization, Structural Adjustment, and Pressure to Conform: Contesting Labor Law Reform in Egypt," *New Political Science* 28, no. 1 (2006): 57.

with a monthly payment for life that was much lower than the pension he would have received had his factory remained state-owned.[129] In other cases, pro-labor laws were simply ignored by the owners of newly privatized firms. The regime was slow to prosecute these firms, and often allowed the transgression to pass without any legal action.[130]

As the privatization process continued in the early 2000s, worker anxiety intensified. The GFTU leadership remained largely indifferent and ineffectual as workers were effectively dismissed through "early retirement" schemes. It also turned a blind eye to abuses within some newly privatized firms, including widespread dismissals of workers and sharp reductions in wages. In response, independent labor activists began to organize wildcat strikes and other labor actions without the permission of the GFTU. In 2004, an NGO that follows labor activism in Egypt reported 267 labor actions including protests, strikes, and work slowdowns. In 2005, the figure reached 246. In 2006, it was 222.[131]

These demonstrations included impassioned appeals for the preservation of public-sector jobs. In this regard, they were a direct challenge to the market liberalism advocated by Egypt's reformers. A close examination of the statements and documents from these labor actions also shows that the workers' demands were very legalistic in character. They were based on a substantial body of worker-friendly legislation from the 1960s and 1970s that ensures job security, regular promotions, and salary increases.[132] Labor activists were calling on factory owners and the government to comply with these legal obligations. For example, consider one of the longest strikes in recent Egyptian history—the 2005 strike at the Qalyub Spinning Company, located in Egypt's delta region. The strike

[129] Pratt, "Maintaining the Moral Economy," 118. Workers who accepted early retirement also lost access to government-provided health care and faced possible eviction from inexpensive company-owned housing complexes. Marsha Pripstein Posusney, "Globalization and Labor Protection in Oil-Poor Arab Countries: Racing to the Bottom?" *Global Social Policy* 3, no. 3 (2003): 277.

[130] Pripstein Posusney, "Globalization," 276–78. Beinin and el-Hamalawy observe that private-sector firms often do not provide health insurance despite their legal obligation to do so. Beinin and el-Hamalawy, "Egyptian Textile Workers."

[131] These figures were gathered by the Land Center for Human Rights. They were compiled by the Egyptian Workers and Trade Union Watch, whose reports are available at http://arabist.net/arabawy/. Accessed August 15, 2007.

[132] These laws are part of a broader web of reciprocal ties between labor and the regime that emerged during the Nasser era. Under this framework, workers would provide uninterrupted labor power that contributed to national economic growth. In exchange, the regime would provide secure employment, good wages, and generous benefits. This arrangement is sometimes called the "moral economy," borrowing a term first employed by E. P. Thompson. See Pratt, "Maintaining the Moral Economy," 112; Pripstein Posusney, *Labor and the State*, 14–22.

involved over four hundred workers and lasted over three months.[133] Interviews with the strike leaders, as well as the documents issued by the strike committee, call for:

- A more transparent process for valuing and selling public-sector firms. The strikers claimed that the mill was being sold for a small fraction of its actual value.[134] In addition, they claimed that the management of the mill had conspired with the government to undervalue the firm, in exchange for large sums of money and vacation homes on the Red Sea coast. The strikers called for the privatization process "to conform with the law" and for accusations of corruption to be "fully investigated by the public prosecutor and brought before the courts."[135]

- Effective implementation of laws that protect workers' jobs and benefits. The strikers pointed out that the government had failed to provide workers with an increase in their annual bonus, despite a clear legal obligation to do so. It also failed to implement laws that guaranteed workers an annual cost-of-living increase, adequate health care, protection from arbitrary dismissal, and a pension sufficient to maintain their standard of living.[136]

- Improved follow-through on promises of state assistance for displaced workers. According to the strikers, the government was legally required to provide subsidized loans and job retraining for workers displaced through privatization. It was also obligated to offer new housing for fired workers who were no longer permitted to live in factory-owned housing. The government had provided some of this assistance, but it was "only a small portion of what is necessary. Many workers continue to be denied their rights from the government."[137]

- Less regime repression of the labor movement and its leaders. According to the strikers, activists in the independent labor movement face "dismissal, arrest, and torture." The strikers call repeatedly for the government to cease its "suppression of the workers and their leaders" and to "respect the voice

[133] Beinin, "Popular Social Movements."

[134] According to a spokesman for the workers, the Qalyub mill was valued at 60 million LE in 1999. In 2003, the government invested 7 million LE in capital improvements. The facility was then sold to a private businessman, Hashim al-Daghri, for 4 million LE. Beinin, "Popular Social Movements."

[135] The strikers' demands are reprinted by the Egyptian Workers and Trade Union Watch at http://arabist.net/arabawy/. Accessed August 15, 2007.

[136] By law, the government is required to pay a pension equal to 80 percent of a worker's salary at retirement. The workers claim that, while 10 percent of workers' monthly wages are deducted for retirement benefits, the company has not paid its matching 20 percent share into the retirement fund since 1992. As a consequence, the retirement fund is not able to support adequate retirement packages. Beinin, "Popular Social Movements."

[137] These demands by the strikers are reprinted by the Egyptian Workers and Trade Union Watch at http://arabist.net/arabawy/. Accessed August 15, 2007.

of the workers." They argue that workers have a constitutional right to express their opinion and to create independent labor organizations. They also claim to have a legal right to strike without the permission of the GFTU. In their view, this right is guaranteed by the International Covenant on Human Rights, which Egypt has signed.[138]

Similar points are raised in the other major strikes of recent years, including the strike at the Egyptian-Spanish Asbestos Products Company (Ora Misr) in 2004; the 2005 air traffic controllers' sit-in, which affected all of Egypt's major airports; the December 2006 strike at the Misr Spinning and Weaving Company; the January 2007 work slowdown by Cairo's railway engineers; and the April 2007 strike at the Mansura-Spain textile factory.[139]

While these labor activists are clearly opponents of market liberalism, they are supporters of legal and institutional changes that would create a more constrained and responsive state. In essence, they are calling for increased transparency in the privatization process, improved accountability of state institutions, and greater respect for the rule of law. Their goal is to harness state power to their cause through the rigorous use of law and, if necessary, the courts. Perhaps surprisingly, the independent labor movement is part of the broader convergence of opposition views around the importance of creating a more constrained, predictable, and law-abiding state. Like the liberal constitutionalists and the Islamic constitutionalists discussed in chapter 4, independent labor activists have grown suspicious of a state that does not serve their interests and acts in a brutal and sometimes whimsical fashion. Nonetheless, the independent labor movement's impact on Egyptian politics should not be overestimated. Labor demonstrations are localized affairs usually triggered by actions at a specific factory. As of early 2008, there was no evidence of coordination among factories in a given industry or cooperation across industries. There was also no indication of significant cooperation between labor activists and any political parties or other political organizations.

• • •

The independent labor movement has not been able to significantly slow or alter the market reform process. Particularly under the Nazif government, market reform has moved forward at a brisk pace. Indeed, the World Bank stated in a 2007 report that Egypt was the world's leading economic

---

[138] All quotations are from ibid. The right to strike was upheld by a Higher State Security court in 1987 (in case 1486). Pratt, "Maintaining the Moral Economy," 123.

[139] For details on the demands made during these strikes, see the Egyptian Workers and Trade Union Watch at http://arabist.net/arabawy. Also, see the website of the Land Center for Human Rights at http://www.lchr-eg.org/.

230 • Chapter Five

reformer.[140] However, Egypt has a long way to go. The same World Bank report concluded that its business environment ranks in the bottom third of the world's economies.[141] In addition, it is unclear whether the bureaucracy has the capacity to implement such extensive changes effectively and quickly. Nonetheless, our goal here is not to evaluate the implementation of economic reform, nor to assess how far Egypt has moved toward creating a market economy. Our purpose is simply to demonstrate that the conception of market liberalism that emerged within the private sector in the 1990s was integrated into the ideology of the ruling party and the policies of the government by 2006. Furthermore, as we will see in the next chapter, the key features of this conception of institutional reform are also found in liberal constitutionalism and Islamic constitutionalism.

[140] World Bank, *Doing Business 2008* (Washington, DC: The World Bank Group, 2007), 2.

[141] Egypt was ranked 126 out of 178 countries. Within the Middle East and North Africa, it was bested by Saudi Arabia, Israel, Kuwait, Oman, Turkey, United Arab Emirates, Jordan, Lebanon, Tunisia, Yemen, West Bank and Gaza, and Algeria. However, Egypt managed to outrank Morocco, Iran, Syria, Iraq, and Sudan. Ibid., 6.

CHAPTER SIX

Liberalism, Islam, and Egypt's Political Future

THE MARKET LIBERALS discussed in the previous chapter call for an accountable state with clearly delineated functions that is constrained by law and by institutions. This state is limited, but it is not weak. In their view, the state must have the authority and the capability to regulate the market, collect taxes, enforce contracts, prevent monopoly behavior, and adjudicate commercial disputes quickly and fairly. It must also have the capacity to build a strong and effective network of social services that provide education, health care, unemployment insurance, and pensions. In addition, it should provide financial and technical support to specific types of businesses that will aid the country's long-term development, such as export-oriented firms, labor-intensive manufacturers, and small- and medium-sized enterprises.

The views of the market liberals share important similarities with those of liberal constitutionalists and Islamic constitutionalists. Most importantly, each of these groups supports the same set of liberal institutional reforms, including: a reduction in the state's dominance of the economy and society; more effective separation of powers within the state, combined with improved checks and balances; a clearer and more coherent legal code that defines the limits of executive power and specifies its relationship to other institutions within the state and society; greater judicial independence and effectiveness; and stronger protection of basic rights. The motives of each group for supporting these reforms differ sharply. Indeed, the fact that groups with such divergent ideological starting points support the same set of institutional changes is quite striking.

One might be tempted to argue that this situation is ripe for the formation of pacts among regime reformers, liberal constitutionalists, and Islamic constitutionalists. Under this scenario, market liberals within the regime would reach out to like-minded reformers in the judiciary and the Muslim Brotherhood to create a broad coalition that supports liberal institutional change. However, this degree of cooperation is unlikely. The Judges' Club carefully preserves its insulation from other social actors in order to protect its reputation for independence and professionalism. As a consequence, it is very reluctant to coordinate its political actions with other groups.[1] Some coordination between the Muslim Brotherhood and the business community is possible, particularly in light of the fact that several prominent members of the Brotherhood are also successful businessmen. However, this relationship is unlikely to develop into extensive cooperation due to philosophical differences between the groups. More specifically, the Brotherhood advocates a significant role for the state in strengthening the piety of individual citizens. The market liberals in the business community are uncomfortable with this degree of state intervention in the private lives of citizens.

As a result of these differences, the most likely scenario for the near future is de facto cooperation among these three groups due to their shared goals, rather than formal collaboration. A "grand coalition" of reformers is probably not in the cards. However, Egypt's path toward liberal reform may be more enduring precisely because it is not contingent on the fractious politics of a broad coalition. De facto cooperation among the judiciary, regime reformers, and the Muslim Brotherhood is not the result of agreements among individual leaders, which could weaken when these leaders disagree or pass from the scene. Rather, it is the result of three groups with different ideological foundations concluding that the same set of institutional changes serves their beliefs and interests. The differences among them may make liberal reform slower than under a grand coalition. But, the distinctness of these three separate groups may make their shared call for institutional reform more adaptable and durable.

WHERE ARE THE DEMOCRATS?

While these three groups advocate liberal institutional reform, they do not exhibit a similar degree of support for broadening the public's participation in politics. For the architects of market liberalism within the business community, democracy is a risky enterprise for several reasons. It raises opportunities for those injured by the reform process—particularly public-sector workers—to organize more effectively and block the implementation of policies that are essential for restructuring the economy. Indeed, the president of the Egyptian Businessmen's Association spoke candidly of the "risk of unrestricted debate by those who lack the requisite knowl-

---

[1] However, the judges have received some support from the Muslim Brotherhood. As noted in chapter 4, the MB participated in demonstrations in 2006 on behalf of two embattled judges. The judges, Ahmad Makki and Hisham Bastawisi, faced disciplinary proceedings for publicly criticizing electoral fraud in the 2005 parliamentary election. The MB also backed the Judges' Club's proposed revisions to the law of the judiciary. Its parliamentary delegation attempted to introduce this proposed law in Parliament, but it was blocked by the ruling NDP.

edge and skill, which could reverse the progress we have made and damage the country's economic growth."[2] In his view, policies that are "overly responsive" to the demands of displaced workers could lead to the reinstatement of tariffs to protect local industries, or the expansion of subsidies to loss-making firms.[3] These steps "would reverse the hard-won progress we have made over the last decade. And, they would harm the country."[4]

The ruling National Democratic Party (NDP) is less blunt. Indeed, it has adopted a host of resolutions and documents expressing its commitment to democracy. For example, the 2004 annual meeting of the NDP issued a policy paper entitled, "The Rights of Citizenship and Democracy." It calls for a "comprehensive concept of reform" that includes political reform.[5] It adds that "the citizenry is sovereign" and that the party must exert a concerted effort to "make each citizen aware of his/her political rights."[6] As part of this effort, the party is committed to improving the fairness of elections, strengthening civil society, and expanding opportunities for public participation in politics. The NDP reiterated these themes in its 2005 electoral platform, as well as in the platform adopted by President Mubarak during the 2005 presidential election.

However, Egypt's leaders have a long history of expressing support for democracy but failing to deliver. Their usual explanation for the slow pace of democratization is that Egyptians are "not yet ready." Husni Mubarak is a prominent advocate of this view. At the beginning of his presidency, Mubarak was asked by a journalist whether he believed Egypt should democratize. He responded, "Certain people are demanding freedom and democracy as in the U.S., France, and Britain. But, I say that these countries reached their current level of democracy because they had good industrial and agricultural bases . . . all their people were educated, and they did not have housing problems. . . . If I had these conditions, I would have allowed freedom and complete democracy with controls without hesitation."[7] He further proposed that the Egyptian people are "not yet able to assimilate full democracy."[8] In his view, "We are dealing with a weary people and we must put controls on everything. When we achieve economic stability, rest assured that we will be afraid of nothing. . . . When will we reach the same standard of democracy as [the U.K., France, and the U.S.]? When we raise our cultural standard."[9]

---

[2] Personal interview with Jamal El-Nazar, March 17, 2005.
[3] Ibid.
[4] Ibid.
[5] *Huquq al-Muwatina wa-l-Dimaqratiyya* (Cairo: Hizb al-Watani al-Dimaqrati, 2004), 1.
[6] Ibid.
[7] Interview in *al-Raya*, February 16, 1983.
[8] Interview in *al-Siyasa*, November 20, 1982.
[9] Interview in the *Arab Times*, December 29–30, 1983.

Twenty-two years later, one of the NDP leaders most associated with political reform—'Ali al-Din Hilal[10]—voiced essentially the same argument. In response to a question about implementing the NDP resolutions that support democratization, he responded:

> As for the time frame for putting reform programmes into effect—this is not the same thing as having a vision for reform. It depends on a whole set of conditions being in place—for instance, the modernization of prevalent cultural structures, which is an integral part of political reform. The values of progress, national resurgence, as well as of science, collective action, dialogue, tolerance and solidarity, all of which are crucial in democratization, must be spread.[11]

Views such as these have led to a dismal record of political reform. One of the clearest recent disappointments was the amendment in 2005 to article 76 of the Constitution, which deals with the procedure for selecting the president. The article initially stated that the president is nominated by Parliament and then confirmed by the people through a referendum. In February 2005, to great fanfare, Mubarak and the NDP agreed to amend the Constitution to allow for competitive presidential elections. The move was hailed in the official media as a watershed that marked the dawn of a new democratic era. However, as the details of the amendment were worked out, the NDP's long-standing fear of genuinely competitive elections resurfaced. The final form of the amendment and the law that implemented it effectively doused any hope of greater competition. They imposed several stringent criteria for nominating a candidate for president, which effectively ensured that only the NDP would be able to field a nominee.[12] Additional amendments to article 76 in 2007 did little to change this situation, or to move Egypt closer to genuinely competitive presidential elections. Much-heralded revisions to the political parties law and the law on political rights were similarly disappointing. They further en-

---

[10] 'Ali al-Din Hilal is also known to Western audiences as 'Ali al-Din Hilal Dassuqi.

[11] Hani Shukrallah, "Change or Be Changed," *al-Ahram Weekly,* June 9–15, 2005. He added in another interview, "You can't have democracy without democrats. You cannot have democracy imposed on authoritarian societies . . . . You have to change the status of women, change the schools. Politics is a reflection of society." Jane Perlez, "Egyptians See U.S. as Meddling in their Politics," *New York Times,* October 3, 2002. At the time of the interviews, Hilal was a member of the General Secretariat of the NDP and a senior member of the policies secretariat of the NDP.

[12] The law required each candidate to have significant support in all the country's elected bodies at both the national and provincial levels. The NDP dominates these bodies through a combination of patronage and careful management of election procedures and results. For further details on the 2005 law governing presidential elections, see "Reforming Egypt: In Search of a Strategy," (Washington, DC: International Crisis Group, October 4, 2005), 4–6. Also, Kristen Stilt, "Constitutional Authority and Subversion: Egypt's New Presidential Election System," *Indiana International and Comparative Law Review* 16 (2006): 335–73.

trenched the NDP's control of the electoral process and rendered meaningful political competition even more difficult.[13]

The NDP's main ideological competitors in the judiciary and the Muslim Brotherhood are also wary of broad public participation in politics. The Judges' Club stresses that citizens have a right to free elections and a right to vote. However, this position is always advanced in highly positivistic terms. Citizens have these rights because they are granted by the law and the Constitution. As was noted in chapter 4, there were many occasions during the debate over conducting the 2005 parliamentary elections when the judges could have made a broader claim about the fundamental right of citizens to participate in their own governance. However, they refrained from doing so. There was no mention of popular sovereignty in any of their documents or public statements, and no effort to assert the normative value of this principle. On the rare occasions when the judges made general assertions about politics and governance, they tended to emphasize the importance of relying on highly educated specialists to interpret and apply the law. They harbor an underlying reticence toward mass politics and a nagging fear that unrestrained popular rule could lead to disorder and injustice.

The Muslim Brotherhood offers the most extensive support for public participation in politics. It proposes that *shura* (consultation) is the foundation of Islamic governance. It argues that, under current conditions, this concept is best achieved through free and fair elections that produce a legislature and executive that are accountable to the people. However, like the judges, the theorists of Islamic constitutionalism fear the potential for disorder in mass politics. Al-Qaradawi, for example, writes that the masses can quickly become "like the waves of an angry sea" that sweep away the country's political institutions.[14] Advocates of Islamic constitutionalism also express concern that publicly elected officials may issue laws that contravene the ethical precepts of Islam. In order to avoid this problem, Abu al-Majd calls for the creation of a constitutional court that serves as a check on the legislature and ensures that its laws conform to *Shari'a*. Al-'Awwa and al-Qaradawi support a similar concept.[15] This view also has followers within the Muslim Brotherhood. During the debate in autumn 2007 over a party platform for the MB, some of the organization's leaders called for the creation of a council of religious scholars that would evaluate

[13] See "Reforming Egypt: In Search of a Strategy," 7–8.

[14] Yusuf al-Qaradawi, *Min Fiqh al-Dawla fi-l-Islam*, 126.

[15] Ahmad Kamal Abu al-Majd, *Natharat Hawla al-Fiqh al-Dusturi fi-l-Islam*, 26; Muhammad Salim al-'Awwa, *Al-Haqq fi-l-Ta'abir*, 10, 35; Al-Qaradawi, *Min Fiqh al-Dawla fi-l-Islam*, 31.

draft legislation and offer opinions on whether it conforms to *Shari'a*. This council would serve as a partial check on the power of elected legislators.[16]

Thus, the NDP, the Judges' Club, and the MB have serious reservations about broad public participation in politics. This stands in sharp contrast to each group's strong support for a more liberal state.

Separating Democracy and Liberalism

This analysis suggests that a consensus has emerged among Egypt's most influential political and legal actors to separate democracy from liberalism. This is an unfamiliar phenomenon to Western political analysts, who often regard "liberal democracy" as a single and indivisible idea. However, democracy and liberalism are separate concepts produced by separate processes. The distinction between them is best understood as the difference between how the leadership of the state is chosen versus how the power of the state is organized. More specifically, democracy is widely understood to mean the regular holding of elections. Huntington offers this definition: "[a] political system [is] democratic to the extent that its most powerful collective decision makers are selected through fair, honest, and periodic elections in which candidates freely compete for votes and in which virtually all the adult population is eligible to vote."[17] This conception of democracy is shared by other influential scholars, including Schumpeter and Przeworski.[18]

Liberalism, in contrast, is a set of institutions and institutional relationships that constrain state power and protect basic rights. It includes a clear legal code that protects the rights of citizens, the separation of powers, checks and balances among these powers, an independent judiciary, and effective legal institutions that implement the law.[19]

---

[16] As noted in chapter 4, the council's opinions would be binding in those areas where the meaning of *Shari'a* is "certain and unchanging." In areas where devout Muslims can disagree, the council's views would be nonbinding and would serve only as a source of information and advice for legislators.

[17] Huntington, *The Third Wave*, 7.

[18] Joseph A. Schumpeter, *Capitalism, Socialism, and Democracy* (New York: Harper Torch Books, 1975), 269; Przeworski et al., *Democracy and Development*, 15.

[19] As noted earlier, this view of liberalism is also known as "classical liberalism." The earliest statement of this view is John Locke's *Two Treatises of Government*. Liberalism has assumed a variety of other meanings in contemporary political discourse. For a discussion of these different forms of liberalism, see Kelly, *Liberalism*. For a thoughtful analysis of how the principles of classical liberalism provide the foundation for constitutional governance, see Walter F. Murphy, *Constitutional Democracy: Creating and Maintaining a Just Political Order* (Baltimore: Johns Hopkins University Press, 2007).

In consolidated democracies, these two concepts reinforce each other so thoroughly that they are merged into a single term—liberal democracy. This should not distract us from the fact that, at earlier stages of democratic development, they are often distinct. For example, consider the history of democracy and liberalism in the United Kingdom. At the start of the nineteenth century, only 1.8 percent of the adult population was eligible to vote. After the passage of the Reform Act of 1832, this figure rose to 2.7 percent. After additional reforms in 1867 and 1884, the figure rose to a mere 12.1 percent.[20] Only in 1930, when women received the right to vote, did the United Kingdom achieve universal adult suffrage and meet the modern standard for being democratic. However, it was a pioneer of liberalism long before this date through achievements such as the Magna Carta (signed in 1215), the Habeas Corpus Act of 1679, the Bill of Rights of 1689, and the Act of Settlement of 1701. Democracy grew in a similarly incremental fashion in the United States. With the adoption of the Constitution in 1789, only white, male property owners were eligible to vote. Thirty-five years later, in 1824, only 5 percent of adult Americans participated in the presidential election.[21] Blacks were enfranchised, in principle, in 1870, but not in fact until the voting rights act of 1964. Women were granted the right to vote in 1920. Despite this slow progress on democracy, the United States was an early and important example of liberalism. The U.S. Constitution was a remarkably comprehensive statement of the importance of limiting state power and protecting individual rights. The specific mechanisms that it employed for dividing and constraining power were major innovations for their day, and remain a model for liberal reformers in the developing world. The constitutions of several American states—particularly Massachusetts and Connecticut—provide even earlier evidence of a strong American commitment to liberalism.[22]

As these two cases show, democracy and liberalism are often the product of different elite calculations. The specific causes of democratization vary so widely that generalizations are difficult.[23] Nonetheless, it is instructive to consider some of the calculations by regime elites that lead to a broadening of political participation. These include: a group within the elite believing that a widening of the franchise will strengthen its hand in clashes with its political rivals (this explains, for example, the decision in the

[20] Fareed Zakaria, *The Future of Freedom: Illiberal Democracy at Home and Abroad* (New York: W.W. Norton, 2003), 50.

[21] Ibid.

[22] In light of the West's much longer experience with liberalism than with democracy, Zakaria argues that the "Western model of government is best symbolized not by the mass plebiscite but the impartial judge." Ibid., 20.

[23] Huntington identifies twenty-seven variables that have been invoked in the literature to explain democratization. Huntington, *The Third Wave*, 37–38.

United States to grant voting rights to women in 1920);[24] elites confronting rising social unrest who calculate that broader political participation will provide a peaceful avenue for venting public anger (democratization in the Philippines in 1986 is an example); or elites calculating that democratic reforms will persuade external actors to provide economic support or military aid (for example, Turkey undertook electoral reforms in the 1990s in an effort to qualify for membership in the European Union).

Liberalism, in contrast, entails a significantly different set of elite decisions. In essence, elites who advocate liberalism are choosing to place limits on state power. One can imagine a variety of scenarios that might lead to this decision, including: property owners who seek to constrain the state in order to protect their property from arbitrary confiscation or taxation; elites calculating that constraints on the state will create a more stable business environment that will stimulate investment; and elites who have suffered from autocratic government choosing to constrain the state in order to prevent future abuses of power.

As this brief discussion suggests, democracy and liberalism are different concepts, produced by different elite calculations, and embodied in different institutions. They can emerge at different times, for different reasons. They may reinforce each other and produce the liberal democracy common in the West, but this is not inevitable.

Indeed, in the Egyptian case, the prospects for democratization are poor. The regime retains a stranglehold on political life which it shows little sign of loosening. Through a combination of patronage and graft, it is able to secure overwhelming victories in electoral contests at both the local and national levels. It also wields a vast array of laws that regulate the formation and actions of political parties, civil society groups, and the press. If these laws prove inadequate, the regime can always invoke emergency powers to arrest any individual or suppress any organization that may pose a threat. Not surprisingly, the political groups that emerge in this environment are weak and fragmented. The country has eighteen opposition political parties, but none has developed a significant national following. In the words of one experienced analyst, they suffer from "[a] lack of vision and intellectual innovation, aging leadership, failure to institute democratic practices within their parties, [and] inability to resolve their internal conflicts . . . over the past twenty-five years, the liberal and leftist parties have not organized a single demonstration in support of democracy or freedom."[25] None of the groups that normally create

[24] David Morgan, *Suffragists and Democrats: The Politics of Woman Suffrage in America* (East Lansing: Michigan State University Press, 1972).

[25] Emad El-Din Shahin, "Democratic Transformation in Egypt: Controlled Reforms . . . Frustrated Hopes," in ed. Nathan J. Brown and Emad El-Din Shahin, *Struggling over Democracy in the Middle East* (Routledge, forthcoming).

pressure for democratization—such as nongovernmental organizations, political parties, labor unions, or social movements—has sufficient size, will, and organizational capability to mount a sustained demand for democracy.[26]

In contrast, the pressures favoring liberal reforms are substantial. As noted above, four of the primary actors in Egyptian politics and law— NDP reformers, business elites, the Judges' Club, and the Muslim Brotherhood—support institutional changes that create a more liberal state. These pressures are reinforced by the country's involvement in a growing web of international economic agreements such as the WTO and the Euro-Mediterranean Agreement. These commitments require Egypt to further limit the scope of state power, improve the accountability of the state, and strengthen the protection of some rights (particularly property rights).

WILL LIBERALISM LEAD TO DEMOCRACY?

There is no definitive theoretical statement of when, and how, liberalism may lead to democracy.[27] Nonetheless, the literature on political development suggests that liberalism sets in motion several processes that can aid democratization. Foremost among these is liberalism's impact on the autonomy of the private sector. A private sector that is dependent on the state for capital and contracts is unlikely to push for democratic reforms. Indeed, its interests are so closely aligned with the regime that it can become one of the most important supporters of authoritarianism.[28] In contrast, a private sector with a high degree of autonomy from the state can

[26] For further discussion of the impediments to democracy in Egypt, see Kienle, *A Grand Delusion: Democracy and Economic Reform in Egypt*. Also, Kassem, *Egyptian Politics*.

[27] Indeed, this question has been the topic of some debate. See Thomas Carothers, "The 'Sequencing' Fallacy," *Journal of Democracy* 18, no. 1 (2007): 12–27; Sheri Berman, "Lessons from Europe," *Journal of Democracy* 18, no. 1 (2007): 28–41; Edward D. Mansfield and Jack Snyder, "The Sequencing 'Fallacy'," *Journal of Democracy* 18, no. 3 (2007): 5–9; Francis Fukuyama, "Liberalism versus State-Building," *Journal of Democracy* 18, no. 3 (2007): 10–13.

[28] The private sector in the Philippines and Indonesia has often exhibited these characteristics. See Rupert Hodder, "Business, Politics, and Social Relationships in the Philippines: A Gentle Revolution?" *South East Asia Research* 8, no. 2 (2000): 93–145; Andrew MacIntyre, *Business and Politics in Indonesia* (Sidney: Allen and Unwin, 1991); Kevin Hewison, *Southeast Asia in the 1990s: Authoritarianism, Democracy, and Capitalism* (St. Leonards, Australia: Allen and Unwin, 1993). There is evidence that some private firms in China (including multinational firms) are also developing these characteristics. See Mary Elizabeth Gallagher, *Contagious Capitalism: Globalization and the Politics of Labor in China* (Princeton, NJ: Princeton University Press, 2005).

be an important ally of democracy.[29] Greater autonomy means reduced dependence on the state for capital, permits, contracts, and distribution networks. A private sector with these characteristics disperses economic power away from the state. It also holds political and economic interests that differ from those of the state. In order to protect these interests, an autonomous private sector is likely to support constraints on state power, improvements in the rule of law, and greater governmental accountability. It is also likely to take steps that increase contestation and broaden public participation in political life. These steps include: building civil society groups that lobby for its interests; funding independent media outlets (newspapers, radio, and television) that advocate its views and present a forum for challenging the state;[30] and participating in electoral politics in order to render Parliament a more effective voice for defending and promoting private-sector interests.

Liberalism can facilitate the development of an autonomous private sector—and thereby aid democratization—in several ways:

Expanding private sources of capital: A powerful state is often able to exert influence over the private sector by controlling the availability of capital. This is usually accomplished through state dominance of the banking sector and extensive regulation of financial activity. Liberal reform erodes these sources of state control. It leads to the privatization of state-owned banks and the establishment of new private banks. It also includes a sharp reduction in the state's regulatory power over financial firms and financial transactions. In addition, liberal reform leads to the formation of stock and bond markets that provide new sources of capital independent of the state.

Strengthening protection of property rights: In order for most businesses to grow, they must borrow investment funds from commercial banks. Banks will lend these funds only if a business can offer collateral to secure the loan. The only collateral available to the typical business is the land and buildings that it owns. In order to use this property as collateral, a firm must have clear and undisputed title to it. Liberal reform includes the establishment of transparent procedures for registering property, unam-

---

[29] See Eva Bellin, "Contingent Democrats: Industrialists, Labor, and Democratization in Late-Developing Countries," *World Politics* 52, no. 2 (2000): 180–82; Eva Rana Bellin, *Stalled Democracy: Capital, Labor and the Paradox of State-Sponsored Development* (Ithaca, NY: Cornell University Press, 2002), 49; Kelly M. McMann, *Economic Autonomy and Democracy: Hybrid Regimes in Russia and Kyrgyzstan* (New York: Cambridge University Press, 2006), 4–5; Linz and Stepan, *Problems of Democratic Transition and Consolidation*, 11–12; Robert A. Dahl, *Polyarchy: Participation and Opposition* (New Haven, CT: Yale University Press, 1971), 51, 57–61.

[30] This funding can range from simply purchasing advertisements to outright ownership of independent media outlets.

biguous laws that govern the ownership and use of property, and judicial institutions that resolve ownership disputes quickly and efficiently. These measures allow businesses to establish clear title to property which, in turn, enables them to borrow capital from private banks and reduce their dependence on financing from the state.

Enhanced protection of property rights can also lead to a broadening of property ownership and the emergence of a property-owning middle class. An economic system that disperses property ownership among a large percentage of the population can have a constructive impact on democracy.[31] This impact arises primarily from the economic self-interest of these myriad property owners, who are subject to property taxes and regulations. They seek to participate more fully in political life in order to minimize government restrictions on their property, to keep their tax bills low, and to ensure that their taxes are used constructively and honestly.

Reducing the scope and arbitrariness of state regulatory power. A key source of state power over the private sector is the vast web of regulations that affect everything from wages to employment policies to prices. These regulations are often enforced selectively, which provides an even greater incentive for businessmen to avoid offending state officials for fear they will retaliate by dredging up an obscure regulation or imposing a hefty fine for a long-forgotten offense. Liberal reform reduces, simplifies, and clarifies the regulatory code governing the private sector. It also strengthens the legal and judicial procedures for challenging unfair application of this code. These developments reduce the arbitrariness of state power and enhance private-sector autonomy.

Facilitating the emergence of small- and medium-sized enterprises. If the private sector is dominated by a few large firms with close ties to the state, it is likely to oppose democratization. These firms develop personal networks with state officials that ensure favorable regulatory treatment, access to subsidized capital and raw materials, and an inside track on contracts from the state and public-sector enterprises. They often utilize their informal ties with the state to gain an advantage over other firms and to

[31] The classic statement of this view is Barrington Moore, *Social Origins of Dictatorship and Democracy: Lord and Peasant in the Making of the Modern World* (Boston: Beacon Press, 1966). Also see: Charles E. Lindblom, *Politics and Markets: The World's Political Economic Systems* (New York: Basic Books, 1977); Dietrich Rueschemeyer, Evelyne Huber Stephens, and John D. Stephens, *Capitalist Development and Democracy* (Cambridge: Polity Press, 1992); Richard Pipes, *Property and Freedom* (New York: Alfred A. Knopf, 1999); James Mahoney, "Knowledge Accumulation in Comparative Historical Research: The Case of Democracy and Authoritarianism," in *Comparative Historical Analysis in the Social Sciences*, ed. James Mahoney and Dietrich Rueschemeyer (Cambridge: Cambridge University Press, 2003), 131–76.

block the emergence of competition.[32] The businessmen who run these firms have little interest in democratic change, which would disrupt the close relationships with state officials that are the foundation of their prosperity. Liberal institutional reform alters this situation by strengthening the economic power of small and medium-sized enterprises (SMEs). The heart of this transformation lies in the adoption of a clear and unbiased legal code, as well as greater transparency and accountability in the allocation of state resources and contracts. These changes reduce the advantages enjoyed by politically well-connected firms and enable SMEs to gain access to a larger share of state resources and to expand their operations. This has several important repercussions for political development. SMEs have a strong interest in strengthening and extending the institutions of liberalism that enable them to "level the playing field" with their larger and better-connected competitors. They also have an interest in invigorating the electoral system, in order to use electoral politics as a means to gain greater influence over the development of policy and to further reduce the advantages enjoyed by larger firms with extensive patron-client ties with the state.[33]

Has liberal reform in Egypt set these processes in motion and helped to create a more autonomous private sector? At least some of the relevant institutional changes are under way. The clearest evidence of change lies in the financial sector, which was substantially restructured by the Unified Banking Law of 2003 (Law 88/2003). Prior to this law, finance was governed primarily by legislation drafted during the Nasser era. Banking was dominated by four large public-sector banks. The government exercised substantial influence over virtually every dimension of decision making by banks, including who was eligible to borrow and the terms of their loan. The government also controlled monetary policy, which meant that the money supply was hostage to the short-term concerns of the political leadership. The Unified Banking Law was a meaningful step toward reducing this degree of state control. It dramatically increased the power and independence of the Central Bank of Egypt (CBE) by shifting it out of the

---

[32] For a useful discussion of this phenomenon in the Philippines, see Paul D. Hutchcroft, *Booty Capitalism: The Politics of Banking in the Philippines* (Ithaca, NY: Cornell University Press, 1998).

[33] The Association of Independent Industrialists and Businessmen (MUSIAD) in Turkey is an example of SMEs playing this political role. See Ayse Bugra, "Class, Culture, and State: An Analysis of Interest Representation by Two Turkish Business Associations," *International Journal of Middle East Studies* 30, no. 4 (1998): 521–39; Ziya Önis and Umut Türem, "Entrepreneurs, Democracy, and Citizenship in Turkey," *Comparative Politics* 34, no. 4 (2002): 439–56; Ziya Önis and Umut Türem, "Business, Globalization, and Democracy: A Comparative Analysis of Turkish Business Associations," *Turkish Studies* 2, no. 2 (2001): 94–120; M. Hakan Yavuz, *Islamic Political Identity in Turkey* (Oxford: Oxford University Press, 2003), 92–96.

Ministry of Economy and giving it the status of an independent economic body. The CBE was given full authority to set monetary policy without interference from the executive branch. The newly independent CBE was further granted the power to supervise and regulate the banking system—a task that had previously fallen to the Ministry of Economy. At the same time, Law 88/2003 revised the prudential regulations governing banks. These new regulations ended the practice of requiring banks to lend money to regime supporters. They also liberated banks from the obligation to finance public-sector enterprises regardless of their economic condition. Other regulatory changes made it easier to form private banks and to offer new financial products without receiving prior government approval. Finally, the new law ended foreign-exchange controls and restrictions on international capital mobility. The regime had used these tools to control the flow of capital to private enterprises and to reward allies by allowing them access to foreign exchange at preferential rates.

In addition to implementing the new banking law, the government privatized one of the four large public-sector banks (Bank of Alexandria) in 2006 and announced plans in 2007 to privatize another (Banque du Caire).[34] It also instructed all public-sector banks to sell the shares they held in joint-venture banks, thereby transferring nearly 20 percent of the deposits in the banking system into the hands of the private sector.[35] By 2007, 60 percent of total deposits in the banking system lay with the private sector. This figure was expected to rise to 75 percent by 2012.[36]

As a result of these changes, total lending to the private sector rose from 197 billion LE in 2001 to 291 billion in 2006.[37] This figure is expected to more than double by 2011. Furthermore, the lion's share of this lending is carried out by private banks. Public-sector banks focus primarily on loans to the government (to finance the growing budget deficit) and to public-sector companies.[38]

There has also been a sharp increase in the size and vibrancy of the Egyptian stock market, which provides large private-sector firms with an additional source of capital that is independent of the state. The Cairo-

[34] *Economist Intelligence Unit, Egypt: Country Report,* August 2007, 22.

[35] This transfer of control is expected to be completed by the end of 2008. *Economist Intelligence Unit, Egypt: Country Report,* August 2006, 21.

[36] "Egypt: Financial Services Forecast," *Economist Intelligence Unit Industry Wire—Forecast,* July 18, 2007.

[37] *Economist Intelligence Unit, Egypt: Country Report,* February 2007, 25.

[38] "Egypt: Financial Services Forecast," *Economist Intelligence Unit Industry Wire—Forecast,* July 18, 2007. Private banks also participate in financing the public deficit, largely through purchasing government bonds. However, government bonds make up a significantly smaller share of their portfolios (less than 30 percent) than for public-sector banks (where the figure exceeds 60 percent).

Alexandria Stock Exchange (CASE) was virtually nonexistent in the early 1990s. By June 2007, its market capitalization stood at 601.8 billion LE ($106 billion), or about 90 percent of GDP. A total of 543 companies were listed on the exchange.[39] This trend of steady growth is likely to continue. The government is eager to make Cairo a regional trading hub and, as a consequence, has adopted a regulatory framework for the CASE that conforms to international norms. These high regulatory standards enabled the CASE to become the first Arab bourse admitted as a full member of the World Federation of Stock Exchanges in 2006.

Egypt has also undergone a meaningful improvement in property rights. As mentioned in chapter 5, liberal reform has included a new law on intellectual property that brings protection in this area up to international standards. The government has also taken substantial steps to facilitate the registration of title to property.[40] In addition, the Ministry of Justice has established a separate office to accelerate formal registration of collateral for use in mortgage loans.[41] These reforms have been accompanied by efforts to invigorate the mortgage market and, thereby, expand ownership of homes and small businesses. At the initiative of the Central Bank, an Egyptian Mortgage Refinance Company was formed in 2007 to increase the amount of capital available for mortgages and to lower the interest rates on these mortgages.[42] Its initial paid-in capital totaled 212 million LE, and it is authorized to expand to 1 billion LE. A total of seven mortgage financing companies were established between 2004 and 2007, where none existed before.[43] The government has also created a Mortgage

---

[39] However, the CASE is dominated by the largest thirty firms, which account for the large majority of trading. Only about 150–200 stocks trade actively. For further details on the CASE and on the sources of portfolio investment in Egypt, see *Economist Intelligence Unit, Egypt: Country Finance 2006*, 61.

[40] It has reduced property registration fees from 13 percent of the value of the property to 3 percent, with a cap of 2000 LE. It has also reduced property taxes from 47 percent to 10 percent, and eliminated the stamp tax applied to property mortgage contracts. It has further modified the law to allow property to be used as collateral without being formally registered with the Registry Office, so long as it is not subject to an ownership dispute, back taxes are not owed, and the property meets local zoning and building regulations.

[41] The office is located within the Mortgage Finance Authority. According to the Authority, this office enables property owners to register their property in no more than one week. See the website of the Mortgage Finance Authority, http://www.mf.gov.eg/. Accessed August 15, 2007.

[42] The company provides long-term capital to mortgage lenders at below-market rates. The company is financed by the CBE and twenty-four other financial institutions (mostly public and private banks), as well as the World Bank.

[43] The most prominent is *Tamwil*, which is affiliated with the construction giant Orascom. "Egypt: Mortgages for the Masses," *Oxford Business Group—Online Business Briefing*, May 23, 2007. "Egypt Finance: Mortgage Lending," *Economist Intelligence Unit Industry Wire—News Analysis*, January 8, 2007.

Guarantee and Subsidy Fund to enable low-income home buyers to afford to purchase a home.[44] These efforts have produced a dramatic increase in mortgage lending, but from a very small base. Total mortgage lending was only 15.8 million LE in June 2005. By June 2006, it had increased almost tenfold, to 148 million LE. By the end of 2006, it had reached 1 billion LE. The minister of investment expects the figure to reach 2 billion LE by the end of 2007.[45] Despite this rate of growth, mortgages still constitute only a small percentage of total lending. Even if the minister's optimistic forecast proves correct, mortgage lending in 2007 will amount to less than 1 percent of total lending to the private sector.[46] Furthermore, Egypt still has a long way to go before it has a large property-owning middle class. As of 2007, only about 30 percent of Egyptians owned the homes in which they lived.[47] Nonetheless, there is a clear trend toward expanding the circle of property owners.[48]

As mentioned in chapter 5, there is also some evidence that the state's regulatory control over the private sector has declined. The tax code has been dramatically simplified. The myriad exemptions for various types of business activities have been discarded in favor of a flat corporate tax rate of 20 percent. The government has also announced a value-added tax that will replace the existing sales tax, which had several different rates depending on the characteristics of the buyer and the seller. The new VAT will have a single, flat rate.[49] Tariffs on imported goods have been cut sharply—from an average tariff of 14.6 percent to 6.9 percent—and the number of goods affected reduced by 90 percent.[50] The labor law has been modified to reduce the government's power to set wages and supervise the resolution of disputes between management and workers. The govern-

[44] The fund provides a subsidy up to 15 percent of the value of the home, with a maximum of 10,000 LE. It defines "low income" as annual salary no higher than 12,000 LE for an unmarried applicant and 18,000 LE for a married applicant. *al-Ahram*, November 7, 2006. A study by the Ministry of Housing in 2006 found that 81 percent of the demand for mortgage loans lies with individuals who make less than 12,000 LE per year. See the website of the Mortgage Finance Authority, http://www.mf.gov.eg/. Accessed August 15, 2007.

[45] *Economist Intelligence Unit, Egypt: Country Report*, May 2007, 31.

[46] This figure amounts to about 8 percent of GDP. *Oxford Business Group—Online Business Briefing*, May 23, 2007. Also, "Real Estate Financing Briefs, *Banking Industry Updates—Egypt*, February 1, 2007.

[47] "Mortgage Finance to Ease Housing Crunch, Says Mohieldin," *Daily News Egypt*, May 16, 2007.

[48] Anecdotal evidence suggests that many more Egyptians would like to own their homes. For example, the Mortgage Finance Authority established a call center and a website in 2006 to answer the public's questions about home and business ownership. In its first six months, the call center received 60,000 calls. Its Internet site had over 100,000 visitors. *Oxford Business Group—Online Business Briefing*, May 23, 2007.

[49] *Economist Intelligence Unit, Egypt: Country Report*, August 2007, 22.

[50] Ibid., February 2007, 22.

ment has also established an "economic court" that will specialize in commercial matters, particularly disputes between businesses and government regulatory authorities.

Notably, the government has backed away from earlier plans to drastically shrink the bureaucracy. It fears that large reductions in staffing would aggravate the country's already severe unemployment problem. The current strategy is to reduce the bureaucracy gradually through attrition and a hiring freeze. However, the power of the bureaucracy has been sharply curtailed. Instead of dismantling it, liberal reformers in the Ministry of Investment have circumvented it by authorizing the creation of "investment zones." Any firm within one of these zones is permitted to deal with a single new government office for all its government-related concerns, rather than having to work through a maze of government agencies and officials. This measure effectively bypasses the normal bureaucracy and provides a "one-stop shop" that handles all of the firm's interaction with the government. Furthermore, these "zones" are quite easy to create—any private-sector firm is eligible to establish one.[51] As a result of these and other reforms, the private sector can accomplish key business tasks with significantly fewer bureaucratic delays. For example, a World Bank study found that the number of procedures needed to start a business fell from thirteen in 2003 to seven in 2007. The amount of time required to navigate the red tape associated with establishing a company fell from forty-three days to nine days.[52]

These developments in the arenas of finance, property rights, and regulatory power indicate that the Egyptian private sector is gaining greater autonomy from the state. However, most private firms remain very small and lack any mechanism for lobbying the state or for participating in political life.[53] A 2004 study prepared for the World Bank found that 95 percent of private enterprises have fewer than ten workers.[54] It also reported that the capitalization of these firms is very small—ninety-eight percent of all private firms in Egypt are capitalized at less than 100,000 LE ($18,000).[55] Seventy-five percent of firms have capitalization of less than

---

[51] Ibid., May 2007, 22; Ibid., August 2007, 28–29.

[52] The cost involved fell from 61 percent of income per capita to 29 percent. All figures are from *Doing Business in 2004: Understanding Regulation* (Washington, DC: World Bank, 2004), 145; and *Doing Business 2008: Comparing Regulation in 178 Economies* (Washington, DC: World Bank, 2007), 118.

[53] There is considerable debate over how to define these firms. For an exhaustive review of this issue in Egypt, see *The Definition of Micro, Small, and Medium Enterprises* (Cairo: Ministry of Foreign Trade, 2004).

[54] Tamer El-Meehy, *The Myth and Reality of SMEs and Employment in Egypt* (Cairo: Entrust Development and Management Consultants, 2004), 8.

[55] Ibid., 10.

10,000 LE ($1,800).[56] These small firms are generally engaged in manufacturing furniture, garments, food, metal products, and wood products. Despite their small size, they are the backbone of private-sector employment. They were responsible for 66 percent of total nonagricultural private-sector jobs in 1996.[57] They also accounted for between 25 percent and 40 percent of GDP.[58]

In light of their key role in generating jobs, the government has placed a high priority on expanding these small firms. Its goal is to create conditions that enable small firms (those with fewer than ten employees) to grow into medium-sized firms (with 11–99 employees). The government has adopted a host of programs to expand these small enterprises by increasing their access to capital, reducing regulatory barriers, and providing training and technical assistance.[59] For example, the Ministry of Investment has modified the laws for forming limited liability companies (LLCs) in order to persuade more small firms to become formally registered. It has reduced the minimum capital requirement to form a LLC to just 1,000 LE (from the previous 50,000 LE) and dramatically simplified the registration process. The goal is to give small enterprises formal legal status, which will enable them to qualify for loans from private banks and to bid more successfully for both public and private contracts.[60]

These measures are still in their infancy. However, there is some fragmentary evidence to suggest that they are having a positive effect. The number of registered firms with capital less than 100,000 LE increased by 14 percent from 2005 to 2006, which indicates that the programs to encourage registration of small firms are working.[61] Preliminary data also suggest that the number of workers per SME is slowly rising—from an average of 2.9 in 1996 to 8.4 in 2006.[62] However, no organizations have emerged to represent the interests of small and medium-sized businesses. Given the large number of firms, and their wide variety of economic activities, it will prove difficult to organize even a small fraction of these businesses.[63] Nonetheless, these obstacles are not insurmountable. Turkey of-

---

[56] Ibid., 11.

[57] Ibid., 9.

[58] Their precise contribution to GDP is difficult to estimate because most of these firms are not registered with the government. As a consequence, they do not report their production or income to any government agency.

[59] For further details, see Hania Moheeb, "15,000 Engines of Growth," *Business Today*, September 2006; Hadia Mostafa, "Introducing the Nilex," *Business Today*, November 2007; "Egypt: Financial Services Forecast," *Economist Intelligence Unit Industry Wire—Forecast*, July 18, 2007.

[60] Nadine el-Sayed, "Cheap and Legal," *Business Today*, March 2007.

[61] *Statistical Review, 2006* (Cairo: Central Bank of Egypt, 2007), 47.

[62] Ibid., 63.

[63] In principle, small and medium-sized enterprises are represented by the Chambers of Commerce. However, in practice, these Nasser-era corporatist bodies are largely moribund.

fers a useful comparison in this regard. A business organization targeted primarily toward SMEs—MUSIAD—emerged in the early 1990s after a group of businessmen from medium-sized firms joined together in the provincial town of Konya.[64] Such a development is possible in Egypt, but there is little indication that it is likely in the near future.

The evidence suggests that liberal reform has begun to transform the private sector, but that this transformation is in its early stages. Most of the changes described above have occurred within the past five years, while several have been adopted only in the past two years. The private sector has not yet become an advocate of democratic reform. Large firms remain wary of the political instability and policy uncertainty that might ensue from democratization. SMEs, while growing in number, remain too diverse and fragmented to advocate effectively for policy or political change.

THE 2007 CONSTITUTIONAL AMENDMENTS AND EGYPT'S POLITICAL FUTURE

The possibility that Egypt's economic reforms are not triggering political change is reinforced by the most recent amendments to the 1971 Constitution, which were adopted by referendum in March 2007.[65] The amendments reaffirm the hybrid character of the regime, but also raise the possibility of a turn toward deeper authoritarianism. They include several features that demonstrate the growing influence of liberals on government policy, particularly economic liberals. Their first target was constitutional language that embraced socialist ideals. The 1971 Constitution described Egypt as a "socialist state based on the alliance of the people's working forces."[66] It further proclaimed that "the people shall control all the means of production"[67] and that "public ownership . . . is the mainstay of the

[64] A few large firms also participated in the formation of MUSIAD. Bugra, "Class, Culture, and State," 521–39; Önis and Türem, "Business, Globalization, and Democracy," 94–120; Yavuz, *Islamic Political Identity in Turkey*, 92–96.

[65] The government claimed that 27 percent of the electorate participated in the referendum, and that the amendments were approved with 76 percent of the vote. Independent observers put the turnout closer to 5 percent. See "Limited Participation in the Referendum on the Constitutional Amendments," *Al-Hayat*, March 27, 2007; "The Opposition Rejects Results of the Referendum and Discusses the Fraud . . . the Egyptian Government: 76% Agreed to the Constitutional Amendments," *Al-Hayat*, March 28, 2007; Mona el-Nahhas, "Awaiting Judgment," *Al-Ahram Weekly*, April 5–11, 2007; Anthony Shadid, "Apathy Marks Constitutional Vote in Egypt," *Washington Post*, March 27, 2007.

[66] Article 1.

[67] Article 24.

strength of the homeland and the basis for the socialist system."[68] All these references to socialism were expunged and replaced with language more amendable to a market economy. The amendment to article 4 proclaims that Egypt's economy is now based on "the development of economic enterprise" and that it "safeguards different forms of ownership."[69] The amendment to article 30 even re-defines "public ownership" to include "individual ownership in the service of the public."[70]

The amendments also create some constraints on executive power. The amended article 74 states that the president may declare a state of emergency only after consulting with the prime minister and the speakers of the Parliament and the *Shura* council. He is also prohibited from dissolving either of these deliberative bodies during a state of emergency. Previously, he faced no such limits on his power. The amended article 82 clarifies the chain of command in case the president is injured or incapacitated, stating that power will pass first to the vice president and then to the prime minister. The amendments also grant Parliament the power to vote on the budget article-by-article, and to change expenditure levels.[71] The Parliament is further granted the authority to review and approve the expenditures carried out during the implementation of the annual budget.[72] In addition, Parliament can dismiss the Cabinet by issuing a vote of no-confidence.[73] The amendments also specify that the president can promulgate regulations and decrees only with the agreement of the Cabinet. He can issue emergency decrees and declare a state of emergency only after consulting with the Cabinet. Previously, he faced no constraint on the exercise of these powers.[74] The significance of these steps should not be exaggerated. The prime minister and all Cabinet members are appointed by the president, and he retains the right to dismiss them. In a similar vein, the measures that enhance the Parliament's power are unlikely to have much impact in the near term in light of the ruling party's

[68] Article 33.

[69] Article 4, amended.

[70] Article 30, amended.

[71] Article 115, amended.

[72] This is accomplished by requiring the government to submit the final account of the budget to Parliament within six months of the end of the fiscal year. See article 118, amended.

[73] Article 127, amended. Previously, a government could be dismissed without the president's agreement only after a public referendum. It should be noted that this expansion of Parliament's power is partially offset by another amendment that simplifies the procedure for dissolving Parliament. The amended article 136 specifies that the president can dissolve Parliament after consulting with the prime minister. Previously, the president could dissolve Parliament only after a referendum. If a Parliament is dissolved, new elections must be held within sixty days.

[74] Article 138, amended.

dominance of this body. Nonetheless, these changes assert the principle of the separation of powers that was lacking in the original constitution. They make it possible for Parliament to play a more active role in constraining the executive, particularly if internal divisions within the ruling party over issues such as economic reform become more pronounced.

Another amendment offers a small improvement in judicial independence by stating that each branch of the judiciary "will take charge of its own affairs."[75] This principle was already present in statutory law (in the judicial authority law of 1984). The amendment gives it constitutional power. However, the amendment allows language to remain regarding a "council," chaired by the president and made up of senior judges, that "oversees the shared interests" of the various branches of the judiciary. The responsibilities of this council are not specified in the Constitution, but the clause clearly seeks to preserve some executive influence (but not control) over the judiciary.[76]

As this discussion suggests, the constitutional amendments contain several features that advance liberalism. However, they make no effort to advance democracy. They do not contain any clauses that strengthen citizens' rights to form nongovernmental organizations or political parties, nor do they decrease the state's control over civil society. The amendment to article 88 sharply reduces the extent of judicial supervision over elections, which is likely to lead to increased opportunities for the ruling party to manipulate election results.[77] The amendments also contain several features that limit political participation, particularly by individuals and organizations that are not to the regime's liking. The amendment to article 62 empowers the government to limit the number of independent candidates who can win seats in either the Parliament or the *Shura* coun-

[75] Article 173, amended. The previous phrasing of this article made no reference to judicial bodies having jurisdiction over their own affairs.

[76] Article 173, amended. The Council's full title is the Supreme Council of Judicial Bodies (SCJB). It consists of the heads of each of the judicial bodies, and is chaired by the president. The SCJB has had very little impact on the judiciary in the past. Indeed, it has not met in over a decade. The Supreme Judicial Council, which is composed entirely of judges, has played a much more important role in judicial affairs.

[77] The amended article 88 states that elections will take place in one day. As a consequence, it will be physically impossible for judges to supervise all of Egypt's polling booths. Rather, their role will be limited to supervising vote counting at regional balloting centers. The amendment further states that the elections will be supervised by a commission made up of "either current or retired judges" and "characterized by independence and impartiality." This commission will be established by the government. However, the Egyptian government's record for creating truly independent electoral commissions is not strong. The commission that it established to supervise the 2005 parliamentary elections made decisions that consistently favored government candidates. See Ihab Salam, "al-Ishraf al-Qada'i wa-l-Riqaba 'ala al-Intikhabat," in *Intikhabat Majlis al-Sha'ab 2005*, ed. 'Amru Hashim Rabi'a (Cairo:Markaz al-Dirasat al-Siyasiyya wa-l-Istratijiyya bi-l-Ahram, 2006), 35–60.

cil. This amendment has important repercussions for the Muslim Brotherhood's participation in politics. Egyptian law has long banned the formation of political parties along religious lines. As a consequence, the
Brotherhood has been unable to form a political party. Its primary strategy
for coping with this problem was to run its candidates as independents.[78]
This strategy produced particularly impressive results in 2005, when MB
independents won 20 percent of the seats in Parliament despite the regime's best efforts to rig the results. The recent amendment to article 62
enables the regime to sharply restrict this avenue for the Brotherhood's
political participation. It is widely expected that the regime will return to
the electoral system in place in 1987, which limited independent candidates to one seat in each of Egypt's forty-eight electoral districts. This
means that, at most, independents could constitute 48 of Egypt's 454
members of Parliament. This low percentage ensures that the MB will
never gain sufficient numbers in Parliament to shape legislation, even if it
has broad public support. Similarly, the amendment to article 76 stipulates
that candidates for the presidency must be nominated by political parties.
As a consequence, it is virtually impossible for the party-less MB to put
forward a presidential candidate.

The amendments include an additional feature that further limits the
Brotherhood's political opportunities. The new article 5 reiterates the
long-standing prohibition on political parties based on religion.[79] However, it adds that "any political activity . . . based on a religious foundation
(*marja'iyya*)"[80] is prohibited. If applied literally, this clause prevents any
organization or individual that invokes any aspect of Islam from participating in political life. Most observers believe that this clause was adopted
primarily to rein in the Muslim Brotherhood. However, the amendment
is cast in remarkably broad language. It not only shuts down the Brotherhood as a political organization—it prevents *any* political group from utilizing Islamic principles in its electoral platform or campaign materials. It
is clearly an effort to sharply narrow the scope of groups that can participate in Egyptian politics, regardless of their level of popular support.

---

[78] Another strategy was to form alliances with existing parties, such as the Wafd in 1984
and the Socialist Labor Party in 1987. However, these alliances proved cumbersome and
unstable as neither participant was prepared to make the long-term compromises needed to
create a truly powerful partnership.

[79] This prohibition had previously been part of statutory law (the political parties law of
1977). The amendment elevates it to constitutional law.

[80] *Marja'iyya* can also be translated as "frame of reference" or "point of reference." As
Brown and Dunne observe, this term is used by mainstream Islamist parties elsewhere in
the Middle East to describe their view of Islam. For example, the Justice and Development
party in Morocco says that it is not a religious party but, rather, a party based on a religious
frame of reference (*marja'iyya*). Nathan J. Brown and Michele Dunne, *Egypt's Controversial*

Supporters of democracy were even more troubled by the amendment to article 179, which enhances the state's power to "safeguard security and public order in the face of the dangers of terrorism."[81] In order to achieve these goals, the government is permitted to take steps that "cannot be hampered" by articles 41, 44, and 45 of the Constitution. These articles assert that citizens may be arrested or detained only with a court order, and that searches, wiretaps, or other monitoring of private communication can be conducted only with judicial authorization. The constitutional amendment effectively empowers the state to suspend indefinitely an individual's constitutional rights in these areas if he is suspected of involvement in terrorist activity. "Terrorism" is not defined.[82] The amendment states that all of the actions taken to confront terrorism will be "under the supervision of the judiciary." However, it is unclear how the judiciary will exercise this supervision if the executive can act without a court order and the victim has no legal recourse for challenging the executive's actions.

The security services have carried out extra-judicial arrests, detentions, and monitoring for decades under the emergency law. These actions were subject to substantial legal challenges in the administrative courts and the Supreme Constitutional Court. In light of this amendment, these challenges will no longer be possible in cases related to the fight against terrorism. The amendment further specifies that the president may refer a person accused of a terrorism-related crime "to any judicial body mentioned in the Constitution or the law." In practical terms, the purpose of this clause is to enable the president to refer these cases to military courts, which offer relatively weak protection of basic procedural rights (such as the right of appeal).[83]

In essence, the amendment to article 179 insulates the security apparatus from most judicial and legal constraints as long as it is engaged in activities related to confronting terrorism. This has considerable potential to shape the development of Egyptian politics. The Egyptian security apparatus is vast. Egypt has 468,500 troops in its military (army, navy, and air force) and another 397,000 employed by the Ministry of Interior (in

---

Constitutional Amendments: A Textual Analysis (Washington, DC: Carnegie Endowment for International Peace, March 23, 2007), 3.

[81] Article 179, amended.

[82] It will be defined in the forthcoming anti-terrorism law. The government has stated that this law will be issued sometime before 2010.

[83] The president has been referring civilian cases to military courts since 1993. However, these transfers were subject to challenge on the grounds that they violated the constitutional right to be tried before one's "natural judge." The amendment to article 179 prevents this type of constitutional challenge.

the central security forces, the national guard, and the border guard).[84] The military enjoyed an annual budget of $2.6 billion in 2005,[85] and reportedly controls a substantial number of economic enterprises that provide additional sources of revenue.[86] The budget of the Ministry of Interior is not publicly available, but some estimates place it as high as $1.5 billion in 2006.[87]

The security apparatus played a substantial role in policy formation and implementation during the Nasser regime. This political role declined steadily under Sadat and Mubarak.[88] However, security officials from both the military and the Ministry of Interior retain close ties with the president and hold important advisory posts throughout the executive branch.[89] In addition, officers from the military and the Ministry of Interior often serve as provincial governors and mayors of major cities.[90] As a consequence, the security apparatus still enjoys substantial political clout without formally holding the reins of power.[91] The amendment to article 179 may be a reflection of this influence, and may indicate that this influence is growing.

The forthcoming anti-terrorism law, expected by 2010, will be the first indication of whether the regime plans to define "terrorism" narrowly and whether it creates meaningful judicial oversight of the security agencies.

[84] *The Military Balance, 2007* (London: International Institute for Strategic Studies, 2007), 221, 223. Some observers claim that the forces controlled by the Ministry of Interior are substantially larger—perhaps as large as 1.4 million. Saad Eddin Ibrahim, "Egypt's Unchecked Repression," *Washington Post*, August 21, 2007; "Bashing the Muslim Brothers," *The Economist*, September 1, 2007, 38. For further details on Egypt's security forces, see Anthony H. Cordesman, *The Military Balance in the Middle East* (Westport, CT: Praeger, 2004), 172–86.

[85] *SIPRI Yearbook 2006: Armaments, Disarmament, and International Security* (New York: Oxford University Press, 2006), 342.

[86] These enterprises reportedly include farms, factories, and trading companies. Robert Springborg, *Mubarak's Egypt: Fragmentation of the Political Order* (Boulder: Westview Press, 1989), 109–18. Also, Stephen H. Gotowicki, "The Military in Egyptian Society," in *Egypt at the Crossroads: Domestic Stability and Regional Role*, ed. Phebe Marr (Washington, DC: National Defense University Press, 1999), 114–16.

[87] Saad Eddin Ibrahim, "Egypt's Unchecked Repression." Ibrahim writes that this figure was reported in the newspaper *Al-Dustur*.

[88] Imad Harb, "The Egyptian Military in Politics: Disengagement or Accommodation?" *Middle East Journal* 57, no. 2 (2003): 269–90; Ibrahim A. Karawan, "Egypt," in *The Political Role of the Military: An International Handbook*, ed. Constantine P. Danopoulos and Cynthia Watson (Westport, CT: Greenwood Press, 1996), 107–21.

[89] Steven A. Cook, *Ruling but not Governing: The Military and Political Development in Egypt, Algeria, and Turkey* (Baltimore: Johns Hopkins University Press, 2007), 63–92.

[90] Kirk J. Beattie, "Egypt: Thirty-Five Years of Praetorian Politics," in *Military Disengagement from Politics*, ed. Constantine P. Danopoulos (New York: Routledge, 1988), 223.

[91] Cook, *Ruling but not Governing*, 73–74.

The problem, of course, is that an ambiguous stance on either of these issues creates the possibility that the leadership of the security apparatus will interpret its powers broadly. A powerful security apparatus with a vague mandate and no clear limits on its power will have a natural tendency to expand its reach.[92]

Currently, the power of the security apparatus is partially counterbalanced by the judiciary, the business community, and the reformist wing of the ruling party. If the security apparatus attempts to broaden its influence into the legal system or economic policy, these strong and well-entrenched constituencies will push back. The Muslim Brotherhood can also be counted on to criticize such steps and to mobilize at least part of public opinion to oppose them. However, it is not difficult to imagine circumstances that could alter this situation. The most likely scenario would involve a high-profile terrorist incident—perhaps an assassination attempt on the president or a bombing that causes substantial civilian casualties. The regime might attribute this attack to jihadists returning from Iraq and Afghanistan, and argue that an expansion of the security apparatus's reach is essential for maintaining public order in the face of this challenge. It might also claim that this violence was orchestrated by al-Qaeda and, as a consequence, the broadening of security powers is part of the global war on terror. Such a claim would partially inoculate the regime from international criticism of its actions. If this scenario occurred, it is unlikely that the institutions of liberalism would be dismantled. They would simply be circumvented by an increasingly powerful and unaccountable security apparatus. Unfortunately, the amendment to article 179 provides a legal framework that could allow this to happen. It creates an opportunity for the *mukhabarat* (security police) state of the 1960s to reemerge.

In several important respects, the security apparatus's expanded autonomy and reach resembles developments in Turkey in the 1980s. In that case, the military gained the formal authority to influence government policy when the 1982 Constitution granted a military-controlled body—the National Security Council (NSC)—a central role in advising the Cabinet.[93] The nature of "security" was then defined so broadly that it em-

---

[92] The conduct of the security services under the emergency law establishes a worrying precedent in this regard. According to the text of the emergency law, it should be invoked only to confront clear and immediate threats to public order. In practice, the security services use it to harass and weaken the regime's political opponents—particularly the Muslim Brotherhood—under the claim that political Islam, in any form, constitutes a threat.

[93] The military held power in Turkey from 1980 to 1983. Article 118 of the 1982 Constitution stated that the Cabinet "shall give priority consideration to the decisions of the National Security Council" concerning whatever measures it deems necessary to ensure the "peace and security of society." For further discussion, see Aylin Guney, "The Military, Politics, and Post-Cold War Dilemmas in Turkey," in *Political Armies: The Military and Nation*

braced virtually every dimension of public policy.[94] As a consequence, the NSC issued decisions that affected topics as varied as the curriculum in public schools, licensing of television stations, the immunity of members of Parliament, appointments to key posts in the bureaucracy, and the formation of electoral alliances in local elections.[95] It is conceivable that Egyptian officials will define "terrorism" in comparably broad terms which, in turn, grant the security apparatus expansive authority to act in the economic, political, and legal arenas with little effective oversight.

In the Turkish case, the political power of the military was reduced by two processes. The first was the deepening of democratic politics. This led in 2002 to the election of a political party (Justice and Development) that enjoyed a strong popular mandate for legal and political change. The second was sustained external demands for reform. The European Union insisted on a reduced role for the military in political life as a condition for EU membership.[96] The combination of these pressures led to a restructuring of the NSC that ensured civilian control.[97] It also led to reforms that granted the Parliament oversight of parts of the military's budget, and removed military officers from the agencies that controlled civilian education and public broadcasting.[98]

Currently, neither of these pressures is present in Egypt. The country does not allow meaningful political competition. In addition, the international community has been unwilling to exert sustained pressure on the Egyptian government to rein in the power of the security apparatus. These

---

Building in the Age of Democracy, ed. Kees Koonings and Dirk Kruijt (New York: Zed Books, 2002), 162–78.

[94] The specific legislation that addressed the concept of "security" was Law 2945 of November 9, 1983. Article 2 of this Law defines national security as the "protection of the constitutional order of the state, its national existence, and its integrity; of all of its interests in the international field, including political, social, cultural, and economic interests." Ergun Ozbudun, *Contemporary Turkish Politics: Challenges to Democratic Consolidation* (Boulder, CO: Lynne Rienner, 2000), 108.

[95] Ümit Cizre Sakallioglu, "The Anatomy of the Turkish Military's Political Autonomy," *Comparative Politics* 29, no. 2 (1997): 158.

[96] Ziya Önis, "Domestic Politics, International Norms, and Challenges to the State: Turkey-EU Relations in the Post-Helsinki Era," in *Turkey and the European Union: Domestic Politics, Economic Integration, and International Dynamics*, ed. Ali Çarkoglu and Barry Rubin (Portland, OR: Frank Cass, 2003), 9–34; and William Hale, "Human Rights, the European Union, and the Turkish Accession Process," in *Turkey and the European Union: Domestic Politics, Economic Integration, and International Dynamics*, ed. Ali Çarkoglu and Barry Rubin (Portland, OR: Frank Cass, 2003), 107–126. Also, Pinar Bilgin, "Turkey's Changing Security Discourses: The Challenge of Globalisation," *European Journal of Political Research* 44 (2005): 175–201.

[97] The NSC was also downgraded to an advisory body that no longer controls its own budget. Cook, *Ruling but not Governing*, 129.

[98] Ibid., 128.

facts suggest that, if the current balance between liberalism and autocracy were to erode, Egypt is likely to turn toward a deeper form of authoritarianism. It would probably be based on a larger role for the security apparatus in political and economic life, under the guise of protecting the country from the dangers of terrorism.

However, there is some cause for optimism. Egypt has embarked on a wide range of institutional changes that strengthen liberalism and which may, with time, lead to political reform. The government's degree of control over the economy is declining. Judicial independence and activism are growing and are likely to accelerate as a younger generation of judges moves into positions of leadership (and the older, more quietest generation retires). A well-organized Islamist movement advocates constraints on state power and improvements in regime accountability. The extent of Egypt's engagement with the global economy is rising and is likely to accelerate, which creates additional pressure to remain on a liberal path. The private sector is also growing in size, complexity, and autonomy. There is every indication that these trends will continue.

The recent constitutional amendments underscore the fact that Egypt is at a turning point in its political development. For a variety of reasons, the regime and the country have undergone meaningful liberal reforms over the past fifteen years. The key issue for the future is whether these reforms will steadily broaden to transform the economy, the legal system, and the polity. Or, will they remain restricted to a few corners of the economy and legal system and merely produce a more efficient and prosperous autocracy?

The United States has a substantial stake in this struggle for Egypt's political future. The emergence of a stable democracy would have several important repercussions. It would provide effective and representative political institutions that could peacefully manage the growing social dislocations and inequality produced by rapid economic growth. It would also help to reconcile the increasing religious and cultural tensions in Egyptian society. In addition, successful democratization would lead to open debate and discussion among secularists and Islamists over the full range of issues confronting Egyptian society. This regular interaction over the nuts-and-bolts of policy is essential for the further development of a moderate conception of Islam that can meet the demands of modern governance. This moderate view of Islamic government has already been charted by the theorists of Islamic constitutionalism and their supporters within the Muslim Brotherhood. It needs to grow and develop through constructive participation in an open and competitive political order. The refinement of moderate Islam into a viable and responsible political force would strengthen the stability and legitimacy of Egypt's regime. It would also provide an important example for Islamist movements throughout the region.

However, U.S. efforts to promote democracy in Egypt have been sporadic and inconsistent. As noted in chapter 1, U.S. policy makers have reached a broad consensus on the value of democratization and its contribution to long-term American security. Nonetheless, the United States still exhibits a tendency to allow short-term tactical concerns to offset this long-term goal. In the near term, the United States needs the assistance of Egypt's regime to deal with pressing regional crises such as the situation in Iraq, the expansion of Iranian influence, and the stagnant peace process between Arabs and Israelis. In order to retain the full cooperation of Egypt's rulers, the United States often softens its demands for political reform. Occasionally, the United States overcomes its reticence and pushes for meaningful political change. For example, in 2004 and 2005, the Bush administration pressured the Egyptian government to democratize. It responded by allowing multi-candidate elections for the presidency in September 2005, and a reasonably free electoral campaign in the run-up to parliamentary elections in November/December 2005. However, Egypt's autocrats blunted the impact of these changes. As noted earlier, the law governing presidential elections was carefully drafted to prevent the emergence of a credible challenger to Mubarak. And, when the opposition showed signs of performing well in the parliamentary elections, the regime simply blocked opposition voters from reaching the polls and tampered with the election results. The United States objected to these actions. However, regional crises soon loomed large (particularly in Iraq and Palestine) and the push for democracy faded. The Egyptian regime quickly returned to politics as usual, including a campaign against critical journalists and a widespread crackdown on the peaceful Islamist opposition.

This pattern has been repeated time and again over the past thirty years: the United States demands meaningful political reform; the regime responds with a half-hearted effort that produces little lasting change, but which ameliorates the U.S. pressure until an important regional issue seizes America's attention. The United States then loses interest in democratization, and the political status quo ante returns. The Egyptian regime is quite skilled at playing this game. It can feign political reform with great conviction, fully aware that it will backtrack after a few months when the United States needs its help on a pressing regional matter.

For these reasons, high-profile efforts to pressure the Egyptian regime to democratize are unlikely to produce lasting results. However, the delinking of liberalism and democracy discussed above may provide an alternative path. This book has argued that a broad consensus has emerged around the importance of liberal reforms that include constraining state power, strengthening the rule of law, and protecting basic civil and political rights. This set of reforms enjoys support among constitutional liberals,

258 • Chapter Six

moderate Islamists, parts of the business community, and the reformist wing of the ruling party. These liberal reforms will not lead inevitably to democracy. However, they can aid democratization by building economic and social constituencies that have interests separate from the state and that enjoy sufficient autonomy to challenge the state without fear of being destroyed. Perhaps the most valuable contribution the United States can make to democratization is to create a framework of incentives and disincentives that keep Egypt on its current path of liberal reform. It can use this framework to strengthen the rule of law, broaden governmental accountability, increase private-sector autonomy, and improve protection of basic civil and political rights. The purpose of these efforts is to firmly support the emergence of a more constrained and law-abiding state with a higher degree of accountability and responsiveness to its citizens. The United States has several tools at its disposal to create this framework, including: military and economic assistance that totals over $1.7 billion per year; support in negotiations for full admission to regional and international trading blocs and agreements; and access to the American market, with the possibility of a Free Trade Agreement between the two countries. The United States must be willing to employ these tools firmly and consistently to oppose a retreat from the rule of law and the weakening of constraints on state power. This retreat is most likely to occur under the pretext of defending the country from the threat of terrorism. The United States should make clear that the effort to confront this threat must take place in accordance with the law and under the jurisdiction of the judiciary. The United States needs to emphasize that a broadening of the arbitrary power of the security services, or a worsening of the human rights situation, will have an immediate effect on aid levels, trade assistance, and market access. Under this approach, the United States is not calling for an immediate transition to democracy. However, it is insisting that authoritarianism not be deepened or broadened.

This approach involves a minimal level of intervention in Egyptian affairs. It focuses on facilitating institutional restructuring that is already under way and that is supported by key reformers within the regime, the business community, the Islamist movement, and the judiciary. It entails reinforcing these domestic pressures for liberal reform, rather than imposing an agenda of political or electoral change. The approach is more durable than the existing strategy precisely because it is less intrusive and it works in concert with local advocates of reform. It is also more likely to attract bipartisan support within American politics and, as a consequence, will prove more sustainable over the long term. At a very minimum, this approach requires the United States to use all the tools at its disposal to prevent a slide into deeper authoritarianism. It also, when possible, involves the United States aiding the spread of liberal institutions and norms throughout the economy, the legal system, and the polity. This posture would help to preserve the existing hybrid regime and buy time for the forces supporting liberal reform to further strengthen the rule of law, increase private-sector autonomy, and improve protection of basic rights. These internal processes of institutional change are the key to creating indigenous pressures for sustained and meaningful democratization.

Bibliography

NEWSPAPERS AND PERIODICALS

Al-Ahali
Al-Ahram
Al-Ahram al-Iqtisadi
Al-Ahram Weekly
Arab Reform Bulletin
Al-Dustur
Al-Hayat
Al-Jumhuriyya
Al-Misri al-Youm

Al-Muhæmah
Al-Musawwar
Nahdat Misr
Ruz al-Yusuf
Al-Sharq al-Awsat
Uktubir
Al-Wafd
Al-Watani

BOOKS AND ARTICLES IN ARABIC

'Abd al-Bir, Faruq. *Dur Majlis al-Dawla al-Misri fi Himayat al-Huquq wa-l-Huriyyat al-'Amma: al-Juz al-Awal.* Cairo: n.p., 1988.

———. *Dur Majlis al-Dawla al-Misri fi Himayat al-Huquq wa-l-Huriyyat al-'Amma: al-Juz al-Thalith.* Cairo: al-Nasr al-Thahabi li-l-Taba'aat, 1998.

———. *Dur al-Mahkama al-Dusturiyya al-Misriyya fi Himayat al-Huquq wa-l-Huriyyat.* Cairo: al-Nasr al-Thahabi li-l-Taba'aat, 2004.

'Abd al-Hafiz, Ahmad. *Niqabat al-Muhamiyyin.* Cairo: Markaz al-Dirasat al-Siyasiyya wa-l-Istratijiyya bi-l-Ahram, 2003.

'Abd Allah, Ahmad Sabr. "Al-Ta'un al-Intikhabiyya." In *Intikhabat Majlis as-Sha'ab 2000,* ed. Hala Mustafa, 37–56. Cairo: Markaz al-Dirasat al-Siyasiyya wa-l-Istratijiyya bi-l-Ahram, 2001.

'Abd al-Mon'am, Ahmad Faris. *Al-Dur al-Siyasi li Niqabat al-Muhamiyyin: 1912–1981.* Cairo: n.p., 1984.

———. *Al-Niqabat al-Mihaniyya wa-l-Siyasa fi 'Ahdi 'Abd al-Nasser wa-l-Sadat.* Cairo: Dar al-Mahrusa, 2005.

'Abd al-Nasser, Jamal. *Awraq 'Abd al-Nasser.* Cairo: Maktabat Madbuli, 1988.

Abu al-Majd, Ahmad Kamal. *Natharat Hawla Al-Fiqh Al-Dusturi fi-l-Islam.* Cairo: Matba'aat al-Azhar, 1962.

———. *Hiwar La Muwajaha.* Cairo: Dar al-Sharuq, 1988.

———. *Ru'ya Islamiyya Mu'asira.* Cairo: Dar al-Sharuq, 1991.

———. "Taqdim." In Ahmad Muhammad Amin, *Al-Dawla al-Islamiyya wa-l-Mabad' al-Dusturiyya al-Haditha.* Cairo: Maktabat al-Sharuq al-Dawliyya, 2005, pp. 7–13.

'Auda, Jihad. *Jamal Mubarak: Tajdid al-Libraliyya al-Wataniyya*. Cairo: Dar al-Huriyya, 2004.

Al-'Awwa, Muhammad Salim. *Fi Usul al-Nitham al-Jin'i al-Islami*. Cairo: Dar al-Ma'arif, 1979.

———. *Al-Aqbat wa-l-Islam*. Cairo: Dar al-Sharuq, 1987.

———. *Fi-l-Nitham al-Siyasi li-l-Dawla Al-Islamiyya*. Cairo: Dar al-Sharuq, 1989.

———. *Azmat al-Mu'ssasat al-Diniyya*. Cairo: Dar al-Sharuq, 1997.

———. *Al-Haqq fi-l-Ta'abir*. Cairo: Dar al-Sharuq, 1998.

Al-Banna, Hasan. *Majmu'aat Rasa'il al-Imam al-Shadid Hasan al-Banna*. Cairo: Dar al-Nashr al-Islami, n.d.

Al-Birnamij al-Intikhabi li-l-Ikhwan al-Muslimin. Cairo: n.p., issued October 15, 2005.

Al-Bishri, Tariq. *Dirasat fi-l-Dimaqratiyya al-Misriyya*. Cairo: Dar al-Sharuq, 1987.

———. *Al-Wad'a al-Qanuni Bayn al-Shari'a al-Islamiyya wa-l-Qanun al-Wad'ai*. Cairo: Dar al-Sharuq, 2003.

———. *Al-Muslimun wa-l-Aqbat fi Itar al-Jama'aa al-Wataniyya*. Cairo: Dar al-Sharuq, 2004.

———. *Minhaj al-Nithr fi al-Nuthum al-Siyasiyya al-Mu'asira li Buldan al-'Alam al-Islami*. Cairo: Dar al-Sharuq, 2005.

Dif Allah, Sayyid. *Nazahat al-Intikhabat wa Istiqlal al-Qada'*. Cairo: Cairo Institute for Human Rights Studies, 2005.

Fuda, Ri'fat. *Dirasat Tahliliyya li Qada' Majlis al-Dawla al-Misri fi Majal al-Ta'un al-Intikhabiyya*. Cairo: Dar al-Nahda al-'Arabiyya, 2001.

Ghanim, Ibrahim al-Bayumi, ed. *Tariq al-Bishri: Al-Qadi, al-Mufakkir*. Cairo: Dar al-Sharuq, 1999.

Al-Ghazali, Muhammad. *Hasad al-Ghurur*. Cairo: n.p., 1978.

Al-Ghazali, Zainab. *Ayyam min Hayati*. Cairo: Dar al-Sharuq, n.d.

Hamrush, Ahmad. *Qisat Thawrat 23 Yuliyu*. Cairo: Madbuli, 1985.

Al-Hizb al-Watani al-Dimaqrati. *Mustaqbal al-Ta'alim fi Misr*. Cairo: Al-Hizb al-Watani al-Dimaqrati, 2003.

———. *Taqrir 'an Mustaqbal as-Siyasa as-Sihatiyya*. Cairo: Al-Hizb al-Watani al-Dimaqrati, 2003.

———. *Taqrir 'an as-Siyasa al-Iqtisadiyya*. Cairo: Al-Hizb al-Watani al-Dimaqrati, 2003.

Al-Hudeibi, Muhammad M. *Al-Islam wa-l-Siyasa*. Cairo: Dar al-Islam li-l-Nashr, 1997.

Imam, 'Abd Allah. *Mathbahat al-Qada'*. Cairo: Madbulis, 1978.

Imam, Samia Sa'id. *Man Yamluk Misr?* Cairo: Dar al-Mustaqbal al-'Arabi, 1986.

Al-'Iryan, 'Isam. *Al-Haraka al-Islamiyya wa-l-Intiqal al-Dimaqrati: al-Tajriba al-Misriyya fi rob'a Qarn*. Al-Mansura: Dar al-Kalima, 2004.

Khalil, 'Abd Allah. *Azmat Niqabat al-Muhamiyyin*. Cairo: Cairo Institute for Human Rights Studies, 1999.

Mubadirat al-Ikhwan al-Muslimin hawwal Mabad' al-Islah fi Misr. Cairo: Dar al-Manara, 2004.

Munisi, Ahmad. "Al-'Anf fi al-Intikhabat." In *Intikhabat Majlis as-Sha'ab 2000*, ed. Hala Mustafa, 209–26. Cairo: Markaz al-Dirasat al-Siyasiyya wa-l-Istratijiyya bi-l-Ahram, 2001.

Al-Murr, 'Awad. *al-Riqaba al-Qada'iyya 'ala Dusturiyyat al-Qawanin*. Cairo: Shirakat al-Jalal li-l-Taba'aat, 2003.

Mustafa, Hala. *al-Dawla wa-l-Haraka al-Islamiyya al-Mu'arada*. Cairo: al-Mahrusa, 1995.

———, ed. *Intikhabat Majlis as-Sha'ab 2000*. Cairo: Markaz al-Dirasat al-Siyasiyya wa-l-Istratijiyya bi-l-Ahram, 2001.

———. "Intikhabat 2000 Mu'shirat 'Amma." In *Initkhabat Majlis as-Sha'ab 2000*, ed. Hala Mustafa, 7–17. Cairo: Markaz al-Dirasat al-Siyasiyya wa-l-Istratijiyya bi-l-Ahram, 2001.

Mu'tamar al-'Adala al-Awal 1986: Al-Watha'iq al-Asasiyya. Cairo: Nadi al-Quda, 1986.

Nadi Al-Quda. *Taqrir Lajna Taqassa al-Haqa'iq 'an Ishraf al-Quda 'ala al-Intikhabat al-Ra'isiyya bi Tarikh 7/9/2005*. Cairo: Nadi al-Quda, 2005.

Najib, Muhammad Fathi. *al-Tanthim al-Qada'i al-Misri*. Cairo: Dar al-Sharuq, 2003.

Nasaar, Mumtaz. *Ma'arakat al-'Adala fi Misr*. Cairo: Dar al-Sharuq, 1974.

Qandil, Amani. *'Amaliyyat al-Tahawwul al-Dimaqrati fi Misr, 1981–1993*. Cairo: Dar al-Amin, 1995.

Al-Qaradawi, Yusuf. *Min Fiqh al-Dawla fi-l-Islam*. Cairo: Dar al-Sharuq, 1997.

Qutb, Sayyid. *Ma'alim fi-l-Tariq*. Cairo: n.p., 1964.

Rabi'a, 'Amru Hashim, ed. *al-Ta'adil al-Dusturi wa Intikhabat al-Ri'asa 2005*. Cairo: Markaz al-Dirasat al-Siyasiyya wa-l-Istratijiyya bi-l-Ahram, 2005.

Ramadan, 'Abd al-'Azim. *'Abd al-Nasser wa Azmat Maris*. Cairo: Ruz al-Yusuf, 1976.

Al-Rif'ai, Yahia. *Sha'un Rijal al-Qada'*. Cairo: Maktabat Rijal al-Qada', 1990–91.

———. *Tashriat al-Sulta al-Qada'iyya*. Cairo: Maktabat Rijal al-Qada', 1991.

Sa'id, Rif'at. *al-Yasar, al-Dimaqratiyya, wa-l-Ta'salam*. Cairo: Mu'ssasat al-Ahali, 1998.

Salam, Ihab. "al-Ishraf al-Qada'i wa-l-Riqaba 'ala al-Intikhabat." In *Intikhabat Majlis al-Sha'ab 2005*, ed. 'Amru Hashim Rabi'a, 35–60. Cairo: Markaz al-Dirasat al-Siyasiyya wa-l-Istratijiyya bi-l-Ahram, 2006.

Al-Sayyid, Ahmad Lutfi. *Al-Muntakhabat*. Cairo: Maktabat al-Anglo al-Misriyya, n.d.

Al-Shubki, 'Amru. "Al-Mustaqilun wa-l-Intikhabat." In *Intikhabat Majlis as-Sha'ab 2000*, ed. Hala Mustafa, 85–104. Cairo: Markaz al-Dirasat al-Siyasiyya wa-l-Istratijiyya bi-l-Ahram, 2001.

Al-Tamawi, Suliman Muhammad. *al-Nathariyya al-'Amma li-l-Qararat al-Idariyya*. Cairo: Dar al-Fikr al-'Arabi, 1984.

'Ubayd, Muhammad Kamil. *Istiqlal al-Qada'*. Cairo: Maktabat Rijal al-Qada', 1991.

Al-'Utayfi, Jamal. *al-'Adala al-Ishtirakiyya*. Appendix to *al-Ahram al-Iqtisadi*, March 1966.

Yasin, Al-Sayyid, ed. *al-Taqrir al-Stratiji al-'Arabi*. Cairo: Markaz al-Dirasat al-Siyasiyya wa-l-Istratijiyya bi-l-Ahram, various years.

BOOKS AND ARTICLES IN ENGLISH AND FRENCH

Abdel-Khalek, Gouda, and Karima Korayem. *Fiscal Policy Measures in Egypt: Public Debt and Food Subsidy.* Cairo: American University in Cairo Press, 2000.

Alashhab, Baher, Georges Flecheux, Asma Khader, and Peter Wilborn. *Clash in Egypt: The Government and the Bar.* Geneva: Center for the Independence of Judges and Lawyers, 1995.

Alba, Pedro, Sherine Al-Shawarby, and Farrukh Iqbal. *Fiscal and Public Debt Sustainability.* Cairo: Egyptian Center for Economic Studies, 2004.

American Chamber of Commerce in Egypt. "The Role of the Private Sector." In *Private Sector Development in Egypt*, ed. Marcelo M. Giugale and Hamed Mobarak, 29–44. Cairo: American University in Cairo Press, 1996.

Amin, Galal. *Egypt's Economic Predicament: A Study in the Interaction of External Pressure, Political Folly, and Social Tension in Egypt, 1960–1990.* Leiden: E. J. Brill, 1995.

Amirah-Fernandez, Haizam. "EU: Barcelona Process and the New Neighborhood Policy." *Arab Reform Bulletin* 4, no. 1 (2006): 5–6.

Arab Human Development Report 2002: Creating Opportunities for Future Generations. New York: United Nations Development Program, 2002.

Arab Human Development Report 2003: Building a Knowledge Society. New York: United Nations Development Program, 2003.

Arab Human Development Report 2004: Towards Freedom in the Arab World. New York: United Nations Development Program, 2005.

Arab Human Development Report 2005: Towards the Rise of Women in the Arab World. New York: United Nations Development Program, 2006.

Armony, Ariel C., and Hector E. Schamis. "Babel in Democratization Studies." *Journal of Democracy* 16, no. 4 (2005): 113–28.

Atherton, Alfred L. *Egypt and U.S. Interests.* Washington, DC: Foreign Policy Institute, 1988.

Al-Awadi, Hesham. *In Pursuit of Legitimacy: The Muslim Brothers and Mubarak, 1982–2000.* New York: Tauris, 2004.

Al-'Awwa, Muhammad Salim. *Religion and Political Structures: An Islamic Viewpoint.* No. 3 Occasional Papers. Birmingham, UK: Center for the Study of Islam and Christian-Muslim Relations, 1999.

Ayubi, Nazih N. *Bureaucracy and Politics in Contemporary Egypt.* London: Ithaca Press, 1980.

———. *The State and Public Policies in Egypt since Sadat.* Reading: Ithaca Press, 1991.

Baker, James A. *The Politics of Diplomacy: Revolution, War, and Peace, 1989–1992.* New York: G. P. Putnam's Sons, 1995.

Baker, Raymond William. *Sadat and After: Struggles for Egypt's Political Soul.* Cambridge, MA: Harvard University Press, 1990.

———. *Islam without Fear: Egypt and the New Islamists.* Cambridge, MA: Harvard University Press, 2003.

El Baradei, Laila. *Do Parallel Structures Resolve the Problems of the Egyptian Government Bureaucracy?* Cairo: Egyptian Center for Economic Studies, 2006.

Baram, Amatzia. "US Input into Iraqi Decisionmaking, 1988–1990." In *The Middle East and the United States: A Historical and Political Reassessment, Fourth Edition*, ed. David W. Lesch, 351–79. Boulder, CO: Westview Press, 2007.

Baylouny, Anne Marie. "Jordan's New 'Political Development' Strategy." *Middle East Report* 35, no. 3 (2005): 40–43.

Beattie, Kirk J. "Egypt: Thirty-Five Years of Praetorian Politics." In *Military Disengagement from Politics*, ed. Constantine P. Danopoulos, 201–30. New York: Routledge, 1988.

———. *Egypt during the Nasser Years: Ideology, Politics, and Civil Society.* Boulder, CO: Westview Press, 1994.

———. *Egypt during the Sadat Years.* New York: Palgrave, 2000.

Beinin, Joel. "Popular Social Movements and the Future of Egyptian Politics." *Middle East Report Online*, March 10, 2005.

Beinin, Joel, and Hossam el-Hamalawy. "Egyptian Textile Workers Confront the New Economic Order." *Middle East Report Online*, March 25, 2007.

Beinin, Joel, and Zachary Lockman. *Workers on the Nile: Nationalism, Communism, Islam, and the Egyptian Working Class.* Princeton, NJ: Princeton University Press, 1987.

Bellin, Eva. "Contingent Democrats: Industrialists, Labor, and Democratization in Late-Developing Countries." *World Politics* 52, no. 2 (2000): 175–205.

———. *Stalled Democracy: Capital, Labor and the Paradox of State-Sponsored Development.* Ithaca, NY: Cornell University Press, 2002.

Berman, Sheri. "Lessons from Europe." *Journal of Democracy* 18, no. 1 (2007): 28–41.

Bianchi, Robert. *Unruly Corporatism: Associational Life in Twentieth-Century Egypt.* New York: Oxford University Press, 1989.

Bilgin, Pinar. "Turkey's Changing Security Discourses: The Challenge of Globalisation." *European Journal of Political Research* 44 (2005): 175–201.

Blackhurst, Richard. "World Trade Organization (WTO) Agreements: Benefits to Egypt." In *Institutional and Policy Challenges Facing the Egyptian Economy*, ed. Heba Nassar and Ahmad Ghoneim, 259–71. Cairo: Center for Economics and Financial Research and Studies, 2003.

Botman, Selma. *The Rise of Egyptian Communism, 1939–1970.* Syracuse, NY: Syracuse University Press, 1988.

Boyle, Kevin, and Adel Omar Sherif. *Human Rights and Democracy: The Role of the Supreme Constitutional Court of Egypt.* London: Kluwer Law International, 1996.

Bratton, Michael, and Nicolas van de Walle. *Democratic Experiments in Africa: Regime Transitions in Comparative Perspective.* New York: Cambridge University Press, 1997.

Brinton, Jasper Yeates. *The Mixed Courts of Egypt.* New Haven, CT: Yale University Press, 1968.

Brown, Nathan J. *The Rule of Law in the Arab World: Courts in Egypt and the Gulf.* Cambridge: Cambridge University Press, 1997.

———. *Constitutions in a Nonconstitutional World: Arab Basic Laws and the Prospects for Accountable Government.* Albany: State University of New York Press, 2002.

Brown, Nathan J., and Michele Dunne. *Egypt's Controversial Constitutional Amendments: A Textual Analysis.* Washington, DC: Carnegie Endowment for International Peace, March 23, 2007.

Brown, Nathan J., and Amr Hamzawy. *The Draft Platform of the Egyptian Muslim Brotherhood: Foray into Political Integration or Retreat into Old Positions?* Washington, DC: Carnegie Endowment for International Peace, January 2008.

Brown, Nathan J., and Hesham Nasr. *Egypt's Judges Step Forward: The Judicial Election Boycott and Egyptian Reform.* Washington, DC: Carnegie Endowment for International Peace, May 2005.

Brownlee, Jason. "The Decline of Pluralism in Mubarak's Egypt." *Journal of Democracy* 13, no. 4 (2002): 6–14.

Bugra, Ayse. "Class, Culture, and State: An Analysis of Interest Representation by Two Turkish Business Associations." *International Journal of Middle East Studies* 30, no. 4 (1998): 521–39.

Bush, George W. *The National Security Strategy of the United States of America.* Washington, DC: The White House, 2006.

Butter, David. "Debt and Egypt's Financial Policies." In *Egypt under Mubarak*, ed. Charles Tripp and Roger Owen, 121–36. London: Routledge, 1989.

Calabrese, John. "Freedom on the March in the Middle East—and Transatlantic Relations on a New Course?" *Mediterranean Quarterly* (2005): 42–64.

Cameron, Maxwell A. *Democracy and Authoritarianism in Peru: Political Coalitions and Social Change.* New York: St. Martin's Press, 1994.

Cannon, Byron. *Politics of Law and the Courts in Nineteenth-Century Egypt.* Salt Lake City: University of Utah Press, 1988.

Carothers, Thomas. "The Observers Observed." *Journal of Democracy* 8, no. 3 (1997): 17–31.

———. *Aiding Democracy Abroad: The Learning Curve.* Washington, DC: Carnegie Endowment for International Peace, 1999.

———. "The End of the Transition Paradigm." *Journal of Democracy* 13, no. 1 (2002): 5–21.

———. "The 'Sequencing' Fallacy." *Journal of Democracy* 18, no. 1 (2007): 12–27.

Carroll, Katherine Blue. *Business as Usual? Economic Reform in Jordan.* Lanham: Lexington Books, 2003.

Case, William. "Can the 'Halfway House' Stand? Semidemocracy and Elite Theory in Three Southeast Asian Countries." *Comparative Politics* 28, no. 4 (1996): 437–64.

———. "Southeast Asia's Hybrid Regimes: When Do Voters Change Them?" *Journal of East Asian Studies* 5, no. 2 (2005): 215–38.

Clark, Janine A. *Islam, Charity, and Activism: Middle-Class Networks and Social Welfare in Egypt, Jordan, and Yemen.* Bloomington: Indiana University Press, 2004.

Cofman-Wittes, Tamara, and Sarah E. Yerkes, "The Middle East Freedom Agenda: An Update." *Current History* 106, no. 696 (January 2007): 31–38.

Cole, Juan R. I. *Colonialism and Revolution in the Middle East: Social and Cultural Origins of Egypt's 'Urabi Movement.* Princeton, NJ: Princeton University Press, 1993.

Cook, Michael. *Commanding Right and Forbidding Wrong in Islamic Thought.* New York: Cambridge University Press, 2000.

———. *Forbidding Wrong in Islam: An Introduction.* New York: Cambridge University Press, 2003.

Cook, Steven A. *Ruling but not Governing: The Military and Political Development in Egypt, Algeria, and Turkey.* Baltimore: Johns Hopkins University Press, 2007.

Cordesman, Anthony H. *The Military Balance in the Middle East.* Westport, CT: Praeger, 2004.

Cromer, Earl of. *Modern Egypt.* Volumes 1 and 2. New York: Macmillan, 1908.

Dahl, Robert A. *Polyarchy: Participation and Opposition.* New Haven, CT: Yale University Press, 1971.

Dalacoura, Katerina. "U.S. Democracy Promotion in the Arab Middle East since 11 September 2001: A Critique." *International Affairs* 81, no. 5 (2005): 963–79.

Davidson, Neil, and Pierre Sebastien. *Egypt: The Sequestration of the Bar.* Geneva: Center for the Independence of Judges and Lawyers, 1998.

Davies, Michael H. *Business Law in Egypt.* Boston: Kluwer Law and Taxation, 1984.

Davis, Eric. "Ideology, Social Classes, and Islamic Radicalism in Modern Egypt." In *From Nationalism to Revolutionary Islam,* ed. Said Arjomand, 134–57. Albany: State University of New York Press, 1983.

El-Dean, Bahaa Ali, and Mahmud Mohieldin. *On the Formulation and Enforcement of Competition Law in Emerging Economies: The Case of Egypt.* Cairo: Egyptian Center for Economic Studies, 2001.

Dekmejian, R. Hrair. *Egypt under Nasir: A Study in Political Dynamics.* Albany: State University of New York Press, 1971.

DeSoto, Hernando. *Dead Capital and the Poor in Egypt.* Cairo: Egyptian Center for Economic Studies, 1997.

———. *Dead Capital and the Poor: Appendices.* Cairo: Egyptian Center for Economic Studies, 1997.

———. *The Mystery of Capital.* New York: Basic Books, 2000.

Diamond, Larry. *Developing Democracy: Toward Consolidation.* Baltimore: Johns Hopkins University Press, 1999.

———. "Thinking about Hybrid Regimes." *Journal of Democracy* 13, no. 2 (2002): 21–35.

Diamond, Larry, Juan J. Linz, and Seymour Martin Lipset. "Introduction: What Makes for Democracy?" In *Politics in Developing Countries: Comparing Experiences with Democracy,* ed. Larry Diamond, Juan J. Linz, and Seymour Martin Lipset, 1–66. Boulder, CO: Lynne Rienner, 1995.

Dillman, Bradford. "Parliamentary Elections and the Prospects for Political Pluralism in North Africa." *Government and Opposition* 35, no. 2 (2000): 211–36.

Dupret, Baudouin. "A Liberal Interpretation of a Socialist Constitution: The Egyptian Supreme Constitutional Court and Privatization of the Public Sector." In *Politics from Above, Politics from Below,* ed. Eberhard Kienle, 167–87. London: Saqi, 2003.

Dupret, Baudouin, and Nathalie Bernard-Maugiron. "A General Presentation of Law and Judicial Bodies." In *Egypt and Its Laws*, ed. Baudouin Dupret and Nathalie Bernard-Maugiron, xxiv–li. London: Kluwer Law International, 2002.

Echagüe, Ana, and Richard Youngs. "Democracy and Human Rights in the Barcelona Process." *Mediterranean Politics* 10, no. 2 (2005): 233–38.

Egyptian Businessmen's Association. "The Role of the Government." In *Private Sector Development in Egypt*, ed. Marcelo M. Giugale and Hamed Mobarak, 12–28. Cairo: American University in Cairo Press, 1996.

Egyptian Center for Economic Studies. *Policy Viewpoint: Priorities for Rapid and Shared Economic Growth in Egypt*. Cairo: Egyptian Center for Economic Studies, 1998.

———. *Policy Viewpoint: Towards More Efficient Telecommunication Services in Egypt*. Cairo: Egyptian Center for Economic Studies, 1998.

———. *Policy Viewpoint: Egypt's Export Puzzle*. Cairo: Egyptian Center for Economic Studies, 2001.

Eisenstadt, Todd A. *Courting Democracy in Mexico: Party Strategies and Electoral Institutions*. New York: Cambridge University Press, 2003.

Eldin, Ziad A. Bahaa, and Mahmud Mohieldin. "On Prudential Regulation in Egypt." In *Financial Development in Emerging Markets: The Egyptian Experience*, ed. Mohamed El-Erian and Mahmud Mohieldin, 111–40. Cairo: Egyptian Center for Economic Studies, 1998.

Emerson, Michael, Senem Aydin, Gergana Noutcheva, Nathalie Tocci, Marius Vahl, and Richard Youngs. "The Reluctant Debutante—The EU as Promoter of Democracy in its Neighborhood." In *Democratisation in the European Neighborhood*, ed. Michael Emerson, 169–230. Brussels: Center for European Policy Studies, 2005.

El-Erian, Mohamed A. *Globalization and the Arab Economies: From Marginalization to Integration*. Cairo: Egyptian Center for Economic Studies, 1997.

El-Erian, Mohamed, and Mahmud Mohieldin, eds. *Financial Development in Emerging Markets: The Egyptian Experience*. Cairo: Egyptian Center for Economic Studies, 1998.

Fahmy, Mahmud. "The Legal and Regulatory Framework of the Capital Market in Egypt." In *Financial Development in Emerging Markets: The Egyptian Experience*, ed. Mohamed El-Erian and Mahmud Mohieldin, 167–84. Cairo: Egyptian Center for Economic Studies, 1998.

Fahmy, Ninette S. *The Politics of Egypt: State-Society Relationship*. New York: RoutledgeCurzon, 2002.

Fawzy, Samiha. *The Business Environment in Egypt*. Cairo: Egyptian Center for Economic Studies, 1998.

———. *Investment Policies and the Unemployment Problem in Egypt*. Cairo: Egyptian Center for Economic Studies, 2002.

———. *Assessment of Corporate Governance in Egypt*. Cairo: Egyptian Center for Economic Studies, 2003.

———. *Public and Private Investment in Egypt: Crowding-Out or Crowding-In?* Cairo: Egyptian Center for Economic Studies, 2004.

Fawzy, Samiha, and Nada Massoud. *The Future of Egypt's Textile and Clothing Exports in Light of New Trade Rules.* Cairo: Egyptian Center for Economic Studies, 2003.

Fergany, Nader. "A Characterization of the Employment Problem in Egypt." In *Employment and Structural Adjustment: Egypt in the 1990s,* ed. Heba Handoussa and Gillian Potter, 25–56. Cairo: American University in Cairo Press, 1991.

Fernandez, Haizam Amirah, and Richard Youngs, eds. *The Euro-Mediterranean Partnership: Assessing the First Decade.* Madrid: Real Instituto Elcano de Estudios Internacionales y Estrategicos, 2005.

Friedman, Alan. *Spider's Web: The Secret History of How the White House Illegally Armed Iraq.* New York: Bantam Books, 1993.

Fukuyama, Francis. "Liberalism versus State-Building." *Journal of Democracy* 18, no. 3 (2007): 10–13.

Galal, Ahmad. *Welfare Consequences of Selling Public Enterprises: An Empirical Analysis.* New York: Oxford University Press, 1994.

———. *Savings and Privatization.* Cairo: Egyptian Center for Economic Studies, 1996.

———. *Which Institutions Constrain Economic Growth in Egypt the Most?* Cairo: Egyptian Center for Economic Studies, 1996.

———. *Social Expenditure and the Poor in Egypt.* Cairo: Egyptian Center for Economic Studies, 2003.

Galal, Ahmad, and Nihal El-Megharbel. *Do Governments Pick Winners or Losers? An Assessment of Industrial Policy in Egypt.* Cairo: Egyptian Center for Economic Studies, 2005.

Galal, Ahmad, and Sahar Tohamy. "Toward an Egypt-U.S. Free Trade Agreement: An Egyptian Perspective." In *Building Bridges: An Egypt-U.S. Free Trade Agreement,* ed. Ahmad Galal and Robert Z. Lawrence, 13–36. Washington, DC: Brookings Institution Press, 1998.

Gallagher, Mary Elizabeth. *Contagious Capitalism: Globalization and the Politics of Labor in China.* Princeton, NJ: Princeton University Press, 2005.

Gallup Editors. *The 2002 Gallup Poll of the Islamic World.* Princeton, NJ: Gallup Press, 2002.

Gamblin, Sandrine. *Contours et Détours du Politique en Egypte: Les élections législatives de 1995.* Paris: Harmattan, 1997.

Gershoni, Israel. "Egyptian Liberalism in an Age of 'Crisis of Orientation': Al-Risala's Reaction to Fascism and Nazism, 1933–39." *International Journal of Middle East Studies* 31, no. 4 (1999): 551–76.

El-Ghobashy, Mona. "The Metamorphosis of the Egyptian Muslim Brothers." *International Journal of Middle East Studies* 37 (2005): 373–95.

Gillespie, Richard, and Richard Youngs, eds. *The European Union and Democracy Promotion: The Case of North Africa.* London: Frank Cass, 2002.

Giugale, Marcelo M., and Hamed Mobarak, eds. *Private Sector Development in Egypt.* Cairo: American University in Cairo Press, 1996.

Gobe, Eric. *Les Hommes d'affaires Egyptiens: Démocratisation et Secteur Privé dans l'Egypte de l'infitâh.* Paris: Karthala, 1999.

Gordon, Joel. *Nasser's Blessed Movement: Egypt's Free Officers and the July Revolution.* New York: Oxford University Press, 1992.

Gotowicki, Stephen H. "The Military in Egyptian Society." In *Egypt at the Cross-roads: Domestic Stability and Regional Role*, ed. Phebe Marr, 105–25. Washington, DC: National Defense University Press, 1999.

Guney, Aylin. "The Military, Politics, and Post-Cold War Dilemmas in Turkey." In *Political Armies: The Military and Nation Building in the Age of Democracy*, ed. Kees Koonings and Dirk Kruijt, 162–78. New York: Zed Books, 2002.

Gutman, A. "Liberalism." In *International Encyclopedia of the Social and Behavioral Sciences*, ed. Neil J. Smelser and Paul B. Baltes, 8784–87. Amsterdam: Elsevier, 2001.

Gutner, Tammi. *The Political Economy of Food Subsidy Reform in Egypt*. Washington, DC: International Food Policy Research Institute, 1999.

Hakimian, Hassan, and Ziba Moshaver, eds. *The State and Global Change: The Political Economy of Transition in the Middle East and North Africa*. Richmond, U.K.: Curzon Press, 2001.

Hale, William. "Human Rights, the European Union, and the Turkish Accession Process." In *Turkey and the European Union: Domestic Politics, Economic Integration, and International Dynamics*, ed. Ali Çarkoglu and Barry Rubin, 107–26. Portland, OR: Frank Cass, 2003.

Hall, Peter. "The Movement from Keynesianism to Monetarism: Institutional Analysis and British Economic Policy in the 1970s." In *Structuring Politics: Historical Institutionalism in Comparative Analysis*, ed. Sven Steinmo et al., 90–113. Cambridge: Cambridge University Press, 1992.

Hall, Peter A., and Rosemary C. R. Taylor. "Political Science and the Three New Institutionalisms." *Political Studies* 44 (1996): 936–57.

Handoussa, Heba. *The Role of the State: The Case of Egypt*. Cairo: Economic Research Forum, 1994.

———. "A Balance Sheet of Reform in Two Decades." In *Institutional Reform and Economic Development in Egypt*, ed. Noha El-Mikawy and Heba Handoussa, 89–103. Cairo: American University in Cairo Press, 2002.

———. *Employment, Budget Priorities and Microenterprises*. Cairo: Egyptian Center for Economic Studies, 2002.

Handoussa, Heba, and Nivine El Oraby. *Civil Service Wages and Reform: The Case of Egypt*. Cairo: Egyptian Center for Economic Studies, 2004.

Handoussa, Heba, and Noha El-Mikawy. "Conclusion: Redefining the Role of the State." In *Institutional Reform and Economic Development in Egypt*, ed. Heba Handoussa and Noha El-Mikawy, 165–71. Cairo: American University in Cairo Press, 2002.

Handy, Howard. *Egypt: Beyond Stabilization: Toward a Dynamic Market Economy*. Washington, DC: International Monetary Fund, 1998.

Harb, Imad. "The Egyptian Military in Politics: Disengagement or Accommodation?" *Middle East Journal* 57, no. 2 (2003): 269–90.

Helmy, Omneia. *Reforming Customs Administration*. Cairo: Egyptian Center for Economic Studies, 2003.

———. *Pension System Reform in Egypt*. Cairo: Egyptian Center for Economic Studies, 2004.

———. *The Efficiency and Equity of Subsidy Policy in Egypt*. Cairo: Egyptian Center for Economic Studies, 2005.

Hewison, Kevin. *Southeast Asia in the 1990s: Authoritarianism, Democracy, and Capitalism*. St. Leonards, Australia: Allen and Unwin, 1993.

Hill, Enid. "The Supreme Constitutional Court of Egypt on Property." *Egypte/ Monde Arabe: Le Prince et son Juge: Droit et Politique Dans L'Egypte Contemporaine*, no. 2 (1999): 55–92.

Hodder, Rupert. "Business, Politics, and Social Relationships in the Philippines: A Gentle Revolution?" *South East Asia Research* 8, no. 2 (2000): 93–145.

Holmes, Stephen. "Constitutionalism." In *The Encyclopedia of Democracy*, ed. Seymour Martin Lipset, 299–306. Washington, DC: Congressional Quarterly, 1995.

El-Hudeibi, Muhammad M. *Politics in Islam*. Cairo: Islamic Home for Publishing and Distribution, 1997.

Huntington, Samuel P. *Political Order in Changing Societies*. New Haven, CT: Yale University Press, 1968.

———*The Third Wave: Democratization in the Late Twentieth Century*. Norman: University of Oklahoma Press, 1993.

Hutchcroft, Paul D. *Booty Capitalism: The Politics of Banking in the Philippines*. Ithaca, NY: Cornell University Press, 1998.

Ikram, Khalid. *The Egyptian Economy, 1952–2000: Performance, Policies, and Issues*. New York: Routledge, 2006.

International Institute for Strategic Studies. *The Military Balance*. London: International Institute for Strategic Studies, 2007.

El-Islam, A. Seif. "Exceptional Laws and Exceptional Courts." In *Egypt and Its Laws*, ed. Nathalie Bernard-Maugiron and Baudouin Dupret, 359–76. New York: Kluwer Law International, 2002.

Ismael, Tareq Y., and Rifa'at El-Sa'id. *The Communist Movement in Egypt, 1920–1988*. Syracuse, NY: Syracuse University Press, 1990.

Joffe, George. *Jordan in Transition*. London: Hurst and Co., 2002.

Karawan, Ibrahim A. "Egypt." In *The Political Role of the Military: An International Handbook*, ed. Constantine P. Danopoulos and Cynthia Watson, 107–21. Westport, CT: Greenwood Press, 1996.

Kassem, Maye. *Egyptian Politics: The Dynamics of Authoritarian Rule*. Boulder, CO: Lynne Rienner, 2004.

Katznelson, Ira. "Structure and Configuration in Comparative Politics." In *Comparative Politics: Rationality, Culture, and Structure*, ed. Mark Irving Lichbach and Alan S. Zuckerman, 81–112. New York: Cambridge University Press, 1997.

Keck, Margaret E., and Kathryn Sikkink. *Activists Beyond Borders: Advocacy Networks in International Politics*. Ithaca, NY: Cornell University Press, 1998.

Kedourie, Elie. *Politics in the Middle East*. New York: Oxford University Press, 1992.

Kelly, Paul. *Liberalism*. Cambridge: Polity Press, 2005.

Kermani, Navid. "From Revelation to Interpretation: Nasr Hamid Abu Zayd and the Literary Study of the Qur'an." In *Modern Muslim Intellectuals and the Qur'an*, ed. Suha Taji-Farouki, 169–92. New York: Oxford University Press, 2004.

Khattab, Mokhtar. *Constraints to Privatization: The Egyptian Experience*. Cairo: Egyptian Center for Economic Studies, 1999.

Kheir-El-Din, Hanaa, Samiha Fawzy, and Amal Rafaat. *Marginal Effective Tax Rates and Investment Decisions in Egypt*. Cairo: Egyptian Center for Economic Studies, 2000.

Kienle, Eberhard. *A Grand Delusion: Democracy and Economic Reform in Egypt*. New York: I. B. Tauris, 2001.

Kissinger, Henry A. "Intervention with a Vision." In *The Right War? The Conservative Debate on Iraq*, ed. Gary Rosen, 49–53. Cambridge: Cambridge University Press, 2005.

Knowles, Warwick M. *Jordan since 1989: A Study in Political Economy*. London: I. B. Tauris, 2005.

Lall, Sanjay. *Strengthening SMEs for International Competitiveness*. Cairo: Egyptian Center for Economic Studies, 2000.

Langewiesche, D. "Liberalism: Historical Aspects." In *International Encyclopedia of the Social and Behavioral Sciences*, ed. Neil J. Smelser and Paul B. Baltes, 8792–97. Amsterdam: Elsevier, 2001.

Levitsky, Steven, and Lucan A. Way. "The Rise of Competitive Authoritarianism." *Journal of Democracy* 13, no. 2 (2002): 51–65.

———. "Autocracy by Democratic Rules: The Dynamics of Competitive Authoritarianism in the Post–Cold War Era." Paper presented at the conference, "Mapping the Grey Zone: Clientelism and the Boundary between Democratic and Democratizing." New York: Columbia University, 2003.

Lia, Brynjar. *The Society of the Muslim Brothers in Egypt: The Rise of an Islamic Mass Movement, 1928–1942*. Reading: Ithaca Press, 1998.

Lindblom, Charles E. *Politics and Markets: The World's Political Economic Systems*. New York: Basic Books, 1977.

Linz, Juan J. *Totalitarian and Authoritarian Regimes*. Boulder, CO: Lynne Rienner, 2000.

Linz, Juan J., and Alfred Stepan. *Problems of Democratic Transition and Consolidation: Southern Europe, South America, and Post-Communist Europe*. Baltimore: Johns Hopkins University Press, 1996.

Locke, John. *Two Treatises of Government*. Cambridge: Cambridge University Press, [1690] 1988.

Lofgren, Hans. "Economic Policy in Egypt: A Breakdown in Reform Resistance?" *International Journal of Middle East Studies* 25 (1993): 407–21.

Lofgren, Hans, and Moataz El-Said. *A General Equilibrium Analysis of Alternative Scenarios for Food Subsidy Reform in Egypt*. Washington, DC: International Food Policy Research Institute, 1999.

Lucas, Russell. "Deliberalization in Jordan." *Journal of Democracy* 14, no. 1 (2003): 137–44.

———. *Institutions and the Politics of Survival in Jordan: Domestic Responses to External Challenges, 1988–2001*. Binghamton: State University of New York Press, 2005.

Lust-Okar, Ellen. *Structuring Conflict in the Arab World: Incumbents, Opponents, and Institutions*. New York: Cambridge University Press, 2005.

Lynch, Marc. "Shattering the 'Politics of Silence.' Satellite Television Talk Shows and the Transformation of Arab Political Culture." *Arab Reform Bulletin* 2, no. 11 (2004): 3–4.

————. *Voices of the New Arab Public: Iraq, Al-Jazeera, and Middle East Politics Today.* New York: Columbia University Press, 2006.

MacIntyre, Andrew. *Business and Politics in Indonesia.* Sidney: Allen and Unwin, 1991.

Magaloni, Beatriz. *Voting for Autocracy: Hegemonic Party Survival and Its Demise in Mexico.* New York: Cambridge University Press, 2006.

Mahoney, James. "Knowledge Accumulation in Comparative Historical Research: The Case of Democracy and Authoritarianism." In *Comparative Historical Analysis in the Social Sciences*, ed. James Mahoney and Dietrich Rueschemeyer, 131–76. New York: Cambridge University Press, 2003.

Mahoney, James, and Dietrich Rueschemeyer. "Comparative Historical Analysis: Achievements and Agendas." In *Comparative Historical Analysis in the Social Sciences*, ed. James Mahoney and Dietrich Rueschemeyer, 3–40. New York: Cambridge University Press, 2003.

Mansfield, Edward D., and Jack Snyder. "The Sequencing 'Fallacy'." *Journal of Democracy* 18, no. 3 (2007): 5–9.

Marsot, Afaf Lutfi al-Sayyid. *Egypt's Liberal Experiment: 1922–1936.* Berkeley: University of California Press, 1977.

McFaul, Michael. "The Fourth Wave of Democracy and Dictatorship: Noncooperative Transitions in the Postcommunist World." *World Politics* 54, no. 2 (2002): 212–44.

McMann, Kelly M. *Economic Autonomy and Democracy: Hybrid Regimes in Russia and Kyrgyzstan.* New York: Cambridge University Press, 2006.

El-Meehy, Tamer. *The Myth and Reality of SMEs and Employment in Egypt.* Cairo: Entrust Development and Management Consultants, 2004.

El-Mikawy, Noha. *The Building of Consensus in Egypt's Transition Process.* Cairo: American University in Cairo Press, 1999.

Mitchell, Richard P. *The Society of the Muslim Brothers.* New York: Oxford University Press, 1993.

Mohieldin, Mahmud. "The Egypt-EU Partnership Agreement and Liberalization of Services." In *Regional Partners in Global Markets: Limits and Possibilities of the Euro-Med Agreements*, ed. Ahmad Galal and Bernard Hoekman, 238–56. Cairo: Egyptian Center for Economic Studies, 1997.

Moore, Barrington. *Social Origins of Dictatorship and Democracy: Lord and Peasant in the Making of the Modern World.* Boston: Beacon Press, 1966.

Morgan, David. *Suffragists and Democrats: The Politics of Woman Suffrage in America.* East Lansing: Michigan State University Press, 1972.

El-Morr, Awad. "The Supreme Constitutional Court of Egypt and the Protection of Human and Political Rights." In *Islam and Public Law*, ed. Chibli Mallat, 229–60. London: Graham & Trotman, 1992.

Moustafa, Tamir. *Law versus the State: The Expansion of Constitutional Power in Egypt, 1980–2002.* Ph.D. Dissertation, Department of Political Science, University of Washington, 2002.

————. *The Struggle for Constitutional Power: Law, Politics, and Economic Development in Egypt.* New York: Cambridge University Press, 2007.

Murphy, Walter F. "Constitutions, Constitutionalism, and Democracy." In *Constitutionalism and Democracy: Transitions in the Contemporary World*, ed. Douglas

Greenberg, Stanley N. Katz, Melanie Beth Oliviero, and Steven C. Wheatley, 3–25. New York: Oxford University Press, 1993.

———. *Constitutional Democracy: Creating and Maintaining a Just Political Order.* Baltimore: Johns Hopkins University Press, 2007.

Nabli, Mustapha K., Jennifer Keller, Claudia Nassif, and Carlos Silva-Jauregui. *The Political Economy of Industrial Policy in the Middle East and North Africa.* Cairo: Egyptian Center for Economic Studies, 2006.

Noland, Marcus, and Howard Pack. *The East Asian Industrial Policy Experience: Implications for the Middle East.* Cairo: Egyptian Center for Economic Studies, 2005.

Norton, Augustus Richard. "Thwarted Politics: The Case of Egypt's Hizb al-Wasat." In *Remaking Muslim Politics: Pluralism, Contestation, Democratization,* ed. Robert W. Hefner, 133–60. Princeton, NJ: Princeton University Press, 2005.

Nosseir, 'Abd al-Rahman. "The Supreme Constitutional Court of Egypt and the Protection of Human Rights." Chicago: Unpublished paper, 1992.

Önis, Ziya. "Domestic Politics, International Norms, and Challenges to the State: Turkey-EU Relations in the Post-Helsinki Era." In *Turkey and the European Union: Domestic Politics, Economic Integration, and International Dynamics,* ed. Ali Çarkoglu and Barry Rubin, 9–34. Portland, OR: Frank Cass, 2003.

Önis, Ziya, and Umut Türem. "Business, Globalization, and Democracy: A Comparative Analysis of Turkish Business Associations." *Turkish Studies* 2, no. 2 (2001): 94–120.

———. "Entrepreneurs, Democracy, and Citizenship in Turkey." *Comparative Politics* 34, no. 4 (2002): 439–56.

Orren, Karen, and Stephen Skowronek. "Institutions and Intercurrence: Theory Building in the Fullness of Time." In *Political Order,* ed. Ian Shapiro and Russell Hardin, 111–46. New York: New York University Press, 1996.

Ottaway, Marina. *Democracy Challenged: The Rise of Semi-Authoritarianism.* Washington, DC: Carnegie Endowment for International Peace, 2003.

Ottaway, Marina, and Thomas Carothers, eds. *Funding Virtue: Civil Society Aid and Democracy Promotion.* Washington, DC: Carnegie Endowment for International Peace, 2000.

Ottaway, Marina, and Meredith Riley. *Morocco: From Top–Down Reform to Democratic Transition?* Washington, DC: Carnegie Endowment for International Peace, 2006.

Owen, Roger. "Egypt." In *The Pivotal States: A New Framework for U.S. Policy in the Developing World,* ed. Robert Chase, Emily Hill, and Paul Kennedy, 120–43. New York: W. W. Norton, 1999.

Ozbudun, Ergun. *Contemporary Turkish Politics: Challenges to Democratic Consolidation.* Boulder, CO: Lynne Rienner, 2000.

Paczynska, Agnieszka. "Globalization, Structural Adjustment, and Pressure to Conform: Contesting Labor Law Reform in Egypt." *New Political Science* 28, no. 1 (2006): 45–64.

Pew Global Attitudes Project. *Views of a Changing World: June 2003.* Washington, DC: Pew Research Center for the People and the Press, 2003.

Pierson, Paul, and Theda Skocpol. "Historical Institutionalism in Contemporary Political Science." In *Political Science: The State of the Discipline*, ed. Ira Katznelson and Helen V. Milner, 693–721. New York: W.W. Norton, 2002.

Pigato, Miria, and Ahmad Ghoneim. *Egypt After the End of the Multi-Fiber Agreement: A Comparative Regional Analysis.* Cairo: Egyptian Center for Economic Studies, 2006.

Pipes, Richard. *Property and Freedom.* New York: Alfred A. Knopf, 1999.

Pratt, Nicola. "Maintaining the Moral Economy: Egyptian State-Labor Relations in an Era of Economic Liberalization." *Arab Studies Journal* 8–9, no. 1–2 (Fall 2000/Spring 2001): 111–29.

Pripstein Posusney, Marsha. *Labor and the State in Egypt: Workers, Unions, and Economic Restructuring.* New York: Columbia University Press, 1997.

———. "Egyptian Privatization: New Challenges for the Left." *Middle East Report* 29, no. 1 (1999): 38–40.

———. "Globalization and Labor Protection in Oil-Poor Arab Countries: Racing to the Bottom?" *Global Social Policy* 3, no. 3 (2003): 267–97.

———. "Multiparty Elections in the Arab World: Election Rules and Opposition Responses." In *Authoritarianism in the Middle East: Regimes and Resistance*, ed. Marsha Pripstein Posusney and Michele Penner Angrist, 91–118. Boulder, CO: Lynne Rienner, 2005.

Przeworski, Adam, Michael E. Alvarez, Jose Antonio Chelbub, and Fernando Limongi. *Democracy and Development: Political Institutions and Well-Being in the World, 1950–1990.* Cambridge: Cambridge University Press, 2000.

Quandt, William B. *The United States and Egypt.* Cairo: American University in Cairo Press, 1990.

———. "American Policy toward Democratic Political Movements in the Middle East." In *Rules and Rights in the Middle East: Democracy, Law, and Society*, ed. Ellis Goldberg, Resat Kasaba, and Joel S. Migdal, 164–73. Seattle: University of Washington Press, 1993.

Radwan, Samir, and Jean Louis Reiffers. *The Euro-Mediterranean Partnership: Ten Years after Barcelona, Achievements and Perspectives.* Cairo: FEMISE and The Economic Research Forum, 2005.

Reid, Donald M. *Lawyers and Politics in the Arab World, 1880–1960.* Minneapolis: Bibliotheca Islamica, 1981.

Riad, Tarek F. "The Legal Environment for Investment in Egypt in the New Millennium." *Arab Law Quarterly* 15, no. 2 (2000): 117–30.

Risse, Thomas, Stephen C. Ropp, and Kathryn Sikkink, eds. *The Power of Human Rights: International Norms and Domestic Change.* New York: Cambridge University Press, 1999.

Roe, Alan R. *The Egyptian Banking System: Liberalization, Competition, and Privatization.* Cairo: Egyptian Center for Economic Studies, 1998.

Rosberg, James H. *Roads to the Rule of Law: The Emergence of an Independent Judiciary in Contemporary Egypt.* Ph.D. Dissertation, Department of Political Science, Massachusetts Institute of Technology, 1995.

Rosefsky-Wickham, Carrie. *Political Mobilization under Authoritarian Rule: Explaining Islamic Activism in Mubarak's Egypt.* Ph.D. Dissertation, Department of Politics, Princeton University, 1996.

Rosefsky-Wickham, Carrie. *Mobilizing Islam: Religion, Activism, and Political Change in Egypt.* New York: Columbia University Press, 2002.

———. "The Path to Moderation: Strategy and Learning in the Formation of Egypt's Wasat Party." *Comparative Politics* 36, no. 2 (2004): 205–28.

Rosenblum, Nancy L. "Liberalism." In *The Encyclopedia of Democracy: Volume 3*, ed. Seymour Martin Lipset, 756–61. Washington, DC: Congressional Quarterly, 1995.

Rueschemeyer, Dietrich, Evelyne Huber Stephens, and John D. Stephens. *Capitalist Development and Democracy.* Cambridge, U.K.: Polity Press, 1992.

Ruggiero, Guido de. *The History of European Liberalism.* Boston: Beacon Press, 1959.

Rutherford, Bruce K. *The Struggle for Constitutionalism in Egypt. Understanding the Obstacles to Democratic Transition in the Arab World.* Ph.D. Dissertation, Department of Political Science, Yale University, 1999.

———. "What Do Egypt's Islamists Want? Moderate Islam and the Rise of Islamic Constitutionalism." *Middle East Journal* 60, no. 4 (2006): 707–31.

Ryan, Curtis R., and Jillian Schwedler. "Return to Democratization or New Hybrid Regime? The 2003 Elections in Jordan." *Middle East Policy* 11, no. 2 (2004): 138–51.

Sadowski, Yahya M. *Political Vegetables? Businessman and Bureaucrat in the Development of Egyptian Agriculture.* Washington, DC: Brookings Institution, 1991.

Safa, Oussama. "Lebanon Springs Forward." *Journal of Democracy* 17, no. 1 (2006): 22–37.

Safran, Nadav. *Egypt in Search of Political Community: An Analysis of the Intellectual and Political Evolution of Egypt, 1804–1952.* Cambridge, MA: Harvard University Press, 1961.

Sakallioglu, Ümit Cizre. "The Anatomy of the Turkish Military's Political Autonomy." *Comparative Politics* 29, no. 2 (1997): 151–66.

Salacuse, Jeswald W. "Back to Contract: Implications of Peace and Openness for Egypt's Legal System." *American Journal of Comparative Law* 28 (1980): 315–33.

Salem, Paul. *Lebanon at the Crossroads: Rebuilding an Arab Democracy.* Washington, DC: Brookings Institution, 2005.

Al-Sayyid, Afaf Lutfi. *Egypt and Cromer: A Study in Anglo-Egyptian Relations.* London: John Murray, 1968.

Schapiro, J. Salwyn. *Liberalism: Its Meaning and History.* Princeton, NJ: Van Nostrand, 1958.

Schedler, Andreas. "The Menu of Manipulation." *Journal of Democracy* 13, no. 2 (2002): 36–50.

———. "The Nested Game of Democratization by Elections." *International Political Science Review* 23, no. 1 (2002): 103–22.

———, ed. *Electoral Authoritarianism: The Dynamics of Unfree Competition.* Boulder, CO: Lynne Rienner, 2006.

Schumpeter, Joseph A. *Capitalism, Socialism, and Democracy.* New York: Harper Torch Books, 1975.

Serag, Mohamed. "A Global Legal Odyssey: Legal Education in Egypt." *South Texas Law Review* 43 (2002): 615–21.

Sfakianakis, John. "The Whales of the Nile: Networks, Businessmen, and Bureaucrats During the Era of Privatization in Egypt." In *Networks of Privilege in the Middle East*, ed. Steven Heydemann, 77–100. New York: Palgrave Macmillan, 2004.

Sharp, Jeremy M. *The Middle East Partnership Initiative: An Overview*. Washington, DC: Congressional Research Service, July 20, 2005.

———. *Egypt: Background and U.S. Relations*. Washington, DC: Congressional Research Service, January 10, 2007.

Shultz, George P. *Turmoil and Triumph: My Years as Secretary of State*. New York: Scribner's, 1993.

Sikkink, Kathryn. *Ideas and Institutions: Developmentalism in Brazil and Argentina*. Ithaca, NY: Cornell University Press, 1991.

Skocpol, Theda. "Why I Am an Historical Institutionalist." *Polity* 28, no. 1 (1995): 103–6.

Skowronek, Stephen. "Order and Change." *Polity* 28, no. 1 (1995): 91–96.

Smith, Andrew R., and Fadoua Loudiy. "Testing the Red Lines: On the Liberalization of Speech in Morocco." *Human Rights Quarterly* 27, no. 3 (2005): 1069–1119.

Springborg, Robert. *Mubarak's Egypt: Fragmentation of the Political Order*. Boulder, CO: Westview Press, 1989.

Steinmo, Sven, and Kathleen Thelen. "Historical Institutionalism in Comparative Politics." In *Structuring Politics: Historical Institutionalism in Comparative Analysis*, ed. Sven Steinmo, Kathleen Thelen, and Frank Longstreth, 1–32. Cambridge: Cambridge University Press, 1992.

Stilt, Kristen. "Constitutional Authority and Subversion: Egypt's New Presidential Election System." *Indiana International and Comparative Law Review* 16 (2006): 335–73.

Stockholm International Peace Research Institute. *SIPRI Yearbook 2006: Armaments, Disarmament, and International Security*. New York: Oxford University Press, 2006.

Subramanian, Arvind. "Egypt: Poised for Sustained Growth?" *Finance & Development* 34, no. 4 (December 1997): 44–45.

Tessler, Mark. "Do Islamic Orientations Influence Attitudes Toward Democracy in the Arab World? Evidence from Egypt, Jordon, Morocco, and Algeria." In *Islam, Gender, Culture, and Democracy*, ed. Ronald Inglehart, 6–26. Willowdale, ON: deSitter Publications, 2003.

Thelen, Kathleen. "Historical Institutionalism in Comparative Politics." *Annual Review of Political Science* 2 (1999): 369–404.

———. "Time and Temporality in the Analysis of Institutional Evolution and Change." *Studies in American Political Development* 14 (2000): 102–9.

———. "How Institutions Evolve: Insights from Comparative Historical Analysis." In *Comparative Historical Analysis in the Social Sciences*, ed. James Mahoney and Dietrich Rueschemeyer, 208–40. Cambridge: Cambridge University Press, 2003.

———. *How Institutions Evolve: The Political Economy of Skills in Germany, Britain, the United States, and Japan*. New York: Cambridge University Press, 2004.

Tignor, Robert L. *Modernization and British Colonial Rule in Egypt, 1882–1914.* Princeton, NJ: Princeton University Press, 1966.

Tohamy, Sahar. *Tax Administration and Transaction Costs in Egypt.* Cairo: Egyptian Center for Economic Studies, 1998.

Vatikiotis, P. J. *The History of Modern Egypt: From Muhammad Ali to Mubarak.* Baltimore: Johns Hopkins University Press, 1991.

Wahba, Mourad M. *The Role of the State in the Egyptian Economy, 1945–1981.* Reading: Ithaca Press, 1994.

Walker, Geoffrey de Q. *The Rule of Law: Foundation of Constitutional Democracy.* Carlton, Victoria: Melbourne University Press, 1988.

Waterbury, John. *The Egypt of Nasser and Sadat: The Political Economy of Two Regimes.* Princeton, NJ: Princeton University Press, 1983.

———. *Exposed to Innumerable Delusions: Public Enterprise and State Power in Egypt, India, Mexico, and Turkey.* Cambridge: Cambridge University Press, 1993.

Whitehead, Laurence. "Three International Dimensions of Democratization." In *The International Dimensions of Democratization: Europe and the Americas,* ed. Laurence Whitehead, 1–24. New York: Oxford University Press, 1996.

World Bank. *Doing Business in 2004: Understanding Regulation.* Washington, DC: World Bank, 2004.

———. *Fostering Higher Growth and Employment in the Kingdom of Morocco.* Washington, DC: World Bank, 2006.

———. *Doing Business 2008: Comparing Regulation in 178 Economies.* Washington, DC: World Bank, 2007.

Yavuz, M. Hakan. *Islamic Political Identity in Turkey.* Oxford: Oxford University Press, 2003.

Youngs, Richard. "Europe's Uncertain Pursuit of Middle East Reform." In *Uncharted Journey: Promoting Democracy in the Middle East,* ed. Thomas Carothers and Marina Ottaway, 229–48. Washington, DC: Carnegie Endowment for International Peace, 2005.

Zaalouk, Malak. *Power, Class, and Foreign Capital in Egypt: The Rise of the New Bourgeoisie.* London: Zed Books, 1989.

Zakaria, Fareed. *The Future of Freedom: Illiberal Democracy at Home and Abroad.* New York: W.W. Norton, 2003.

Zaki, Moheb. *Civil Society and Democratization in Egypt: 1981–1994.* Cairo: Ibn Khaldoun Center and Konrad Adenauer Stiftung, 1995.

Ziadeh, Farhat Jacob. *Lawyers, the Rule of Law, and Liberalism in Modern Egypt.* Stanford, CA: Hoover Institution, 1968.

Zogby, James J. *What Arabs Think: Values, Beliefs, and Concerns.* New York: Zogby International, 2002.

El-Zoheiri, K., and W. Rady. "Press Law." In *Egypt and Its Laws,* ed. Nathalie Bernard-Maugiron and Baudouin Dupret, 345–57. New York: Kluwer Law International, 2002.

Index

'Abd al-Aziz, Zakariyya, 32, 150–51, 159, 161

'Abd al-Nasser, Jamal, 21, 32, 41; assassination attempt on, 81; Bar Association and criticism of, 42–43; death of, 43; economic policies of, 140, 200 (*See also* nationalization *under this heading*); education policies during, 46; "massacre of the judges" during administration of, 56–57; Muslim Brotherhood and, 79–82, 131; nationalizations during administration of, 42, 53, 132, 133; power concentration by, 131; "socialist legality" and legal reforms of, 141, 151, 162, 192; state power institutionalized during, 2; trade policies of, 200; 1967 War and, 82, 193

'Abduh, Muhammad, 99, 101

Abu al-Fatuh, 'Abd al Mon'am, 87–88, 130, 163, 175n217

Abu al-Majd, Ahmad Kamal, 30, 98, 99, 100, 104, 107, 108n117, 109, 112, 113, 117–18, 121, 122, 124, 129–30, 164, 181, 235

Abu al-Nasr, Hamid, 89

Abu Bakr, 108n117, 110, 117, 166

Abu Zayd, Nasr Hamid, 69, 108n121, 115n161

accountability of government, 28, 126; during crises, 185; as horizontal rather than vertical, 75; Islamic constitutionalism and, 126–27, 128, 164, 166–67, 195–96; as Islamic principle, 113; Islamic principle of *shura* (consultation) and, 110–11, 127, 167; Judges' Club and, 191; judiciary and, 52, 60–61, 75, 162, 191; liberal constitutionalism and, 195–96; and monitorial responsibility of the governed, 111, 119, 171; Muslim Brotherhood and, 1, 172–73, 177, 185, 191; private sector and, 240; U.S. pressures for greater, 6, 18; WTO and increased, 202

administrative judiciary (administrative courts and High Administrative Court):

and civil and political rights, 65–71; constraint of state power and, 53–56, 59–61; elections and, 72–73; emergency law limited by rulings of, 54; Emergency State Security Courts decisions reviewed by, 62–63; judicial independence and, 62–64; political parties and, 71–74; property rights and, 59; public participation in politics and, 71–75; religious freedom decisions of, 70; rule of law and, 62–64; state power and, 59

Advance Democracy Act, 9

Al-Afghani, Jamal al-Din, 99

'Akif, Muhammad Mahdi, 77, 163–64, 180, 182

El Alfi, Moataz, 211n57

Algeria, 4, 14

'Amara, Muhammad, 83

American Chamber of Commerce in Egypt (AMCHAM), 205–12

Anglo-Egyptian Accord (1936), 40

apostasy, 69, 70, 114, 115n161

'Aqd (contract), 109

Arab Human Development Reports (AHDR), 11–12

Arab Socialist Union (ASU), 42, 82

Asfur, Muhammad, 43, 47–48

Assaad, Assaad S., 211n57

assassination: attempt on Nasser, 81; of Al-Banna, 79; of Sadat, 83

Atherton, Alfred, 6

authoritarianism: Egypt as authoritarian regime, 1–2, 256, 258; hybrid regimes and characteristics of, 16–17, 19n82. *See also* autocracy

autocracy: Arab popular rejection of, 13; critical junctures and weakening of, 29; in hybrid regimes, 16, 17, 21, 24; Nasser regime and concentration of power, 131; as source of radical Islam, 6–7, 167; survival strategies of, 15–16, 18, 20, 257. *See also* monarchies; state power; statism in Egypt

legal profession: increase of law school graduates, 46–47; liberal constitutionalism in Egypt and, 30; role of in Egyptian nationalism, 36–39. *See also* Bar Association (*Niqabat al-Muhamiyyin*)

legitimacy: critical junctures and loss of, 25–26; respect for law as foundation of, 144; 1967 War and crisis of, 82

Levitsky, Steven, 19, 20–21

liberal constitutionalism: Egypt's autocratic regime and, 30–31; elites and liberal reform, 34; Islamic constitutionalism compared to, 126, 190–96; Judges' Club and, 32; judiciary and, 30, 49–76; legal profession and, 30, 32, 36–38; liberalism and, 32–33, 37; market liberalism and shared ideals of, 231

liberalism: Bar Association and, 42–49; compared and contrasted to Islamic constitutionalism, 121–22; as constructed by Egyptian judiciary, 161–62; defined, 17n72, 32, 236; as distinct from democracy, 17n72, 31, 236–39, 257–58; ECES recommendations and, 217–18; as elite calculation, 238; as facilitator of democratization, 239–42; historical roots of in Egypt, 32–42; Islamic constitutionalism and, 121–22; Judges' Club and liberal reform, 151–52; judiciary and principles of, 162–63; Muslim Brotherhood and, 189–90, 190n267. *See also* liberal constitutionalism; market liberalism

Liberal Party, 84, 92

Liberation Rally, 81

Linz, Juan J., 17

Lipset, Seymour Martin, 17

Lucas, Russell, 22

Lust-Okar, Ellen, 22

Lynch, Marc, 13–14

Madi, Abu-l-'Ila, 97

Magaloni, Beatriz, 22

Al-Maghrabi, Ahmad, 211n57, 223

Mahoney, James, 24

Makki, Ahmad, 146, 151, 152, 158, 160, 184, 232n1

Mansur, Muhammad, 211n57, 223

March 30 declaration (1968), 43, 142

"March 14th " movement in Lebanon, 14

marja'iyya (frame of reference), 251

market liberalism, 31; accountability of government and, 231; Egyptian Center for Economic Studies (ECES) and development of, 211–23; investment and, 197–98; labor movement as response to, 224–30; legal reforms, 197–99; pace of market reforms, 229–30; private sector and, 198, 204–18; privatization and, 197–98; property rights, 202–4; regulation and state intervention challenged by, 199, 212; rule of law and, 199, 201–2, 215–16; separation of powers and checks and balances and, 213–14, 231; social welfare programs and, 215; state power and, 231; WTO and market-oriented reforms, 199–203, 210

Mashur, Mustafa, 89, 163

maslaha (public interest) doctrine in Islamic legal thought, 69, 103, 192

Al-Mataar, 'Abd al-Nasir, 43

Matwalli, 'Abd al-Hamid, 43

McCain, John, 7

media: censorship and state as moral actor, 170; Islamic extremism challenged through, 84; Judges' Club use of, 158; liberalism and Egyptian print culture, 41–42; media advocacy groups, 19; Muslim Brotherhood and freedom of, 174; Nasser regime and state control of, 132; role of Arab media in democratization, 13–14; Supreme Press Council and regulation of, 94. *See also* freedom of the press

Mexico, 21

Middle East Partnership Initiative (MEPI), 7–9, 18–19

military, 252–53; Muslim Brotherhood's opposition to governmental involvement of the, 172; political change as response to military defeat, 25

military coup (1952), 5, 79–81, 131

military courts, 87–88, 173, 252n83

Ministry of Interior, 72, 73, 184, 252–53

Ministry of Investment, 246, 247

Ministry of Justice, 144–45, 173, 177

Ministry of Religious Endowments, 80, 94–95, 104n104

Ministry of Social Affairs (MOSA), 66, 94, 147n78

Mohanna, 'Umar, 211n57

Mohieldin, Mahmud, 211n59, 220, 222–24

nationalization: of al-Azhar University, 172; growth of public sector during, 133; Muslim Brotherhood and, 80n10; during Nasser regime, 42, 53, 132, 133; Nasser's statist regime and, 133; property rights and, 42, 52–53, 59; Wafd party and Egyptian, 39–41

national security: Emergency State Security Court and, 62–63; judiciary and "acts of sovereignty" in interest of, 55–56; judiciary and limits to powers of exceptional courts, 62–63; as rationale for broadening powers of security apparatus, 254–55; as rationale for Law on Personal Status, 54; State Security Court and matters of, 51, 56; terrorism and, 252–55

National Security Strategy (U.S. 2006), 7

"natural judge" concept, 56n104, 60n123, 143, 173, 194, 252n83

natural law, Shari'a as comparable to, 121

Al-Nazar, Jamal, 205

Nazif, Ahmad, 31, 223, 229–30

New Islamists, 101

New Wafd Party, 71–72, 84, 92

NGOs. See non-governmental organizations (NGOs)

non-governmental organizations (NGOs), 94; and arbitrary treatment by government, 66; regulation and restriction of, 65–66, 150–51; restrictions on, 206. See also civil society groups

Nour, Mounir Abdel, 211n57

Nuh, Mukhtar, 89, 96, 97, 130, 163

Nuqrashi, Mahmud, 40–41

Obama, Barack, 9

Obey, David, 9n37

oil, 3, 224; economic impacts of oil boom, 135–36, 139; political impacts of oil boom, 90–91; as strategic interest, 5

ordinary judiciary: appointment of judges to, 50n69, 50n70; Court of Cassation, 51; role of, 51

Organizational Law: of 1883, 33; of 1913, 34

Ottaway, Marina, 17

Paris Club, 137, 138

Parliament: absence of legislatures in classical Islamic political thought, 112–13; budgeting role of, 249; Constitutional amendments revising powers of, 249–50;

emergency law and concentration of presidential power, 1; Fundamental Law and powers of, 33; Islamic constitutionalism and, 126, 128; judicial supervision of election to, 72; as mechanism for shura (consultation), 118; Muslim Brotherhood on role of, 177–78; Muslim Brotherhood on strengthening of, 173; procedural reforms proposed by Muslim Brotherhood, 185; provisions in Constitution of 1923, 38–39

participation in politics, 28; Constitutional limits to, 250–51; as fundamental right, 74; Islamic constitutionalism and, 30, 117–21, 122; judiciary and defense of, 71–75; mass politics as threat to social order, 74–75; Muslim Brotherhood and, 176–78, 235–36; Muslim Brotherhood and restrictions on, 251; Nasser and restrictions on, 132; Parliamentary system and, 177–78; private sector business interests and, 246; as religious obligation, 119; religious organizations prohibited from, 187, 251; SCC and defense of, 64–65; shura (consultation) as mechanism for, 117–18, 176–77, 195; skepticism toward unrestricted democracy, 232–35; women's right to, 165–66, 174–75, 180n247

pensions, 215, 222, 226–27, 228

People's Assembly, 72–73

Pierson, Paul, 24

pluralism, 98, 119, 129, 164–65, 166

political participation. See participation in politics

political parties, 15; as allies of Muslim Brotherhood, 92; al-Wasat, 90; as constraint on state power, 113; government regulation of, 2, 84, 87n34, 178; as instrument of control, 74; international party foundations, 19; Islamic constitutionalism and multi-party system, 119; multi-party system, 44, 171; Muslim Brotherhood and, 84, 90, 95, 171, 178; Nasser and single party system, 132; prohibition against religious organizations operating as, 84, 251–52; as relatively weak in Egypt, 238–39; resistance to market liberalism by Left wing, 224–25; SCC and defense of right to form, 71–72

positive law (man-made law), 103–4, 107–8, 118, 128